BETWEEN HOSTILE SHORES

BETWEEN HOSTILE SHORES

Mediterranean Convoys 1941–1942

BRITANNIA NAVAL HISTORIES OF WORLD WAR II

UPP
University of Plymouth Press

This edition first published in the United Kingdom in 2013 by
University of Plymouth Press, Portland Square, Plymouth University
Plymouth, Devon, PL4 8AA, United Kingdom.

Paperback   ISBN 978-1-84102-354-0
Hardback   ISBN 978-1-84102-353-3

© University of Plymouth Press 2013

The rights of this work have been asserted in accordance with the Crown
Copyright, Designs and Patents Act 1988.

A CIP catalogue record of this book is available from the British Library.

Publisher: Paul Honeywill
Commissioning Editor: Charlotte Carey
Series Editors: G. H. Bennett, J. E. Harrold, R. Porter and M. J. Pearce
Editor: Miranda Spicer
Publishing Assistant: Maxine Aylett

Historical content courtesy of Britannia Museum, Britannia Royal Naval
College, Dartmouth, TQ6 0HJ.

Cover image © Edward Stables 2013

Typeset by University of Plymouth Press in Janson 10/14pt.
Printed and bound by Short Run Press, Exeter, United Kingdom.

The historical documents reproduced here appear as unedited text, apart
from minor changes made to date formats and corrections to typing errors
found in the original.

Mixed Sources
Product group from well-managed
forests, controlled sources and
recycled wood or fibre
www.fsc.org   Cert no. SGS-COC-005998
© 1996 Forest Stewardship Council
FSC

© Richard Porter 2012

Britannia Royal Naval College

A majestic landmark, which towers above the harbour town of Dartmouth in Devon, Britannia Royal Naval College was designed by royal architect Sir Aston Webb to project an image of British sea power. A fine example of Edwardian architecture, the College has prepared future generations of officers for the challenges of service and leadership since 1905.

The Britannia Museum opened in 1999 to safeguard the College's rich collection of historic artefacts, art and archives and promote greater public understanding of Britain's naval and maritime heritage, as a key element in the development of British history and culture. It also aims to instil a sense of identity and ethos in the Officer Cadets that pass through the same walls as their forbears, from great admirals to national heroes to royalty.

www.royalnavy.mod.uk/The-Fleet/Shore-Establishments/BRNC-Dartmouth

Contents

Foreword 8

Introduction 10

Abbreviations 30

Overview 31

PART I

Battle summary No. 18

Selected Convoys (Mediterranean) 1941 34

PART II

Battle Summary No. 32

Selected Convoys (Mediterranean) 1942 89

PART III

Review of Damage to His Majesty's Ships

3 September 1941 to 2 September 1942 260

Biographies 358

Britannia Naval Histories of World War II Series 360

Foreword

Vice Admiral
Sir Richard Ibbotson

The Mediterranean in 1941 and 1942 was a crucial maritime theatre, but has not attracted a great deal of historical analysis thus far. It deserves more, partly because of the importance of operations like Excess, Halberd and Pedestal, partly because of battles like Sirte, but mostly because the lessons and implications are enduring, and merit understanding by current and future generations of our maritime nation. *Between Hostile Shores* therefore provides an important contribution to our naval history.

My operational experience in a different era was dominated by three persistent and seemingly timeless realities; the need to control sea lines of communication, while coping with extended supply lines and operating without air superiority. For my generation, these facets were a stark reality both for the Falklands, and for stages of the successive Gulf conflicts. I am intrigued that these were the key themes in the Mediterranean in 1941–1942. They chime with both the operational realities and the priorities of a post-Cold War Royal Navy far more than I might have imagined as a young watchkeeper and principal warfare officer, when the Royal Navy's focus was predominantly on deep-water anti-submarine warfare in cold northern waters.

Events of the last two decades have again turned our maritime eye to the Mediterranean. Like many other Naval Officers, the leadership and focus on training provided by Somerville and Cunningham have inspired me. The Royal Navy rightly prides itself on professionalism and leadership. The events covered here are testament to the importance and validity of such a focus. These qualities gave the two Admirals' ships the ability to fight through, against real, long-term adversity, unrelenting pressure and frequent loss.

The lessons that may be drawn from this book therefore remain wholly relevant today, and are brought together in the introduction with real style and vigour. I commend it wholeheartedly.

Introduction

Michael Pearce

In the two and a half years between Italy's declaration of war on 10 June 1940 and the end of December 1942, Mediterranean convoy battles were fought largely to sustain the beleaguered island of Malta. Other supply and troop convoys were run to Greece, some all the way through the Mediterranean to the Royal Navy's Egyptian base at Alexandria, but all were routed via Malta. During 1941 and 1942, the Royal Navy had to fight convoys through the western Mediterranean for almost the entire 1000 miles from Gibraltar to Malta, in the teeth of Axis efforts to oppose them with aircraft, submarines, mines, fast coastal torpedo craft and the threat of the modern and powerful Italian surface fleet. Convoys were also run to Malta from Alexandria but the 900-mile voyage through the eastern Mediterranean became even more hazardous than the western route after May 1941, with the Luftwaffe operating from air bases in Crete and the Dodecanese, as well as from Libya, Sicily and Italy. This enabled Axis aircraft, particularly dive-bombers, to dominate the sea from north, south and west. Even so, convoys continued in both directions. If Malta had fallen or been neutralised, Axis armies in North Africa would have had unrestricted access to supplies, fuel, munitions, equipment and reinforcements, free from the attacks that British naval and air forces, based on the island, were able to bring to bear. In these circumstances, Rommel's Afrika Korps might have reached Cairo and the Suez Canal, possibly sweeping on even further east, to the oilfields of Iraq and the Gulf.

Malta's fine natural harbour, and strategic position astride the trade routes in the narrowest part of the central Mediterranean, made the island the main base for the Royal Navy's Mediterranean Fleet from early in the 19th century, notwithstanding Sicily being only 60 miles away. Malta's importance increased further in 1869 when the Suez Canal opened, making the Mediterranean the favoured route for British trade with the East and communications with the Indian Empire and Australia. This remained the case 70 years later, in March 1939, when the British erected on Malta the first shore-based radar installation outside the UK. After Italy's opportunistic declaration of war, the Mediterranean initially became the main supply route for British forces based in Egypt, but when Hitler committed German air and ground forces, the longer, but more secure, route around Africa became increasingly important, especially in the build-up to the pivotal Battle of El Alamein. This was fought at a time when land-based Axis air power on both shores prevented large-scale British use of the Mediterranean supply route.

The Royal Navy's ability to fight convoys through the Mediterranean hinged on Britain's possession of Gibraltar, which held then, as now, the key strategic position controlling access to a largely land-locked sea. With this in mind, Hitler sought Spanish support in September 1940 for an attack on Gibraltar. He was confident of persuading General Franco, the fascist dictator of Spain, to cooperate, or even take part in an assault to seize the fortress, given that Germany had provided Franco with substantial support during the recent Spanish Civil War. At that time, Hitler had supplied the Nationalist Army and Air Force with modern equipment and sent the Condor Legion to fight against the Republicans. Hitler therefore pushed ahead with Operation Felix, a plan devised in June 1940 by Chief of the German Army Operations Staff, General Alfred Jodl, to capture Gibraltar by sending troops through Spain from occupied France. But, to Hitler's surprise and disappointment, Franco initially prevaricated and then rejected his proposals. British Intelligence received firm information that Franco would not only refuse permission for German troops to pass through Spain but that the Spanish army would resist if the Germans tried to do so by force. After Hitler and Mussolini failed in a final joint effort to change Franco's mind, Hitler reluctantly suspended Operation Felix in March 1941 and turned his attention to the forthcoming invasion of Russia. Finally, from October 1941, British Intelligence was able to confirm that Wehrmacht divisions on the Franco-Spanish frontier were being withdrawn. The British guarantee to continue Spain's sea-borne imports, especially essential foodstuffs from the US and Canada, was, in their view, the major influence on Franco's attitude. But of equal importance was the fact that Franco still felt shock and dismay at Hitler's cynical expediency in agreeing to a Soviet-German non-aggression pact the previous year, which the Caudillo regarded as an unforgivable betrayal of their hitherto joint anti-communist ideals. The inability of the Axis to occupy or neutralise Gibraltar was a significant strategic failure that compromised their successful prosecution of the war. The resulting freedom enjoyed by Britain to maintain the naval base at Gibraltar and assemble and sail convoys from its relatively secure harbour, ensured that Malta remained a viable threat to Axis supply convoys between Italy and North Africa, even at the height of air attacks on the island.

The invasion and occupation of Malta itself was another obvious strategic objective that the Axis failed to achieve. Italy had developed plans for this as early as 1935 and updated them in June 1940 – a time when the island's air defences were negligible. But the plans were not acted on. Perhaps Mussolini expected the British to follow France and surrender to Hitler and, even if they did not, he was confident that Spain would join the Axis and seize

Gibraltar. This would remove any need for Italy to invade Malta. In June 1941, Hitler rejected a proposal for an immediate assault on Malta, partly due to heavy losses of German parachute troops a month earlier during the assault on Crete, but also to concentrate available forces for the invasion of Russia later that month. Early in 1942, major figures within the Axis high command judged that their war objectives would be best served by the invasion and occupation of Malta. Mussolini, Grand Admiral Erich Raeder and Field Marshal Albert Kesselring all sought to convince an initially reluctant Hitler until, in February 1942, he finally agreed that an assault should be made by nearly 100,000 German and Italian troops supported by the Italian battle fleet. Facing them were 26,000 poorly equipped and badly fed British and Maltese troops with 10 tanks. Planning for the invasion, Operation Herkules, was a rare example of cooperation between the three major Axis powers, in that a Japanese representative shared knowledge gained from island assaults in South East Asia. But when Kesselring informed Hitler in April 1942 that air attacks had isolated and neutralised Malta, enabling the invasion to take place, this coincided with Rommel's advance towards Cairo and the Suez Canal. Rommel readily accepted that Malta should be invaded but argued that his campaign in North Africa should be given priority; Hitler agreed and postponed the invasion of Malta until after Egypt had fallen. But, from May, Malta was heavily reinforced by large numbers of Spitfires flown in from British and US aircraft carriers and these prevented the Luftwaffe and Regia Aeronautica from gaining air supremacy over the island. Then, in July, Rommel's advance was stopped at El Alamein and many troops training for the Maltese expedition were sent to North Africa as reinforcements; finally, when General Bernard Montgomery's reinforced, resupplied and revitalised Eighth Army attacked and defeated Rommel in October 1942, the need to support the shattered Panzer Army, Afrika consumed the last of them and the invasion of Malta was abandoned.

The success of relatively light naval and air forces based on Malta in disrupting and destroying Axis supply convoys to North Africa was attributed at the time to high quality air reconnaissance carried out from the island. In reality, it was a flow of secret tactical intelligence, known as ULTRA, provided by code breakers at Bletchley Park from their decrypts of intercepted Axis Enigma signals traffic. This gave the British the invaluable operational advantage of deploying cruisers, destroyers, submarines and strike aircraft from Malta to the exact positions of Axis supply convoys, allowing them to wreak havoc on the routes from Naples and Taranto to North Africa. The need to protect this vital source of intelligence from compromise resulted in the British not taking action against Axis convoys, whose positions had been provided by ULTRA unless reconnaissance aircraft despatched to the enemy's position had been sighted by them. ULTRA intelligence also assisted the British in a more subtle way, as their successes against Axis convoys sowed mistrust and discord between the Axis partners, with Germany always suspecting the existence of a highly placed traitor in the Italian Navy – a misconception that the British did nothing to dispel. The need to obscure the real source of critical ULTRA information was of paramount importance and British Intelligence invented a ficticious agent in Naples, sending signals in a code that the Germans could break, thanking him for vital operational intelligence and saying that payments sent to him would be increased. The contribution made by ULTRA to the war in the Mediterranean is not mentioned in these Battle Summaries, as Britain's ability to decipher and act on Enigma intercepts remained highly classified until 1974, when it finally crept into the public domain, but its importance should not be underestimated.

In 1940, Mediterranean convoy operations undertaken by the Royal Navy achieved their objectives and led to successful, if not decisive, clashes with the Italian surface fleet. Indeed, by the end of 1940, after six months of war with Italy, Britain had cause to feel reasonably confident about its position in the Mediterranean – particularly after three Italian battleships were sunk or disabled in Taranto on 11 November by Fleet Air Arm Swordfish torpedo bombers from HMS *Illustrious*. This coup was followed on 8 December by Lt. Gen. Sir Richard O'Connor's astonishingly successful offensive by 30,000 British and Empire troops against 80,000 Italians under Marshal Graziani at Sidi Barrani, resulting in the loss, within a few days, of 38,000 Italian troops, 50 tanks and 400 guns. The reinforced British Western Desert Force then advanced over 500 miles into Libya, took 130,000 prisoners and knocked out or captured 380 tanks, only stopping at El Agheila on 7 March 1941, when the British War Cabinet took a political decision to transfer 57,000 troops from North Africa to fight the Axis in Greece. This fatally weakened British forces in Libya, to the extent that Rommel's newly arrived Afrika Korps was able to launch an offensive on 31 March and quickly push the remaining two poorly equipped British divisions back eastwards.

Before this, in early January 1941, Hitler's first response to Mussolini's appeals for assistance had been the despatch of Luftwaffe units to southern Italy and Sicily, including Fliegerkorps X from Norway. The dive bombers of this unit were trained in anti-shipping techniques and, specifically, to sink the first radar-equipped aircraft carrier HMS *Illustrious*, operating in the eastern Mediterranean as part of Admiral Sir Andrew Cunningham's Mediterranean Fleet. Fliegerkorps X calculated that it would require four direct hits to sink the *Illustrious* and the Operation Excess convoy gave them an opportunity to try as early as 10 January. Low-level torpedo bomber attacks drew the few Fulmar fighters from the *Illustrious* down to sea level, much as would happen on a larger scale to the Japanese fighter defence during the Battle of Midway a year and a half later. Ju. 87 Stukas then attacked the carrier with armour-piercing bombs, scoring seven direct hits and a damaging near-miss. Cunningham, watching from the bridge of his flagship, HMS *Warspite*, could only ruefully admire the skill shown by the pilots. However, the *Illustrious* reached the dubious refuge of Valletta's Grand Harbour under her own power, where the Stukas scored another direct hit and a second near-miss. These 10 bombs, seven 550 kg and three 250 kg, killed 126 of her ship's company and caused structural and fire damage to the upper levels of the ship, but they did not sink her and she soon sailed at 21 knots for Alexandria and then on to Norfolk Navy Yard for permanent repairs in the US.

The temptation to seek to score a significant tactical and propaganda victory by sinking HMS *Illustrious* seems to have seduced Fliegerkorps X away from the main strategic objective of preventing the re-supply of Malta. Not one of the 14 merchant ships in Operation Excess and three related convoys was lost. Nevertheless, the aircraft of Fliegerkorps X made the central and eastern Mediterranean extremely hazardous for British ships during the first half of 1941, until part of the unit was diverted to support Germany's invasion of Russia. In the meantime, the Royal Navy had to undertake costly evacuations of British and Allied troops from Greece and Crete, virtually without air cover during April and May 1941 and had four cruisers and eight destroyers sunk, with three battleships, one fleet carrier, six cruisers and seven destroyers damaged, most at the hands of Fliegerkorps X Stukas. These severe casualties more than offset the sinking of three heavy cruisers and two destroyers, with damage to the new battleship *Vittorio Veneto*, inflicted on the Italian Navy during the Battle of Matapan in March. The remaining convoys in 1941 were fought through with surprisingly small losses among the merchant ships – although in September's Operation Halberd, Italian torpedo bombers disabled the 12,500 ton Blue Star Line fast cargo liner *Imperial Star*, which finally had to be sunk by the destroyer HMS *Oribi*, prompting an intriguing observation in the Battle Summary that the *Imperial Star* was carrying 'valuable and secret stores' that could not be exposed to the risk of capture. This clandestine cargo was new radar equipment to augment the installations on Malta, carried in addition to the ship's normal load of 420 military personnel, crates of bombs and ammunition, kerosene, meat and provisions. All the personnel were taken aboard British destroyers but her important cargo was lost with her.

The particular and overriding vulnerability of British Mediterranean convoys during 1941 and 1942 was their lack of adequate air cover, making the voyage to Malta, from Gibraltar or Alexandria, a perilous gauntlet to be run by merchant ships and their naval escorts alike. At the start of the war, the RAF in the eastern Mediterranean was very short of all types of aircraft, particularly modern fighters and, by May 1941, there were only 13 fighters fit for action in the Western Desert. Admiral Cunningham made repeated requests for additional aircraft to be sent to Air Chief Marshal Sir Arthur Longmore, the Air Officer Commanding, Middle East, emphasising the pressing need for Hurricanes and Spitfires to defend Malta and Egypt, long range Beaufighters to cover British convoys and a strike force to attack the Axis supply lines, but it was some time before the situation at home allowed these to be sent. The Royal Navy's own Fleet Air Arm was in no better shape: the fleet carrier HMS *Formidable* being reduced to four serviceable aircraft in May 1941, without reserves of naval aircraft or flying personnel, following operations off Tripoli and the successful two-way Operation Tiger convoys. These delivered urgently needed reinforcements of tanks direct from Gibraltar to Alexandria, while two oil tankers and five supply ships reached Malta from Alexandria.

Aircraft carriers were a vital part of the Royal Navy by 1941 but each carried too few fighters at that time to protect the ship itself from concentrated air attack, let alone provide sufficient air cover for a fleet or convoy, while those fighters that were operated, such as the Fairey Fulmar, had inadequate performance when compared with shore-based aircraft that they faced in combat. Nevertheless, they were fought with skill, courage and determination, shooting down significant numbers of attacking aircraft, while breaking up and disorganising many raids. The Royal Navy had not wrested control of its integral Fleet Air Arm from the fiercely independent Royal Air Force until 1937 and there was the expectation that aircraft carriers would provide reconnaissance and spotting support for the guns of the fleet, rather than a strike force. The specifications for naval aircraft designs had therefore been undemanding, even unimaginative, except perhaps for the forward-looking, but poorly performing, Blackburn Skua dive-bomber; even the Fairey Swordfish, later a celebrated torpedo bomber and lethal submarine hunter, was originally intended only for spotter-reconnaissance duties. During the late 1930s, Admiralty planning accepted that the impending European war would require British aircraft carriers to operate without adequate numbers of high performance fleet fighters in hostile waters dominated by enemy shore-based air power. This prescient assumption became the predominant influence on the design of a new class of fleet carriers to follow the one-off *Ark Royal*. The *Illustrious* class were designed from the outset with protective armour on the flight deck and hangar sides. The corollary of this aspect of the design was a reduction in the number of aircraft carried and the class has been criticised for its limited aircraft capacity compared with the *Ark Royal* and, especially, US fleet carriers. However, the ability of *Illustrious* class carriers to resist air attack was amply demonstrated in the Mediterranean where bombs that did manage to penetrate their armour failed to reach vital machinery spaces and vulnerable lower decks.

During the Operation Excess convoy, HMS *Illustrious* suffered perhaps the worst bomb damage survived by any carrier in World War II. The ruggedness of the class was also dramatically shown in the Pacific in 1945 when several ships, including the *Illustrious*, shrugged off direct hits from Kamikaze (sometimes multiple hits), suffering only minor structural damage and remaining operational.

The Royal Navy was thinly spread by the end of 1941, after the serious losses and battle damage suffered during the year. In only five weeks during November and December, the battleships *Barham* and *Prince of Wales*, the battlecruiser *Repulse*, the aircraft carriers *Ark Royal* and *Audacity*, and the cruisers *Neptune*, *Galatea* and *Sydney* were all sunk. Even at this time, Royal Navy light cruisers and destroyers maintained pressure on Rommel's supply line, particularly oil tankers. Force K from Malta destroyed a convoy early in November and three British and a Netherlands destroyer torpedoed and sank two Italian light cruisers a month later, as they attempted a high-speed run from Palermo to Tripoli, carrying urgently needed petrol. However, Britain's situation deteriorated even further on the night of 18/19 December, when six members of the Italian 10th Light Flotilla penetrated Alexandria Harbour, using two-man 'chariots' or manned slow-speed torpedoes, and planted mines that severely damaged both HMS *Queen Elizabeth* and HMS *Valiant*, Admiral Cunningham's two remaining battleships. This left only light cruisers and destroyers to counter the Italian battle fleet and thereby altered the balance of power in the eastern Mediterranean. However, the Royal Navy's reaction to this apparent disaster was phlegmatic: at a staff meeting held aboard his listing flagship the following morning, Admiral Cunningham said, "Now we've got to bluff them that we've got a Fleet". Admiral Sir Henry Moore, the duty member of the Board of Admiralty and a friend of Cunningham's, merely observed, "Well, we'll have to do without them", on being woken from his bed in the Admiralty basement with the news that both ships would be out of action for months. The only light at the end of the Royal Navy's dark tunnel of 1941 was that Hitler and Mussolini rashly declared war on the US following the Japanese attack on Pearl Harbor – now there was the likelihood of future US participation.

It was against this unpromising background, with continuing losses in all theatres of war, that the Mediterranean convoy battles of 1942 were fought. They had to compete for scarce resources with the primary lifeline of Atlantic convoys to and from the US and Canada, as well as with Arctic convoys to Russia and the struggle to assemble a scratch collection of available warships into an Eastern Fleet to face the rampaging Japanese in the Indian Ocean. Rommel advanced steadily eastwards during the first half of 1942 until, by the middle of the year, he had pushed the British back as far as El Alamein, deep into Egypt and less than 100 miles from the naval base at Alexandria. Even though this enabled German bombers to operate from airfields along the North African coast, the need to fight convoys through to Malta became ever more urgent as the year wore on. The island continued to suffer appallingly from air raids, averaging 10 a day in March, while the garrison and population were reduced almost to starvation level rations. Polio, TB, dysentery and scabies ravaged civilians and service personnel alike, while the spectre of widespread scurvy was held at bay only by emergency supplies of vitamin C tablets being flown in. Apart from the perpetual shortage of food, there was, in particular, a lack of medical supplies, fuel and ammunition for defending fighters and shells for anti-aircraft guns. In April 1942, King George VI awarded the island, and its entire population, the George Cross, Britain's highest award for civilian gallantry, in recognition of their fortitude. But in the same month, the then Governor, Lt. Gen. William Dobbie, informed the Chiefs of Staff in London that the island would run out of food, ammunition and fuel in a matter of weeks and then there would be no choice but to surrender.

In tactical terms, the point had been reached when the cost of keeping Malta supplied outweighed any damage the island could inflict on the Axis war effort at that time. However, things were not that simple, given past sacrifices to keep Malta 'in the war' and the critical need for Britain to avoid another defeat at a bleak time in her war fortunes. Also, strategically, there was the intention to use Malta as a base to maintain ULTRA-informed attacks on Rommel's supply lines and to keep the door open for future Allied action in North Africa and against Sicily and Italy. In any event, whether or not the game was strictly worth the candle, the obdurate and indomitable Winston Churchill was determined that Malta should never be forced into surrender. Therefore, further supply convoys were run to the embattled island, despite there being no battleships or aircraft carriers in the Mediterranean Fleet. The passage of these convoys gave rise to bitter struggles against air, submarine and surface attack, with Malta's suppressed air defences able to provide little support. Two convoys failed to arrive and the surviving ships of another, 'MW10' from Alexandria, were sunk in Valletta Harbour before they could be unloaded. The spirited defence of 'MW10' led to the second Battle of Sirte on 22 March 1942, described by Admiral Cunningham as "one of the most brilliant naval actions of the war", when the able but irascible Rear Admiral Philip Vian successfully drove off the Italian battleship *Littorio* and three cruisers, with only a weak force of small light cruisers and destroyers. Belying the Mediterranean's fair-weather image, the running battle was fought in near gale-force winds and increasingly heavy seas. These hampered the manoeuvring and gunnery of both sides, reducing the performance of British radar sets because of 'sea clutter' interference from wave crests and causing a 152mm gun of the *Littorio*'s secondary armament to burst because of water in the barrel. The conditions became so bad by the following morning that two Italian destroyers were overwhelmed in the high seas and sank, leaving only 18 survivors between them.

The Operation Pedestal convoy in August 1942 was almost the last chance to resupply Malta and prevent surrender. By this time, Spitfires and long-range Beaufighters had been sent to the island, together with a striking force of Beaufort torpedo bombers and Wellington bombers. Nevertheless, 36 additional Spitfires were flown in from the old carrier HMS *Furious* to provide reinforced air cover for the convoy's final approaches to the island. Eleven British and two US fast merchant ships sailed from Gibraltar, with the *Ohio*, a new fast oil tanker of particularly strong construction, transferred to British registry from an understandably reluctant Texaco, after the personal intervention of President Roosevelt; her master and crew replaced by British merchant seamen. In common with the other merchantmen, the *Ohio* was provided with additional anti-aircraft guns but her safe arrival was considered to be so critical to Malta's survival that her machinery was modified on the Clyde to make it more shock-resistant. The powerful heavy escort of three fleet carriers and two battleships included HMS *Rodney*, which took the opportunity to use her 16-inch main armament, the biggest guns in the Royal Navy, as spectacular and intimidating anti-aircraft weapons. The convoy suffered serious losses of merchant ships and naval escorts, including the fleet carrier HMS *Eagle*, sunk by a U-boat and bomb damage to another fleet carrier, HMS *Indomitable*, a sister ship of the *Illustrious*. But Malta's surrender was postponed by the five scarred survivors, which staggered into Grand Harbour – including the shockingly battered *Ohio* with her desperately needed cargo of fuel oil and kerosene. Blackened by fire, her engine room flooded and her rudder blown off, still carrying the wreckage of a downed Stuka on her twisted deck, she had limped slowly towards Valletta for several hours. Having been torpedoed and bombed, her back was broken and she was only held in one piece by a destroyer lashed to each beam with another steering at her stern. She finally entered port with her upper deck awash and stayed afloat just long enough to discharge the last of her cargo before sinking to the bottom of Grand Harbour.

Target Date, when Malta's surrender would be unavoidable, was continually put back during 1942 as surviving remnants of convoys, particularly from Operation Pedestal, reached the island, while large submarines delivered a steady trickle of essential fuel and supplies, known as the 'Magic Carpet Service'. In addition, aviation fuel and other key supplies were brought in by heavily escorted fast naval supply ships, with more carried in fast minelayers sailing independently, including HMS *Welshman* disguised as a Vichy French destroyer. Destroyers delivered spare aero-engines, with HMS *Fortune* being so overloaded with this vital deck cargo that she was in danger of capsizing. Malta's situation began to improve after November, when Rommel's retreat from El Alamein allowed the British to provide air cover from re-occupied Libyan airfields, while large-scale Anglo-American landings, Operation Torch, in French North Africa re-focused Axis attention on the opposite end of the Mediterranean. In late November, the Operation Stoneage convoy delivered four ships without loss from Alexandria, moving Target Date back to January 1943, and, from December 1942, almost uncontested convoy operations finally lifted the siege of Malta, although supply ships continued to be convoyed to the island until mid-1944.

The two Battle Summaries reproduced here were written during World War II, produced as Admiralty training documents originally classified as 'Confidential' under the Official Secrets Act. Battle Summary No 18, *Mediterranean Convoys 1941*, was issued in early 1944 as CB (Confidential

Book) 3081(11) and covers three convoys in January, July and September. Battle Summary No 32, *Malta Convoys 1942*, was issued in Autumn 1945 as CB 3081(25) and covers four convoy operations, including Operation Pedestal. The security classification of both documents was downgraded to 'Restricted' in the early 1950s, before they were updated and rewritten to include information from German and Italian archives and revised British records. A new edition of both Battle Summaries was produced as a combined volume and issued in 1957 as BR (Book of Reference) 1736 (11), entitled *Selected Convoys (Mediterranean) 1941–1942* in the Naval Staff History of the Second World War series. This was printed only in small numbers and was not intended to be available to the public, being classified as 'Restricted', although it was finally declassified in the early 1970s.

Despatches from senior Royal Navy officers in command during Mediterranean convoy battles were submitted to the Admiralty as formal accounts of the actions, and these were published as a *Supplement to the London Gazette* in August 1948. Before this, the despatches were made available to the writers of the Mediterranean Convoy Battle Summaries, but excerpts are included in this volume as they are historically important in their own right, being accounts written immediately after the battles in the words of those who were there.

Extracts from another Admiralty official document, *Review of Damage to His Majesty's Ships (3rd September 1941 to 2nd September 1942)*, are also included. Originally written in 1943, it was an internal working document for the Directorate of Naval Construction, some in typescript and some in longhand, at a time when resources were scarce. It was intended to provide technical details and an analysis of battle damage suffered by selected warships, in order to give the Royal Navy operational, damage control and constructional information. The document was originally classified 'Confidential', as CB 4263A, and issued in very small numbers with a limited distribution, but was later downgraded to 'Restricted' and, finally, declassified. In the normal course of events, all copies would have been destroyed but one was recognised as an extremely scarce and important historical source, and was lodged in the Britannia Royal Naval College archive. The detailed plans and drawings are especially valuable in illustrating the scale and effects of the damage suffered by each ship. The extracts include generic technical assessments of damage to Royal Navy warships, plus detailed descriptions of damage incurred by the following four ships during the Mediterranean convoy operations:

HMS *Nelson*: (Battleship)	Torpedoed by Italian aircraft on 27 September 1941, during the Operation Halberd convoy, causing damage that was patched up in Gibraltar and then fully repaired during a refit in Rosyth Dockyard that lasted until April 1942.
HMS *Queen Elizabeth*: (Battleship)	Suffered severe mine damage on 19 December 1941, in Alexandria Harbour, that was temporarily repaired there, enabling her to sail in June 1942 to Norfolk Navy Yard for a refit that lasted a year. Similar damage to her sister ship HMS *Valiant*, caused at the same time, is not covered as it was less severe; she was repaired at Alexandria by May 1942.
HMS *Liverpool*: (Cruiser)	Torpedoed by Italian aircraft on 14 June 1942, during the Operation Harpoon convoy, causing damage that was patched up at Gibraltar, allowing her to sail for permanent repairs in Rosyth that were completed by July 1943.
HMS *Indomitable*: (Aircraft carrier)	Bombed by Stukas on 12 August 1942, during the Operation Pedestal convoy, causing damage that was temporarily repaired at Gibraltar, allowing her to sail for a refit in Liverpool that lasted until February 1943. She returned to the Mediterranean in time to be damaged again on 16 August 1943 – this time by torpedo – while supporting the Allied invasion of Sicily.

Bibliography

Bagnasco, E. & de Toro, A., (2011), *The Littorio Class*, Seaforth Publishing.

Beevor, A., (2012), *The Second World War*, Weidenfeld & Nicholson.

Brown, D. K., (2000), *Nelson to Vanguard, Warship Design and Development 1923–1945*, Chatham Publishing.

Burt, R. A., (2012), *British Battleships 1919–1945*, Seaforth Publishing.

Bush, Capt. E., (1958), *Bless Our Ship*, George Allen & Unwin.

Cunningham of Hyndhope, Viscount, (1951), *A Sailor's Odyssey*, Hutchinson.

Debono, C., (2010), *Radar Stations During Wartime Malta*, Times of Malta, Valetta.

Douglas-Hamilton, J., (1990), *The Air Battle for Malta*, Airlife Publishing.

Friedman, N., (1988), *British Carrier Aviation*, Conway Maritime Press.

Greene, J. and Massignani, A., (1998), *The Naval War in the Mediterranean 1940–1943*, Chatham Publishing.

Grove, E., (1993), *Sea Battles in Close Up Vol 2*, Ian Allan.

Hinsley, F. H. et al, (1979 & 1981), *British Intelligence in the Second World War Vols 1 & 2*, HMSO.

Holland, J., (2003), *Fortress Malta*, Orion Books.

Howse, D., (1993), *Radar at Sea, The Royal Navy in World War 2*, Macmillan Press.

Ireland, B., (1993), *The War in the Mediterranean*, Arms and Armour Press.

Lenton H. J. & Colledge J. J., (1964), *British Warship Losses of World War II*, Ian Allan.

Macintyre, D., (1964), *The Battle for the Mediterranean*, Batsford.

McCart, N., (2000), *The Illustrious and Implacable Classes of Aircraft Carrier 1940–1969*, Fan Publications.

Pack, S. W. C., (1973), *The Battle for Crete*, Ian Allan.

Pack S. W. C., (1975), *The Battle of Sirte*, Ian Allan.

Piekalkiewicz, J., (1992), *Rommel and the Secret War in North Africa 1941–1943*, Schiffer Publishing.

Parkes, Dr O., (1966), *British Battleships*, Seeley Service.

Shankland, P. & Hunter, A., (1961), *Malta Convoy*, Collins.

Smith, P., (1970), *Pedestal: the Malta Convoy of August 1942*, William Kimber.

Spooner, T., (1996), *Supreme Gallantry: Malta's Role in Allied Victory 1939–1945*, John Murray.

Stephens, M., (1991), *The Fighting Admirals*, Leo Cooper.

Thomas, D. A., (1999), *Malta Convoys*, Leo Cooper.

Warner, O., (1967), *Cunningham of Hyndhope, Admiral of the Fleet*, John Murray.

Woodman, R., (2000), *Malta Convoys 1940–1943*, John Murray.

C.B. 3305 (1)   BR 1736 (11)

NAVAL STAFF HISTORY
SECOND WORLD WAR

BATTLE SUMMARIES Nos. 18 and 32

SELECTED CONVOYS
(Mediterranean)
1941 – 1942

T.S.D. 30/51
Training and Staff Duties Division (Historical Section),
Naval Staff, Admiralty, S.W.1

The two Battle Summaries superseded by this volume were originally issued in 1944 and 1945, and were contained in two separate books. In the present volume they have been largely rewritten to include information from the opposing side and other sources not available at the time they were produced. They have also been amended in matters of detail, where such have proved in error. The Introduction and Chapters VII and VIII are entirely new.

Part I of the ensuing book contains the story of three convoys in 1941, when the arrival of German air forces to stiffen the Italians greatly complicated the problem. (This was formerly Battle Summary No. 18.)

Part II deals with the attempts to relieve Malta in the critical conditions of March, June and August, 1942 (former Battle Summary No. 32).

It must be remembered that all these events took place in the early days of radar. Few ships were fitted with sets other than for the detection of high-flying aircraft, and fewer still for fighter direction.

Plans illustrating the events described have been redrawn to include up-to-date information and will be found at the end of the volume, together with a reference chart of the Mediterranean Sea.

January 1956

CONTENTS
Part I – Convoys in 1941, Battle Summary No. 18

Chapter I
Operation "Excess"
Background and Object of Operation 35
Defence Measures 36
Passage, 6–9 January 38
Torpedo-Boat Action 40
Enemy Air Attacks: *Gallant* Mined 40
Illustrious Damaged 42
Movements, 10–12 January 47
Loss of *Southampton*: *Gloucester* Damaged 48
End of Operations 50

Chapter II
Operation "Substance"
Object and Plan 51
Start of Operations 55
Air Attacks: *Fearless* Sunk, *Manchester* and *Firedrake* Damaged 55
M.T.B., Attacks, 23–24 July 61
Arrival at Malta 63
Passage to Gibraltar 64
Movements of Mediterranean Fleet 65
Remarks on Operation 65

Chapter III
Operation "Halberd"
Plan of Operation "Halberd" 70
Passage, 24–26 September 72
Italian Reactions 75
Enemy Air Attacks: *Nelson* Damaged 75
Italian Fleet at Sea 77
Night Attacks on Convoy 80
Westerly Passage of Empty Transports 83
Return Passage to Gibraltar 85
British Submarine Operations 86
Remarks on Operation 87

Part II – Convoys in 1942, Battle Summary No. 32

Chapter IV
Operation "M.G.1"

General Situation 92
Plan of Operation "M.G.1" 93
Passage of Convoy M.W.10 94
Rear-Admiral Vian's Tactical Intentions 95
Surface Action, Gulf of Sirte: First Contact 96
German Air Attacks on Convoy 102
Movements of Italian Fleet 102
Surface Action – Second Phase 104
Arrival of Convoy M.W.10 at Malta: Air Attacks and Damage 115
Submarine Attacks on Italian Forces 117
Return of Admiral Vian to Alexandria 118

Chapter V
Operation "Harpoon"

Situation in Malta: Operations "Harpoon" and "Vigorous" 120
Plan of Operation "Harpoon" 121
Passage, 11–14 June 122
Italian Reactions 123
Air Attacks 123
Damaged *Liverpool* Returns to Gibraltar 126
Further Air Attacks: 3 M.S. Sunk 126
Movements of Italian Surface Forces 129
Surface Action off Pantellaria 134
Loss of *Bedouin* 138
Arrival at Malta: Mine Damage 139

Chapter VI
Operation "Vigorous"

Plan of Operation "Vigorous" 141
Sailing of Convoys 145
Air, Submarine and M.T.B. Attacks 146
Movements of Italian Fleet: British Air and S/M Attacks:
        Trento Sunk 148

C-in-C. Mediterranean's Instructions 152
Threat of Italian Fleet: Further Air Attacks on Convoy 153
Convoy Recalled to Alexandria: *Hermione* Sunk by U-Boat 155
Return Passage of Italian Fleet 155

Chapter VII
Operation "Pedestal"

Strategical Situation 158
Planning and Plan of Operation "Pedestal" 159
Preparations: Passage, U.K. to Gibraltar 162
Operation "Bellows": Loss of *Eagle*: First Air Attack 163
Enemy Intentions 167
Air Attacks 169
S/M Attack in Narrows: *Nigeria*, *Cairo*, *Kenya*, *Ohio* Torpedoed:
      Dusk Air Attack 172
M.T.B. Attacks: Loss of *Manchester* and 4 M.S. 174
Movements of Italian Cruisers: *Bolzano* and *Attendolo* Torpedoed ... 175
Air Attacks on Force "X" and Convoy: Further Damage 176
Arrival at Malta 178
Return Passage of Forces to Gibraltar 180
Conclusion 181

Chapter VIII
Comment and Reflections

Strategical Conditions 183
Comparison with Arctic Convoys 184
Planning and Preparation: Security 185
Tactical Aspect 186
"By-products" 189

Epilogue

Epilogue 193

Appendices

Appendix A 194
Appendix B 199
Appendix C 201
Appendix D 203
Appendix E 207

Appendix F 211
Appendix G 214
Appendix H 217
Appendix I 219
Appendix J 222
Appendix K 229
Appendix L 235
Appendix M 237
Appendix N 241
Appendix O 243
Appendix P 245
Appendix Q 247

Endnotes 249

Abbreviations

A.A.	anti-aircraft
A/C	aircraft
A/S	anti-submarine
A.S.V.	air-surface vessel (radar)
C.-in-C.	Commander-in-Chief
C.S.	Cruiser Squadron
D. of S.T.	Director of Sea Transport
E-boat	motor torpedo boat
F.A.A.	Fleet Air Arm
H.A.	high angle (gunnery)
L.A.	low angle (gunnery)
M.S.	merchant ship
M/S	mine-sweeper/sweeping
M.T.B.	motor torpedo boat
N.I.D.	Naval Intelligence Division
P.M.	Prime Minister
R.A.	Rear-Admiral
R.A.(A)	Rear-Admiral, Aircraft Carriers
R.A.F.	Royal Air Force
R.F.A.	Royal Fleet Auxiliary
R.O.	Record Office (Admiralty)
R/T	radio-telephony
S.O.O.	Staff Officer, Operations
T.S.D.S.	two-speed destroyer sweep (minesweeping)
U.K.	United Kingdom
V.A.	Vice-Admiral
V.H.F.	very high frequency
W/T	wireless telegraphy

Overview

The passage of a convoy through narrow waters in the face of determined attacks by aircraft, submarines, surface craft and mining is one of the most hazardous and arduous operations of maritime warfare.

This was the problem which immediately confronted Great Britain on the declaration of war by Italy in June 1940.

It was at once apparent that the regular flow of slow merchant shipping through the Mediterranean was impracticable, and the bulk of supplies for Alexandria and the Middle East was diverted round the Cape of Good Hope. But occasions arose in which the urgency of the situation in the Middle East necessitated the running of fast convoys through the Mediterranean, and there was always Malta – at once the linchpin of British strategy and its "Achilles heel". Malta, within 60 miles from Sicily and roughly a thousand miles alike from Gibraltar and Alexandria, had to be kept supplied either from the east or from the west; and it was on the ability of the British Navy, with the help of the Air Force, to achieve this that the security of the island depended.

The problem had been much debated in the years prior to 1939, and investigations in which the R.A.F. took part had been held at the Royal Naval Staff College and elsewhere. Broadly speaking, the result of these pre-war investigations had been to confirm the R.A.F. in their view that enemy air power would render the undertaking impossible; while the Navy, though not convinced of the truth of this conclusion, was very well aware of the hazards such operations would involve.

Within a few days of the outbreak of war with Italy, Admiral Sir Andrew Cunningham put the matter to the test, and by the end of 1940 it was felt that the measure of the enemy had been taken. Brushes between Italian heavy ships and the Mediterranean Fleet in July[1] and Sir James Somerville's Force "H" in November[2] had led to the precipitate withdrawal of the enemy on each occasion, and the attacks of the Italian air force, though severe, had inflicted little damage and, together with submarine attacks, could be regarded as an acceptable war risk.

At the beginning of 1941, however, a "potent new factor" made itself felt. Strong German air forces were based in Sicily; and from then onwards operations in the Central Mediterranean became hazardous in the extreme. It was found possible, nevertheless, to maintain the supply of Malta throughout that year.

The beginning of 1942 saw a change greatly in favour of the enemy, which continued throughout the greater part of the year. In the first place, serious losses in capital ships in the late autumn of 1941[3] and the necessity to form the Eastern Fleet on the outbreak of war with Japan had reduced the Mediterranean Fleet to a handful of cruisers and destroyers. The *Ark Royal*, too, had been sunk in November, leaving only the old carriers *Eagle* and *Argus* available to work with Force "H".

Conditions in Malta itself and the events of the land campaign in Libya, too, rendered the supply of the island very much more difficult. In December 1941 air attacks on Malta were stepped up and continued to increase in severity till May 1942. Desperate though the island's needs, even if supplies could be got there, to land them during the heavy assaults from the air in April and May was out of the question, as was plainly shown by the fate of the ships which arrived towards the end of March. As for the fighting on land, the Germans and Italians advanced from Agheila to Gazala between 21 January and 7 February, thereby depriving the Fleet of the valuable advanced base of Benghazi and ships in the Central Mediterranean of the air cover which the Royal Air Force had provided from airfields in Cyrenaica; Tobruk fell a week after the convoy operations in mid-June, and by the end of that month the German and Italian forces had crossed into Egypt and were facing the British Army at El Alamein, less than 50 miles from Alexandria. There they stayed until the last week in October, when there began that great British advance which reached Tripoli in three months and went on to Tunis.

In these difficult circumstances, up to August six convoys – four from the east and two from the west – met with indifferent success. Two convoys from Egypt, one in January and one in March – the latter only to be virtually destroyed after arrival – reached Malta; but an attempt in February failed, and the fourth convoy in June was forced to turn back. Two convoys from the west, one in June (synchronised with the one from Egypt) and one in August, both sorely reduced by losses on the way, reached the island. After that the Home Fleet, from which the bulk of the escorts came, was fully occupied with the convoys to North Russia; several of the destroyers that escorted the

August convoy in the Mediterranean went straight back to serve with the Arctic convoys in September.

Then came calls on the Home Fleet in connection with the landings in Algeria at the beginning of November, and it was not till 20 November – the day the Army took Benghazi – that another convoy from Egypt arrived at Malta. The crisis was then passed and others followed in December.

Altogether 60 supply ships sailed for Malta under escort during the year: 30 arrived, 20 were lost and 10 had to turn back. An aircraft carrier, two cruisers, an A.A. ship and nine destroyers[4] were lost in these operations, whilst other warships were seriously damaged.

Apart from the regular convoys, the most pressing needs of Malta were supplied by submarines, which carried twenty small cargoes to the island during the year, and by the fast minelayers *Welshman* and *Manxman*, which made six passages sailing alone. Some 350 fighter aircraft arrived also, flown off from H.M. ships *Argus, Eagle* and *Furious* and from U.S.S. *Wasp*.

Chapters I, II and III[5] of the ensuing battle summary describe the passages of three military convoys from Gibraltar in 1941. There were other similar operations during that year, but the three described have been chosen as illustrating the different sorts of opposition that had to be faced and overcome. In none of these operations did the convoys suffer attack from a hostile fleet, though on one occasion heavy ships approached within 50 miles or so. But the threat was always present, and attacks by submarines, torpedo-boats, and especially aircraft in varying forms threw a heavy strain on both warships and merchant ships.

Chapters IV to VII[6] deal with the convoys run in the worsened conditions of March, June and August, 1942. The losses and setbacks to these were mainly due to the enemy's strength in the air; but behind this was the great numerical superiority of the Italians in surface ships which, had they been more enterprising, could scarcely have failed to inflict material damage on more than one occasion, and, as things were, by its mere existence prevented the arrival of Convoy M.W.11 from Egypt in June. The Italians always had three or four battleships ready for service and a considerable force of large cruisers and destroyers. The convoys in the western basin had the support of a battleship or two, lent from the North Atlantic or Home Fleet; but in the eastern basin cruisers and destroyers alone were available as escorts. How a weaker force outfaced material superiority, and also when it had to abandon the attempt, emerges from the story.

Part I

Operation "Excess"

Background and Object of Operation

On 28 October, 1940, the Italians had crossed the Albanian frontier and invaded Greece, expecting an easy victory over the ill-equipped Greek army. Things did not go according to plan, however; the Italians failed in their thrusts, and in mid-November the Greeks, supported by the R.A.F., went over to the offensive. By 28 November they had driven the Italians back to within 50 miles of Durazzo; then severe winter weather held up the offensive, though the Greeks held their positions till early in April, when the Germans came to the rescue of their Allies.

From the naval point of view the Italian attack on Greece enabled our Mediterranean Fleet to use Suda Bay as a much-needed advanced base.

Naturally, assistance to the Greeks in every feasible form became one of our main concerns in the eastern Mediterranean, and in January 1941 an operation was staged to pass a military convoy named "Excess" from Gibraltar through the Mediterranean. It consisted of four ships, three for the Piraeus with stores for the Greek Army and one with stores for Malta – in all, 39,500 gross tons. Small as at first sight it might appear, the operation employed nearly all our naval strength in the Mediterranean, namely Force "H" from Gibraltar under Vice-Admiral Sir James Somerville and the bulk of the Mediterranean Fleet from Alexandria under Admiral Sir Andrew Cunningham. When the convoy reached the narrow waters between Sicily and Tunisia, the Gibraltar force turned back, leaving the transports to go on with a small escort to meet the Mediterranean ships beyond the Narrows. Admiral Cunningham took advantage of the occasion to ensure the passage of three subsidiary convoys (Operation MC.4) between Egypt and Malta. These consisted of two ships from Alexandria to Malta (M.W.5½) two fast ships from Malta to Alexandria (M.E.5½), and six slow ships from Malta to Port Said and Alexandria (M.E.6). The first of these three convoys went to Malta during the passage of the fleet westward to meet Convoy "Excess"; the other two left Malta as the fleet was returning, the fast ships joining Convoy "Excess" near Malta and keeping it company so far as their ways lay together, while the slow ships went eastward along a parallel route farther south.[7]

The most dangerous part of the voyage was that between Sardinia and Malta. There for a stretch of some 400 miles (26 hours at 15 knots) ships were exposed to attack from enemy air stations in Sardinia and Sicily, less than 150 miles away. Submarines and surface torpedo craft were a constant menace, and mines too were a possible danger. Attack by large surface ships was less likely, though potentially more dangerous, especially if the Italians attacked the convoy with battleships on one side and cruisers on the other, which Admiral Somerville thought possible.[8] They had no lack of forces for such an attack; for they had two or possibly three battleships and a dozen cruisers ready for service. To guard against this danger, Admiral Somerville asked for a third capital ship and some cruisers to strengthen Force "H", which otherwise would have consisted only of the *Renown* and *Malaya*, the *Sheffield* and *Bonaventure* (a new type of anti-aircraft cruiser), the aircraft carrier *Ark Royal*, and a screen of 11 destroyers. Failing this addition, he proposed three counter-measures, first, a maximum concentration of submarines, suitably disposed in the western basin; secondly, the operation of an air striking force from Malta against the Italian fleet on critical days; and finally, a feint movement of heavy forces from the eastern Mediterranean towards the Narrows on the afternoon and night before the most critical day of the voyage. Admiral Cunningham thought the Italian superiority in cruisers did not greatly matter, provided the safe arrival of the convoy was the single purpose of the expedition, as difficulties in the service of convoys arose in his opinion chiefly from the handicap of a divided object. To meet the contingency, however, he detached two cruisers, the *Gloucester* and *Southampton*, to join Convoy "Excess" for the dangerous passage between Sardinia and Malta, which left him four cruisers and an old anti-aircraft ship to serve the other convoys. He also decided that, instead of making a "feint movement," he would join Convoy "Excess" himself, a few miles east of the Narrows (*i.e.*, 100 miles west of Malta), with the battleships *Warspite* and *Valiant*, the aircraft carrier *Illustrious*, and some destroyers.[9]

Defence Measures

There were three critical stages in the passage from Sardinia to Malta, and the following were the escorts allotted to protect Convoy "Excess" in those areas.

Sardinia to the Narrows (130 miles)
 Capital ships, 2 – *Renown* (Flag, Vice-Admiral Sir James Somerville),
        Malaya

Aircraft carrier, 1 – *Ark Royal*
Cruisers, 4   – *Sheffield, Bonaventure, Gloucester* (Flag Rear-Admiral Renouf), *Southampton*
Destroyers, 12   –   (including one from the Eastern Mediterranean)

Through the Narrows (150 miles)
Cruisers, 3   – *Bonaventure, Gloucester, Southampton*
Destroyers, 5

The Narrows to Malta (110 miles)
Capital ships, 2 – *Warspite* (Flag, Commander-in-Chief), *Valiant*
Aircraft carrier, 1 – *Illustrious*
Cruisers, 3   – *Bonaventure, Gloucester, Southampton*
Destroyers, 13

In addition, three submarines were stationed near Sardinia while Convoy "Excess" was passing that island – the *Pandora* off the east coast and the *Triumph* and *Upholder* to the southward, as shown in Plan 1.

For the protection of the Malta-Egypt convoys there remained available the cruisers *Orion* (Flag, Vice-Admiral Pridham-Wippell), *Perth, Ajax* and *York;* the anti-aircraft ship *Calcutta;* two destroyers and four corvettes.

The Royal Air Force also took part in the operation. Aircraft from Gibraltar furnished anti-submarine patrols while the convoy was passing through the Straits, and aircraft from Malta reconnoitred Italian ports, an area north and west of Sicily, and the Narrows. The reconnaissance was not, however, on a big scale, and Admiral Somerville reported that he was "obliged to rely solely on carrier reconnaissance for information of the presence of enemy surface vessels in the area south and east of Sardinia." He added that "the danger of surprise contacts with enemy surface forces will continue until existing shore-based reconnaissance can be augmented." The orders made no provision for the air striking force he had proposed, nor for protection by shore-based fighters, nor for attack upon the enemy's air stations during the passage of the convoys.

The operation was marked by the first appearance of German aircraft in large numbers in the Mediterranean. Admiral Cunningham reported afterwards that the enemy had probably some 400 or 500 German bombers[10] at Catania in Sicily and at African air stations, apart from the many Italian aircraft within reach of the convoys. Their air force operating from Sicily made a great effort to destroy the *Illustrious*; and the dive-bombing attack on her and the *Warspite* and *Valiant* was pressed home with grim determination.

Passage, 6–9 January

Convoy "Excess", consisting of four ships, left Gibraltar before dark in the evening of 6 January, escorted by the *Bonaventure* and four destroyers. At first they steered westward to mislead spies, turning back in the night in time to pass Europa Point after moonset and before daylight next morning; the ruse was successful though the *Bonaventure* reported that fishing craft and merchant ships must have seen the convoy going east again while the moon was still up. At dawn on 7 January, the *Bonaventure* parted company to return to Admiral Somerville, who sailed about that time with the rest of the ships which were to form the escort from Sardinia to the Narrows.

All that day the convoy followed the Spanish coast as if bound for a Spanish port; the wind was light, the sea was calm; that night the convoy crossed to the coast of Africa and steered eastward for the Narrows, keeping 30 miles or so off shore. 7 January was to be Day One of the operation. The Admiral had arranged to overtake the convoy and its four destroyers in the night of 7/8 January, and then to keep some distance north and east of them until the morning of 9 January, in order to screen them from enemy aircraft, unless he had reason to believe that Italian ships were at sea to the west of Sardinia; in this case he would join the convoy with his whole force. In any case the convoy was to be joined by the *Bonaventure* in the morning of 8 January, and by the *Malaya* and two more destroyers in the evening.[11] As it turned out, air reconnaissance from Malta in the forenoon of 8 January located two or possibly three Italian battleships at Naples, three cruisers at Messina, and four cruisers at Taranto – the other cruisers were probably at Brindisi and Naples. When morning dawned on 9 January, the Admiral was ahead of the convoy with only the *Renown*, *Ark Royal*, *Sheffield* and five destroyers. At 0500,[12] in 37° 45' N., 7° 15' E., the *Ark Royal* flew off five Swordfish aircraft for Malta, some 350 miles away, all of which arrived safely. The Admiral then turned back to meet the convoy, joining it about 0900, roughly 120 miles south-west of Sardinia. The *Ark Royal* had seven reconnaissance aircraft, one anti-submarine and three fighters up. At 0918 an aircraft made an enemy report of two cruisers and two destroyers to the eastward. These ships turned out to be Force "B" under Rear-Admiral Renouf from the Mediterranean Fleet; and an hour later Admiral Renouf joined the convoy with the cruisers *Gloucester* and *Southampton* and a destroyer.[13]

Admiral Renouf had sailed from Alexandria at 1300 on 6 January with troops for Malta on board his cruisers. They arrived in the Grand Harbour at 0915/8, disembarked the troops, and sailed at 1345 in the afternoon. They passed Pantellaria that evening, sighting five mines 15 miles west of the island. The moon was bright and the weather fine. A signal station on the island had apparently challenged him. Apart from this minor incident there was nothing to suggest that the enemy knew anything of the operation until just before the junction of the three groups of ships. At 0900/9, however, an Italian aircraft closed Admiral Renouf's force, making off when fired at; another shadower, sighted about 1000, escaped from the *Ark Royal*'s fighter patrol. At 1320, in 37° 38' N., 8° 31' E., by the *Gloucester*'s reckoning, bombers appeared on the scene and made their attack.

The convoy of four ships was steaming at the time in two columns in line ahead, 1,500 yards apart, the *Gloucester* and *Malaya* leading the columns, with the *Bonaventure* and *Southampton* as sternmost ships and seven destroyers in the screen ahead. The *Renown* and *Ark Royal*, screened by the *Sheffield* and five destroyers, were stationed "in close support" on the convoy's port quarter. The mean line of advance was 088°, and the ships were zigzagging at 14 knots. The enemy consisted of ten Savoia bombers. The *Sheffield* detected them 43 miles off (the maximum working range of her radar), fine on the starboard bow, and they came in sight fourteen minutes later, flying down the starboard side of the convoy out of range at a height of about 11,000 ft. Twelve minutes later still, at 1346, having worked round broad on the bow, they began their attack, coming in from 145°, the bearing of the sun. All the ships opened a heavy fire, which Admiral Somerville considered much more accurate than on previous occasions. Admiral Renouf thought the barrage from the *Renown* and her consorts, bursting over the convoy, diverted the enemy from their original course. On the other hand, Captain Egerton of the *Bonaventure* remarked that most of the shells burst well below the aircraft. Eight aircraft dropped bombs, some of which fell near the *Gloucester* and *Malaya* but did no harm, while the rest fell clear. The other two bombers turned away during the approach, perhaps upset by the ship's fire, and a Fulmar from the *Ark Royal* shot them down; they crashed within sight of the *Malaya*, and three men of their crews were picked up. The other fighters lost touch with the enemy in the clouds during the attack; except for one possibly shot down by the *Bonaventure*, the rest of the bombers got away.

Nothing more happened that afternoon, 9 January, though the fighter patrol reported sighting another party of Savoia aircraft from Cagliari half an hour after the attack. Nor was there even a hint of danger from the Italian fleet. The *Ark Royal* had had seven aircraft up all the forenoon, reconnoitring as far as the Skerki Bank and back to the south-east coast of Sardinia, and two aircraft left her at 1600 to search a hundred miles ahead of the convoy. They saw nothing; and a "nil" report had also come at midday from the Royal Air Force flying boat on patrol north and west of Sicily. At dusk, in 37° 42' N., 9° 53' E., some 30 miles westward of the Narrows and north of Bizerta, Admiral Somerville parted company to go back with Force "H" proper to Gibraltar, where he arrived on 11 January after an uneventful passage. Admiral Renouf in the *Gloucester* took the convoy on with the three cruisers and five destroyers of Forces "B" and "F".[14]

Torpedo-Boat Action

They had a quiet night, passing Pantellaria after moonset and giving the island as wide a berth as possible, while keeping in deep water to lessen the danger of mines. But next morning at 0720/10, just as dawn broke, they encountered two Italian torpedo boats, the *Vega*[15] and *Circe*[15], some three miles off on the port beam, in about 36° 30' N., 12° 10' E., a dozen miles south and east of Pantellaria. The *Jaguar*, port wing ship in the screen, and the *Bonaventure*, stationed astern of the columns, sighted the strangers at the same time. Thinking they might be destroyers of Admiral Cunningham's force, which the convoy was due to meet, both British ships reported the enemy by signal to Admiral Renouf before attacking, and the *Bonaventure* challenged them. Then she fired a star shell, turned for the enemy at full speed, and engaged the right-hand ship of the pair. Admiral Renouf turned the convoy away from the danger, while the *Southampton*, *Jaguar* and *Hereward*, hauling out from their stations on the engaged side, made for the enemy. By the time they arrived the *Bonaventure* had shifted her attention to the other Italian (the *Vega*), which came towards her at full speed to attack. She fired her torpedoes, which the *Bonaventure* avoided; and between them the four British ships quickly stopped the enemy, but did not sink her, though the *Bonaventure* alone fired 600 rounds. In the end the *Hereward* torpedoed her, some forty minutes after the fight began. The first Italian had disappeared.[16]

Enemy Air Attacks: *Gallant* Mined

At 0800 on 10 January, Admiral Cunningham arrived on the scene with Force "A", before the little fight was finished (see Appendix A). Half an hour later, when the Fleet had turned south-east again in the wake of the convoy, the destroyer *Gallant* in the screen had her bows blown off by a mine. The *Mohawk* took her in tow, and they steered for Malta, escorted by the *Bonaventure* and *Griffin*, which were joined later by Admiral Renouf with the *Gloucester* and *Southampton*. Two Italian torpedo aircraft attacked whilst the cripple was getting in tow, but the fire of the *Bonaventure* and *Mohawk* forced them to drop their torpedoes at long range without effect. Between 1130 and 1800, as the two crawled along at five or six knots, with the escort zigzagging at 20 knots, they were attacked or threatened ten times by aircraft, nearly all German high-level bombers, which came in ones, twos or threes. Fortunately the *Bonaventure* always managed to give warning, and the ships' fire generally spoilt the attacks; for, though the enemy dropped their bombs in five out of the ten attempts, there was only one moment of real danger – at 1300, when three German dive-bombers succeeded in slightly damaging the *Southampton* by a near-miss. The *Gallant*, with the *Bonaventure*[17], *Mohawk* and *Griffin*, reached Malta safely the next forenoon.

The ships with Admiral Cunningham had a similar experience on a larger scale. The enemy had good intelligence of the Admiral's movements, for their aircraft had found him on 7 January (the day he sailed from Alexandria) and again on 9 January, and finally at 0930/10, an hour and a half after his joining Convoy "Excess". In the course of the afternoon, heavy dive-bombing attacks were pressed home with skill and determination, mainly directed against the *Illustrious*. They attacked chiefly with German dive-bombers, though there was one attempt by a pair of Italian torpedo aircraft and one by Italian high-level bombers. Had some of the dive-bombers attacked the convoy instead of the supporting men-of-war, said Admiral Cunningham, all four transports must inevitably have been sunk. As it was, out of 70 or 80 aircraft altogether engaged, only three high-level bombers attacked the convoy and without effect. On the other hand, the *Illustrious* was disabled, and her services were lost to the fleet for many months.

At noon the transports were steering south-eastward, zigzagging at 14 to 15 knots, with an escort of three destroyers – joined at 1320 by the *Calcutta* which arrived before the bombing of the convoy itself began. The *Warspite*, *Illustrious* and *Valiant* were steaming in line ahead on the convoy's starboard quarter, course 110°, zigzagging at 17 and later at 18 knots, with seven destroyers in the screen. The weather was clear, with high cloud; a fresh breeze was blowing from south-south-west, roughly at right-angles to the mean line of advance.[18]

The fleet was in 35° 59' N., 13° 13' E., some 55 miles west of Malta, when the battle began with an attack by two Savoia torpedo aircraft, which were detected six miles away on the starboard beam at 1220. They came in at a steady level, 150 feet above the water, and dropped their torpedoes about 2,500 yards from the battleships. They were sighted a minute before firing, and the ships received them with a barrage from long- and short-range guns, altering course to avoid the torpedoes, which passed astern of the rearmost ship, the *Valiant*. Five Fulmars from the *Illustrious* had been patrolling above the fleet, but one had returned on board, disabled while assisting to destroy a shadower some time before the attack; the other four fighters chased the torpedo planes as far as Linosa Island, about 20 miles to the westward, and claimed to have damaged both of them.

Directly after this attack, while the ships were re-forming the line, a strong force of aircraft was reported at 1235 coming from the northward some 30 miles away. The Fulmars, of course, were then a long way off, flying low, and with little ammunition left after their two engagements; indeed, two had fired all they had. They were ordered back over the fleet, and the *Illustrious* sent up four fresh aircraft besides reliefs for the anti-submarine patrol. This meant a turn of 100° to starboard into the wind to fly off; the enemy came in sight in the middle of the operation, which lasted about four minutes, and the ships opened fire. The fleet had just got back to the proper course of 110°, and the Admiral had made the signal to assume loose formation, when the new attack began. The enemy had assembled astern of their target "in two very loose and flexible formations" at a height of 12,000 feet.

Illustrious Damaged

They were Junkers dive-bombers, perhaps as many as 36, of which 18 to 24 attacked the *Illustrious* at 1240, while a dozen attacked the battleships and the screen. They came down in flights of three on different bearings, astern and on either beam, to release their bombs at heights of 1,500 to 800 ft.: "a very severe and brilliantly executed dive-bombing attack," said Captain Boyd of the *Illustrious*. The ships altered course continually, and, beginning with long-range controlled fire during the approach, shifted to barrage fire as the enemy dived to the attack. They shot down at least three aircraft, while the eight Fulmars shot down five more, at a cost of one British fighter; even the two that had no ammunition left made dummy attacks, and forced two Germans to turn away. But, as Captain Boyd pointed out, "at least twelve" fighters in the air would have been required to make any impression on the enemy, and double that number to keep them off. The *Illustrious* was seriously damaged. She was hit six times, mostly with armour-piercing bombs of 1,100 pounds.

They wrecked the flight deck, destroyed nine aircraft on board, put half the 4.5-in. guns out of action, and did other damage, besides setting the ship on fire fore and aft and killing and wounding many of the ship's company. The *Warspite*, too, narrowly escaped serious injury, but got off with a split hawsepipe and damaged anchor.[19]

The ship being useless as a carrier and likely to become a drag on the fleet, Captain Boyd decided to make for Malta. The Commander-in-Chief gave her two destroyers for escort, one from his own screen and one from the convoy's, and she parted company accordingly. She had continual trouble with her steering gear, which at last broke down altogether, so that she had to steer with the engines, making only 17 to 18 knots speed, though on first leaving the fleet she had worked up to 26 knots. Meanwhile, those of her aircraft which were already in the air at the time of the attack flew to Malta, anti-submarine Swordfish as well as Fulmars – some of the fighters had a further turn of service later in the day.

Despatches: Supplement to *The London Gazette*, Published by Authority
The following Despatch was submitted to the Lords Commissioners of the Admiralty on 19 March, 1941 by Admiral Sir Andrew B. Cunningham, G.C.B., D.S.O., Commander-in-Chief, Mediterranean Station.

Wednesday 11 August 1948, Operations M.C.4 and M.C.6

The dive-bombing attacks by German aircraft were most efficiently performed and came as an unpleasant surprise. The results of short range A.A. fire were disappointing, though it has been subsequently learned that this fire was in fact more effective that it appeared, and the Germans suffered considerable loss.

Nevertheless, it is a potent new factor in Mediterranean war and will undoubtedly deny us that free access to the waters immediately surrounding Malta and Sicily which we have previously enjoyed, until our own air forces have been built up to a scale adequate to meet it.

The dive-bombing attacks on the 3rd Cruiser Squadron on the afternoon of 11 January – resulting in the loss of *Southampton* – were a complete surprise, delivered at a time when the ships concerned believed themselves to have drawn clear of the threat of air attack, and when officers and men were doubtless relaxing their vigilance to some extent after a very strenuous four days.

This damaging attack served to emphasise the importance of including an R.D.F. ship [ship fitted with radar equipment] in detached units whenever possible.

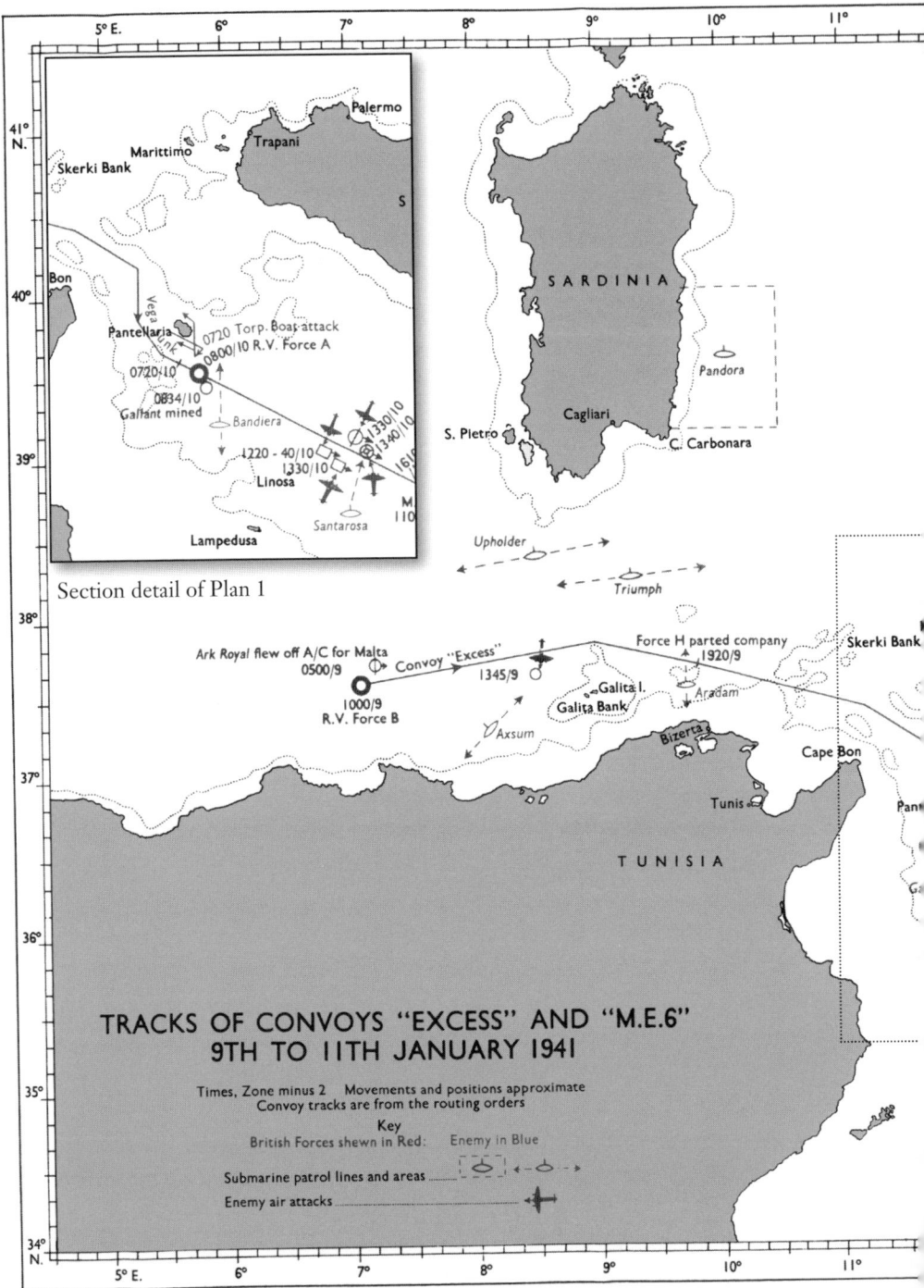

Section detail of Plan 1

TRACKS OF CONVOYS "EXCESS" AND "M.E.6"
9TH TO 11TH JANUARY 1941

Times, Zone minus 2   Movements and positions approximate
Convoy tracks are from the routing orders

Key
British Forces shewn in Red: Enemy in Blue

Submarine patrol lines and areas

Enemy air attacks

C.B.H. 22729

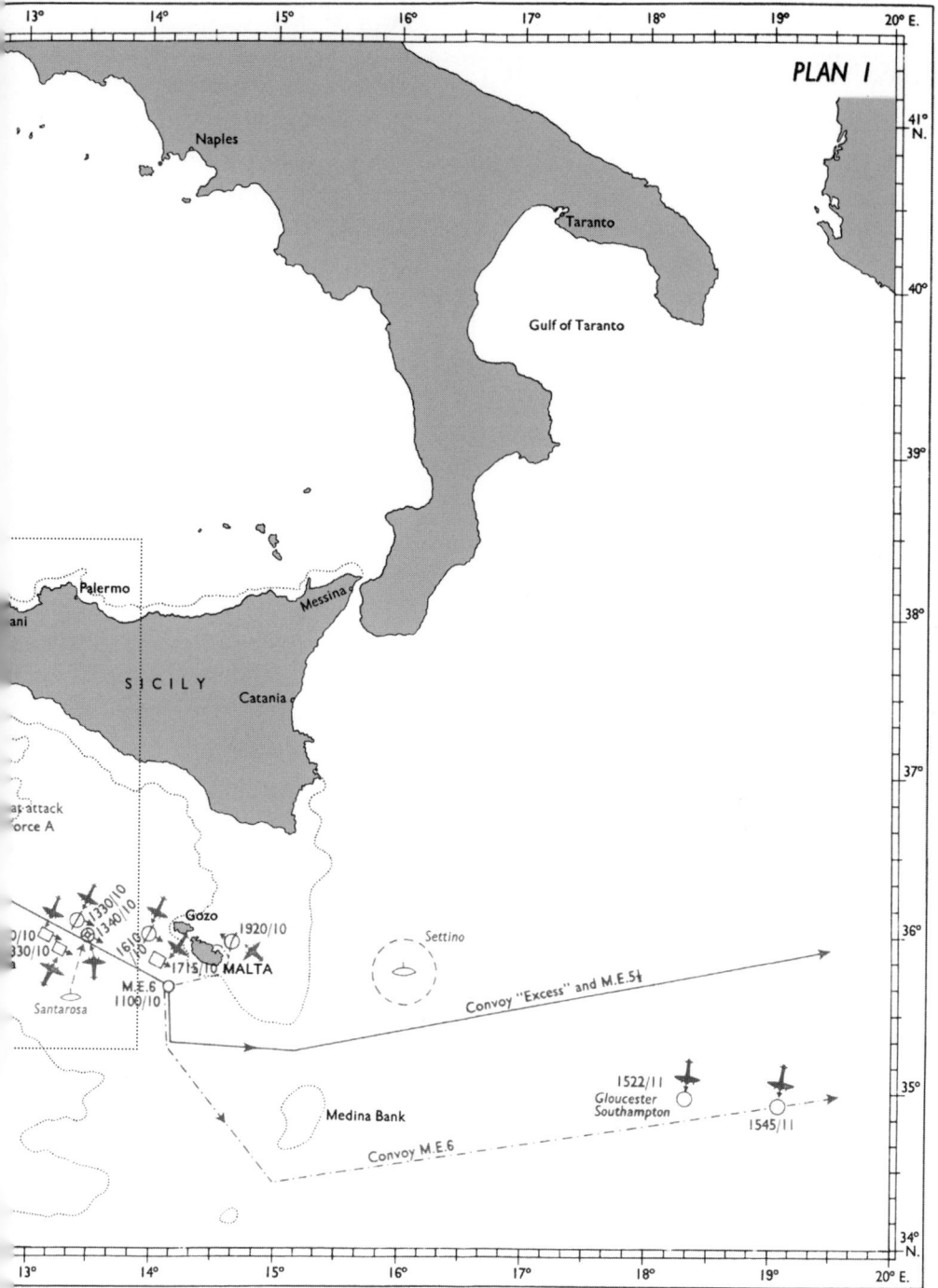

PLAN I

Naples

Taranto

Gulf of Taranto

Palermo

Messina

ani

S I C I L Y

Catania

attack
orce A

1330/10

1340/10

160/0

0/10

330/10

Gozo

1920/10

1715/10 MALTA

M.E.6
1100/10

Santarosa

Settino

Convoy "Excess" and M.E.5↓

Medina Bank

1522/11
Gloucester
Southampton

1545/11

Convoy M.E.6

A third attack came at 1330 on the afternoon of 10 January. By this time the *Illustrious* was 10 miles north-eastward of the battleships; and owing to their manoeuvres during the previous attacks, while the convoy was steaming steadily on, the battleships were nearly as far from the transports, which were themselves attacked at 1340 (see Plan 1). The enemy were high-level bombers, probably Italian, though there may have been some Germans among them. Seven of them attacked the *Illustrious*, and seven more the battleships, while three attacked the convoy. They were detected in good time, the *Valiant* being able to warn the *Illustrious* by signal before the latter sighted her assailants; and the ships received them with a heavy fire as they appeared at a height of 14,000 or 15,000 feet. Even the *Illustrious*, then turning in circles out of control, with only half her guns fit for service, was able to spoil the enemy's aim. All the bombs fell wide. The *Calcutta*, which had arrived but a short time before the attack and was now stationed astern of the transports, hit and perhaps destroyed one bomber.

More serious in its results was a second dive-bombing attack upon the *Illustrious* at 1610. Again the *Valiant* detected the enemy and gave timely warning. There were 15 Junkers bombers, escorted by five fighters, but only nine dropped bombs, the others being kept at arm's length by the fire of the *Illustrious* and her two destroyers. Six aircraft attacked from astern and on either quarter, followed by three that attacked from the starboard beam. Captain Boyd said "this attack was neither so well synchronized nor so determined as that at 1240"; yet one bomb hit, and there were two near misses, resulting in more damage and loss of life. However, the ship was well under control by this time, able to alter course to avoid bombs, and with eight 4.5-in. guns and some pom-poms in action, though smoke and haze from a fire still burning in the hangar interfered with the aim of guns on the lee side. She and the *Jaguar* destroyed at least one enemy aircraft between them.[20]

A few minutes after the attack on the *Illustrious* the six aircraft she had driven off approached the battleships, but again retired on coming under fire. The turn of the battleships for a second dive-bombing attack came an hour later, at 1715, when 17 Germans attacked as before, except that they dropped their bombs at a greater height. The *Valiant* had detected them 50 miles away, so the ships were once more prepared; and they received the enemy in the same way, with controlled fire during the approach and a barrage as they spiralled down into the dive. No bombs hit, but splinters from near misses killed a man in the *Valiant*, and a bomb fell very near the *Janus* without exploding. The ships may have destroyed one aircraft by gunfire. Three Fulmars of the original patrol from the *Illustrious*, directed by wireless from the *Valiant*, came out from Malta and damaged three bombers returning from the attack.[21]

This turned out to be the end of the ordeal for Convoy "Excess" and its supporting ships of war, but not for the *Illustrious* which had one more encounter with the enemy before she reached Malta. About 1920, a little more than an hour after sunset and in moonlight, some aircraft approached from seaward, when she was only 5 miles from the entrance of the Grand Harbour. She had warning from Malta that aircraft were about, and she sighted two – probably torpedo planes. She and her escorting destoyers fired a blind barrage, on which the enemy disappeared. Directly afterwards, the *Hasty* got an Asdic contact and fired depth charges, but whether it was a submarine is uncertain. The *Illustrious* entered harbour about 2100, accompanied by the *Jaguar*, which had passengers to land. Further trials were in store for her in the thirteen days of hurried repairs that followed at a port within easy reach of the enemy's air power.[22]

Movements, 10-12 January

In the meantime, after the mild attack at 1340/10, Convoy "Excess" went on its way unhindered, escorted by the *Calcutta* and a screen of destroyers. Its movements then became involved in those of the Malta–Egypt convoys, which were being run under cover of the main operation with the special support of Vice-Admiral Pridham-Wippell's four cruisers of Force "D", the *Orion*, *Perth*, *Ajax* and *York*. The first of these convoys, the two ships of M.W.5½, had left Alexandria for Malta on 7 January, some hours after Admiral Cunningham sailed westward with Force "A" to meet Convoy "Excess". Both ships had reached Malta without adventure in the morning of 10 January, escorted by the *Calcutta*, *Diamond* and *Defender*. On arrival, the *Calcutta* joined the six slow ships bound for Port Said and Alexandria, Convoy M.E.6, which had just sailed with four corvettes to go east by a route parallel to but south of that followed by Convoy "Excess". At the end of the searched channel they met Admiral Pridham-Wippell, who had been cruising north and east of the incoming convoy the night before, and now took charge of ME.6; the *Calcutta* was ordered to join Convoy "Excess", and arrived in time to defend it from the Italian bombers, as already described.

The last convoy, M.E..5½, two fast ships bound for Alexandria, also left Malta in the morning of 10 January under escort of the *Diamond*;[23] they were to join Convoy "Excess" and proceed in company till they reached the point where the ships for Alexandria must turn southward to clear Crete, while Convoy "Excess" stood on for the Piraeus. The two convoys met that afternoon; and the transport *Essex* left Convoy "Excess" to go to Malta, escorted by one destroyer, which rejoined the fleet after seeing her into harbour.

Admiral Pridham-Wippell stayed with the eastgoing Convoy M.E.6 until dark on 10 January, and then went on with the *Orion* and *Perth* towards a rendezvous with the Commander-in-Chief appointed for next day. But the battleships, owing to the air attacks in the afternoon, were considerably behind time and a long way astern of Convoy "Excess", so Admiral Cunningham ordered Admiral Pridham-Wippell to go north of Convoy "Excess" for the night so as to be between the convoy and possible attack by Italian ships from Taranto or Brindisi. Meanwhile, the battleships also kept to the northward, and gaining ground during the night arrived some 25 miles north of the convoy by daylight, on 11 January, at which time Admiral Pridham-Wippell joined the Commander-in-Chief, who then kept both forces within a few miles of the convoy.

Loss of *Southampton*: *Gloucester* Damaged

These arrangements for the protection of Convoy "Excess" left the six ships of Convoy M.E.6 some 70 to 90 miles to the south and west of the battle fleet with only the *York*[24] and the four corvettes for escort. In the forenoon of 11 January, therefore, the Commander-in-Chief sent his Walrus aircraft to Admiral Renouf, telling him to overtake and support the convoy with the *Gloucester*, *Southampton* and *Diamond* with which he was then steering for Suda Bay, having left the disabled *Gallant* off Malta some hours before. The order reached Admiral Renouf a little after midday, and he shaped course accordingly, steaming at 24 knots against the convoy's 9 or 10 knots, and sending up his aircraft to find the convoy. At 1522, when his ships were some 30 miles astern of it, in 34° 56' N., 18° 19' E., they were suddenly attacked by a dozen German dive-bombers. Fortune was against them. The attack came as an entire surprise, and, according to Captain Rowley of the *Gloucester*, "aircraft were not sighted until the whistle of the first bomb was heard". Six bombers attacked each cruiser, diving steeply from the direction of the sun and each releasing a 550-lb bomb at heights of 1,500 ft to 800 ft. The ships opened fire with 4-in. guns and below, increasing speed and altering course to avoid the attack; but two bombs, or perhaps three, hit the *Southampton*, exploding in "A" boiler-room and the gunroom flat and doing disastrous damage. The *Gloucester* too, was damaged by a bomb which hit her forward 6-in. director tower and penetrated five decks, fortunately without exploding; she was also hit by splinters from a couple of near misses. Half an hour later seven high-level bombers attacked, but the ships saw them and opened fire in good time, and the bombs fell wide. At about the same time a solitary aircraft dropped two bombs between the columns of the convoy, then in 34° 54′ N., 19° 7′ E.

Admiral Renouf had immediately reported the damage to the cruisers by signal to the Commander-in-Chief, who turned to the south-westward to close them, sending Admiral Pridham-Wippell ahead with his two cruisers and two destroyers. Before they arrived, however, Admiral Renouf reported that the *Southampton* must be abandoned and that he would sink her, so the battleships turned east again. The *Southampton* had caught fire badly on being hit. For a time the ship's company fought the fire successfully and kept the ship in action and under control: indeed, she steamed at 20 knots during the second air attack and for an hour longer. Then the fire spread; it was found impossible to flood certain magazines, and after striving nearly four hours to save the ship, officers and men had to give it up. Shortly before 1900 fresh fires were breaking out, water and fire-fighting appliances had failed, and the *Diamond* was ordered alongside to take off the crew.[25] As soon as this was accomplished, a torpedo was fired into her by the *Gloucester*, which, however, did not sink her. The *Diamond* then went alongside the *Gloucester* to transfer survivors; but at 2050 ships were seen approaching and she cast off, lest they were enemy. They proved to be Admiral Pridham-Wippell's force; the *Southampton* was sunk by three torpedoes from the *Orion* and the transfer of survivors was completed by 2220,[26] when course was shaped to rendezvous with the Commander-in-Chief next morning. Meanwhile, the ships for Alexandria had left Convoy "Excess" during the evening of 11 January, the *Calcutta* putting into Suda for oil, while the three ships of Convoy "Excess" with their destroyer screen stood on for the Piraeus, where they arrived safely next morning, 12 January.

End of Operations

On the morning of 12 January, the *Orion*, *Perth*, *Gloucester* and the three destroyers joined the Commander-in-Chief at a rendezvous off the west end of Crete, meeting there also Rear-Admiral Rawlings with the *Barham*, *Eagle*, *Ajax* and their destroyer screen. Under the original plan, the fleet was then to have begun a series of attacks on the Italian shipping routes; but the disabling of the *Illustrious* put an end to the chief part of the plan, so Admiral Cunningham took the *Warspite*, *Valiant*, *Gloucester* and some destroyers straight back to Alexandria. Eventually bad weather prevented Admiral Rawlings from carrying out his share of this operation. Admiral Pridham-Wippell went to the Piraeus with the *Orion* and *Perth*, embarked some troops from ships of Convoy "Excess" there, and took them to Malta – a task the *Southampton* was to have done. Meanwhile, the six ships of Convoy M.E.6, the last to reach port, arrived at their destinations on 13 January. A signal was received on 17 January from the Governor of Malta, expressing high appreciation of the work of the fleet and sympathy for the losses suffered in bringing much-needed aid to Malta.

Not a single ship of the 14 in the four convoys had been lost; but the fleet had had to pay a heavy price for their safety. German dive-bombers had appeared on the scene, presenting "a potent new factor" in the Mediterranean, where the fleet's unquestioned supremacy over the Italian airmen had hitherto enabled it to do its work without undue risk. From that day a heavy menace hung over the Sicilian route, and the voyage to Malta became one of perilous hazard.[27]

Operation "Substance"

Object and Plan

The spring of 1941 saw great changes in favour of the Axis in the strategical situation in the eastern Mediterranean. In Libya German–Italian forces had launched an offensive which compelled General Wavell's army – depleted in order to send assistance to Greece – to relinquish all the ground gained in the winter with the exception of Tobruk, and carried the Axis forces as far as the Egyptian frontier town of Sollum. At the same time the Germans overran Yugoslavia, and the following month occupied Greece and Crete.

The Mediterranean Fleet suffered very heavy loss and damage in these operations, which offset its success in the Battle of Matapan in March. But more serious was the deterioration in the air situation, owing to the possession by the enemy of airfields in Cyrenaica and Libya and their denial to the British. Moreover, the enemy had gained Benghazi as a useful supply base for his armies in addition to Tripoli, while the Mediterranean Fleet had lost its valuable advanced base at Suda.

In the western Mediterranean there had been no great change in the situation, and it was therefore natural that when Malta's needs became compulsive the attempt to reinforce the island should be made from this direction.

Accordingly an operation known as "Substance" was planned to take place in July. The object was to take six storeships and a troopship, known as Convoy G.M.1, from Gibraltar to Malta and at the same time to protect the passage of seven other transports, Convoy M.G.1, going empty from Malta to the westward.

Admiral Somerville was to accompany the convoy from Gibraltar with his whole force as far as the Narrows between Sicily and Tunisia, as he had done in January; but this time Force "H" was to be strengthened considerably by ships that brought out the transports from home. Rear-Admiral Syfret, in the *Edinburgh*, was then to take the convoy through the Narrows to Malta with a detachment of cruisers and destroyers known as Force "X".[28] Meanwhile, the empty transports from Malta, sailing on 23 July, the day the east-going convoy

OPERATION "SUBSTANCE"
TRACKS OF CONVOY G.M.I AND FORCE "H"
22ND - 24TH JULY 1941

Times, Zone minus 2   Movements and positions approximate
Based on plans in M. 012938/41 and Italian Official History
Key
British Forces shewn in Red: Enemy in Blue

Submarine patrol lines and areas
Enemy air attacks

PLAN 2

Section detail of Plan 2

reached the Narrows, were to pass through that area the same night, but by a different route. After parting with Admiral Syfret, the main body of Force "H" cruised south-west of Sardinia to await the return of Force "X" and to "endeavour to distract attention" from the empty ships on their passage westward, "but keeping if possible out of the range of shore-based fighters". To support these operations, Admiral Cunningham arranged a diversion in the eastern Mediterranean by which he led the enemy to believe their ships would risk meeting the Mediterranean Fleet should they put to sea to attack the convoys.

Admiral Somerville had two capital ships, *Renown* and *Nelson*, the aircraft carrier *Ark Royal*, four cruisers, the *Edinburgh*, *Manchester*, *Arethusa* and *Hermione*, the minelayer *Manxman* (serving as a cruiser), and seventeen destroyers – including one employed to escort an oiler from which the destroyers of the fleet were to oil during the voyage. There were also eight submarines at sea, patrolling off Sardinia, Sicily and Naples during the critical days of the operation (see Plan 2). The convoy of empty transports had only one destroyer for escort.

As the Italians were believed to have five battleships fit for service (three of them at Taranto) and no fewer than ten cruisers divided between Taranto, Messina and Palermo, the empty transports ran considerable risk in going from Malta westward without a stronger escort. But there was no help for it. It was not possible to give them better protection without running the gauntlet of the Narrows twice or calling on the Mediterranean Fleet.

The Royal Air Force was able to give more help than in January. Aircraft from Gibraltar furnished anti-submarine patrols for the first two days of the passage east, and others reconnoitred areas between Sardinia and Africa, while aircraft from Malta reconnoitred between Sardinia and Sicily, besides watching the Italian ports. Malta also provided fighters to protect Force "X" and the convoy after the *Ark Royal* had left them. Fortunately, according to the latest intelligence, there were no longer any German aircraft in that part of the Mediterranean. The Italians had apparently some 50 torpedo aircraft and 150 bombers (of which 30 were dive-bombers), roughly half of each type being stationed in Sardinia and half in Sicily.

The transports bound for Malta and most of the other ships of war that joined Admiral Somerville for the occasion came from England with the *Nelson*; the rest, including Admiral Syfret's flagship the *Edinburgh*, were already at Gibraltar with Force "H". In order to conceal the convoy's passage into the Mediterranean, it was arranged that as many ships as possible should go through the Strait of Gibraltar in the night of 20/21 July, without entering harbour. Some ships had to fuel, however, and others had passengers to embark; for there were 5,000 troops going to Malta in the convoy, and part of these troops had to be divided among ships of the escort at Gibraltar. The ships that had to go into harbour were to leave the convoy in two groups in time to arrive on 19 and 20 July respectively; and the passengers were to remove into their new ships after dark on those days. The oiler *Brown Ranger*, too, with her escorting destroyer, was to leave Gibraltar in the night of 20/21 July to join the convoy next morning. Admiral Somerville was to sail last, with the *Renown*, *Ark Royal*, *Hermione* and eight destroyers, leaving harbour in time to clear the Strait before dawn on 21 July.

Start of Operations

The six storeships entered the Mediterranean in the night of 20/21 July as arranged, escorted by Admiral Syfret with the *Edinburgh*, *Nelson*, *Manxman* and five destroyers. The ships that left Gibraltar that night were held up by fog. The *Manchester*, *Arethusa* and the other three destroyers joined the convoy in the morning, as did the *Brown Ranger* and her escort; unfortunately the troopship *Leinster* ran on shore whilst turning out of Gibraltar Bay, and 1,000 troops thus missed their passage. Admiral Somerville overtook the convoy at midday,[29] 21 July; and having adjusted the destroyer screens with a view to economy of fuel, he stretched ahead and to the northward, so the fleet went east in two groups at varying distances apart, with Sunderland flying boats from Gibraltar giving anti-submarine protection to each group. Next day, 22 July, Admiral Syfret's ten destroyers oiled at sea, two at a time, a task that took about ten hours, after which the oiler *Brown Ranger* went back to Gibraltar. An Italian aircraft seems to have reported the ships with Admiral Somerville in the morning, but did not apparently find the convoy, then nearly a hundred miles away to the south-westward. A little before midnight a submarine attacked the *Renown*, which was able to avoid the torpedoes through a timely warning from the *Nestor*.

Air Attacks: *Fearless* Sunk, *Manchester* and *Firedrake* Damaged

Admiral Somerville joined the convoy again at 0800/23, as the fleet was approaching the dangerous part of its voyage past Sardinia. The ships took up Cruising Disposition No. 16 (see Plan 3), with the *Renown, Ark Royal, Hermione* and their destroyers "formed as a flexible port column of the convoy with the object of providing anti-aircraft protection whilst still remaining free to manoeuvre for flying". The mean course was 090°, ships zigzagging, and the speed of advance 13½ knots. The sea was calm, the sky was clear, and a light breeze was blowing from the north-east.

Shadowing aircraft had already reported the position of the fleet that morning, and heavy attacks soon followed. The first came about 0945, a well-timed combination of nine high-level bombers and six or seven torpedo bombers approaching from the north-east. The *Ark Royal* had eleven fighters up, which met the bombers about 20 miles from the fleet, and shot down two for the loss of three Fulmars. The other seven bombers came on, working round the head of the screen of destroyers to attack the convoy from the starboard beam at a height of some 10,000 feet; their bombs fell harmlessly among the leading ships as they altered course to avoid the attack. The torpedo aircraft were more successful. They came from ahead out of the sun, flying low, and as the destroyers opened fire they divided into groups of two or three to attack the convoy on both sides. Two aircraft attacked the *Fearless*, stationed ahead in the screen, dropping their torpedoes at ranges of 1,500 and 800 yards from a height of 70 feet; the destroyer avoided the first torpedo, but was hit by the second, set on fire, and completely disabled. Other aircraft went on to press home their attacks on the convoy itself. One of them, dropping its torpedo between two transports, hit the *Manchester* as she was turning to regain her station after avoiding two torpedoes fired earlier; this time she reversed her helm once more, but without avail. The ships had opened a long-range controlled fire at the bombers; and they fired a barrage with both long- and close-range guns against the torpedo aircraft, bringing down three of them.

The *Manchester* could use only one engine out of four, and as at first she could steam only 8 knots (she afterwards worked up to 12), the Admiral ordered her back to Gibraltar with the *Avon Vale* for escort. That evening, about 100 miles on the way to the westward, the two ships were attacked by three torpedo aircraft, but their guns kept the enemy at a safe distance. They reached Gibraltar on 26 July without further adventures except an abortive attack by a submarine on 24 July.[30]

The *Fearless*, however, was done for. By order of the Admiral, another destroyer torpedoed and sank her.

Despatches: Supplement to *The London Gazette*, Published by Authority
The following Despatch was submitted to the Lords Commissioners of the Admiralty on 4 August, 1941 by Vice-Admiral Sir James F. Somerville, K.C.B., D.S.O., Flag Officer Commanding, Force H.

Torpedo Bombing and High Level Bombing Attack on Fleet, a.m. 23 July

The first group of enemy aircraft was detected at 0910 bearing 055°, 60 miles. This developed into a well synchronised torpedo bomber and high level bombing attack which commenced at 0942 and was completed in approximately four minutes. Six torpedo planes attacked from ahead and concentrated on the convoy while eight high level bombers crossed from south to north dropping their bombs amongst the convoy.

The torpedo bombers approaching low down from ahead were engaged with barrage fire by the destroyer screen. This fire appeared effective and on coming within range the enemy split into two groups of three, one group altering course to port, the others to starboard. One of the starboard group followed by one of the port group attacked *Fearless* who was stationed in the starboard bow position on the screen. The remaining two aircraft of the port group pressed home their attack on the port bow of the convoy which took avoiding action. There is no clear record of any torpedoes having been dropped by the remaining two aircraft of the starboard group, but *Manchester* observed two tracks from port and one from starboard before a final torpedo approaching from port hit her.

Loss of *Fearless*

The two aircraft which attacked *Fearless* released their torpedoes from a height of 70 feet at a range of about 1,500 and 800 yards respectively. Avoiding action was taken and the first torpedo passed about 90 yards ahead. The torpedo from the second aircraft ran shallow. Course was shaped to comb the track but when abreast the stern on the port side, at a distance of about 30 feet, the torpedo broke surface, altered course to port, and hit the ship abreast the 3-inch gun.

Both engines were put out of action, the rudder was jammed at hard-a-port, all electric power failed due to the switchboard being demolished and an extensive fuel fire was started aft. One officer and 24 ratings were killed outright or died later. *Fearless* reported she was entirely disabled. As she was badly on fire and I did not consider the detachment of a second destroyer to attempt towing was justified under the circumstances, I ordered *Forester* to take off survivors and then sink the ship. This was effected by one torpedo at 1055.

CRUISING DISPOSITION No. 16
AS USED ON THE 23rd JULY 1941

PLAN 3

Fearless

Nelson

Edinburgh

Manxman

Renown

Ark Royal

Manchester

Hermione

Arethusa

0   6000

Scale of Yards

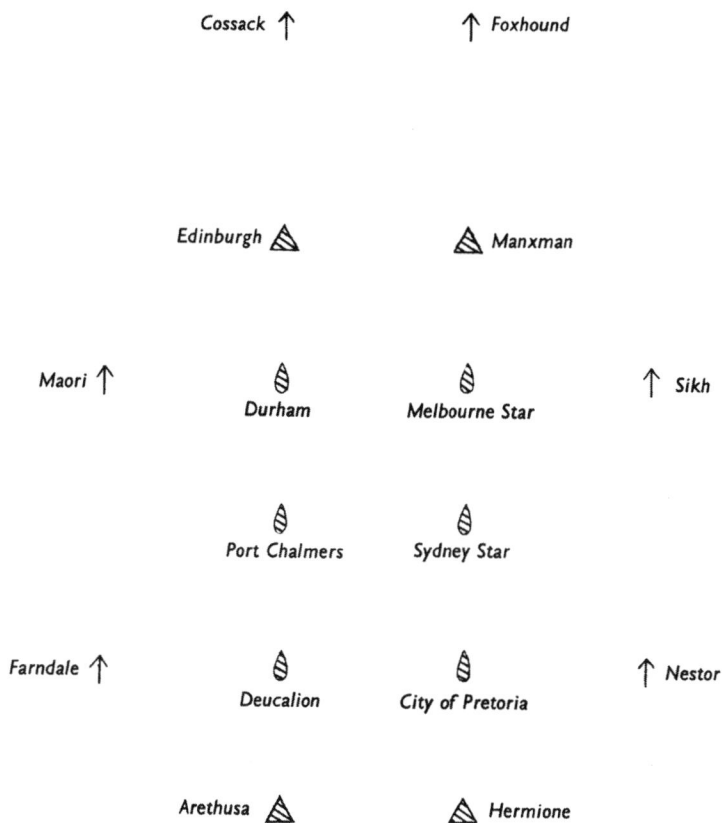

CRUISING DISPOSITION No. 17
FOR THE NIGHT OF 23rd — 24th JULY 1941

PLAN 4

Cossack ↑   ↑ Foxhound

Edinburgh ◬   ◬ Manxman

Maori ↑   Durham   Melbourne Star   ↑ Sikh

Port Chalmers   Sydney Star

Farndale ↑   Deucalion   City of Pretoria   ↑ Nestor

Arethusa ◬   ◬ Hermione

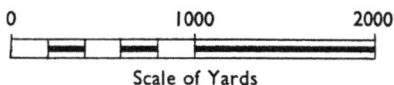

0   1000   2000

Scale of Yards

Note:—
Until she was disabled and had to leave the convoy, the *Firedrake*
occupied the station in which the *Cossack* is shown. The *Foxhound*
and *Firedrake* had sweeps streamed.

At 1010/23, half an hour after the first engagement, five more bombers tried to attack the convoy, crossing this time from north to south. Five fighters from the *Ark Royal*, though unable to reach within 1,000 feet of the enemy, forced them to drop their bombs at a great height and mostly outside the screen. Again, about 1645, five torpedo bombers led by a seaplane came in from the northward; but three Fulmars caught them nearly 20 miles away, shot down two, and drove off the rest. Soon afterwards the fleet arrived off the entrance to the Skerki Channel. There the *Nelson* joined Admiral Somerville, the *Hermione* joined Admiral Syfret in place of the *Manchester*, and the destroyers took up their proper stations, six with Force "H" and eight with Force "X". At 1713 Admiral Somerville hauled round to the westward, while Admiral Syfret stood on, forming Cruising Disposition No. 17 (see Plan 4) for the passage through the Narrows. For an hour more, until the Royal Air Force Beaufighters arrived from Malta to relieve them, the *Ark Royal* kept Fulmars up to attend the convoy. When the Beaufighters did arrive, they did not identify themselves, apparently through lack of experience, and were engaged by gunfire from the fleet.

There was still nearly five hours to go before dark, and the convoy had to suffer yet further attacks from the air that day. Four torpedo bombers arrived from the eastward at 1900, flying low and working round from ahead to the starboard side of the convoy. They approached in pairs in line abreast, and kept the *Sikh* (on the starboard bow of the screen) between them and their target until nearly the moment for attack, thereby hampering the fire of other ships. They dropped their torpedoes at long range from a height of 50 feet, and nearly hit the *Hermione*, sternmost ship in the starboard column. To avoid the attack, each column of the convoy turned 90 degrees outwards; and the men-of-war opened barrage fire from all guns that would bear. The barrage fell short, but the fire from the cruisers, though it possibly endangered the destroyers as much as the enemy, probably caused the Italians to drop their torpedoes early, and may have brought down one aircraft.

This attack scattered the convoy, which took some time to re-form. At 1945, soon after the ships were again on their course and in station, about seven bombers appeared from ahead at a height of some 14,000 feet to attack the convoy on the port side. The convoy altered 40 degrees to port together by signal; and the escort opened a controlled fire – with some hesitation, for the Italian aircraft looked very like Beaufighters, several of which had lately joined, while others were expected. The bombing was reported as extremely accurate; several bombs fell near the *Edinburgh*, which was leading the port column, and a near-miss abreast a boiler-room disabled the *Firedrake*, the port destroyer of two that were sweeping ahead of the convoy. She could no longer steam, so Admiral Syfret ordered her back to Gibraltar in tow of the *Eridge*.

They had an anxious passage, being shadowed by aircraft continuously during daylight hours, but were not again attacked; on 25 July the *Firedrake* managed to raise steam in one boiler and slipped the tow; they entered harbour on 27 July.[31]

M.T.B., Attacks, 23–24 July

Soon after leaving the Skerki Channel in the evening of 23 July, the convoy hauled up to the north-east towards the coast of Sicily, instead of standing on for Pantellaria, as Convoy "Excess" had done in January and as the enemy evidently expected it to do. The object of this "long and tortuous route," as Admiral Syfret called it, was to lessen the danger from mines; but it also saved the convoy from an air attack at dusk, which was his principal anxiety. The result was excellent. The Italians did not shadow the convoy after their attack at 1945, and therefore missed this alteration of course, which was made at 2000. An hour or so later, as it was growing dark, enemy aircraft searched diligently for the convoy along its old line of advance. Again, in the hour before midnight, the convoy several times sighted flares, some 20 miles off to the southward, which the Admiral supposed to be towed by aircraft in an attempt to find the convoy. As for mines, the only evidence of their presence was the parting of the *Foxhound*'s sweep apparently by a mine, soon after the turn southward into the known Italian convoy route to Tripoli a little after midnight.

The principal feature of the night took the form of attacks by Italian motor torpedo boats in the early hours of 24 July, while the convoy was passing Pantellaria. They seem to have made three distinct attacks, between 0250 and 0315, all from the port bow; and for twenty minutes more some of these craft were hovering about the convoy. Their number was uncertain, estimated at half a dozen all told, though some ships thought it was more; actually there were only two. Admiral Syfret considered the enemy did not expect the meeting, and did not attack resolutely. They were hard to see, but could be heard to start their engines, and gave themselves away by using high speed. "One felt," he said, "they would have achieved more success had they kept quiet whilst and after firing their torpedoes." Nevertheless, they succeeded in torpedoing the *Sydney Star*, the middle transport in the starboard column, though she reached Malta. They were thought to have lost one or perhaps two boats sunk by the fire of the escort, but actually none was sunk.

The *Cossack*, ahead of the port column, was the first to find the enemy. She detected three objects on the port bow by radar about 0245, and a few minutes later heard the starting of engines and saw two boats close on the port beam, one of which she lit up by searchlight and engaged with 4.7-in. and smaller guns. The *Edinburgh*, leading the port column, heard and sighted the same boat at about the same time; she turned towards the enemy, increased speed, and opened fire with pom-poms and Oerlikon guns. The *Manxman*, leading the starboard column, also sighted this boat; lit up by crossed searchlight beams from the *Edinburgh* and *Cossack*, she made "a perfect target," to be fired at "unseen ourselves and almost at leisure." Between them the three ships might have sunk this boat, but it was she that torpedoed the *Sydney Star*. Meanwhile, the other boat ran down between the screen of destroyers and the port column of transports, and was engaged by the *Farndale*, and by the *Arethusa* and *Hermione* in the rear of the convoy, and was probably damaged. In the second attack, at 0305, the *Foxhound* and *Cossack* apparently fired on a boat crossing from starboard to port, and the *Foxhound* tried to ram; then the *Edinburgh*, lighting the target with her searchlight, smothered it with fire from small guns at a range of 1,500 or 2,000 yards, and thought she had sunk it with a full broadside of 6-in. fire. At 0315 the *Edinburgh* again saw a boat on her port beam. The enemy went ahead, crossed the bows of the *Cossack*, which tried to ram, and eventually escaped past the convoy after firing a torpedo that nearly hit the *Cossack*.[32]

Commanders Stokes (*Sikh*) and Courage (*Maori*), whose destroyers were stationed abreast the columns thought that they would have been more useful ahead of the convoy, where there was more room to manoeuvre, and where they could hope to beat off such attacks before the enemy could fire torpedoes. As it was, Commander Courage in the *Maori* dared not fire lest he should hurt a friend, for the enemy was passing between his ship and the transports; and Commander Stokes in the *Sikh* was in the same station on the disengaged side. Admiral Syfret, however, considered that small torpedo craft might well pierce an extended screen, and that the *Maori* ought to have closed still nearer to the convoy to stop the enemy from passing inside her.

On being torpedoed, the *Sydney Star* had dropped astern and was found by the *Nestor*, which was stationed on the starboard beam of the convoy. Commander Rosenthal put his destroyer alongside the transport, took her troops and part of her crew on board, and persuaded her master to try to reach Malta. In an hour or so the two ships were under way, the transport making 12 knots despite serious leaks in her holds. Torpedo aircraft twice threatened attack between 0615 and 0650/24, the second hour of daylight, so the *Nestor* called for help, on which Admiral Syfret sent back the *Hermione*, which had no passengers on board. At 1000, eight German dive-bombers and two high-level bombers attacked, their bombs falling close to the escorting ships; and the *Hermione* shot down one dive-bomber. This was the last attack they had to face. The three ships arrived at Malta early in the afternoon.[33]

Arrival at Malta

The main body of the convoy went on its way unhindered after the attacks by motor boats, except for an attempt by three torpedo bombers about 0700, probably some of those which the *Nestor* and *Sydney Star* had seen. These aircraft dropped their torpedoes at a safe distance, however, when fired on by the destroyers in the screen ahead. According to the orders, Admiral Syfret was to leave the convoy at this stage of the voyage, if the situation as regards Italian surface forces were considered satisfactory, and go on to Malta with the cruisers and some of the destroyers. There they were to land passengers and stores, complete with fuel, and return to Admiral Somerville as soon as possible, while the remaining destroyers, keeping the transports company to Malta, were also to rejoin Force "H" as soon as they could. Admiral Syfret felt easy about the surface danger, as all the Italian ships were reported in harbour the day before; but he was anxious about the air. The Beaufighters at Malta had no previous experience of working with ships, and their tactics and their failure to identify themselves the evening before made the Admiral doubt their ability to protect the convoy. "At one time", he said, "it appeared that all our efforts to get the convoy to Malta might be frustrated unless all cruisers and destroyers remained with the convoy to the end." However, it was urgently necessary to save time, and at 0745 the *Edinburgh*, *Arethusa* and *Manxman* left the convoy and pressed ahead at high speed to Malta, where they arrived at midday, 24 July. The transports and destroyers arrived about four hours later, having been attacked once by a torpedo aircraft since the separation. All four cruisers sailed again in company the same evening, followed by five destroyers, which overtook the cruisers in the morning of 25 July – the sixth destroyer had to stay at Malta to make good defects. Instead of returning by the way they had come, both groups of ships kept south of Pantellaria and close along the African coast, and joined Admiral Somerville north-westward of Galita Island about 0800/25.

Passage to Gibraltar

After parting with the convoy in the evening of 23 July, Admiral Somerville had taken Force "H" westward at 18 knots until the afternoon of 24 July, going as far west as longitude 3° 30' E. He then turned back to meet Admiral Syfret, first sending from the *Ark Royal* to Malta six Swordfish aircraft, which left the carrier in 37° 42' N., 7° 17' E., at 0100/25. After their junction, Forces "H" and "X" made the best of their way towards Gibraltar. Fighter patrols from the *Ark Royal* shot down a shadowing aircraft soon after the fleet shaped course westward, losing a Fulmar in doing so; but another shadower had already reported the fleet, and high-level bombers from the east and torpedo bombers from the north appeared about 1100. The *Ark Royal* had four fighters in the air, and sent up six more. They prevented the bombing attack, shooting down three aircraft out of eight at a cost of two Fulmars, while the ships watched the enemy jettison their bombs 15 miles away. The torpedo attack came to nothing too; for the enemy gave up their attempt and retired while still several miles from the fleet, though the fighters did not succeed in intercepting them. Two days later, 27 July, the fleet reached Gibraltar.

There remains to tell of the seven empty transports going from Malta to Gibraltar. Six sailed in the morning of 23 July, escorted by the *Encounter*, but the seventh was held up for some hours through an accident when leaving harbour. At dusk, when a few miles east of Pantellaria, the six ships divided into pairs according to their speeds, and continued separately, keeping close along the shore of Tunisia. The *Encounter* at first escorted the middle pair, but joined the leading ships the following evening, 24 July, when past the Galita Bank. Italian aircraft, both bombers and torpedo bombers, attacked all these ships on 24 July to the southward of Sardinia, not far from where the *Fearless* and *Manchester* had been torpedoed the day before. They made their first attempt on the second pair of transports and the *Encounter*, four torpedo aircraft attacking at 1230 and four bombers at 1250; the bombs fell close, but no ships were hit. Next came the turn of the leading pair, which was attacked farther westward by two bombers that came singly at 1330 and 1400, the second nearly hitting the *Breconshire*. Finally, when the third pair of transports reached about the same position in the evening, it was attacked by torpedo bombers and the *Hoegh Hood* was damaged, though she arrived at Gibraltar within a few hours of her consort on 27 July, the same day as the fleet. The four faster ships had arrived the day before. The seventh ship, delayed at Malta, arrived on 28 July.

Movements of Mediterranean Fleet

On the two critical days, 23 and 24 July, the Mediterranean Fleet carried out the proposed diversion in the eastern Mediterranean. Admiral Cunningham had arranged that Vice-Admiral Pridham-Wippell should sail from Alexandria on 23 July with two battleships and several cruisers and destroyers, and steer to the westward to suggest that he was bound for the central Mediterranean. The surface ships, however, were to turn east again after dark "with a view to the fleet's being lost by enemy reconnaissance", leaving two submarines to make a series of fictitious signals in the morning of 24 July from positions Admiral Pridham-Wippell might have reached had he continued westward. All went as intended: enemy aircraft shadowed the fleet in the afternoon and evening of 23 July, as it was hoped they would, and the submarines made their signals. Admiral Cunningham said "nothing of interest occurred during the operation, but it is understood that the diversion was successful, and that the enemy was left with the impression that the Mediterranean Fleet was entering the central Mediterranean".

Remarks on Operation

The transports all reached their destinations without hindrance from the Italian fleet. Admiral Somerville remarked that the enemy's inactivity may have been due to the work of the Allied submarines, which were patrolling in the zones shown in Plan 2 from the morning of 22 July to the evening of 26 July. None of them sighted large ships of the enemy, but some made their presence known by attacking enemy convoys when going to their stations or during their patrol. For instance, the *Olympus* attacked a small convoy on 21 July on her way to her station; and although he had little hope of success Lieutenant-Commander Dymott "considered it worth firing at extreme range, as ... a hit would have furthered my object"; and he attacked a merchant ship off Ischia on 23 July.

As for the dangers the transports did encounter, Admiral Syfret drew certain conclusions about the attacks from the air:–

(i) "Shore-based fighters need careful training and a clear understanding of fleet requirements to enable them to work with the fleet."

(ii) "Italian high-level bombing is accurate, unless the formation is broken up by fighters."

(iii) "Italian torpedo bombers will not face determined barrage, and use torpedoes with a long- or medium-range setting."

Of the merchant ships he remarked: "That the operation was successfully carried out is due in no small measure to the behaviour of the merchant ships in convoy. Their manoeuvring and general conduct was excellent, and caused me no anxiety whatever. I had complete confidence that orders given to them by me would be understood and promptly carried out. Their steadfast and resolute behaviour during air and E-boat attacks was most impressive and encouraging to us all."

Despatches: Supplement to *The London Gazette*, Published by Authority
The following Despatch was submitted to the Lords Commissioners of the Admiralty on 4 August, 1941 by Vice-Admiral Sir James F. Somerville, K.C.B., D.S.O., Flag Officer Commanding, Force H.

General

Outstanding points in this operation were:–

Effective work of Fulmars.

The Fulmars of *Ark Royal* contributed in no small measure to the safe arrival of the convoy at its destination. On 23 July formations of enemy aircraft were intercepted on three occasions. On the first occasion, two were shot down for certain and another two probably destroyed, whilst the survivors which reached the fleet were in no state to carry out an accurate attack. On the second occasion as the Fulmars were about to intercept, the bombers released their bombs on the destroyer screen and immediately withdrew. Finally an attempted T/B attack was completely broken up and driven off, leaving two aircraft shot down with another damaged and possibly lost.

On 25 July, the only enemy formations to approach the fleet were once again thoroughly routed. A force of torpedo bombers withdrew before the fighters could reach it and the only high level bombing attack was intercepted about 15 miles from the fleet, when four enemy planes were destroyed for certain with one probably destroyed and two more damaged. All bombs were jettisoned.

One Italian officer survivor stated he had been shot down by a Hurricane. It is evident that the enemy hold our Fleet Air Arm fighters in higher esteem than do our own Fulmar pilots.

Comments

It was with considerable surprise that I learned on arrival at Gibraltar that a number of women and children had been embarked in the ships of Convoy M.G.1. Had I known this earlier, I should certainly have sent a destroyer to escort each group.

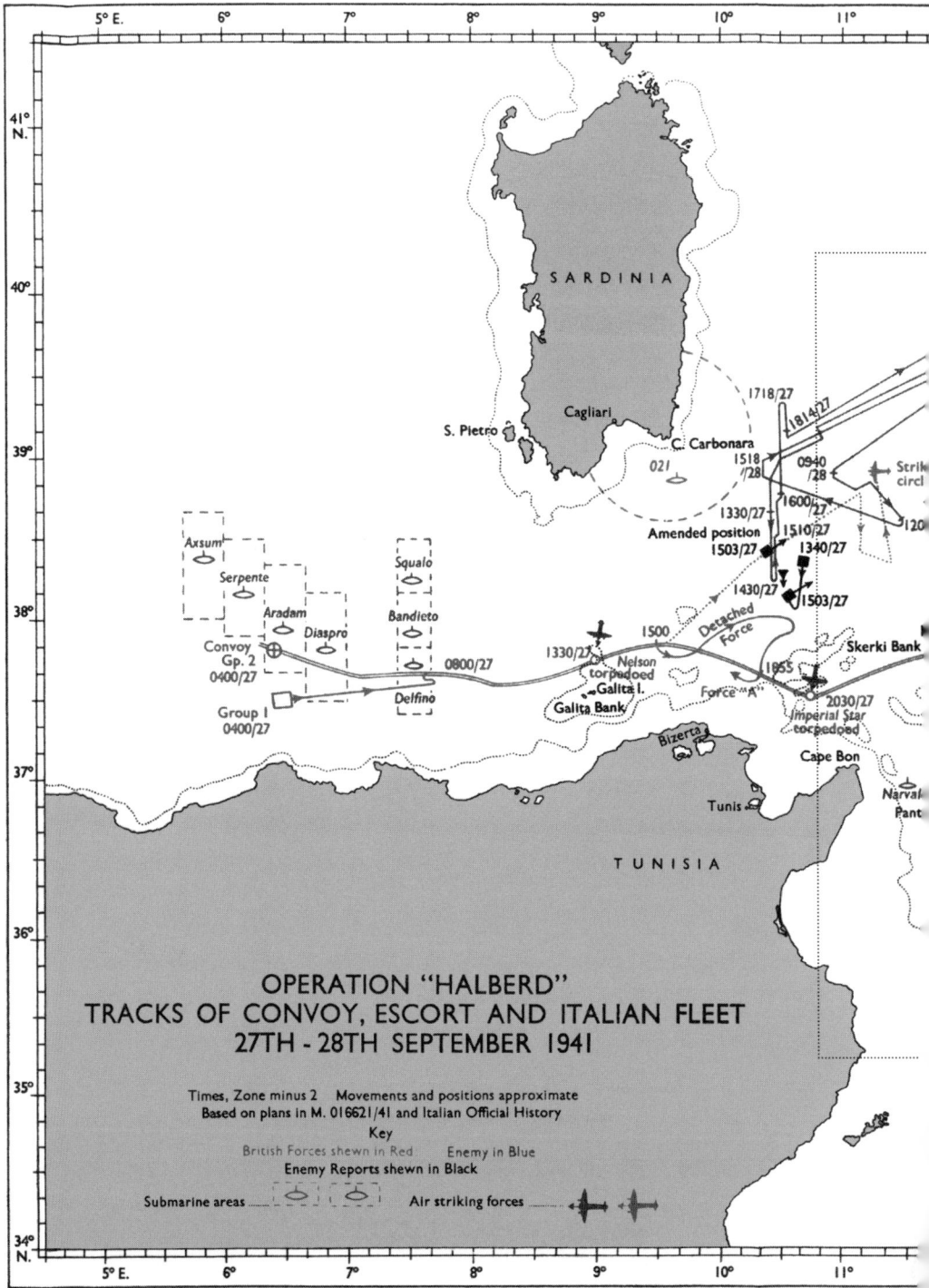

OPERATION "HALBERD"
TRACKS OF CONVOY, ESCORT AND ITALIAN FLEET
27TH - 28TH SEPTEMBER 1941

Times, Zone minus 2   Movements and positions approximate
Based on plans in M. 016621/41 and Italian Official History
Key
British Forces shewn in Red   Enemy in Blue
Enemy Reports shewn in Black

Submarine areas ....   Air striking forces ....

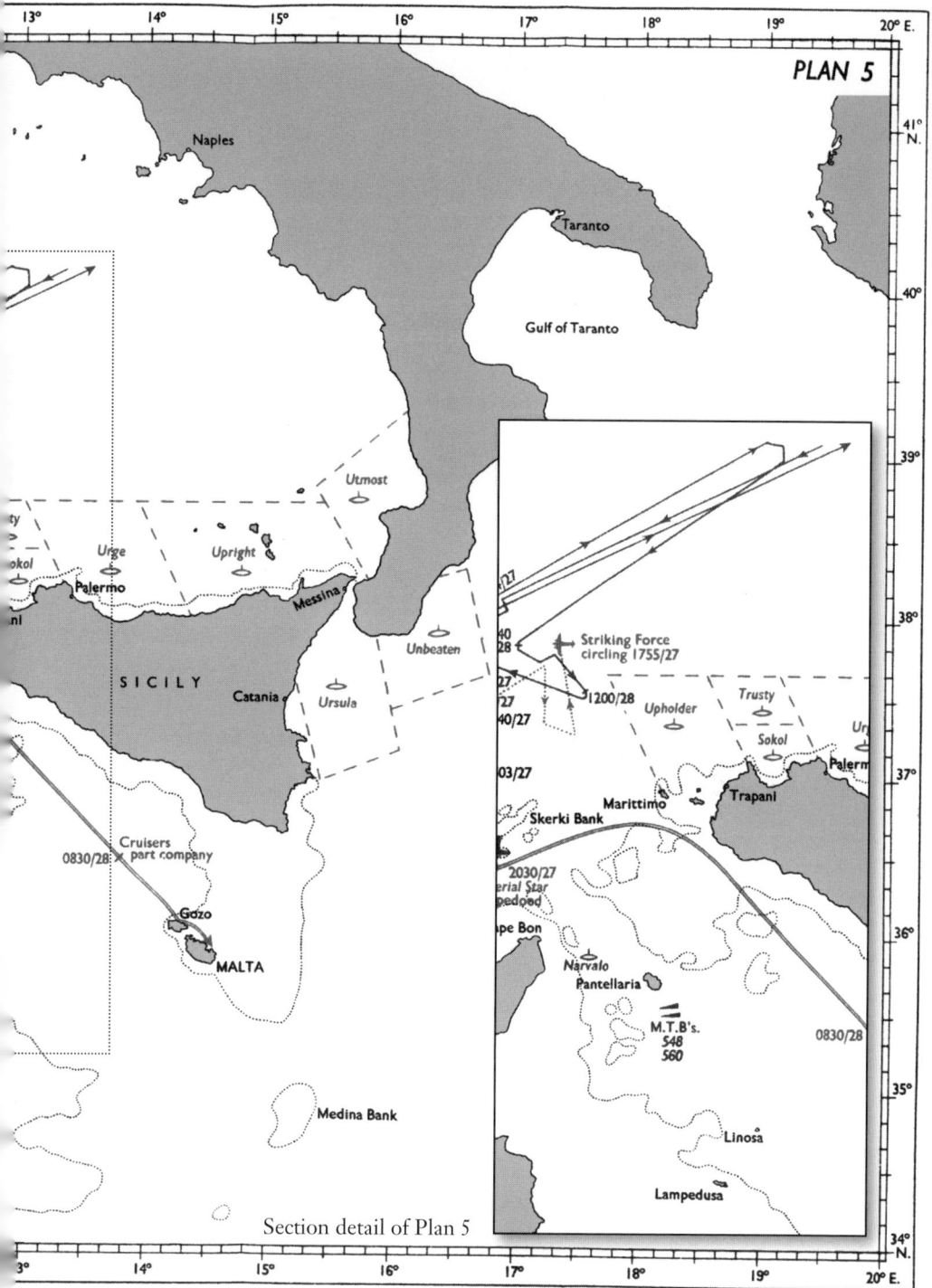

PLAN 5

Section detail of Plan 5

Operation "Halberd"

Plan of Operation "Halberd"

Operation "Halberd" was very like Operation "Substance" in July; but on this occasion part of the Italian fleet appeared at sea between Sardinia and Sicily. There were nine transports with troops and stores (Convoy G.M.2) to go to Malta and three empty ships (Convoy M.G.2) to come back to Gibraltar, and Admiral Somerville gave them protection with Force "H" on the same lines as before. Force "H" was greatly strengthened for the occasion, and had three capital ships – the *Nelson* (flag, Vice-Admiral Somerville), *Prince of Wales* (flag, Vice-Admiral Curteis) and *Rodney*, with the aircraft carrier *Ark Royal*, five cruisers, *Kenya* (flag, Rear-Admiral Burrough), *Edinburgh* (flag, Rear-Admiral Syfret), *Sheffield*, *Hermione*, *Euryalus*, and eighteen destroyers. On reaching the Narrows the east-going convoy went on to Malta with all the cruisers and half the destroyers (Force "X"), under Rear-Admiral Burrough, while the main body (Force "A") drew off to the westward to wait for Admiral Burrough's return and to distract the enemy's attention from the empty ships coming from Malta.[34] There were nine submarines off Sardinia, Sicily, and southern Italy in the stations shown on Plan 5 and aircraft of the Royal Air Force from Gibraltar and Malta provided anti-submarine patrols, reconnaissance and fighter protection.

Despatches: Supplement to *The London Gazette*, Published by Authority

The following Despatch was submitted to the Lords Commissioners of the Admiralty on 9 October, 1941 by Vice-Admiral Sir James F. Somerville, K.C.B., D.S.O., Flag Officer Commanding, Force H.

Convoy M.G.2 (Malta to Gibraltar) – Departure of First Ship from Malta

A signal was received from the Vice-Admiral, Malta at 1141, stating that a few Army and R.A.F. personnel with their wives had been embarked in the three ships of M.G.2 at their own risk, and at the request of H.E. the Governor of Malta. I feel that I should have been consulted about this, since a moral obligation arose to give these ships some degree of close protection. It was my intention, however, not to depart substantially from the priorities laid down by the Admiralty for Operation "Substance", *viz.*, that the safe return of the escorting forces was of more importance than the safe arrival of empty shipping.

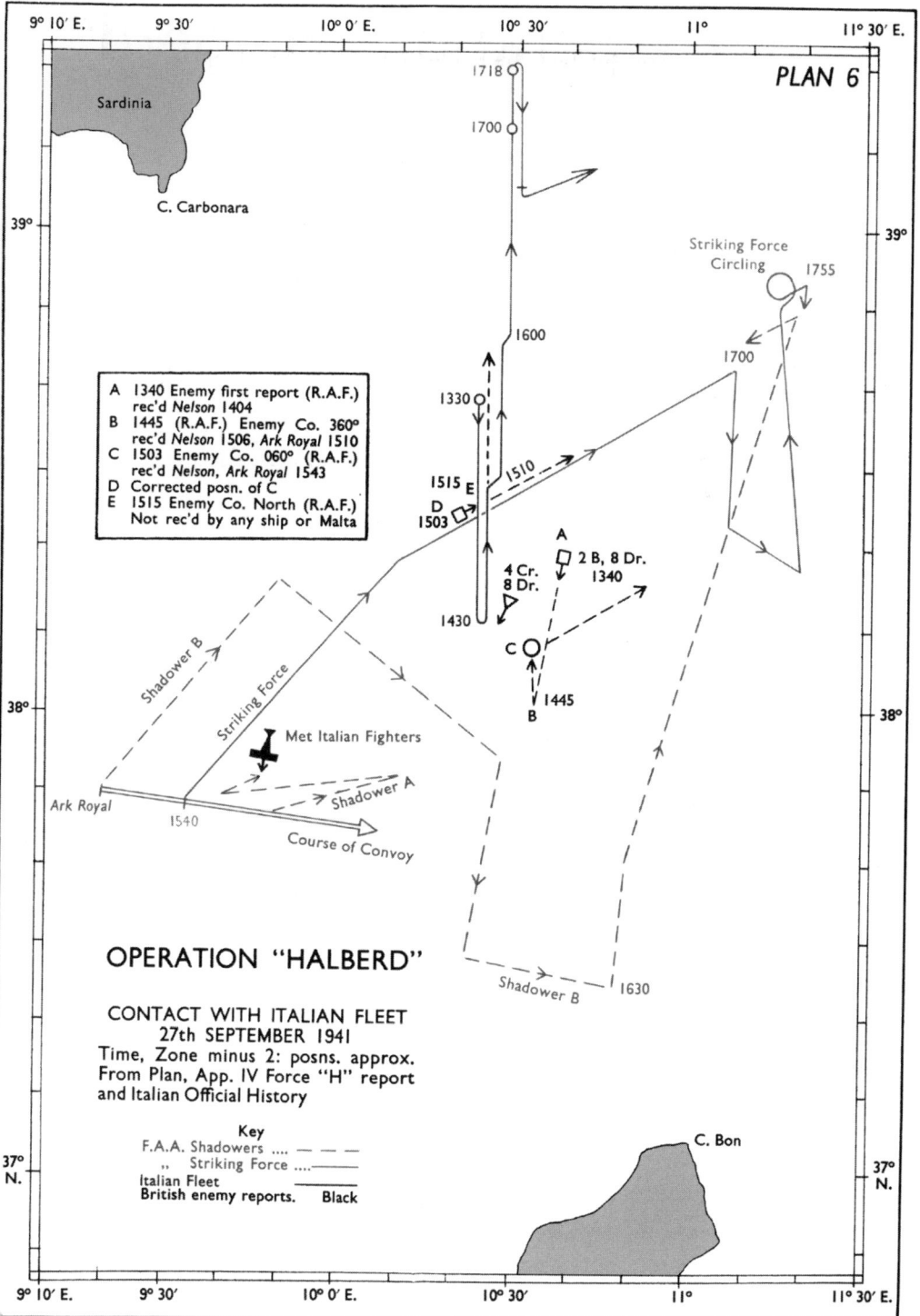

PLAN 6

9° 10′ E. 9° 30′ 10° 0′ E. 10° 30′ 11° 11° 30′ E.

Sardinia

C. Carbonara

39°

1718

1700

Striking Force
Circling

1755

1700

1600

1330

1510

A 1340 Enemy first report (R.A.F.)
   rec'd *Nelson* 1404
B 1445 (R.A.F.) Enemy Co. 360°
   rec'd *Nelson* 1506, *Ark Royal* 1510
C 1503 Enemy Co. 060° (R.A.F.)
   rec'd *Nelson*, *Ark Royal* 1543
D Corrected posn. of C
E 1515 Enemy Co. North (R.A.F.)
   Not rec'd by any ship or Malta

1515 E

D
1503

A
2 B, 8 Dr.
1340

4 Cr.
8 Dr.

1430

C
1445
B

Shadower B

Striking Force

Met Italian Fighters

38°

Ark Royal

1540

Shadower A

Course of Convoy

Shadower B

1630

OPERATION "HALBERD"

CONTACT WITH ITALIAN FLEET
27th SEPTEMBER 1941
Time, Zone minus 2: posns. approx.
From Plan, App. IV Force "H" report
and Italian Official History

C. Bon

37°
N.

Key
F.A.A. Shadowers .... — — —
   „   Striking Force ....———
Italian Fleet
British enemy reports. **Black**

9° 10′ E. 9° 30′ 10° 0′ E. 10° 30′ 11° 11° 30′ E.

.B.H. 22729

71

Admiral Cunningham had supported Operation "Substance" in July by sending the Mediterranean Fleet to sea to show itself, and by having dummy signals made from submarines on its pretended track. His proposal in September appeared in the following signal he made to Admiral Somerville on 22 July (1050B/22): "I do not intend to follow any hard and fast plan, but will keep Mediterranean Fleet at short notice from 0800 on Day Two [26 July] with the idea of proceeding to sea and being observed steaming westward as soon as your forces are sighted by enemy; my intention is to prevent German air force turning west from Libya." With this in view he sailed from Alexandria on 26 July with the *Queen Elizabeth, Valiant, Barham,* and some cruisers and destroyers, returning to harbour next day. He did not sight any enemy aircraft, nor was there any sign that the enemy knew the fleet had gone to sea; accordingly, in the night of 26/27 July signals were made by wireless to ensure that this diversion should have effect.

Passage, 24–26 September

The transports from home went out escorted by the *Prince of Wales,* two cruisers, and some destroyers under Vice-Admiral Curteis, with the troops (about 2,600) divided among the transports and such men-of-war as were going to Malta. As they approached Gibraltar, the escorting ships took turns to go ahead into harbour to complete their fuel and rejoin, arriving and sailing again in the dark; and ships already at Gibraltar joined the convoy, which entered the Mediterranean in the night of 24/25 September with the *Prince of Wales,* four cruisers, and seven destroyers. Meanwhile, Admiral Somerville had sailed from Gibraltar westward in the *Nelson* with a screen of destroyers before dark on 24 Sepember. His flag was left on board the *Rodney* at Gibraltar, and farewell signals were openly exchanged between the two ships as if the *Nelson* were going home and the *Rodney* taking her place; but the Admiral turned east again in the night to overtake the convoy, while the *Rodney* sailed eastward likewise with the *Ark Royal, Hermione,* and the rest of the destroyers. "This ruse," said Admiral Somerville, "appears to have created the desired impression." Another opportunity to mystify and mislead enemy spies was given by the presence of some extra transports that accompanied the convoy from home; these ships were bound for Freetown, but they were sent into Gibraltar during the night of 24/25 September to show themselves next day in the hope of lulling suspicion had the convoy's passage through the Strait been detected.

The whole fleet assembled inside the Strait at 0900[35]/25, and divided again into two groups to sail separately until 27 September, when they would join forces for the critical passage past Sardinia. Admiral Somerville, with the *Nelson, Ark Royal, Hermione* and six destroyers (Group I), stretched ahead of the convoy and went eastward along the African coast to give shadowing aircraft the impression that only "the usual" Force "H" was at sea.[36] His passage was uneventful on 25 September; but at 0932 next day the *Nelson* sighted a shadowing aircraft, flying very low 10 miles off to the south-east, which had not been detected by radar. Owing to a complete failure of radio-telephony in the fighter leader's aircraft, delay occurred in vectoring the fighters and no interception took place. An enemy report was intercepted at 0935, and this was re-broadcast by an Italian station twenty minutes later. At 1537 two aircraft were sighted low down to the eastward by the *Zulu, Nelson* and *Hermione.* They were thought to be Hudsons, but shortly afterwards an Italian enemy report went out. On the first occasion of sighting, Group I was in roughly 37° 30' N., 4° 30' E., some 250 miles south-westward of Cagliari; in the afternoon it was about 25 miles farther east. At this time the Admiral was steering to the westward to reduce his distance from the convoy, and did not turn east again till dusk.

Group II, under Admiral Curteis, with the convoy of nine transports, kept at first north-eastward along the coast of Spain, turning south-east on approaching the Balearic Islands – a track "through an area which experience suggested was reasonably clear of merchant ships and civil aircraft." At 1700/25, in 36° 36' N., 1° 58' W., the *Sheffield, Duncan* and *Gurkha*, all in the screen ahead, attacked a submarine with depth-charges.[37] On 26 September the twelve destroyers with the convoy oiled in pairs from the *Brown Ranger* as the destroyers with Admiral Syfret in July had done – the *Brown Ranger* had sailed from Gibraltar ahead of the convoy and returned there at dusk on 26 September after fulfilling her task. That afternoon, an aircraft with Spanish colours appeared suddenly out of the clouds over Group II and was thought to have reported the convoy to the enemy.

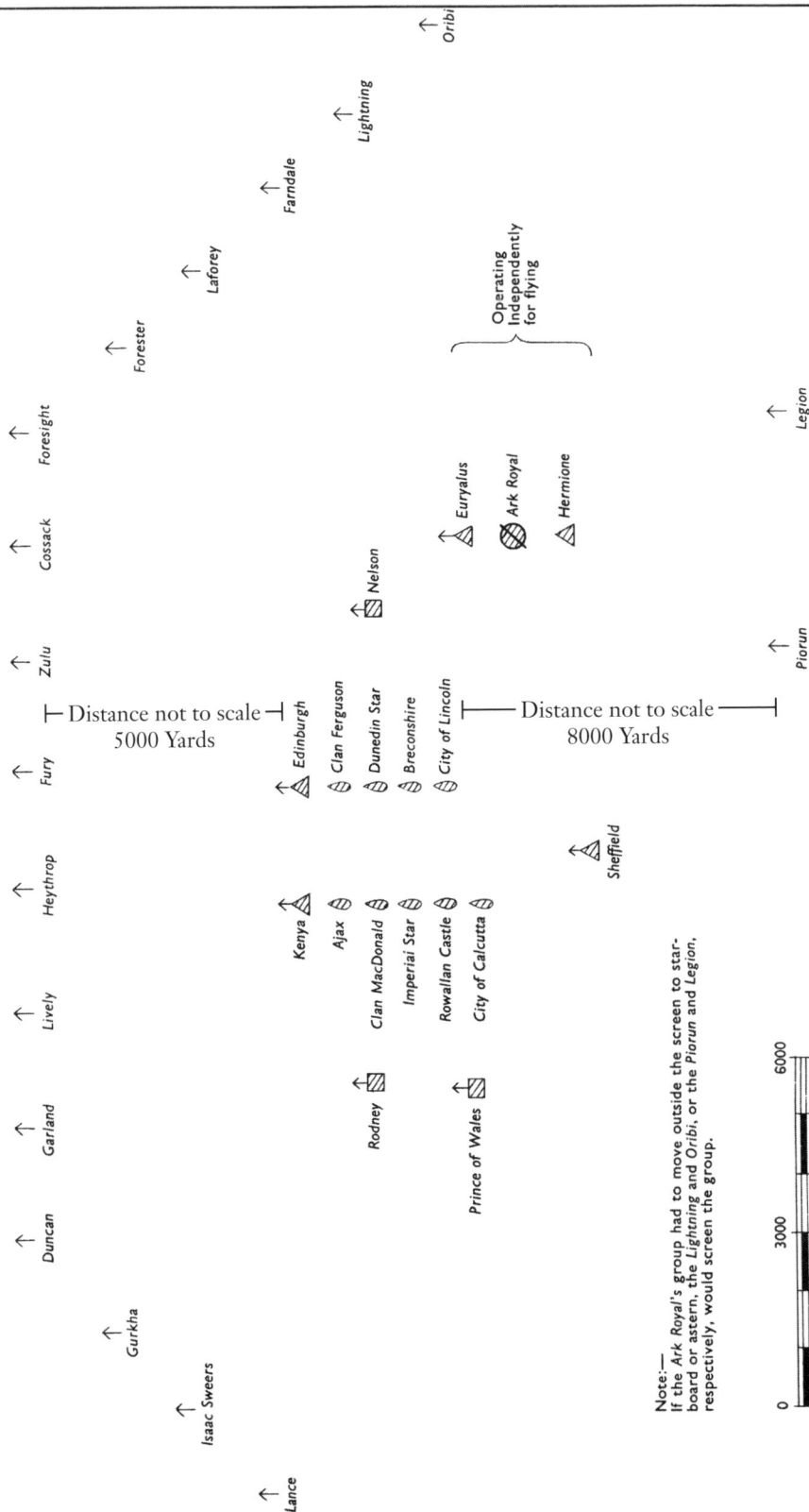

CRUISING DISPOSITION No. 16A AS USED ON THE 27th SEPT. 1941

Lance ←

Isaac Sweers ←

Gurkha ←

Duncan ←   Garland ←   Lively ←   Heythrop ←   Fury ←   Zulu ←   Cossack ←   Foresight ←   Forester ←   Laforey ←   Farndale ←   Lightning ←   Oribi ←

Rodney ←▨   Kenya ◁▨

Prince of Wales ←▨   Ajax ◁
Clan MacDonald ◁
Imperiai Star ◁
Rowallan Castle ◁
City of Calcutta ◁

Edinburgh ◁▨   Nelson ←▨

Clan Ferguson ◁
Dunedin Star ◁
Breconshire ◁
City of Lincoln ◁

⊢ Distance not to scale ⊣
5000 Yards

⊢ Distance not to scale ⊣
8000 Yards

Sheffield ◁▨

Euryalus ◁▨
Ark Royal ⊘
Hermione ◁

Operating
Independently
for flying

Piorun ←   Legion ←

Note:—
If the *Ark Royal*'s group had to move outside the screen to starboard or astern, the *Lightning* and *Oribi*, or the *Piorun* and *Legion*,
respectively, would screen the group.

0   3000   6000

Scale of Yards

Italian Reactions

Meanwhile the Italians had received early information of the departure of the British forces from Gibraltar. The Naval Staff at first formed the opinion that the British were contemplating a landing at Pantellaria, or perhaps a bombarding operation against the Ligurian coast. Accordingly, submarine patrols were redisposed and arrangements were made with the Air Force to intercept and attack. The battleships *Littorio*, wearing the flag of the Commander-in-Chief, Admiral Iachino, and *Vittorio Veneto*, with the 6-in. cruisers *Abruzzi* and *Attendolo*, were ordered to proceed to Maddalena; and the 8-in. cruisers *Trento* (flag, Vice-Admiral Lombardi), *Trieste* and *Gorizia* were ordered to Spezia.

Later, when it appeared that the operation was not directed towards the Ligurian coast, these orders were modified, and at 0315/27 September, Admiral Iachino received orders for the whole force to rendezvous 50 miles east of Cape Carbonera, Sardinia, at noon that day.

This concentration was duly effected, and Admiral Iachino then had with him two battleships, three 8-in. and two 6-in. cruisers and 14 destroyers. Believing at this time that the British force only consisted of one battleship (though reports suggested that another might be at sea), a carrier, two cruisers and five destroyers, he decided to seek action, and shaped course to the southward at 24 knots in order to intercept the British force.

Enemy Air Attacks: *Nelson* Damaged

To return to the British.

The two groups met again about 0800/27; and the fleet assumed Cruising Disposition No. 16A, with all three battleships formed on the convoy, yet free to move independently, and the *Ark Royal* with the cruisers *Euryalus* and *Hermione* following on the weather quarter (see Plan 7). Whatever the enemy may have learnt through the air and submarine contacts of the previous two days, they soon knew all they needed to know; for their shadowing aircraft reported the fleet as the ships were taking their new stations in the morning, and at least once later in the forenoon. The expected air attacks came in three phases between 1255 and 1405, all by Italian torpedo bombers, mainly of types BR.20 and S.79. It was a calm, sunny day with patches of thundercloud at 1,000 feet and a very light breeze varying between south-west and west. The ships were zigzagging, speed about 12 knots, mean line of advance 075°. The mean position of the attacks was roughly 37° 45' N., 9° E. – some 90 miles to the southward of Cagliari.

The first to attack were a dozen torpedo aircraft, of which a half reached the fleet, escorted by six GR.42 fighters. They were discovered to the north-east at 1255, on which the *Ark Royal's* patrol of eight Fulmars was ordered to intercept. The Fulmars met the enemy 10 miles from the fleet, the torpedo planes being low near the water with their escort 7,000 feet above them. The British fighters succeeded in shooting down one torpedo plane and driving off others without the Italian fighters interfering; but one Fulmar, separated from the rest in the clouds, met the Italian fighters, and was damaged in the encounter and eventually shot down by the *Prince of Wales* on its return to the fleet. Meanwhile, six torpedo planes persevered, attacking the fleet from the port side about 1300 and dropping their torpedoes at a range of 5,000 yards from the convoy at a height of 300 feet. The convoy and escorting ships made large turns towards the enemy and fired a barrage. No ship was hit, though the *Rodney, Lance* and *Isaac Sweers* had narrow escapes. On the other hand, the fleet shot down three enemy aircraft and the Fulmars yet another, which was retiring from its attack – making five all told in this phase.[38]

Towards the end of this engagement, seven more Fulmars were sent up by the *Ark Royal*, steaming fast down wind for the flying off and passing ahead of the *Nelson*. There were thus 14 fighters in the air to meet the next attack, which came from the starboard side of the fleet just before 1330; yet despite this unusually strong protection it was during this phase of the battle that the enemy gained their one success in daylight. Three aircraft, out of six or seven that attacked, pressed through the destroyers' barrage and made for the flagship. The first dropped its torpedo from a height of 200 feet, only 450 yards from the *Nelson*, fine on her starboard bow. She had turned towards the enemy to comb the torpedo tracks, steaming 18 knots or over, and had just steadied on a course when she saw the torpedo, too late to avoid it. It hit her on the port bow, limiting her speed eventually to 15 knots.[39] The aircraft was shot down by the *Prince of Wales* and *Sheffield* as it flew away. The second plane dropped its torpedo from a greater height and at twice the range, missing the *Nelson* by a hundred yards. The *Laforey* and other destroyers shot down the third plane as it passed over the screen. The rest of the enemy attacked the fleet from the starboard quarter; but the Fulmars intercepted them, spoilt their aim, and shot one down. On the other hand, one Fulmar was unfortunately shot down by the *Rodney*.

The third phase of the attack followed close on the heels of the second. About 1345 some 10 or 11 planes, flying very low, came in sight 10 miles away to the southward. Most of them retired on being fired at by the fleet, but three or four tried to work round to point ahead of the convoy, which made a large turn to port to meet the attack; the aircraft, diverted by the destroyers' fire, dropped their torpedoes outside the screen without effect, though the *Lightning* was narrowly missed by a torpedo fired at a range of 500 yards. Three of the aircraft that had originally turned away then came back from abaft the beam to attack the *Ark Royal;* none dropped torpedoes, and one was shot down by the *Ark Royal* and *Nelson* and another by Fulmars. At 1358 an aircraft outside the screen, right ahead of the *Nelson*, dropped a torpedo, which the *Cossack* was able to avoid with the help of her Asdic set. An Italian fighter "performing aerobatics" over the destroyers, evidently to make a diversion for the torpedo planes, was either shot down or failed to pull out of a dive.

Further attacks threatened as the afternoon wore on; but they came to nothing, the enemy being generally driven off by Fulmars a long way from the fleet. Out of 30 aircraft that attacked that day, only 18 got within firing-range and gained one hit; six were shot down by the guns of the fleet, besides the four brought down by fighters. This was largely due to the disposition of the destroyers, which turned back most of the enemy, shooting down two, so that only four aircraft got past the screen and none reached a good position for a shot at the convoy. But it meant some risk to the destroyers; several reported being endangered by the fire of big ships and transports astern, and the *Oribi* had two men wounded by splinters of British shells.

Italian Fleet at Sea

The attack from the air was still going on when news came of the Italian fleet. According to the latest intelligence (an air report of 26 September from Malta), the Italians had three battleships, six cruisers and some destroyers at Taranto, and two battleships, one cruiser and some destroyers at Naples. Then, at 1404/27, Admiral Somerville received a report timed 1340/27, by a Royal Air Force aircraft scouting from Malta, that two battleships and eight destroyers were in 38° 20' N., 10° 40' E., steering 190° at 20 knots, which put them about 74 miles 070° from the *Nelson* at 1404. Twenty minutes later a further signal timed 1350 reported four cruisers and eight destroyers 15 miles west-south-west of the enemy battle fleet, and making the same course and speed.[40] The appearance of an enemy fleet to the eastward, on the route of the convoy, altered the whole situation. Admiral Somerville considered that the enemy, believing he had only one capital ship, intended either to meet him at the western end of the Narrows or to draw the British heavy ships north-east, so that the convoy should lie open to attack by lesser forces in the Narrows at dusk. He decided to make for the enemy at his best speed with his three battleships and a few destroyers, leaving his three large cruisers and the bulk of the flotilla with the convoy, while the *Ark Royal*, the two anti-aircraft cruisers and two destroyers were to keep near it; the carrier was to send up two aircraft at once to shadow the Italian fleet, and a striking force armed with torpedoes as soon as it could be got ready. This arrangement would place the battleships between the convoy and the enemy, and enable the latter to be brought to battle should they make for the convoy. At 1408, therefore, he ordered the *Ark Royal* to prepare a striking force and to fly off shadowing aircraft, and at 1417 he ordered the battleships to form on the *Nelson* which was already stretching ahead of the convoy.[41]

But it soon became apparent that the *Nelson's* injuries would prevent her going more than 15 knots, and the Admiral revised his plan. At 1446 he ordered Admiral Curteis, with the other two battleships, two cruisers and two destroyers, "to drive off the enemy," while the *Nelson* stayed with the convoy. Admiral Curteis proceeded accordingly at 27 knots, with the *Edinburgh* and *Sheffield* five miles ahead of the *Prince of Wales* and the *Rodney* following as fast as she could.

Actually, the enemy had altered course to 360° a quarter of an hour previously and was then steering directly away from the British. Though Admiral Iachino had received a signal from the Naval Staff giving him "freedom of manoeuvre," his instructions permitted him to "engage only in conditions of decisive superiority". But visibility was poor, being limited by mist to about 5 miles, and he was uncertain as to the position and composition of the British forces; he knew, however, that they included a carrier, and the fighter escort from Cagliari which he had requested had not turned up. In these circumstances he did not feel sure of his "decisive superiority" and at 1430 altered course towards Sardinia, hoping that the fighter protection would materialise and that air reconnaissance reports would soon clarify the situation.

It was not long before Admiral Curteis received news of this change of course.

At 1521 a report came from the Royal Air Force reconnaissance aircraft that the Italian battleships had turned to 360° at 1445[42]; and at 1530 another signal timed 1503 made their course 060° and put them several miles to the northward of their position as previously reported. This made it clear to Admiral Curteis that he could not hope to force an action. It was possible, however, that the enemy might still come down between the Skerki Bank and Marittimo, to raid the transports when it grew dark, or attack them from the westward, having decoyed the British squadron northward. In these circumstances, Admiral Curteis decided to "close the passage between Skerki and Marittimo, while keeping well placed to fall back on the convoy," and he proceeded accordingly. About 1700, however, he received orders from Admiral Somerville to rejoin the convoy, "just as I was reaching a position," he said, "from which I could cover a movement either to the eastwards or westwards without fear of the enemy's winning the race." An hour or so later his detachment returned to the fleet.

Admiral Somerville had recalled him because he believed the Italians had abandoned any idea of a fight and were retiring. Even if the *Ark Royal's* aircraft succeeded in reducing the enemy's speed, he thought it too late for Admiral Curteis to gain touch before dark, when a "successful issue was highly problematical"; moreover, he considered it essential that the cruisers and destroyers should return to the convoy before dark. This view was confirmed by events.

Neither shadowers nor striking force from the *Ark Royal* found the enemy. The two shadowers left the *Ark Royal* at 1448, being informed that the enemy was 60 miles 078°, steering 190°. As mentioned above, two important signals then came in from a Royal Air Force reconnaissance aircraft. The first, made at 1445, reported that the Italians had altered course to 360°. This was received by the *Ark Royal* at 1510, but wireless congestion arising from the issue of the new orders detaching Admiral Curteis delayed its transmission to the shadowers. The other signal, timed 1503, reported the enemy's course as 060°, and amended the position in the original report (1340), making it 14 miles to the northward. This amended position was within 6 or 7 miles of the actual position, but the course 060° was merely a brief alteration to the eastward, to avoid a reported submarine. This was received by the *Ark Royal* at 1543, and the amended position and new course were passed to the striking force by wireless.[43] A few minutes before, at 1540, the striking force of twelve Swordfish had flown off, escorted by four Fulmars, with an estimated position of the enemy 54 miles 056°, steering 360°. Having reached the enemy's estimated position on the 060° course and seen nothing, they turned at 1700 and searched to the southward, then turned north again for 40 miles, but failed to locate the enemy, who had altered back to 360° at 1510 and by that time was some 50 miles to the westward of them at the extreme limit of radar range. Just before 1800 they reported their failure, and were ordered to return. Six landed on just after sunset and six after dark, all very short of petrol. The *Ark Royal*'s shadowers were equally unsuccessful. Shadower A, proceeding to the eastward, met seven Italian fighters and was badly damaged and had to return. Shadower B had not received the 1445 report of the enemy's alteration of course to 360°, though he received the 1503 report of the amended position and of the enemy's being on course 060°. His A.S.V. set failed about 1700, and a visual search was unsuccessful. He returned after having been five hours and five minutes in the air.

The Italian Fleet, meanwhile, had continued to the northward till about 1700, when, on receipt of an encouraging signal from the Naval Staff,[44] Admiral Iachino altered course to south; but at sunset, just after 1800, he received orders to proceed to the east of Sardinia for the night and to await fresh instructions; he shaped course accordingly in an east-north-easterly direction.

Night Attacks on Convoy

Soon after Admiral Curteis had rejoined, at 1851, the fleet reached the mouth of the Narrows, where the convoy was to part company with Force "A" and continue its voyage under Admiral Burrough. When the news first came of the Italian fleet, Admiral Somerville had considered whether the convoy should steer southward along the coast of Tunisia instead of keeping east towards Sicily as arranged; but Admiral Burrough preferred the Sicilian route for the following reasons: "(a) The bolder course seemed more likely to deceive the enemy; (b) the convoy would be clearly silhouetted under the moon, while moving to the southward, and off the Tunisian coast could take no avoiding action; (c) convoy and escort in single line ahead from Cape Bon to south of Kelibia Light would extend to about seven miles, and would be very vulnerable to either aircraft or E-boat attack; (d) time of arrival at Malta would be delayed; (e) the enemy would be more likely to conduct a search to the south-west than to the north-east." Admiral Somerville agreed, "in view of the enemy's hurried withdrawal to the north-east," and at 1855/27 they separated. The three battleships, the *Ark Royal* and the nine destroyers of Force "A" turned away westward. The five cruisers and nine destroyers of Force "X" took the convoy on, forming in Cruising Disposition No. 17 before dark (see Plan 8), and steaming at 14 to 15 knots.

CRUISING DISPOSITION No. 17   PLAN 8
AS USED ON THE NIGHT OF 27th — 28th SEPT. 1941

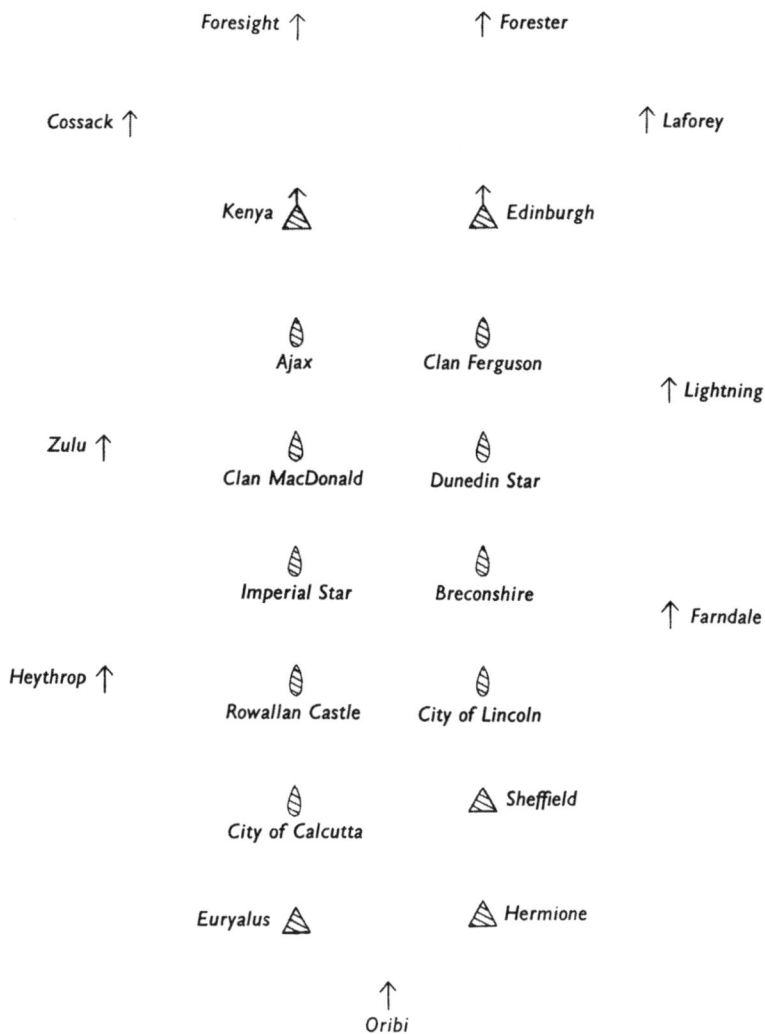

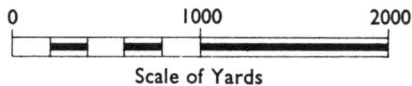

Foresight ↑   ↑ Forester

Cossack ↑   ↑ Laforey

Kenya ⌂   ⌂ Edinburgh

Ajax   Clan Ferguson

                                             ↑ Lightning

Zulu ↑

Clan MacDonald   Dunedin Star

Imperial Star   Breconshire

                                             ↑ Farndale

Heythrop ↑

Rowallan Castle   City of Lincoln

City of Calcutta   △ Sheffield

Euryalus △   △ Hermione

↑
Oribi

0		1000		2000

Scale of Yards

Note:—
The *Foresight* and *Forester* had sweeps streamed

C.B.H. 22729

81

Enemy aircraft were still about. Several Italian fighters had come within 20 miles or so of the fleet some little time before the convoy parted company, and for an hour the few Fulmars still available for patrol were engaged in keeping the enemy at a distance, lest they should observe the separation. Other Italian aircraft (probably fighters) approached the convoy between 1915 and 1930 as it passed through the Skerki Channel, but turned away when the cruisers opened fire. As soon as it grew dark, however, their torpedo bombers came, attacking the convoy repeatedly in ones, twos or threes between 2000 and 2040.

The sky was clear, with a half-moon shining on the starboard quarter, whereas the attacks were all on the port side: "an impossible night to see the birds, as any wildfowler will agree" said Commander Graham of the *Zulu*. And indeed, though the *Oribi* shot down one aircraft and the *Kenya* claims to have destroyed another with her 6-inch barrage, the ships had little chance of keeping the enemy at arm's length by their fire, hampered too as they were by the danger of hurting friends. Captain Hutton, of the *Laforey*, described the attack thus: "The appearance from the disengaged side of streams of shell of all calibres fired from H.M. ships and merchant ships was spectacular, but its effectiveness looked doubtful; some of it was quite indiscriminate, and revealed the convoy clearly to any other aircraft which may have been in the vicinity". There were luckily not much above a dozen aircraft there, or the convoy would probably have suffered heavily.

The *Cossack* (see Plan 8) sighted aircraft on the port side at 2027, and at 2029 a torpedo was dropped on the port bow of the *Sheffield*, which five minutes later had to turn with full helm to starboard to avoid another dropped on her port beam. At 2032, in 37° 31' N., 10° 46' E., the transport *Imperial Star* was struck by a torpedo on the port side aft. The *Oribi* was attacked at 2036, the torpedo being dropped 800 yards away just abaft the port beam, and avoided by the ship's turning stern on; her pom-poms and Oerlikon guns shot down the attacking aircraft.

The *Heythrop* went alongside the *Imperial Star*, took on board her 300 soldier passengers, and rejoined the convoy. The *Oribi* took her in tow and steered for Malta, distant 220 miles, Lieutenant-Commander McBeath deciding that she should go on rather than go back to Gibraltar. But the big transport's injuries made her unmanageable; with both screws and rudder gone and her stern deep in the water through the flooding of an engine-room (she was drawing 38 feet aft), she would only steer in circles. After two hours' towing they had to give it up; it was impracticable to tow her without tugs; and as she had valuable and secret stores on board, and there was risk of capture owing to her position, it was decided to sink her. The ship was scuttled with depth charges at 0340/28; a huge fire broke out aft, and the *Oribi* shelled her to spread the blaze. When it seemed clear that she must soon be entirely gutted, the destroyer left her and went on to Malta alone. There was no trace of her the next day.

Towards the end of these moonlight actions, at 2030/27, the *Hermione* had parted company to shell the harbour and base at Pantellaria as a diversion. She reached her firing position north of the island about 0130/28, and fired 122 high-explosive shells in five minutes at ranges of 12,000 to 13,500 yards by the light of starshell, causing columns of smoke to rise in the area fired at; she also dropped smoke floats a few minutes before opening fire "to give the impression that the convoy was passing." The bombardment was plainly visible to the convoy 50 miles away. The batteries on shore returned the *Hermione*'s fire without effect, and she joined Admiral Burrough again at 0630.

After the torpedo attack at 2030 the convoy had a quiet night. Some aircraft were detected over 20 miles off an hour after the last attack, searching for the convoy farther south, others approached from the northward a little before midnight, others again crossed astern from the southward, but none came near enough to be dangerous. The moon set a few minutes after midnight, and thenceforward the night was uneventful. At 0615/28, Fulmars and Royal Air Force fighters from Malta arrived, "to give excellent protection," said Admiral Burrough, "for the remainder of the passage." About 0830, having heard by signal from Malta that no enemy ships were near his track, Admiral Burrough went on ahead with four cruisers to gain time for landing passengers and refuelling. He entered the Grand Harbour at 1130 with guards and bands paraded amidst the cheers of the whole city, assembled in crowds on the shore. Admiral Syfret, with the *Edinburgh* and the destroyers, brought the convoy into harbour a couple of hours later. They had several threats of attacks by Italian aircraft during the forenoon, but the Malta fighters drove off the enemy each time. The only ship lost was the *Imperial Star*.

Westerly Passage of Empty Transports

Of the three transports that were to go from Malta empty to Gibraltar under cover of this operation, the *Melbourne Star* sailed on 26 September alone and reached Gibraltar without adventure on 29 September. The other two, *Port Chalmers* and *City of Pretoria*, left Malta together on 27 September, going through the Narrows westward along the coast of Tunisia the same night as the outgoing convoy passed through eastward farther north. Up to sunset that day a corvette had kept them company, but afterwards they sailed without escort. Soon after leaving Malta they had been seen and reported by enemy aircraft; and when passing Pantellaria at night they encountered a motor torpedo boat, with which the *Port Chalmers* exchanged fire. In the morning of 28 September the transports separated, the faster *Port Chalmers* going on at full speed and arriving at Gibraltar early on 30 September. Italian aircraft approached both ships several times during 28 September, but the transports, flying French colours, carefully refrained from firing at the aircraft. In the evening, however, three torpedo planes attacked the *City of Pretoria*; and she may have been attacked by a submarine at the same time. The transport hoisted her proper colours, fired at the aircraft, avoided their torpedoes, and made off under a smoke screen. Again in the night of 29/30 September a submarine may have attacked her off the coast of Spain, but she reached Gibraltar unharmed a few hours after the *Port Chalmers*.

Admiral Somerville remarked on their conduct that "the able and resolute handling of both *Port Chalmers* and *City of Pretoria* in successfully driving off enemy attacks deserves high praise. Both masters showed excellent restraint in withholding fire at enemy aircraft, while there was a chance of their false colours being effective, and also in keeping wireless silence when attacked, except on the one occasion when *City of Pretoria* was attacked by torpedo bomber aircraft and her report might possibly have brought fighter assistance if *Ark Royal* had been in the vicinity."

The Admiral had not tried to give these ships direct protection. "In view of the low speed of *Nelson*," he wrote, "I did not consider that action to afford close support . . . was justified, since this would have involved an unacceptable reduction in the destroyer screen then available. I wished also to convey the impression that a general withdrawal of forces to the westward was in progress and would be continued." After leaving Admiral Burrough in the evening of 27 September, therefore, he took Force "A" westward at 14 knots, the flagship's best speed. The following morning, the Royal Air Force reconnoitring aircraft reported the Italian fleet still cruising between Sardinia and Sicily, and there it remained all day, far from either part of the British fleet, finally withdrawing to the E.N.E. at 1518 that afternoon. Enemy aircraft shadowed Force "A" too, and at least once signalled a report;

this was to some extent welcome to Admiral Somerville, who remarked, "By keeping the battleships concentrated until dark I hoped to have concealed damage to *Nelson*, and that consequently enemy surface vessels would keep clear while Force "X" made the passage westward from Malta." But as soon as it grew dark, having then arrived roughly in the longitude of Algiers, Admiral Somerville parted company. The speed of the *Nelson* had to be reduced to 12 knots at 2010 to lessen the strain on the bulkheads, the ship being down 8 feet by the bows with 3,500 tons of water in her. She arrived at Gibraltar with three destroyers on 30 September. Admiral Curteis had turned east with the *Prince of Wales*, *Rodney*, *Ark Royal* and six destroyers to meet Admiral Burrough.

Return Passage to Gibraltar

Having landed passengers and stores and filled up with fuel at Malta, the ships of Force "X" sailed again in the evening of 28 September. Instead of keeping to the northward as he had come, Admiral Burrough went back along the African shore, and joined Admiral Curteis about 1030/29, when the combined force steered for Gibraltar, following a route different from that which Admiral Curteis had "already covered twice in thirty-six hours." The fleet divided into two groups at dusk that day, 29 September, Admirals Curteis and Burrough stretching ahead with some ships which entered harbour on 30 September, while Admiral Syfret arrived with the rest on 1 October.

The fleet's passage through the western basin was punctuated by a number of submarine attacks. There were six certain contacts or attacks between the evening of 28 and morning of 30 September, as well as other contacts not definitely submarine. The first took place at 1942/28, shortly before Admiral Somerville left the fleet, and the *Duncan* attacked with depth-charges, but without visible effect. Next morning, Admiral Curteis encountered two submarines on his way back to meet Admiral Burrough's force – the first about daybreak, the second two hours afterwards. In the first encounter, at 0612, two torpedoes passed under the *Gurkha*, which with the *Isaac Sweers* hunted the submarine unsuccessfully; in the attack at 0810 the *Gurkha* dropped a 14-charge pattern and may have damaged or destroyed the enemy. There was another attack in the afternoon, at 1645, by which time the fleet had arrived within some 40 miles of the *Duncan's* contact of the day before; the *Legion* and *Lively* hunted for an hour a submarine whose conning tower had broken surface and which had fired torpedoes at the fleet, but they could not claim any result. Lastly, there were two encounters on 30 September, perhaps with the same submarine. Between about 0330 and 0400, Admiral Curteis had indications of a submarine's presence on the surface, and heard what were probably torpedoes exploding at the end of their run, though the screening ships did not find the enemy. At 0930, when Admiral Syfret reached a position a little to the northward of this attack, the *Gurkha* and *Legion* hunted a submarine; and as Admiral Somerville recorded it, "there appears to be no reasonable cause to doubt" their full success.[45] It is now confirmed that the *Adua* was sunk on this occasion.

British Submarine Operations

None of the nine Allied submarines on patrol had the luck to sight the Italian battleships. But Lieutenant-Commander Cayley in the *Utmost* attacked three cruisers in the afternoon of 26 September as they were steering northward towards Naples, having come through the Messina Strait, screened by eight destroyers and escorted by flying boats. Fortune, however, did not favour the *Utmost*; for one of the destroyers nearly rammed her, perhaps indeed passed over her, just as she was about to fire; and the high speed of the enemy, estimated at 28 knots, spoilt the chance of catching up with the director angle and making a second attempt. Lieutenant-Commander Cayley then tried to report the enemy by wireless, but nobody seems to have received his signal. In the evening of 27 September the *Trusty* and *Upholder* had orders from Malta to shift their stations to the Bay of Naples, south-west of Ischia and Capri respectively, in the hope of intercepting the Italian battleships going back to port; they saw nothing, though they reached their new stations in good time: the enemy entered harbour early on 29 September, but may well have approached Naples by the route north of Ischia. On 28 September the *Urge* was moved away from the coast near Palermo to the probable track of cruisers returning to Messina, but again to no purpose. The Dutch *0.21* diving close off the south-east corner of Sardinia, cannot have been far from the enemy that afternoon, yet all she saw was a single destroyer, which passed inside her and went into Cagliari Bay.

Some submarines attacked merchantmen and torpedo craft; but Lieutenant Norman in the *Unbeaten*, south of the toe of Italy, refrained on 27 September for fear of "compromising *Unbeaten*'s position for fleet operation." Admiral Cunningham thought this a mistake, "since the enemy must pass through" that area "whether he knows submarines are present or not." On the other hand, the Admiral of Submarines said that "an observed attack . . . might well have ruined any chances of H.M.S. *Unbeaten*'s achieving her object of attacking or reporting Italian surface units," and that even a fleet tanker was not "a worthy target" in the circumstances.[46]

Remarks on Operation

The most dangerous part of the convoy's voyage proved to be the moonlight passage through the Narrows, when the *Imperial Star* was torpedoed and lost. Admiral Somerville said of this danger that "it cannot be emphasized too strongly that, if operations of this character are carried out during moonlight, the hazards are increased to a very considerable extent. Had the enemy concentrated his torpedo aircraft in attacking from dusk onwards, he might well have succeeded in torpedoing a large proportion of the convoy." In comparison, the danger from the air during daylight was much less serious, the determined and successful attack on the *Nelson* notwithstanding; nor, in the Admiral's words, did the Italian fleet ever constitute a serious threat. Admiral Somerville noted "the excellent co-operation" by the Royal Air Force, whose fighters' services to the convoy Admirals Burrough and Syfret specially remarked on.[47] Apart from that, the bombing and machine-gun attacks on airfields in Sardinia and Sicily on 27 and 28 September "undoubtedly reduced to a considerable extent the scale of air attack which the enemy intended to launch."

These three operations – "Excess", "Substance" and "Halberd" – brought 29 ships through the Narrows (apart from the 10 ships of the Malta-Egypt convoys in January) with a loss of one sunk and two damaged. The cost to the fleet was by no means small. It amounted to one battleship *(Nelson)* damaged; one aircraft carrier *(Illustrious)* severely damaged; one cruiser *(Southampton)* sunk and two damaged *(Gloucester, Manchester)*; one destroyer *(Fearless)* sunk and two damaged *(Gallant, Firedrake)*. These losses weighed little at the time against the joyous cheers that rose from the walls of Valetta as the ships entered the beleaguered harbour. England had not forgotten them. Her Navy still held the pathways of the sea.

Despatches: Supplement to *The London Gazette*, Published by Authority
The following Despatch was submitted to the Lords Commissioners of the Admiralty on 4 August, 1941 by Vice-Admiral Sir James F. Somerville, K.C.B., D.S.O., Flag Officer Commanding, Force H.

General Remarks

Failure to locate enemy battlefleet.

The operation orders stated clearly that the primary object of the operation was the safe arrival of the convoy at its destination, and any action taken to deal with enemy surface forces in the vicinity must be related to the achievement of this object.

At no time did the enemy surface forces constitute a serious threat. On the other hand enemy air forces remained a potential and serious threat throughout the day and well after moonset. Under these circumstances the maintenance of fighter patrols assumed an importance which could not be ignored. Light variable winds added to the difficulties with which *Ark Royal* was confronted, and I consider that her Commanding Officer acted throughout with great judgement and a well balanced appreciation of the situation.

Had the shadowing aircraft from Malta been able to maintain observation on the enemy battlefleet for a longer period the two reconnaissance Swordfish should have experienced no serious difficulty in making contact. Unfortunately, communications, due to atmospherics and congestion, were difficult. Congestion was due in part to the damage sustained by *Nelson* involving a last minute alteration of the pre-arranged plan to deal with the situation. With a force occupying a front of 12 miles the delay caused by V/F communication was unacceptable.

Failure of Malta and H.M. Ships to receive the all important signal timed 1515 on 27 September, undoubtedly contributed largely to the failure of the striking force to locate the enemy battlefleet. It appears now that whilst the enemy was at pains to withdraw as quickly as possible he was probably concerned to keep under a C.R.42 umbrella furnished from Cagliari.

Part II

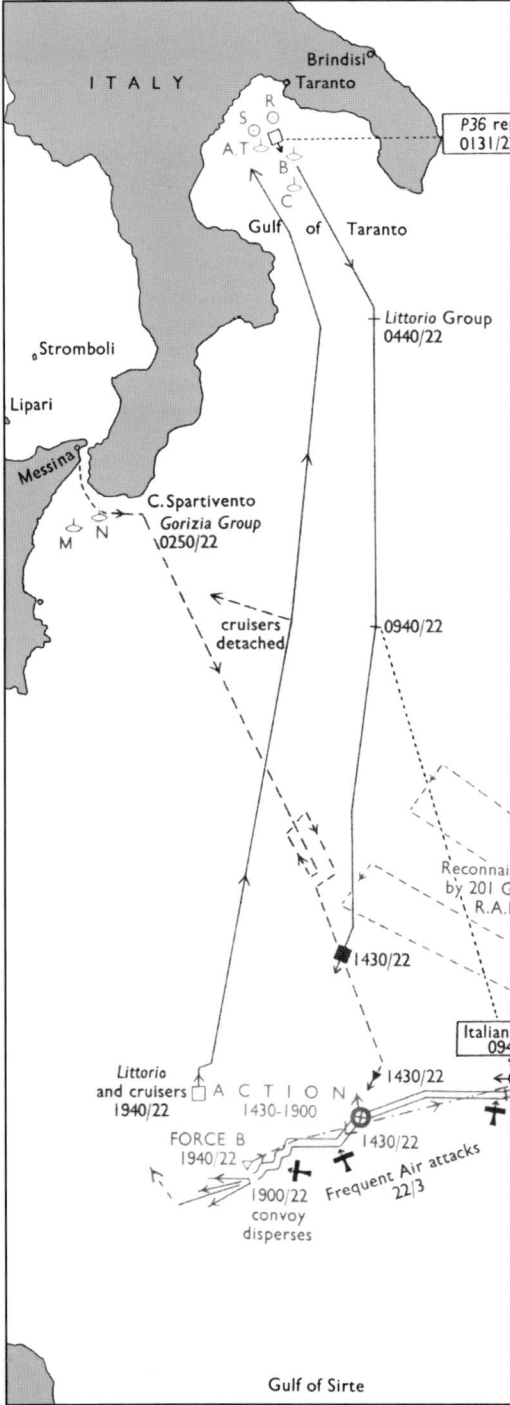

Section detail of Plan 9

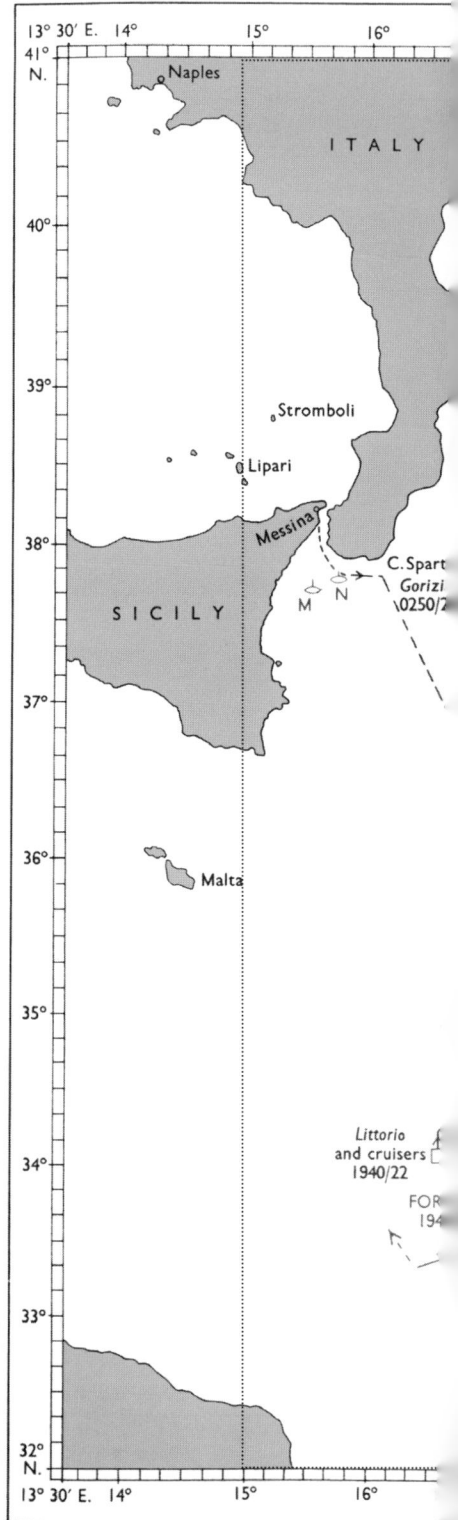

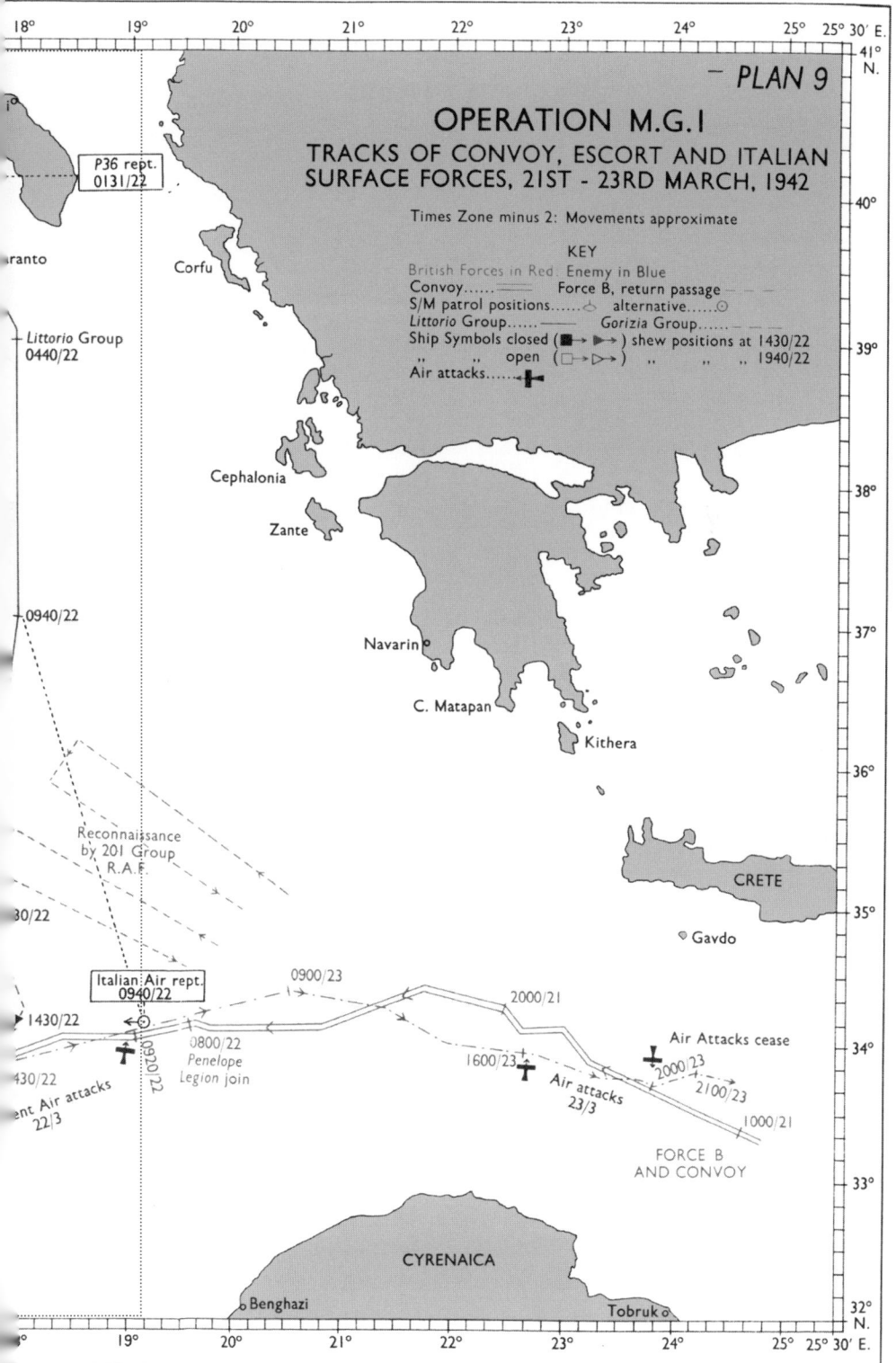

- PLAN 9

OPERATION M.G.I
TRACKS OF CONVOY, ESCORT AND ITALIAN
SURFACE FORCES, 21ST - 23RD MARCH, 1942

Times Zone minus 2: Movements approximate

KEY

British Forces in Red. Enemy in Blue
Convoy......   Force B, return passage
S/M patrol positions......   alternative.....
Littorio Group......   Gorizia Group......
Ship Symbols closed (■→ ▶→) shew positions at 1430/22
     ,,   ,,   open (□→ ▷→) ,,   ,,   ,, 1940/22
Air attacks......

P36 rept.
0131/22

ranto

Corfu

Littorio Group
0440/22

Cephalonia

Zante

0940/22

Navarin

C. Matapan

Kithera

CRETE

Reconnaissance
by 201 Group
R.A.F.

30/22

Gavdo

Italian Air rept.
0940/22

0900/23

2000/21

1430/22

0800/22
Penelope
Legion join

0920/22

Air Attacks cease

430/22

1600/23

2000/23

Air attacks
23/3

2100/23

ent Air attacks
22/3

1000/21

FORCE B
AND CONVOY

CYRENAICA

Benghazi

Tobruk

Operation "M.G.1"

General Situation

In March 1942 the naval situation in the Mediterranean – and, indeed throughout the world – was more difficult than at any time hitherto during the war. The quarter ending that month saw a higher tonnage of merchant shipping sunk in the Atlantic than in any previous period, and this was on the increase; in the Arctic, the protection of the convoys to North Russia was throwing a very severe strain on the Home Fleet, due to the advent of daylight after the winter darkness and a redisposition of the German Fleet; and the tremendous events in the Far East following the Japanese entry into the war in December 1941, made themselves felt everywhere, and not least in the Mediterranean. In the eastern basin, neither capital ships nor carriers were available in the British Fleet, while Italy had four or five battleships fit for service and strong forces of shore-based aircraft at her disposal. In the western basin, Force H was preparing for the operation which resulted in the occupation of Diego Suarez (Madagascar) in May.

An attempt to send a convoy from Alexandria to Malta in February had failed, two ships being destroyed and the third disabled by air attack. But the Commander-in-Chief, Admiral Sir Andrew Cunningham, determined to try again, employing his whole strength of cruisers and destroyers under Rear-Admiral Philip Vian to fight the way through and with shore-based fighter aircraft patrolling overhead at times more than 300 miles from their base. This operation, known as M.G.1, was the last planned by Admiral Cunningham before he gave up the command of the station to Admiral Sir Henry Harwood in April; and it led to a brilliant action known as the Battle of Sirte[48] between surface ships in which Rear-Admiral Vian, using methods like those proposed by Kempenfelt long ago, showed the power of a weak squadron to parry attempts by much stronger forces.[49] Unfortunately, only a small fraction of the cargoes "carried to Malta at such risk and price," said Admiral Harwood, was safely discharged. One ship was bombed and sunk by aircraft the day after the battle; another was towed disabled into Marsaxlokk and never reached the Grand Harbour, though a part of her cargo was recovered; continual air attacks after their arrival hindered unloading the other two, and they were sunk eventually with their holds still nearly full.

Plan of Operation "M.G.1"

The ships available for the escort were three cruisers, an anti-aircraft ship, with ten "Fleet" and six (originally seven) Hunt-class destroyers from Alexandria, besides a cruiser and a destroyer from Malta that were to meet the convoy west of Crete.[50] The "Hunts" were to carry out an antisubmarine search between Alexandria and Tobruk in the night of 19/20 March, the night before the convoy sailed, and during daylight on 20 March; they were then to oil at Tobruk, and to join the convoy in the morning of 21 March. The sweep was unfortunate, for the *Heythrop* was torpedoed by a submarine on 20 March and sank whilst on her way to Tobruk in tow a few hours later. The convoy itself was to leave Alexandria with a small escort in the morning of 20 March, Rear-Admiral Vian following with the main body in the evening to catch up with the convoy next morning at the eastern end of the passage between Cyrenaica and Crete, whence earlier convoys had suffered heavy air attacks. Having met the two ships from Malta in the morning of 22 March, the convoy was to proceed at full strength until dark that day, steering well to the southward of the natural course for Malta. At nightfall Rear-Admiral Vian was to turn back for Alexandria with his three cruisers and the "Fleet" destroyers (Force "B"), while the convoy finished its voyage with the ships from Malta, the anti-aircraft ship and the "Hunts," reaching its destination at dawn on 23 March. Admiral Cunningham reckoned upon interference by surface ships during daylight on 22 March or the night following. "Should this occur," ran his order on the subject, "it is my general intention that the enemy should, if possible, be evaded until darkness, after which the convoy should be sent on to Malta with the destroyer escort, being dispersed if considered advisable, and the enemy brought to action by Force "B". The convoy should only be turned back if it is evident that the enemy will otherwise intercept in daylight and east of longitude 18° E."

Four vessels of the Malta submarine flotilla and one from Alexandria – the *Proteus* – were also employed against surface attack, two on patrol south of the Strait of Messina, three off Taranto. The submarines off Taranto had each two stations: "A", "B" and "C" up to 22 March; "R", "S" and

"T" farther inshore, on 23 March (see Plan 9). Only *P.36* saw anything of the Italian fleet on its sailing; she sighted some destroyers and had hydrophone effect of bigger ships standing out of the Gulf of Taranto in the night of 21/22 March, and thus was able to give timely warning to Rear-Admiral Vian. On the other hand, three submarines had opportunities for successful action before the operation began, while waiting to fulfil their part in protecting the convoy. On 14 March, *P.34* of the Messina patrol sank a submarine off Punto di Stilo, north-east of Cape Spartivento; and the *Unbeaten* sank another on 17 March on her regular station, Position "N". Lastly, the *Upholder*, being sent into the Adriatic to kill time, sank a submarine within 2 miles of the port of Brindisi on 18 March. She had also a long shot in a very rough sea on 23 March at the Italian battleship *Littorio* returning to Taranto after the action of the previous day, but was unsuccessful, as will be told in its place.

Both the Army in Libya and the Royal Air Force helped to defend the convoy against attack from the air. The Army made feint advances on 20 and 21 March, to threaten enemy airfields, and thus to divert aircraft from attacking the convoy; these movements proved very successful, in particular the shelling of Martuba landing-ground on the second day of the advance. The Royal Air Force was to attack air stations in Cyrenaica and Crete to keep aircraft grounded.[51] Fighter patrols were to accompany the convoy "as far as possible" – a duty nobly performed until 0900[52]/22, when the aircraft were over 300 miles from their base. Air reconnaissance was to be flown both from Libya and Malta; but in the event heavy enemy attacks on the airfields prevented reconnaissance from Malta. Torpedo striking forces were also arranged for – Beauforts from Libya and a naval air squadron from Malta.

Passage of Convoy M.W.10

The convoy, known as M.W.10, consisting of the commissioned supply ship *Breconshire* and three merchant ships, sailed from Alexandria in the morning of 20 March with the anti-aircraft ship *Carlisle* and six destroyers, Rear-Admiral Vian following in the evening with the *Cleopatra* (flag), *Dido*, *Euryalus* and four destroyers. The two forces met some 70 miles northward of Tobruk in the forenoon of 21 March, by which time five of the six "Hunt" destroyers from Tobruk had also joined the convoy, and all proceeded westward together at 12 knots with relays of fighter aircraft overhead. The sixth destroyer from Tobruk, held up there by a fouled propeller, joined in the evening; and at 0800/22, the *Penelope* and *Legion* joined from Malta in 34° 10' N., 19° 30' E. The force was thus complete and well on its way, having passed through the danger area between Crete and Cyrenaica without attack. By this time, however, Rear-Admiral Vian knew that he was unlikely to be left in peace much longer. Some German transport aircraft, crossing from Libya to Crete, had reported the convoy the previous evening,[53] and at 0518 that morning the following signal (timed 0131/22) had come from Submarine *P.36:* "Three destroyers and hydrophone effect of heavier ships in 40° 08' N., 17° 07' E., course 150° at 23 knots."

This force was actually the battleship *Littorio*, wearing the flag of the Commander-in-Chief, Admiral Iachino, and four destroyers, which had sailed from Taranto shortly after midnight and was steaming to the southward with Convoy MW.10 as its quarry, after being joined by two 8-inch cruisers (*Gorizia, Trento*), a 6-inch cruiser (*Bande Nere*) and four destroyers under Admiral Parona from Messina.

P.36's signal indicated to Admiral Vian that air attacks must be expected at any moment, whilst an Italian fleet might appear in the afternoon. The air attacks began at about 0930, just half an hour after the last fighter patrol had to leave the convoy, and continued at intervals till dark. It was estimated that all told some 150 aircraft were employed, torpedo- and high-level-bombers, shadowers and spotting aircraft. The forenoon attempts were not dangerous, however, being only a few torpedo shots at long range by Italian S.79 aircraft – "futile attacks," as Captain Nicholl of the *Penelope* called them, on which "there are no particular remarks to make." The convoy was protected by a double screen, an inner air warning screen of cruisers and destroyers stationed close in with an anti-submarine screen of destroyers two miles ahead; and the half-dozen or so of torpedoes dropped were all released beyond the outer screen without effect. On the other hand, the attacks by German bombers later in the day were much more serious; most of the ships of war were away engaging the Italian fleet, and the merchantmen and their actual escort were hard put to it to avoid damage.

Rear-Admiral Vian's Tactical Intentions

At 1230, Rear-Admiral Vian assumed his organization for a surface action and signalled his intention to form the striking force on a northerly course, should the enemy appear. He was determined that the convoy should go to

Malta, "even if enemy surface forces made contact." In this organization, the ships were ordered in divisions as follows: –

1st   *Jervis* (Captain Poland, D.14), *Kipling, Kelvin, Kingston*

2nd *Dido* (Captain McCall), *Penelope, Legion*

3rd *Zulu* (Commander Graham), *Hasty*

4th *Cleopatra* (flag), *Euryalus*

5th *Sikh* (Captain Micklethwait, D.22), *Lively, Hero, Havock*

6th *Carlisle* (Captain Neame), *Avon Vale* (smoke-laying)

On the enemy's approach, the ships of the first five divisions were to stand out from the convoy and concentrate by divisions as a striking force (see Fig. 1). Meanwhile, the 6th Division would prepare to lay smoke across the wake of the convoy; and the remaining destroyers – *Southwold* (Commander Jellicoe), *Beaufort, Dulverton, Hurworth* and *Eridge* – which already formed part of the inner screen, would be redisposed as a close escort. In case the Rear-Admiral decided against an immediate close engagement, he had a special signal to "carry out diversionary tactics using smoke to cover the escape of the convoy," when the convoy was to turn away, while the concentrated divisions laid smoke screens at right-angles to the bearing of the enemy, reversing course in time to attack with torpedoes as the enemy reached the smoke. A month previously, the cruiser squadron and some of the destroyers had practised the manoeuvre required – "to move out from a cruising disposition designed to meet air attack into a disposition suitable for surface action with the least possible delay."

They were soon to carry it out in earnest.

Surface Action, Gulf of Sirte: First Contact

The first sign of the enemy's approach came at 1332, when a shadowing aircraft dropped four red flares ahead of the convoy. Then at 1410 the *Euryalus* reported smoke to the northward, and at 1427 four ships bearing 015°, while the *Legion* at the same time reported one ship bearing 010°, distant 12 miles. At first the enemy were thought to include three battleships, but they proved to be cruisers – it was thought one 8-inch and three 6-inch ships – and they had arrived a couple of hours sooner than was expected.[54] As we have seen, some Italian ships had sailed from Taranto about midnight, 21 March, and *P.36* had detected them at 0131/22, but had been unable to make a definite report of their composition; nor did she report a second contact with heavy ships two hours later.[55] Whether the force that now appeared had come indeed from Taranto, at a higher speed than Rear-Admiral Vian allowed for, or was a separate force from Naples or Sicily, was not known. The Rear-Admiral must have learnt of its coming so soon with mixed feelings. On general grounds he would have liked to put off the meeting till the evening and as late in the convoy's passage as possible. Yet he wrote that "it was clear that the enemy must be driven off by dark"; for the ships of Force "B" could not oil at Malta, and so could not afford to be entangled in operations at night far to the westward; nor could the convoy afford to continue long off its proper course, when every hour's delay increased the danger from the air on the morrow.

As soon as he received the second report from the *Euryalus*, Rear-Admiral Vian made his special manoeuvring signal and the ships of the striking force drew off to the north "exactly as detailed in the operation orders," forming divisions in line ahead, while the convoy and its close escort were sent away south-westward. A few minutes afterwards, at 1433, the divisions turned east to lay smoke, with a freshening south-easterly wind to blow the smoke across the wake of the merchantmen.[56] The four Italians, hitherto standing towards the convoy in a very loose line abreast, appeared to turn south-east beam on to open fire,[57] though still out of range, and at 1442 they altered right round to north-west. By that time they were recognized as cruisers only, so Rear-Admiral Vian made the signal to steer towards them, leading the way with the *Cleopatra* and *Euryalus*. At 1456 these two ships began a concentrated shoot on the 8-inch cruiser at a range of about 20,000 yards, but the Italians turned away north soon after fire was opened and at 1508 this engagement ceased. The Italian 6-inch ship then turned back for a few minutes,[58] and straddled the two British ships in a sharp exchange of fire at extreme range; at 1515, however, she hauled away again to join her consorts. Owing to the interference of their own smoke, few of the other British ships even saw the enemy during this brief action; the only other ship engaged was the *Lively*, which fired an occasional round from her 4-in. guns as she made out a target through the smoke. The enemy having gone off, Rear-Admiral Vian steered to rejoin the convoy. There was no apparent damage on either side, but the Rear-Admiral felt able to report to the Commander-in-Chief at 1535, "Enemy driven off."[59] An hour later he overtook the convoy.

OPERATION M.G.I
SURFACE ACTION, 22 MAR. 1942

BASED ON BRITISH AND ITALIAN PLANS

Times Zone minus 2: movements approximate

NOTE. For the sake of clearness only the tracks of Convoy MW 10, *Cleopatra* and *Littorio* are shewn continuously. Close escort (*Hunt* class) is not shewn.

KEY

British Forces in Red: Enemy in Blue

Convoy MW 10 *Breconshire*, *Clan Campbell*, *Talabot* Escort, *Southwold*, *Beaufort*, *Dulverton*, *Hurworth*, *Eridge*	
1st Div. *Jervis*, *Kipling*, *Kelvin*, *Kingston*	J
2nd ,, *Dido*, *Penelope*, *Legion*	D
3rd ,, *Zulu*, *Hasty*	Z
4th ,, *Cleopatra* (Flag), *Euryalus*	
5th ,, *Sikh*, *Lively*, *Hero*, *Havock*	S
6th ,, *Carlisle*, *Avondale*	C

Open fire _____ Cease fire ____

Littorio (Flag C.-in-C.) from Italian report _____

Italian cruisers from Italian report _____

,, ,, as observed by British _____

Ship symbols closed (⊗) approx. posns. at 1425, 1640, 1740, 1840

,, ,, open (⊗) ,, ,, ,, 1515, 1705, 1805

Air attacks ✛

NOTE

The *Sikh's* Gunnery report emphasises that at 1820 the range of the *Littorio* had fallen to about 6000 yds., but the contemporary plan places her about 19,000 yards off at the time. It seems probable that in fighting the *Littorio* off the *Sikh* actually made good a course considerably further to the west and north than is shewn in the plan from about 1800, and after turning at 1820 to the smoke-laying course, did not get so far to the northward before altering back to the south westward. The 6000 yard arc from the *Littorio's* 1820 position is shewn in red.

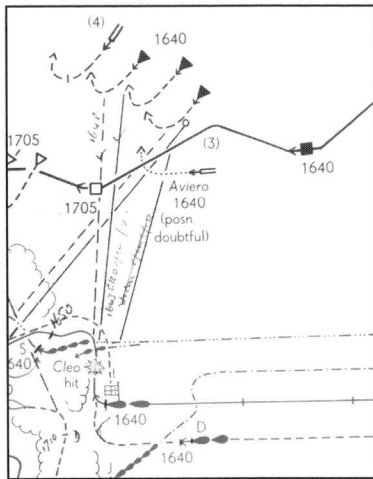

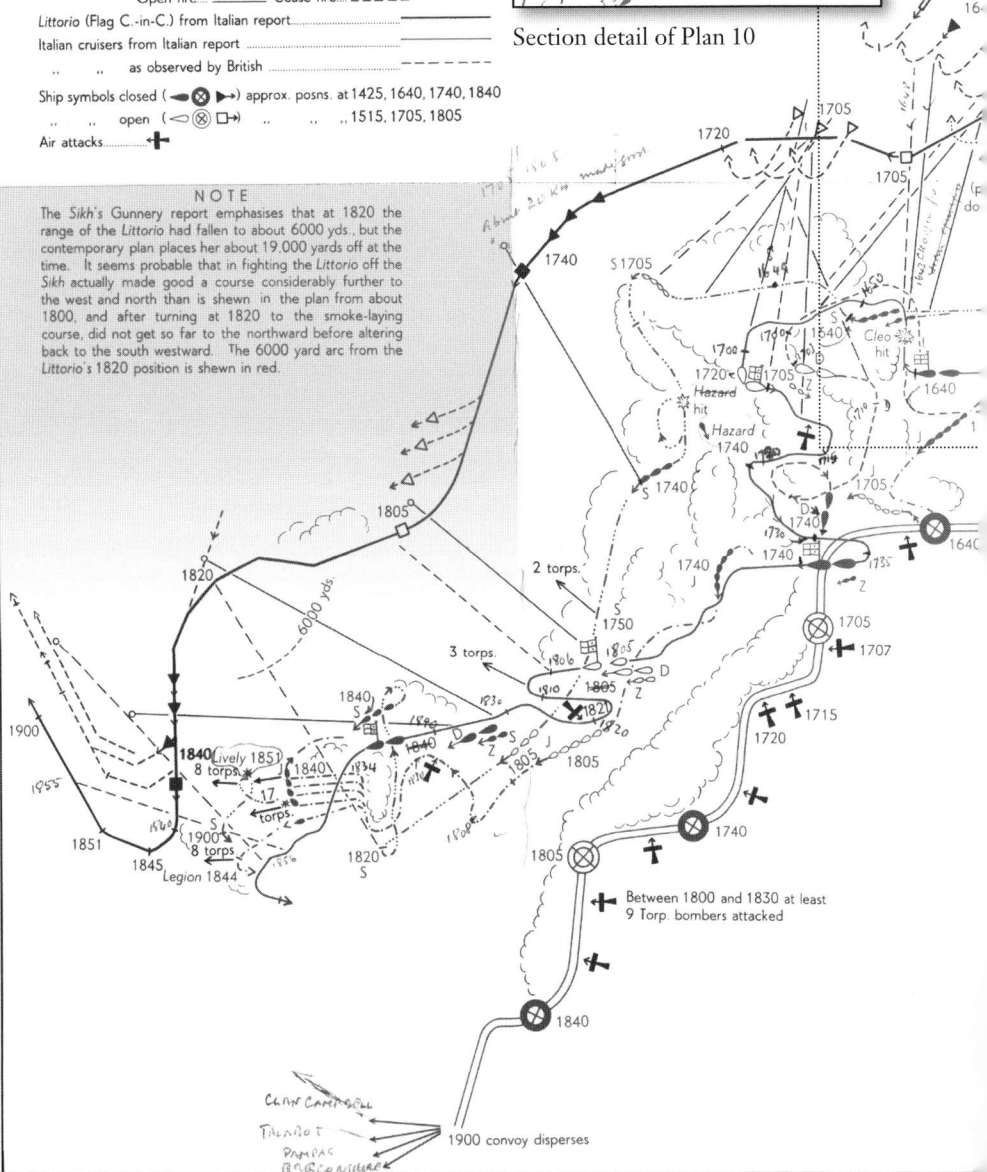

Section detail of Plan 10

Aviero 1640 (posn doubtful)

Cleo hit

Hazard hit

Hazard 1740

6000 yds.

2 torps.

3 torps.

1840 *Lively* 1851
8 torps

17 torps

1900
8 torps

1845 *Legion* 1844

Between 1800 and 1830 at least 9 Torp. bombers attacked

CLAN CAMPBELL
TALABOT
PAMPAS
BRECONSHIRE

1900 convoy disperses

Littorio, 3 dests.

26°

Gorizia, Trento, Bande Nere, 4 dests.

To join *Littorio*

1515

Dests. 4
posn. doubtful

1504

1600

1449

1454

1448

1445

1437

1456

1425

1618

Cruisers, R.V.

1433

1429

A

S 1515

Z

D

1515

1515

1500

1500

1456

1453

1500

1500

Zulu
Hasty
1600

1450

1500

1442

Zulu

Euryalus

Sikh
Havock
Hero
Lively
1600

1547

Sikh

*Ivo Avondale
and Avondale*

Jervis
Kipling
Kelvin
1600

Kingston
Legion

1425

Penelope

Carlisle

1600

Cleopatra
Euryalus
Dido

1515

Dido

1600

Jervis

Penelope

TRUE
NORTH

1505 Carlisle and
Avondale collide
in smoke

1530

1445

Carlisle
1600 Avondale

1500

Convoy
M.W.10
and 'Hunts'

1609

1551

1535

1524

1515

Wind SE, 25 knots
(increasing)
Sea, rough,
moderate
Swell

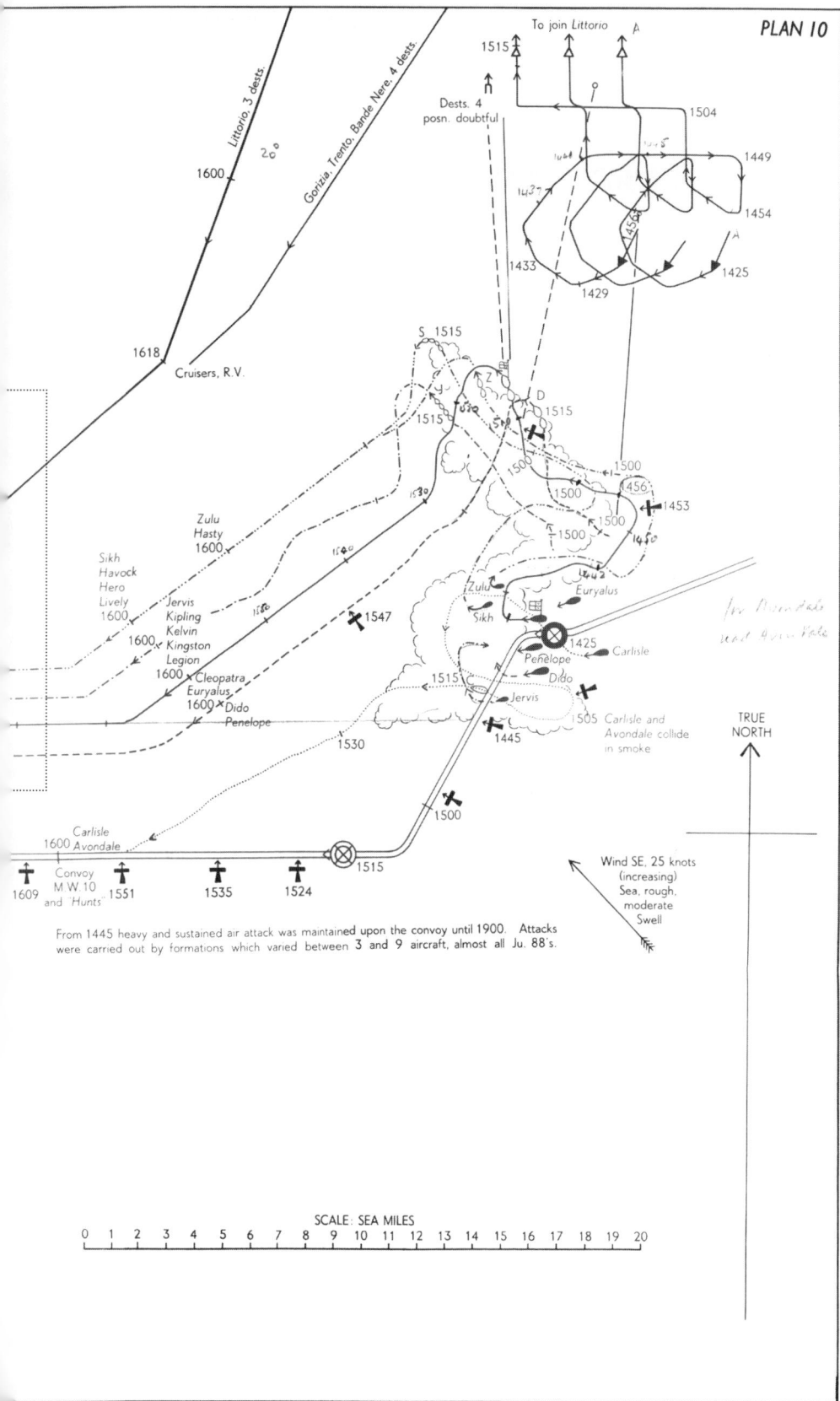

From 1445 heavy and sustained air attack was maintained upon the convoy until 1900. Attacks
were carried out by formations which varied between 3 and 9 aircraft, almost all Ju. 88's.

SCALE: SEA MILES

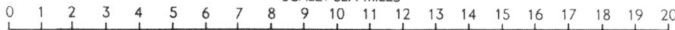

0 1 2 3 4 5 6 7 8 9 10 11 12 13 14 15 16 17 18 19 20

▽

▽ Italian Cruisers

▽

▽

N

W — E

Wind

Wind S.E. 25 knots (increasing later). Sea rough with moderate swell. Sunset 1904.(Zone −2).

Note :- Smoke was being made by all ships not with the convoy from 1430 to 1520, and from 1640 to 1913

Note

Ships are shewn concentrating in divisions and standing out from the convoy. The ships of the 5th Destroyer Flotilla are not shewn : Five screened the convoy throughout the action, and the sixth joined Carlisle.

Zulu, Hasty.

Sikh, Lively,
Hero, Havock.   Euryalus

Cleopatra▽   ◦Talabot

Breconshire   Clan Campbell

Penelope   Pampas ▽Carlisle

Legion

Dido

Scale : Sea miles

Jervis, Kipling,
Kelvin, Kingston.

| 0 | 1 | 2 | 3 | 4 | 5 | 6 | 7 | 8 |

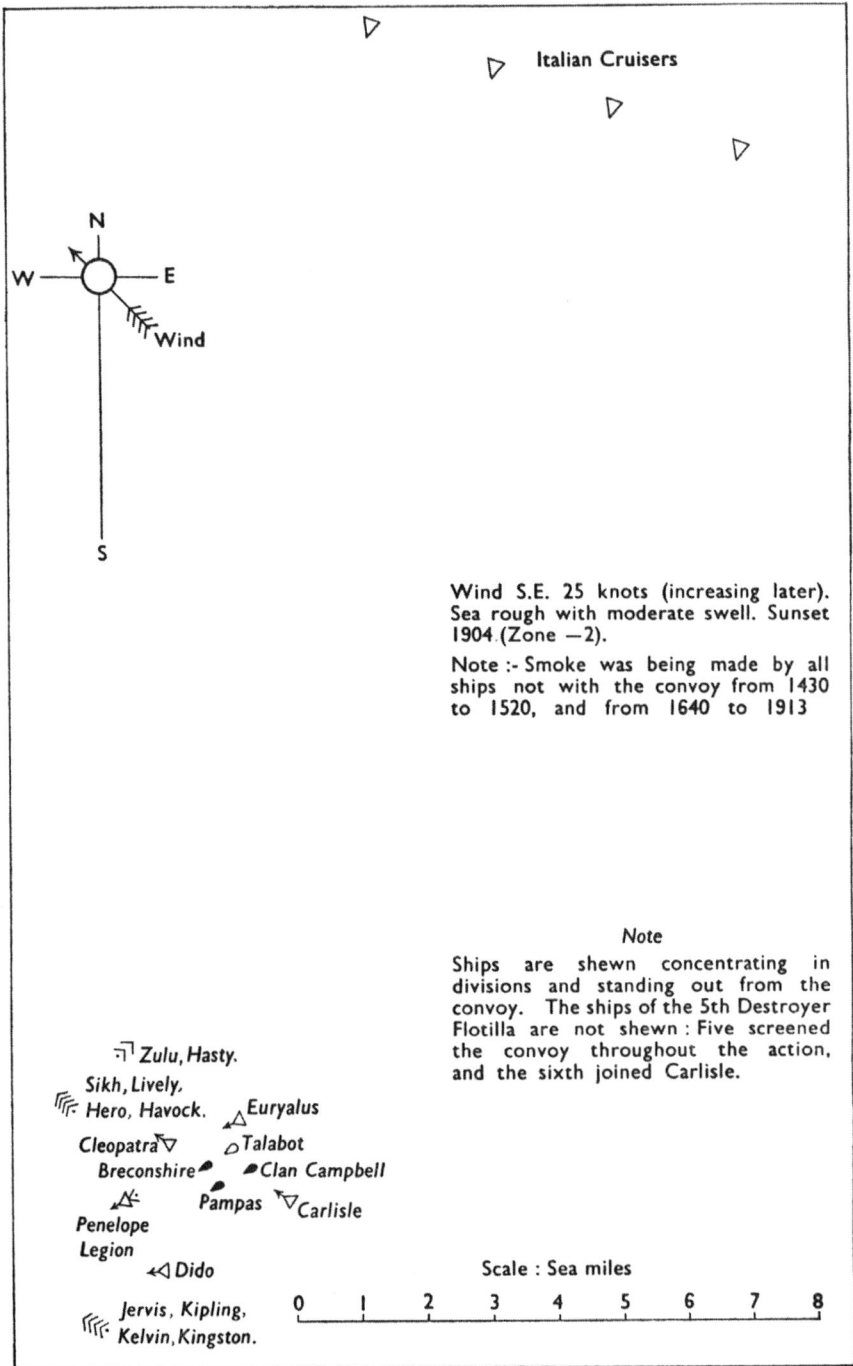

Fig. 1. First sighting by *Euryalus*, 1427

Italian Cruisers

Sikh

Cleo. Eury. Zulu

Jervis Dido Pen.

Legion

Avon Vale Carlisle

Scale : Sea miles

0   1   2   3   4   5   6   7   8

Convoy (under
heavy air attack)

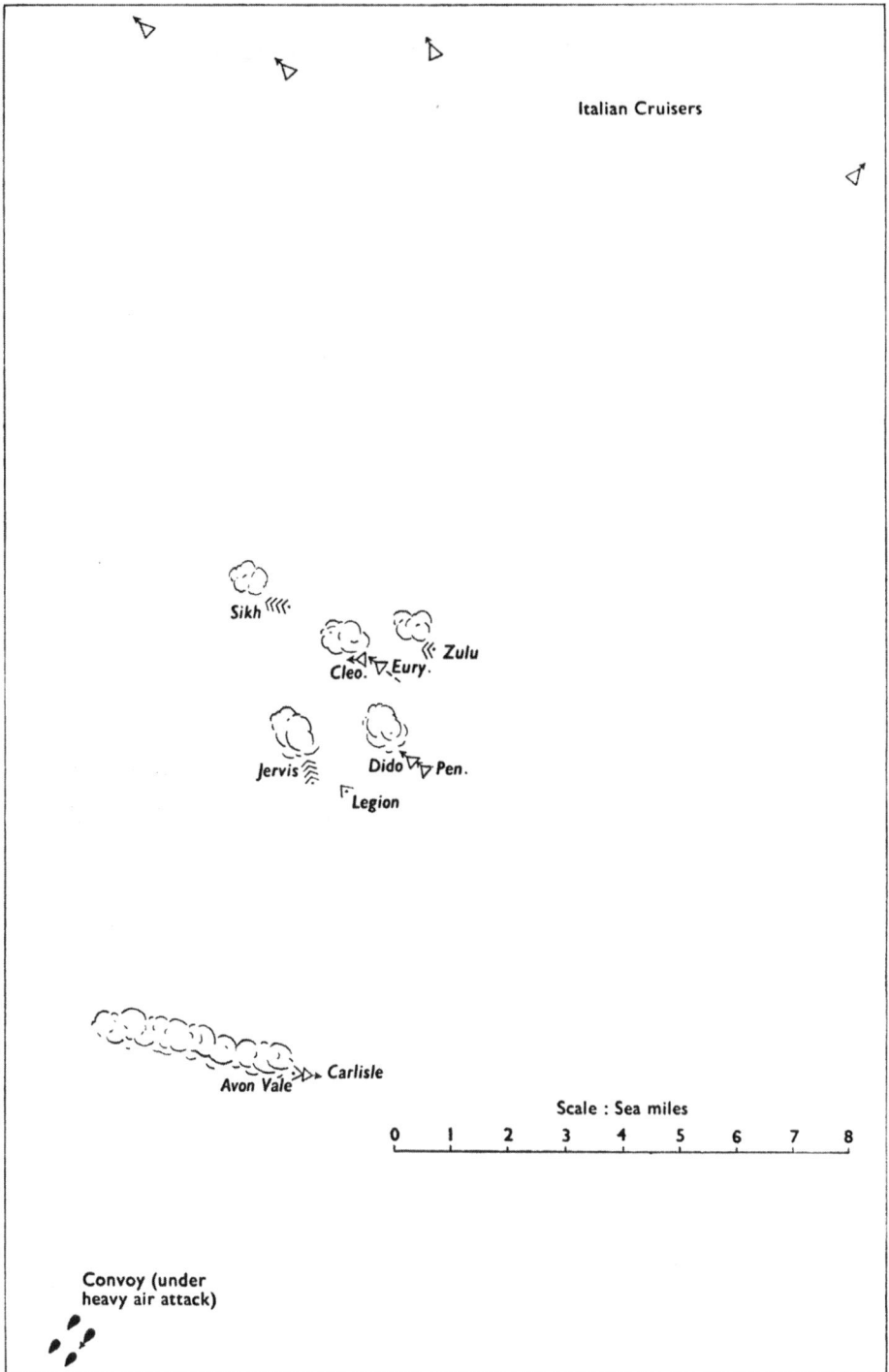

Fig. 2. Enemy withdraws to Northward, 1500

German Air Attacks on Convoy

The *Carlisle* and *Avon Vale* – the special smoke-laying division – had already joined the convoy. They had turned at about 1520, when they saw that the striking force was coming south again and that the convoy was being attacked from the air. Some single aircraft had dropped bombs harmlessly among the ships of the striking force during the engagement with the Italian squadron, and the *Carlisle* had a narrow escape from bombs while still laying smoke to the southward[60]; but "a heavy and sustained" assault upon the convoy had begun at 1445. The enemy were German Ju.88 bombers, varying in number from three to nine aircraft at a time, and they made both high-level and diving attacks from 9,000 ft. The steady shooting of the escort and the skilful handling of the convoy spoilt the attacks, which were entirely unsuccessful. Commander Jellicoe of the *Southwold* gave particular credit to the guns' crews on the forecastles of the destroyers, "who were fighting their guns under most difficult conditions" in the heavy sea then running "and were drenched from the start." Rear-Admiral Vian remarked that "whilst the striking force was rejoining, the sound of the 4-inch fire from the Hunts and *Carlisle* was most impressive, resembling continuous pom-pom fire, even though heard at a distance of 8 to 10 miles." But it was very expensive in ammunition; a little after 1600, as the striking force was coming up, the *Carlisle* reported having used one-third of her outfit, while the *Southwold* signalled, "Nine attacks so far; 40 per cent of 4-inch ammunition remaining." Accordingly, the Rear-Admiral ordered the five ships of the 1st Division to join the escort.[61]

Movements of Italian Fleet

Meanwhile Admiral Iachino's force, the *Littorio* and four destroyers, had been coming down from the northward on course 190° at 28 knots. The first enemy report he received came in from a shore-based aircraft at 0955 and placed a considerable naval force in 34° 10' N., 19° 10' E., steering 270° at 14 knots.

Admiral Iachino was determined to keep his forces to the westward of the enemy, in order to bar the passage to Malta, arguing that if (as actually occurred) the convoy turned to the southward, the delay would expose it to further air attack, and might give him another opportunity for surface attack next day. This decision governed his tactics throughout the day.

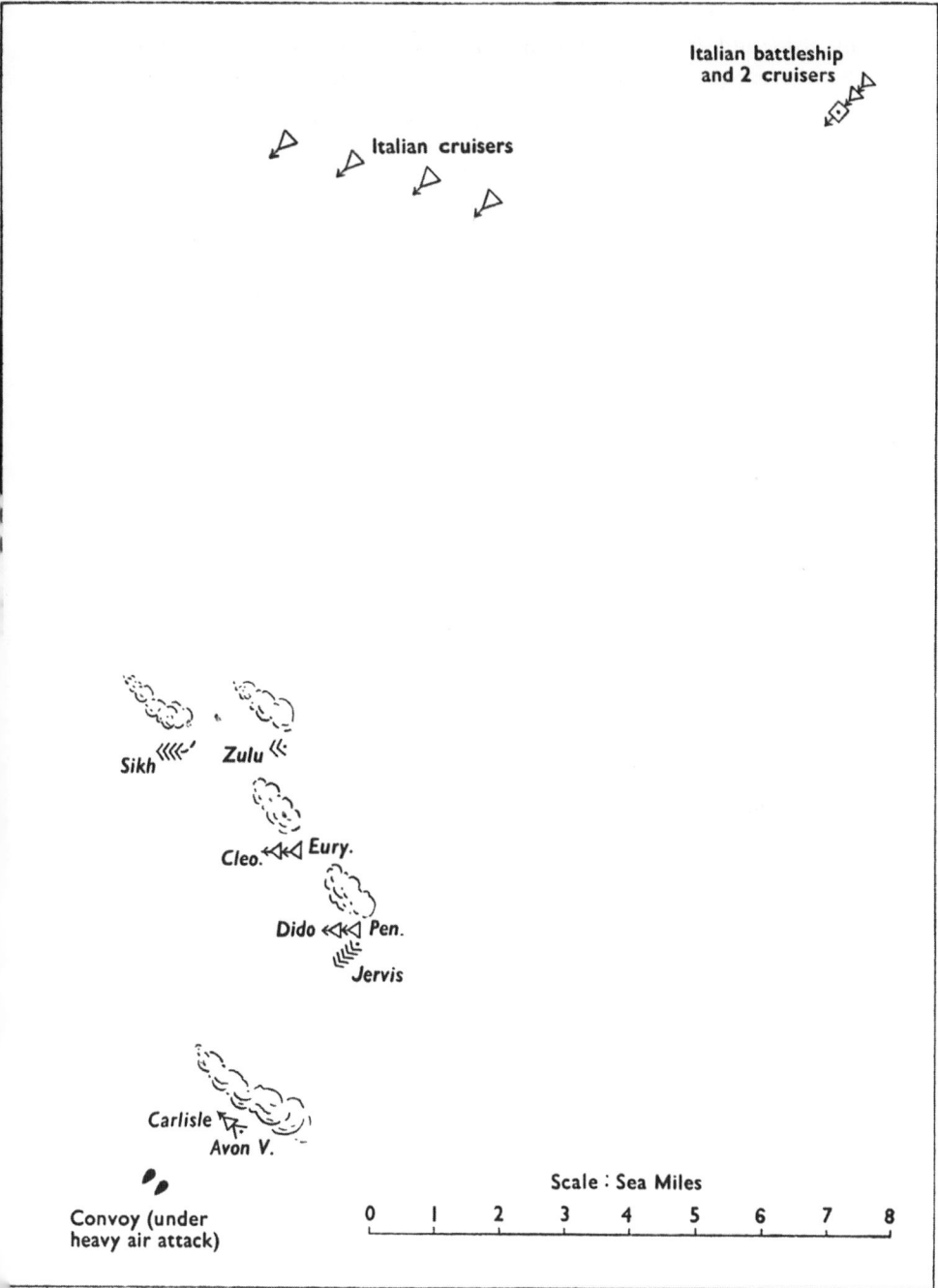

Italian battleship
and 2 cruisers

Italian cruisers

Sikh   Zulu

Cleo. Eury.

Dido Pen.

Jervis

Carlisle
Avon V.

Convoy (under
heavy air attack)

Scale : Sea Miles

0   1   2   3   4   5   6   7   8

Fig. 3. Second contact, 1640

Accordingly, as enemy reports came in, he gradually hauled round to the south-westward, altering from 180° to 200° at 1353 and finally to 230° at 1618. At 1530 Admiral Parana's three cruisers joined him and were stationed in line abreast 5,500 yards to port of the *Littorio*. At the same time one of the *Littorio*'s destroyers, the *Grecale*, had trouble with her steering gear and was ordered back to Taranto. An hour later (1631), in very bad and shortening visibility aggravated by "vast masses of smoke spread by the English vessels,"[62] the enemy came in sight. They were some 10 miles farther west than expected, and 12 minutes later the *Littorio* altered course to 270°.

Surface Action – Second Phase

To return to Admiral Vian: no sooner had the striking force overhauled the convoy than Italian ships came in sight again to the north-east. This time it was a truly formidable force, which eventually appeared to consist of one *Littorio*-class battleship, two 8-inch cruisers, and four smaller ships, all thought to be 6-inch cruisers. There followed sporadic fighting for some two and a half hours, from about 1640 to 1900, the British striking force laying smoke east and west to bar the way, while the Italians tried to work round the smoke to reach the convoy, which made off to the southward – still heavily attacked from the air. Rear-Admiral Vian wrote of the "enormous area of smoke, which lay well in the existing weather conditions of a 25-knot wind from south-east. The enemy tried to make touch with the convoy by passing round the western end of the smoke, to leeward, and was therefore effectually held away from the convoy, as he would not approach the smoke, which was drifting towards him." He remarked, too, that "the enemy's most effective course of action was to pass to windward of the smoke," that is to the eastward; but they preferred what seemed the shortest way between the convoy and its destination. While the smoke screen thus fulfilled its main purpose of protecting the convoy, besides to some extent shielding the British ships of war from the fire of their stronger opponents, it naturally hampered the British ships' gunnery and restricted their view of the enemy's motions, and indeed of their consorts. The increasing sea had also its effect, the ships washing down fore and aft, and the bridges and director control towers of even the cruisers being drenched with spray, whenever they were steaming to windward. Meanwhile, the Italians had some assistance from spotting aircraft, which pointed out the positions of British ships in the smoke; on the other hand, they had the disadvantage of the lee gage, and one ship at least was seen to use only her upper – "B" and "X" – turrets in consequence. Certainly the British force had the better of the encounter and gained its object.

The first sighting report had come from the *Zulu* at 1637 – four unknown ships bearing 042°, distant 9 miles; and this was followed at 1640 by a report from the *Euryalus* of three cruisers bearing 035°, distant 15 miles. As the situation developed, however, it appeared that the westward group of Italian ships were two 8-inch and two 6-inch cruisers,[63] some 10 miles away, with one battleship and two cruisers[64] farther east and about 15 miles from the British flagship, both groups steering a south-westerly course at high speed. As soon as the second report was received the divisions of the British striking force stood away to the northward to meet the enemy, as they had two hours before, only this time without a signal to proceed – except the 1st Division, which held on for a time towards the convoy according to Rear-Admiral Vian's previous orders. The *Cleopatra* and *Euryalus* led out on course 010° and started immediately to lay smoke. At 1643 they opened fire at a range of some 20,000 yards on the westernmost Italian, an 8-inch cruiser, the British ships firing individually instead of attempting a concentration as they had in the earlier engagement. The 8-inch ship and a 6-inch cruiser at once returned the fire, and the latter hit the bridge of the *Cleopatra* with her second salvo.[65] The Italian battleship, outside the British ships' range, opened fire also at this time, a splinter from a 15-inch shell hitting the *Euryalus*. At 1648 Rear-Admiral Vian turned westward into his smoke and ceased fire. Meanwhile, the *Dido* and *Penelope* had come into action against the Italian cruisers, as had the four destroyers of the 5th Division, but the *Zulu* and *Hasty* did not find a target within their reach.

The *Dido* and *Penelope* could not see their fall of shot, owing to the smoke and spray; neither they nor the *Cleopatra* and *Euryalus* could claim hits at this stage of the fight. When the Admiral turned away, they followed after him, losing sight of him as he entered the smoke. Captain McCall of the *Dido* thus described the situation: "The smoke was at that time extremely dense; 15-inch guns could be heard firing at no great distance, occasional large splashes were seen, and the positions of destroyers were obscure; so that a very exciting period ensued until we emerged from the smoke, steering an easterly course, at 1703, when three enemy cruisers were sighted in line ahead on a south-westerly course with the battleship close to them on an opposite course."[66] Captain Micklethwait, of the *Sikh*, believed that his division scored hits on "what was thought to be two destroyers," which soon turned north and disappeared. These were probably two of the *Littorio*'s destroyers which Admiral Iachino had sent in to attack with torpedoes; seeing them quickly straddled, he ordered them to disengage. No hits were scored by either side. The four British destroyers were some way to the westward of the British cruisers; and at 1649, just after their first encounter, they sighted two cruisers and the battleship to the north-east 6 miles away, as it seemed to Captain Micklethwait, so he hastened westward to gain a favourable position for attacking with torpedoes. At 1659, three cruisers appeared on about the same bearing only 5 miles off – possibly the western group of Italians again; and, turning up north-westward, Captain Micklethwait engaged these ships through the smoke till 1705, when the battleship came in sight once more farther east. Then he altered away "to avoid punishment."[67]

Rear-Admiral Vian hauled round gradually to the south-eastward at about 1700. For the next ten minutes or so his two ships fired at the flashes of the enemy's guns to the northward, or at ships dimly seen through the smoke, at a range of some 14,000 yards, still without apparent effect. The *Dido* and *Penelope*, having turned to the eastward about the same time as the flagship, were now ahead of her, and when they cleared the smoke they engaged the Italian cruisers, which were steering to the south-west 13,000 yards away, with the battleship east of them, steering something north of west. The *Dido*, opening at 1704, fired nine broadsides at an 8-inch ship and claimed at least two hits; the *Penelope*, coming later out of the smoke, fired a few rounds at a 6-inch ship, possibly hitting her with the first salvo.[68] But the two British cruisers had come under fire from the battleship; "and as we were getting rather far from the smoke screen," Captain McCall bore away south, finding shelter in the smoke at 1712 and sighting the flagship soon afterwards. The Rear-Admiral turned west at 1714 and south-eastward at 1720, continuing so till 1730 and firing a few rounds at a ship seen through the smoke at 1727, though he considered afterwards that the target was out of range. At 1730 he turned east for five minutes, with the other cruisers and the *Zulu* and *Hasty* conforming generally to his movements, "in search of two enemy ships not accounted for, and which I thought might be working round in the rear" to reach the convoy from to windward. The Italians in fact did not change from their plan of cutting off the convoy by steering the most direct course the smoke screen allowed. And, as it turned out, Rear-Admiral Vian's stretch to the eastward at 1730, short as it was, nearly gave them their chance. Captain Micklethwait's division of destroyers kept them at bay.

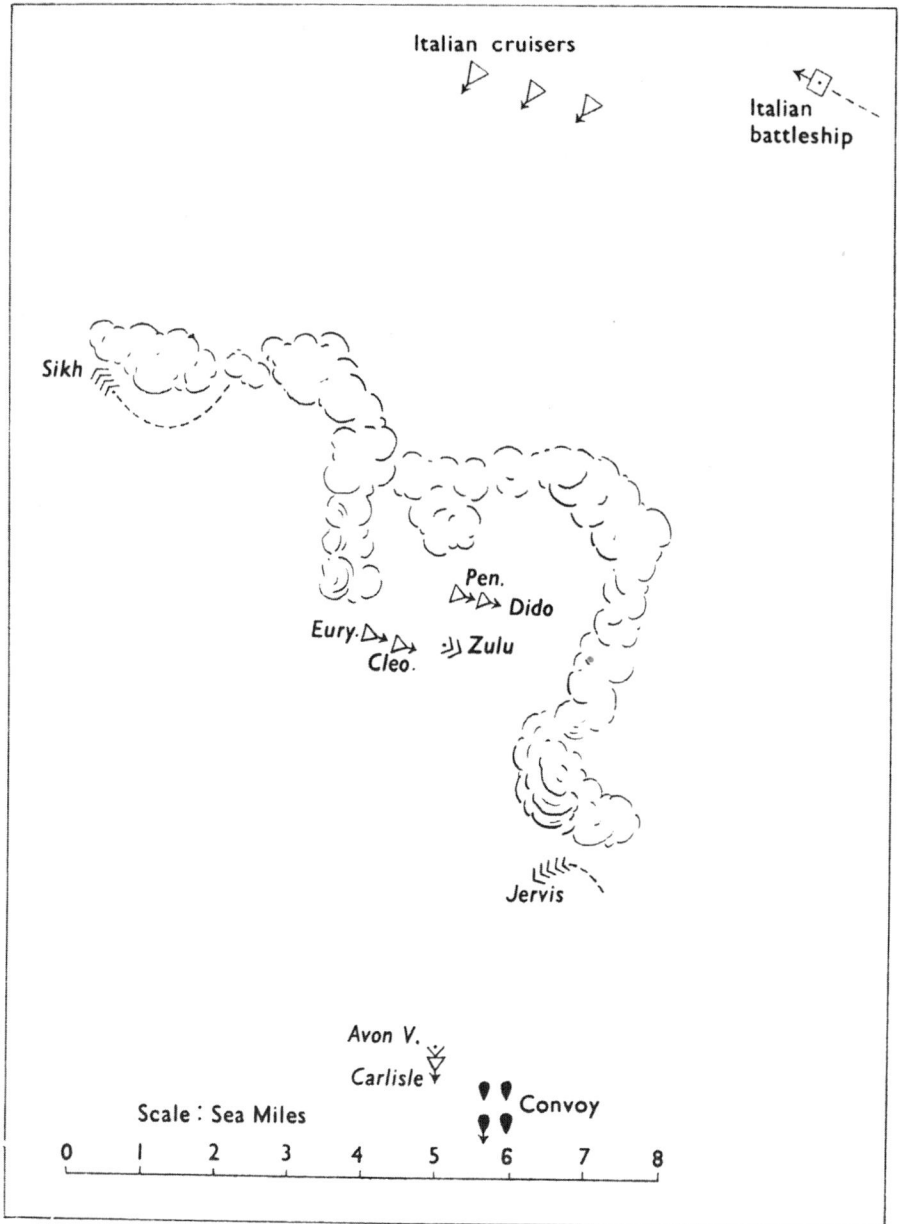

Fig. 4. Enemy attempts to get Leeward of smoke, 1705

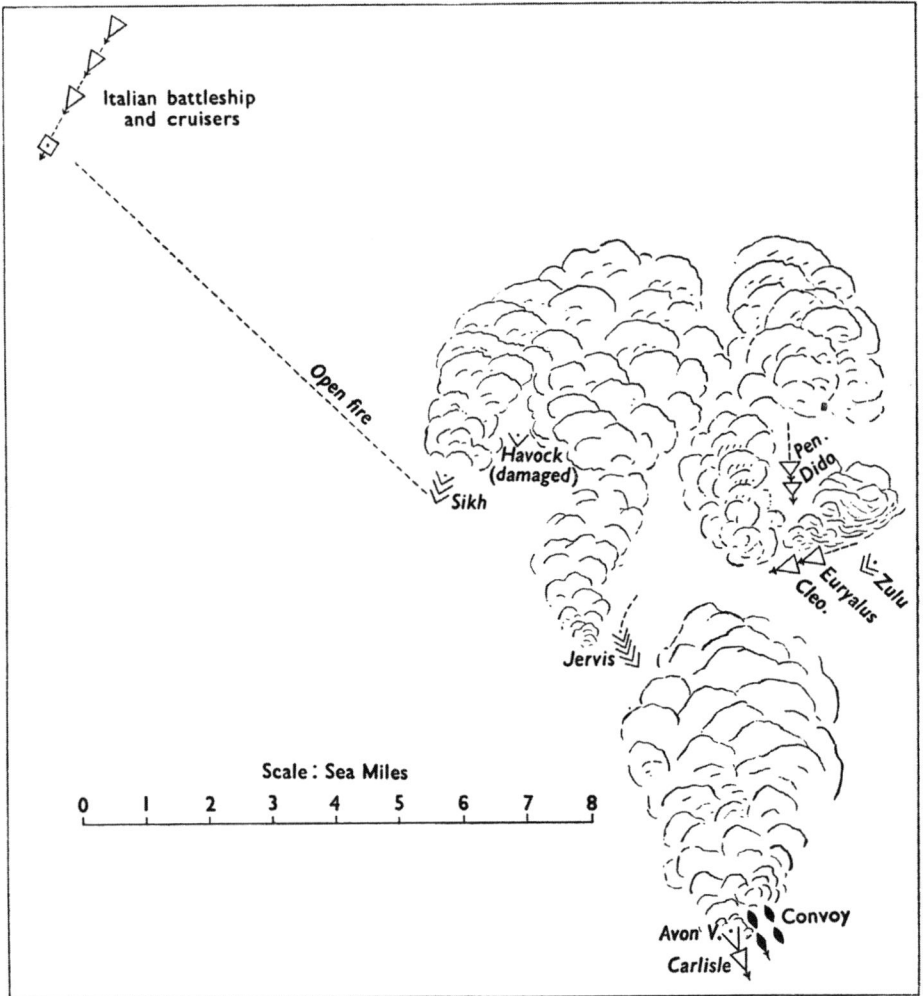

Fig. 5. 5ᵗʰ Division holding off the enemy, 1740

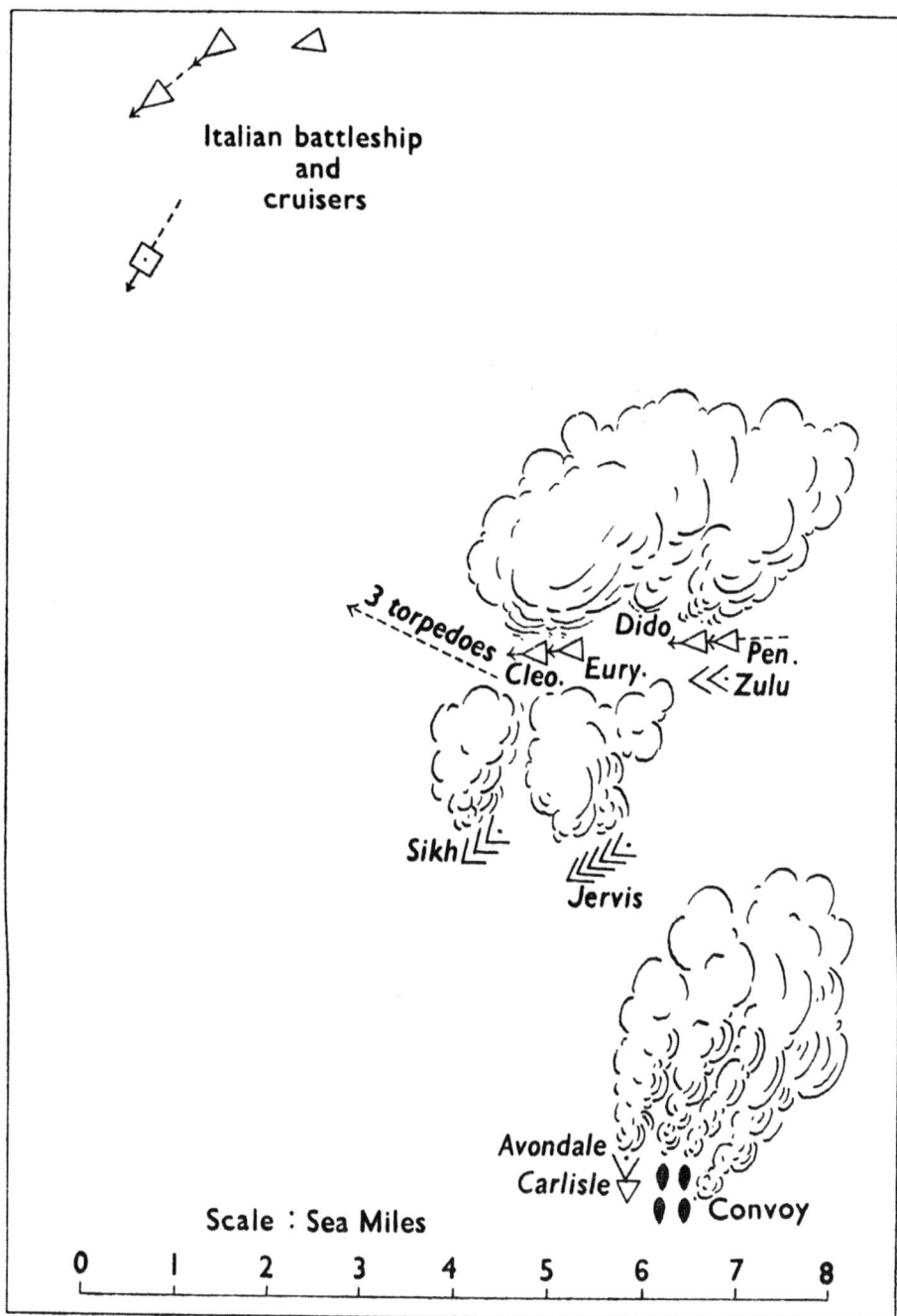

Fig. 6. Torpedo attack ordered, 1805

These ships had been standing to the southward since 1705, watching the enemy at a distance of 10 miles or so. They had not escaped punishment; for at 1720 a near miss from a 15-inch shell damaged a boiler in the *Havock*, reducing her speed to 16 knots,[69] and she had to be sent to join the convoy. None the less, the other three destroyers turned northward a few minutes after this with a view to attacking with torpedoes; but, deciding the conditions were not yet favourable, Captain Micklethwait turned away again and shaped course to the southward to keep between the Italians and the convoy, laying smoke all the while. At 1740 they sighted the battleship again 16,000 yards off to the north-west, steering to the southward at high speed, and they opened fire on her with their 4.7-inch and 4-inch guns. Seas were sweeping over their forecastles, they were moving heavily in the swell, and smoke too interfered with shooting, while the range was far too great to observe the fall of shot of such light calibre guns. Indeed the *Lively* and *Hero*, astern of the *Sikh* and with her smoke between them and the enemy, could seldom see what was happening, though the *Lively* opened fire whenever she had a target to aim at.[70] According to the Italians, the *Littorio* was frequently straddled and turned to the south-west to open the range. She of course returned the fire, and at 1748 straddled the *Sikh*, which then fired two out of her four torpedoes, "in order to avoid sinking with all torpedoes on board and in the hope of making the enemy turn away," but to no effect. By 1800 the Italians were drawing ahead on the convoy; it looked as if they might gain their object after all. Captain Micklethwait made a signal to the convoy to steer south (its former course being south-westerly), while he endeavoured to extend the smoke screen westward, still continuing his "somewhat unequal contest" with the enemy.

In the meantime the British cruisers had come back. Rear-Admiral Vian had turned again at 1735, when some 6 miles south-eastward of the 5th Division and 14 miles from the Italians. At 1742 the *Cleopatra* fired a few salvoes at the battleship at extreme range: then for twenty minutes smoke covered all, and the ships with the Rear-Admiral tried in vain to cut their way through it to see the enemy. At 1759 he made the general signal, "Prepare to fire torpedoes under cover of smoke." At 1802 the *Cleopatra* cleared the smoke, sighted the battleship 13,000 yards off, and opened fire with all turrets; while the *Euryalus*, still in smoke astern of her, fired by radar. Then at 1806 the *Cleopatra* turned to port and fired her three starboard torpedoes as the battleship disappeared again behind the drifting smoke. No hits were seen, and no other ship fired. By the time they were out of the smoke, the opportunity had passed; the enemy had turned away and was hiding in a smoke screen of her own. But Rear-Admiral Vian believed it was his flagship's torpedoes that impelled the Italian to alter course, "further delaying the moment at which she might sight the convoy and slightly relieving the pressure on the 5th Division."[71] After the attack the Rear-Admiral went east again, not yet easy in his mind about the missing Italian cruisers, which might be still working to windward; at 1817, however, he could see there were none of the enemy in the north-east quarter, so he turned round once more to support the destroyers of the 5th Division. Their fight ended – for the time being – at 1819. Captain Micklethwait then hauled right round to the northward to lay a new screen of smoke.[72]

It was now the turn of the 1st Division under Captain Poland. At 1631, before the Italians came in sight, this division had been ordered to join the convoys to strengthen its anti-aircraft fire. The five destroyers set off accordingly; but when Captain Poland received the news of the enemy's approach, and two words of a mutilated signal from the flagship, he decided to follow the convoy at a distance, laying smoke between it and the enemy, instead of joining it. His first view of the battle came at 1745, gun flashes appearing to the north-west through the smoke laid by the 5th Division, which he could see was under heavy fire from 15-inch guns. At 1808 he received a signal timed 1758 from Captain Micklethwait that put the Italians only 8 miles[73] from the convoy, and four minutes later he altered up from south-west to north-west to close the enemy. An attack by some torpedo aircraft deflected him from his course for some minutes, but at 1834, then steering north, he sighted the battleship west-north-west 12,000 yards away and determined to attack immediately with torpedoes. The division turned together to west, which brought the ships into line abreast, and increased speed to 28 knots, the 4.7-inch ships as they ran in carrying out a concentration shoot, for which hits were claimed; the *Legion*, mounting 4-inch guns, withheld her fire till the range came down to 8,000 yards. The enemy were steering south, and three cruisers in line ahead were now in sight astern of the battleship; all returned the British destroyers' fire, but their shooting, said Captain Poland, "was very erratic." At 1840 the first cruiser, an 8-inch ship, turned away 90° to starboard, while the other two cruisers turned in a few points to port.[74]

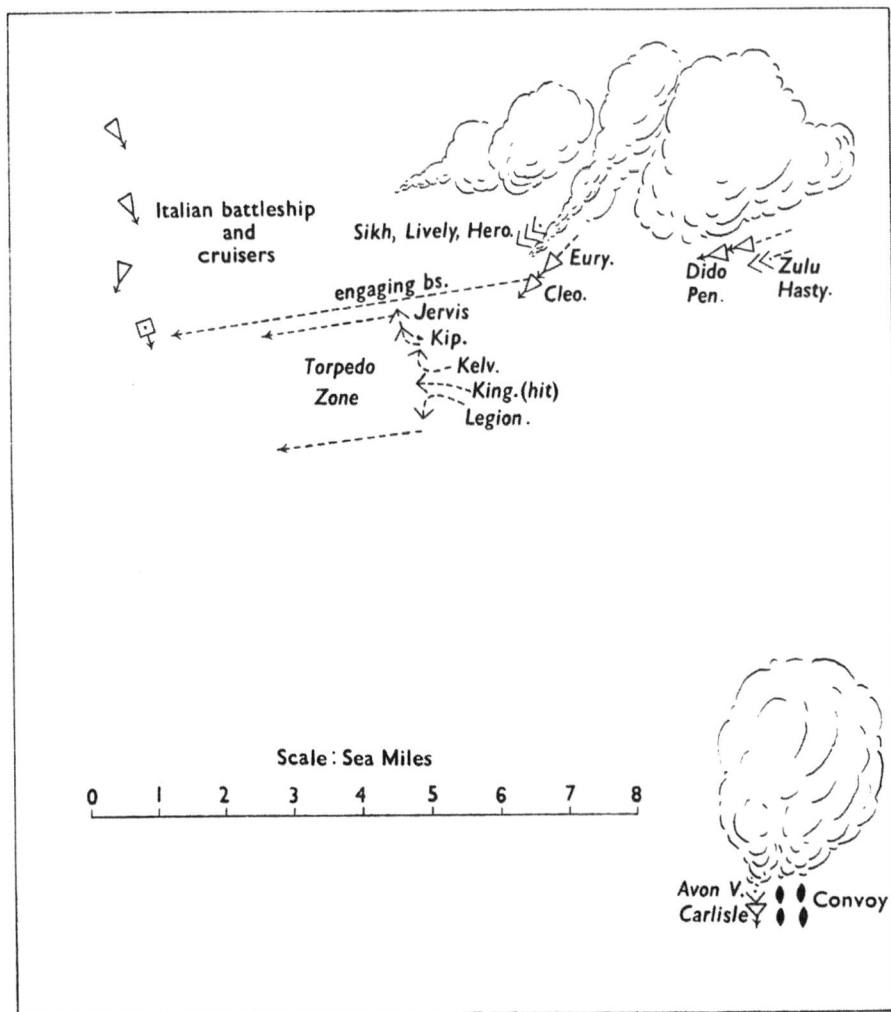

Fig. 7. Torpedo attack by 1st Division, 1841

At 1841, with the range down to 6,000 yards, the destroyers turned and fired torpedoes, the *Jervis*, *Kipling*, *Kelvin* and *Kingston* turning to starboard, the *Legion* to port. A 15-in. shell hit the *Kingston* as she was about to turn[75], yet she managed to fire three torpedoes. Altogether they fired twenty-five, all of which were avoided by the Italians, though at the time it was thought that one had hit the *Littorio*, which had turned away when she saw the destroyers firing, and withdrew to the north-westward, accompanied by the cruisers. The British ships retired to the eastward under smoke.[76]

During the attack the 1st Division was supported by the guns of the *Cleopatra* and *Euryalus* on the return of these ships from the eastward. This partly accounted for the erratic shooting of the Italians, whose one hit was that which crippled the *Kingston*; as Captain Grantham of the *Cleopatra* reported it, "The enemy battleship was firing in divided control, the forward turrets at the destroyers ahead and the after turret rather wildly in the rough direction of the *Cleopatra* and *Euryalus*." Having turned at 1817, Rear-Admiral Vian brought his division west with the *Dido* and *Penelope*, the *Zulu* and *Hasty* following at some distance astern. The *Cleopatra* sighted an enemy cruiser at 1830, and they exchanged a few salvoes at 20,000 yards, but were interrupted by smoke laid by the 5th Division on its northward stretch. Five minutes later all four Italians came in sight; thenceforward, for some twenty minutes, the *Cleopatra* engaged the battleship whenever smoke allowed, and the 8-inch cruiser at other times, and the *Euryalus* also engaged the battleship. At 1841, range 12,500 yards, the battleship was seen to be on fire from a hit abaft her after turret; and more hits were observed as she retired after the destroyers' attack. The last shots were fired at 1856; but about the same time the 5th Division attacked with torpedoes. After breaking off their gun action at 1819, the three ships still in company had laid smoke on a northerly course till 1835, and then turned south-west again. Their stretch to the north, however, had given them a good start for an attack when the Italians retired north-west, and Captain Micklethwait seized upon the opportunity. Unluckily, as he turned to fire at 1855, smoke hid the target from all except the *Lively*, which fired all eight torpedoes, though without success. Once again the enemy scored one hit with their guns, a splinter of a 15-inch shell entering the *Lively* on her waterline as she was about to fire.[77]

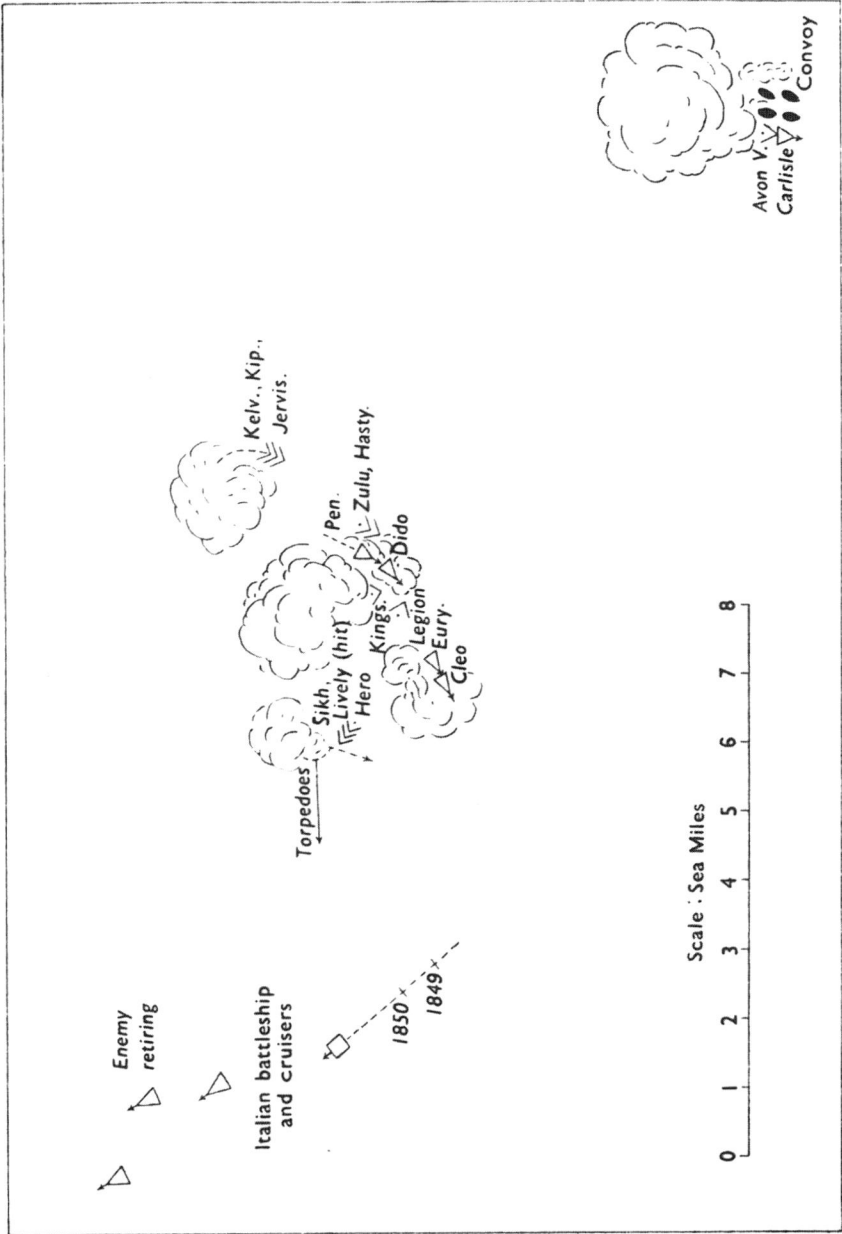

Fig. 8. Enemy breaks off the action, 1855

The battle was over. Four weak cruisers and eleven destroyers had held at bay a capital ship, three cruisers and 7 destroyers for nearly two and a half hours in stormy weather, obliging them, in the words of Kempenfelt, "to think of nothing but being on their guard against your attack" – for that is what it amounted to. And at last, as the sun was setting that Sunday evening, 22 March, the British force saw the enemy abandon their object and steer away homewards. Yet the Italians do not seem to have suffered much material damage. They received a few hits from guns of 4-inch up to 6-inch calibre, mostly on the battleship, but they seem to have been overawed by the constant readiness of Rear-Admiral Vian and his ships and by the threat of sudden torpedo attack coming out of the smoke; it was certainly the determined attack by the 1st Division that finally turned them back. In achieving this result the British ships fired 36 torpedoes and a great deal of gun ammunition; over 1,550 rounds were expended by the cruisers and about 1,300 by the destroyers. Much of the gunfire was inevitably ineffective, for the range was often uncertain and the shell splashes invisible owing to smoke, the state of the weather and the long range at which the action was for the most part fought.[78] By taking advantage of every opportunity, however, the British ships proved their constant eagerness to fight, and deterred the Italian fleet from running risks with them.

Arrival of Convoy M.W.10 at Malta: Air Attacks and Damage

All this time the convoy and its close escort had been under attack from the air. An occasional German bomber and one or two flights of Italian torpedo aircraft had attacked or threatened attack on ships of the striking force, sometimes requiring the attention of the cruisers' 5.25-inch guns to get quit of them; the *Euryalus* shot down one aircraft at 1733 and another at 1906. But instead of combining air attack with surface action to disable the striking force and so clear the way to the convoy, the enemy chose to spend the weight of their attack from the air directly upon the convoy. Up to about 1800, the aircraft were German Ju.88 bombers, after which some Italian S.79 and German He.111 torpedo aircraft attacked. The bombers generally came singly and down wind, on the port side of the convoy, approaching at about 8,000 ft. and releasing their bombs at 2,000 to 3,000 ft. They attacked with resolution and skill, considering the strength of the wind, but accomplished nothing beyond almost exhausting the ammunition of the escort, though that indeed helped towards success next day. These four hours of continual air attack in that heavy weather tested the British skill in gunnery and seamanship and the endurance of the ships' companies. Many aircraft were kept at arm's length or induced to drop bombs or torpedoes at a safe distance. Five were shot down, of which the *Breconshire* and *Pampas* each accounted for one, while the others fell to the *Carlisle* and the six destroyers.[79]

As soon as the Italian ships had disappeared, Rear-Admiral Vian collected his force and steered to close the convoy, 10 miles or so to the southward.

At 1940, in the growing darkness with the convoy not yet in sight, the Rear-Admiral decided to shape course for Alexandria with Force "B" and to send the convoy to Malta under the arrangements laid down in the operation orders. The two ships from Malta, the *Penelope* and *Legion*, parted company accordingly to overtake the convoy and return to their base; the *Havock* had joined the convoy already, and the *Kingston* was on her way to do so, both too badly damaged in the action to go back to Alexandria in the face of a rising gale. Rear-Admiral Vian proceeded eastward with the remaining three cruisers and eight destroyers. Captain Hutchison, of the *Breconshire*, the convoy commodore, had in fact complied with the operation orders on his own initiative at 1900, dispersing the ships on diverging courses with a destroyer or two apiece for escort, each ship to make her best speed so as to reach Malta as early as possible next morning; they had been intended to arrive at dawn, but the Italian fleet, by forcing the convoy south of its route, had given the German bombers a second chance, as Admiral Iachino had foreseen. Aircraft appeared as soon as it was light on 23 March, in spite of the thick weather; and the ships had to run the gauntlet of attacks all the way to the entrance of the Grand Harbour, with their escorts, desperately short of ammunition, firing only when the danger became immediate.

The first ship of the convoy to arrive was the *Talabot*, at 0915, and she was closely followed by the *Penelope*, each ship accompanied by a destroyer. "We proceeded up harbour," reported the *Havock*, "to the cheers of the populace." Both merchantmen had had narrow escapes two hours earlier, two bombs actually hitting the *Pampas* without exploding, and their last assailants were driven off only a few minutes before they passed the breakwater. But that was the end of Fortune's favours. The *Breconshire*, with the *Carlisle* and three destroyers in company, arrived within 8 miles of the harbour at 0920, having survived a score of attacks only to be hit and disabled at last. The *Carlisle* prepared to take her in tow, circling round her meanwhile to keep off the enemy, for aircraft continued to attack. The *Penelope*, however, coming up later, decided herself to tow the *Breconshire*, as the *Carlisle* was almost out of ammunition; but the great draught of the damaged ship and the heavy swell running made towing impossible; so she was anchored, and three destroyers stayed to protect her. Finally, the *Clan Campbell* was hit at 1030, when some 20 miles short of her destination, by a bomb dropped from a height of only 50 ft.; she sank quickly, but her escort, the *Eridge*, saved most of her crew. For the time being, all the ships of war escaped injury except the *Legion*, which was damaged by a near miss and had to be beached in Marsaxlokk.

The three surviving ships of the convoy were lost within a few days of their arrival, as well as some of the men-of-war that brought the convoy in. Actually, the first loss was due to a mine, the *Southwold* being sunk by a mine on 24 March, while standing by the *Breconshire* outside Grand Harbour. The *Breconshire* herself reached Marsaxlokk in tow on 25 March, in spite of bad weather, but sank there on 27 March after further damage from bombs; she had suffered continual attack for four days. The *Legion* was sunk from the air on 26 March, soon after reaching the dockyard from Marsaxlokk. The *Talabot* and *Pampas* were hit that day too; and the former had to be scuttled, lest her cargo of ammunition should explode, while all the latter's holds but two were flooded. Last of all, Submarine *P.36* was bombed and sunk on 1 April, and the *Kingston* on 11 April. But the loss of cargoes was worse in the circumstances, perhaps, than the loss of ships. Only 5,000 tons out of nearly 26,000 tons carried in the convoy was safely landed, including some oil fuel saved from the *Breconshire*. And it was several months before supplies in large quantities again reached Malta.

Submarine Attacks on Italian Forces

Attempts on the homeward bound Italian Fleet were made without success. A torpedo striking force of Beaufort aircraft, sent from Libya in the evening of 22 March, and No. 828 Naval Air Squadron from Malta were unable to make contact with the enemy before dark, so were recalled by order of Admiral Cunningham without having attacked. There were still the submarines, but the state of the weather gave them little chance of success. It was "visibility very poor in heavy rain and high seas," said one; and finding it impossible to patrol at periscope depth they generally had to keep listening watch down at 70 ft. The *Upholder*, however, in Position "S" off Taranto (see Plan 9), detected hydrophone effect of ships to the southward in the evening of

23 March. After closing for a quarter of an hour, she sighted "dull shadows," of the bridge and funnels of a battleship. Two minutes later, at 1738, she fired her four torpedoes at 4,000 yards, though Lieutenant-Commander Wanklyn considered it "a forlorn hope" to fire under those conditions; all missed, the Italian apparently zig-zagging away during their run. In the night of 24/25 March two cruisers were reported by aircraft about 120 miles east-north-east of Malta, steering for the Strait of Messina at 15 knots. The *Unbeaten*, then some 45 miles west of the reported position, on her way back to Malta from patrol, was ordered to intercept them. Her best speed in that weather was 7 knots, and she eventually had to abandon the chase, though for an hour she saw flares dropped by aircraft beyond the horizon.

The Italians did not get away scatheless, however. During the night of 22/23 March the weather got worse and worse; by midnight speed had to be reduced to 16 knots. The *Littorio* held on for Taranto, but the cruisers and most of the destroyers made for Messina. The *Bande Nere*[80] and all the destroyers suffered severe damage in the gale; two of the latter – the *Scirocco* and *Lanciere* – sank next day. Most of the damage was ascribed by Admiral Iachino to too-light hull construction, inefficient water-tight arrangements, scuttles, etc., and vulnerability of pumping arrangements. Even the *Littorio* shipped large quantities of water, which put the electric firing machinery of one of her 15-in. turrets out of action for some time.

Return of Admiral Vian to Alexandria

The ships of Force "B" had an arduous passage back to Alexandria, though suffering rather from the dangers of the sea than from the violence of the enemy. Rear-Admiral Vian wished to go as far as possible through "Bomb Alley" between Cyrenaica and Crete before daylight, but the easterly gale forced him to reduce speed considerably, and at dawn on 23 March he had only reached the longitude of Benghazi; moreover, all the destroyers except one had fallen astern, while most of them had suffered damage from the weather. On the other hand, though shadowing from the air began early, the force was spared attack until the afternoon, when the worst of the gale was past. No doubt the weather was the cause of this respite, though fighter aircraft of the Royal Air Force managed to give the ships protection all day at very long distances from their base. There were half a dozen attacks in all, usually by single aircraft, between 1610 and dusk. Two only were dangerous: at 1610, six Ju. 87 aircraft bombed the *Lively*, which was a mile astern of the force, and she had to "act the part," as the Rear-Admiral put it, to avoid being hit; at 1900, three S.79 aircraft attacked the *Zulu* with torpedoes, but also without success. The damage suffered by the *Lively*, in the battle and in the gale, prevented her from keeping station when better weather after dark allowed Rear-Admiral Vian to increase speed, so he detached her to Tobruk. The rest of the ships arrived at Alexandria at midday on 24 March, "honoured to receive the great demonstration" they were given for their victory.

Commenting on this operation, the Commander-in-Chief, Admiral Sir Henry Harwood, remarked on the good handling of the merchant ships and the excellent work done by the Naval liaison officers embarked in them. "There can be no doubt," he wrote, "that the defeat of the heavy air attacks on the convoy on 22 March was due in no small measure to the excellent seamanship and discipline displayed by the merchant ships."

"During the action on 22 March, the determination and team-work of all ships more than fulfilled the high standard that had been expected. This, combined with the resolute leadership and masterly handling of the force by Rear-Admiral Philip L. Vian, K.B.E., D.S.O., produced a heartening and thoroughly deserved victory from a situation in which, had the roles been reversed, it is unthinkable that the convoy or much of its escort could have survived."

Operation "Harpoon"

Situation in Malta: Operations "Harpoon" and "Vigorous"

After the convoy in March 1942 a few special cargoes reached Malta in submarines and in the fast minelayer *Welshman*, but the fortress had to wait till the middle of June for the next attempt to supply it on a large scale. This was chiefly due to the unceasing assaults on Malta from the air; as Admiral Sir Henry Harwood, the new Commander-in-Chief, Mediterranean, wrote in his report of the operation in March, "It is evident that before another Malta convoy is run, air superiority in the island must be assured." Accordingly, strong reinforcements of fighter aircraft were sent to Malta, flown off from the *Eagle* and U.S.S. *Wasp*. By the middle of May the bombing attacks had slackened, largely as a result of great air battles on 9 and 10 May, when the enemy lost heavily both in bombers and in their fighter escorts; more British fighters arrived early in June.[81] In these improved circumstances it was decided to make another attempt to supply the island, and a double operation was planned: a convoy of six ships from the United Kingdom through the Strait of Gibraltar – Operation "Harpoon" – and another of eleven ships (Convoy M.W.11) from Egypt – Operation "Vigorous" – the two convoys being timed to reach Malta on consecutive days. This, it was hoped, would divide the attention of the enemy between the two convoys while they were on passage. Mining of the harbour approaches had greatly increased since March[82] (when the *Southwold* was lost), and as Malta was almost entirely without resources to deal with this danger, it was arranged that minesweepers should accompany the convoys to sweep them into harbour, and subsequently to strengthen those stationed at Malta.

The result of these operations was disappointing. In the end two ships of the western convoy only arrived, while the eastern convoy had to give up the attempt and turn back to Alexandria. Although the actual losses in merchant ships were all due to air attack, the principal cause of ill success was probably the lack of surface force, which submarines and aircraft were unable to replace.

The main strength of the Italian fleet – battleships and cruisers based on Taranto – was employed against the eastern convoy. Though they did not meet, the threat of attack by a battle fleet diverted the convoy from its course for so long that, under repeated attacks from the air, the ships of the close escort ran so far short of ammunition as to preclude the convoy's going on. In the same way two cruisers and five destroyers from Sardinia, meeting the western convoy south of Pantellaria with only an anti-aircraft ship and nine destroyers, held it up for three hours. Air attacks during the action and soon afterwards, beyond the reach of effective protection by fighter aircraft from Malta, sank one merchantman and disabled two, which had to be sunk but might have been saved except for the presence of Italian ships.

Though complementary to each other, these operations were entirely separate. For the sake of clearness, therefore, Operation "Harpoon" only will be described in this chapter and Operation "Vigorous" in the next; but it should be borne in mind that they were actually taking place at the same time.

Plan of Operation "Harpoon"

The plan for Operation "Harpoon" was similar to that adopted in the latter part of 1941. The convoy sailed from the United Kingdom with an escort of Home Fleet ships under Vice-Admiral Curteis, who conducted the operation, ships of the North Atlantic Station from Gibraltar strengthening the escort as the convoy entered the Strait.[83] As before, the heavy ships (Force "W") turned back on reaching the Skerki Channel at the entrance of the Sicily-Tunis Narrows, while the convoy went on with a smaller escort (Force "X"), and an oiler with her own escort (Force "Y") cruised on a rendezvous to fuel ships of the convoy escort during the passage. The escort, however, was much weaker than those it had been possible to provide in the previous summer and autumn. There was only one capital ship, the *Malaya;* and the aircraft carriers *Eagle* and *Argus,* both old ships, had between them hardly the capacity of the *Ark Royal* which had been lost in November, 1941. Furthermore, instead of a respectable squadron of cruisers for the last stage of the passage, there was only the anti-aircraft ship *Cairo,* besides smaller ships. The full strength as follows: – [84]

Force "W"
Capital ship, 1 (*Malaya*)
Aircraft carriers, 2 (*Eagle, Argus*)
Cruisers, 3 (*Kenya* – flag, Vice-Admiral Curteis – *Liverpool, Charybdis*)
Destroyers, 8.

Force "X"
    A.A. ship, 1 *(Cairo*, Captain C. C. Hardy, S.O.)
    Destroyers, 9
    Minesweepers, 4.

Force "X" had instructions to "bear in mind the conflicting requirements of the safe arrival of the convoy and the need for economy of fuel, and to a lesser extent of ammunition, so that no extra ship need enter Malta." The *Cairo* and destroyers, in fact, were to return without entering harbour, unless they had to replenish fuel and ammunition.

Six minesweeping motor launches, as well as the four fleet sweepers, accompanied the convoy and were to join the Malta command on arrival. The *Welshman*, with a special cargo, also accompanied the convoy as far as the Narrows, but then went on alone at 28 knots. Four submarines were stationed on a line between Sardinia and Sicily.

The Royal Air Force at Gibraltar provided anti-submarine patrols for the first part of the passage inside the Strait. Malta provided air reconnaissance, long- and short-range fighter protection, and torpedo striking forces by Royal Air Force and naval aircraft so far as resources allowed; but "Malta's major effort" was required for Operation "Vigorous" to the eastward.

Passage, 11–14 June

Operation "Harpoon" commenced with the departure of the convoy (WS19Z) from the Clyde on 5 June. It soon became apparent that several of the merchant ships were not capable of maintaining the scheduled speed of 14 knots,[85] but by "cutting corners" the Mediterranean was entered up to time during the night of 11–12 June, the ships of the Home Fleet escort oiling at Gibraltar in reliefs during the passage through the Strait. Nearly 2,000 miles to the east the preliminary movements of operation "Vigorous" were taking place at the same time. The North Atlantic ships of the escort joined that night and next morning, as did one of the convoy – the tanker *Kentucky* – which was already at Gibraltar.

By 0800,[86] 12 June, the force was at full strength and proceeding to the eastward at 12 to 13 knots. That day passed without incident, except the sighting of a Spanish merchant ship in the evening. On 13 June, however, the convoy was shadowed continuously by German and Italian aircraft, and reported by a submarine, despite the efforts of the fighter and anti-submarine patrols from the *Eagle* and *Argus*, which destroyed one Italian Cant. Z1007.

This was the day appointed for meeting Force "Y" and refuelling the escort, but delay occurred through the oiler being some 25 miles off her rendezvous,[87] and oiling was not finished till late at night, the *Cairo* and eleven destroyers completing from the *Brown Ranger* and three destroyers from the *Liverpool* to save time.[88]

At 2245/13, intelligence of cruisers and destroyers leaving Cagliari was received, and the convoy was believed to have been reported by a submarine[89] at 0242/14; otherwise the night passed without incident. At dawn shadowing aircraft appeared once more. The convoy was then approaching the danger area for attack from the air stations in Sardinia, where it was believed the enemy had some 40 bombers and 35 torpedo aircraft.

Italian Reactions

At this stage it will be convenient to take note of the situation as it appeared to the Italians, and how they proposed to deal with it. Information of the departure of the "Harpoon" forces from Gibraltar had reached the Italian Naval Staff in the morning of 12 June, and early next day air reconnaissance in the eastern Mediterranean reported the departure of a large convoy from Alexandria. Appreciating that these movements were both directed towards the supply of Malta, they at once set in train measures to deal with the situation. The bulk of the Italian Fleet was then at Taranto, a detachment of two 6-in. cruisers – the *Eugenia di Savoia* and *Montecuccoli* – and five destroyers being at Cagliari. It was decided that the Taranto forces should be used in the eastern Mediterranean against the convoy from Egypt, which from the number of ships reported was deemed to be the more important of the two. These operations will be described in the following chapter.

To deal with the "Harpoon" Convoy, a large number of submarines was disposed in the western basin and off Malta (by the morning of 15 June 20 submarines were so deployed). Concentrated air attacks south of Sardinia and also after passing Cape Bon were planned; and the Cagliari cruiser force was to attack the convoy at dawn on 15 June. In addition, torpedo boats and coastal motor boats were to attack in the Sicilian Channel; but, as things turned out, the weather and the darkness of the night precluded these latter attacks.

Air Attacks

To return to the "Harpoon" Convoy: at 1000/14, the first radar warning came, and at about the same time fighters from the *Eagle* shot down an Italian torpedo aircraft, one of a number gathering for an attack some 20 miles away. It was a bright clear morning, with hardly a cloud in the sky. There was little wind, but such as there was came from nearly astern, west to northwest; and this made it difficult for the British fighter crews, especially those working from the twenty-five-year-old *Argus*, with her small margin of speed, unless she were to haul right round to the wind and so leave the shelter of the destroyer screen. The convoy was steering east in two columns in line ahead, the flagship *Kenya* leading the port column and the *Liverpool* the starboard with the *Malaya* and *Welshman* in line ahead astern of the convoy. The motor launches also followed the convoy, adding to the volume of close-range fire and available for rescue work. The carriers were to port of the convoy, manoeuvring independently, each with her A.A. escort and a destroyer, viz., *Eagle*, *Cairo*, *Wishart*, and *Argus*, *Charybdis*, *Vidette*. The remaining fifteen destroyers and four fleet sweepers formed an all-round screen spread from 3 to 3½ miles from the convoy – an unusual extension that "proved satisfactory," said Vice-Admiral Curteis, "and all ships fired both outwards and inwards with a freedom which would have been impossible with a closer screen."[90]

The attacks began at 1030. The first was a shallow dive-bombing attack by two groups, each of four or five Italian fighter-bombers (CR.42), one approaching from astern at 12,000 ft. and diving to 6,000 ft., the other coming out of the sun ahead at 6,000 ft. and dropping bombs at 3,000-4,000 ft. Their target was the *Argus* and her consorts on the port beam of the *Malaya*, and one bomb fell close to the *Charybdis*. Two of the enemy were shot down after their attack by a section of the *Eagle's* Fulmars, which were controlled by the *Argus* and afterwards landed on board her, the policy being to employ the Hurricanes from the *Eagle* as a high fighter force and the Fulmars from the *Argus* as a low force.[91]

A much more serious attempt followed half an hour later, when some 28 Savoia torpedo aircraft escorted by 20 Macchi fighters carried out a combined attack with 10 Cant. high-level bombers. The Savoias approached from the northward in two waves of equal strength, the first at 1110 and the second soon afterwards. The first wave passed through the screen on the port beam 500 ft. or so above the water, rounded the rear of the convoy, and attacked from the starboard side, splitting into groups before firing. They dropped torpedoes at a height of 100 ft. and a range of 2,000 yards; and they hit the *Liverpool*, leading the starboard column, as she turned to meet the attack, and also the Dutch ship *Tanimbar* in the rear, the latter sinking within a few minutes. The second wave, attacking the port column, dropped their torpedoes first and at longer range, perhaps deterred by the heavy gunfire; their aim being further upset by an emergency turn towards them ordered by Vice-Admiral Curteis, they did not secure a hit. The Cant. bombers came also in two formations, flying in out of the sun ahead some 10,000 ft. up. They seem to have aimed their attacks at the *Eagle* on the port bow and at the *Argus* on the quarter of the convoy, but none of their bombs fell dangerously near.

A little before noon, several torpedo aircraft made harmless attacks at long range. They were probably stragglers turned back from the earlier attacks by gunfire and anxious only to be rid of their torpedoes.

On the whole the Italians seem to have attacked gallantly. Captain Russell of the *Kenya*, for instance, remarked on their outstanding bravery, and Captain Armstrong of the *Onslow* called the attacks unexpectedly impressive, though other officers were not so kind. On the other hand, had their timing been more exact and the two torpedo attacks delivered together instead of one after the other, they would probably have proved more successful. The British fighters shot down three Italian fighters and three torpedo aircraft, which was a notable achievement in view of what Captain Rushbrooke of the *Eagle* called "the most inadequate measure" of protection that was all his ship and the *Argus* could provide; for they had at most six Hurricanes and four Fulmars in the air at a time, whereas the enemy had a score of shore-based fighters attending on the striking force. Three British aircraft were lost, one being shot down by a ship in the screen. The convoy and escort destroyed seven of the enemy, all Savoia 79, both long- and close-range fire taking their toll. Captain Waller of the *Malaya* remarked on the efficiency of the 6-inch barrage in inducing the Italians to drop torpedoes prematurely. He also lamented the idleness of his 15-inch guns for want of suitable ammunition against aircraft. Captain Philip of the *Argus* made the same point, and indeed went further: "A modern edition of the old carronade for use at short range," he said, "might well provide a successful solution; in short, all that is needed for these insolent aircraft is a big blast from something."[92]

Despatches: Supplement to *The London Gazette*, Published by Authority
The following Despatch was submitted to the Lords Commissioners of the Admiralty on 24 June, 1942 by Vice-Admiral Sir Alban T. B. Curteis, K.C.B., Senior Officer, Force T.

Fighters

The number of fighters in the air never exceeded 6 Hurricanes and 2 Fulmars. This number is quite inadequate and the Hurricane is not sufficiently strongly armed to deal with types such as the Ju. 88. Twenty fighters armed with cannon in the air would have made a vast difference.

The achievements of the pilots of *Eagle* were magnificent while the ground staff deserve high praise for the way in which they managed to keep aircraft in the air in excess of the numbers it had been thought possible to operate.

Damaged *Liverpool* Returns to Gibraltar

The *Liverpool* had been hit in the engine room and she could only steam at the rate of 3 or 4 knots on one shaft. She was ordered back to Gibraltar, towed by the *Antelope* and screened by the *Westcott*, a long voyage that for the first twenty-four hours or so was punctuated by air attacks. At 1640, some three and a half hours after proceeding, five C.R. 42 fighter-bombers attacked from astern out of the sun, luckily without hitting, though one or two bombs fell near enough to increase the ship's list. At 1800, the tow having parted, there was a harmless attempt by eleven high-level bombers followed by an equally harmless attempt by seven torpedo aircraft, the latter heavily escorted by fighters; the *Liverpool* and *Westcott* each destroyed a torpedo plane. At 2015, when once more in tow, she was attacked by five high-level bombers, their bombs again falling wide. At 2230, six torpedo aircraft made a twilight attack at very long range, only to lose one of their number to the cruiser's barrage. Then at 1420/15, three torpedo aircraft made a final unsuccessful attempt, after which the ships were not again molested. Two tugs arrived from Gibraltar the same afternoon; and at sunset one of them took over the tow, releasing the *Antelope* to join the *Westcott* as an antisubmarine screen, which had become the more urgent service. On 16 June some corvettes arrived. Apart from a shadowing submarine that night, which was thrown off after dark, the rest of the voyage passed without incident. The *Liverpool* reached Gibraltar in the evening of 17 June.

Further Air Attacks: 3 M.S. Sunk

The fruitless attacks on the damaged *Liverpool* in the afternoon and evening of 14 June evidently occupied the remaining aircraft available in Sardinia; for after its hard service in the forenoon that day the convoy went freely on, except for shadowers, until it came within the reach of Sicilian air stations in the evening. Then at 1820, German bombers first appeared, about 10 Junkers 88 aircraft approaching the convoy from astern at 10,000 ft. and diving to 6,000 ft. to make the attack. "As is usual in the Mediterranean," remarked Vice-Admiral Curteis, "it was very difficult to see these till they had reached the bombing position, and gunfire was ineffective." Both the carriers had narrow escapes, the *Argus* in particular; a bomb pitched fine on her port bow, dived under the ship, and burst under the starboard bow. No ship was damaged, however, nor were any bombers brought down, though the six British fighters on patrol harassed the enemy and forced several to jettison their bombs. One Fulmar was lost.

As in the morning, the shallow dive-bombing attack preceded a heavy combined torpedo and bombing attack; but in the evening the lapse of time was greater, and dive-bombers as well as high-level bombers took part in the massed attack. It was a combination of Italians and Germans: 16 Savoia 79 torpedo planes, strongly escorted by Macchi fighters, with 10 Junkers 88 and 15 Junkers 87 bombers. The first to appear were the Savoias, which approached from the north-east – to port – at about 2000, flying well above the water; they worked round the stern of the convoy outside gun range to glide down and attack on the starboard side. In the meantime, a few minutes after the S. 79s had been sighted, two groups of Ju. 88s came in from ahead at 12,000 ft. and dropped their bombs without effect as they flew across the screen and along the columns of the convoy. Next, the Ju. 87 dive-bombers arrived on the port bow and attacked the port wing of the screen, diving from 7,000 ft. to 1,000 ft., and narrowly missing the *Icarus* and *Wrestler*, though they had probably hoped to reach the *Eagle*, which was to port of the convoy; the coming of the dive-bombers, said Captain Armstrong of the *Onslow*, "entirely took the screen's attention away" from the torpedo aircraft. These last closed to attack at about 2020. The Vice-Admiral had ordered three emergency turns to port to keep the sterns of the convoy towards the aircraft, thus giving them but poor targets. Most of them concentrated on the *Malaya*, *Argus*, *Charybdis* and *Vidette*, then together some two miles out on the starboard quarter, and they managed to drop three torpedoes within 300 yards of the carrier, though her handiness enabled her to avoid them.[93]

The *Malaya*'s distance from the convoy was due to an encounter with an enemy submarine. The *Middleton* in the screen ahead had sighted a periscope during the dive-bombing attack. She dropped a depth-charge, and was followed by two other destroyers which hauled out of the screen to drop charges over the position of sighting, but without making asdic contact "owing to the numerous wakes in the vicinity." The submarine evidently went deep under the advancing merchantmen, for her periscope next appeared broad on the starboard bow of the *Malaya* astern. The battleship was turning to starboard to meet the air torpedo attack then developing, and she continued her turn towards the submarine until the periscope disappeared close ahead of her; then she reversed her helm to rejoin the convoy, making a warning signal to the *Speedy*, which was in the screen on the starboard quarter. The *Speedy* had seen the destroyer dropping charges, and she gained a good asdic contact and attacked, firing continuously at aircraft all the time; Lieutenant-Commander Doran claimed that he destroyed the submarine.[94]

This was the last encounter before the force divided at the Narrows. Compared with the big air attacks from Sardinia in the morning, the attempts between 2000 and 2020 were timed in better combination, and some officers considered the torpedo attack more vigorously carried out. Yet the evening attacks were fruitless, which must be chiefly ascribed to the convoy's emergency turns away, for neither gunfire nor fighter aircraft were nearly as successful as in the morning. Radar warning of the enemy's approach gave time to increase the British air patrol from four to eight fighters; but they were busily engaged with the far more numerous Italian fighters, and could do little to spoil the attacks. They shot down two torpedo aircraft, however, and the ships' fire destroyed a third. Three British fighters were lost – one in action, one unfortunately shot down by the fleet, and one which crashed when landing down wind. Altogether, on 14 June, the 16 Hurricanes and 6 Fulmars carried shot down 11 enemy aircraft, and damaged and drove away others, at a cost of 7 British aircraft. The *Eagle* and *Argus* lacked adequate equipment for fighter-direction; and they could only maintain 10 aircraft at the most in the air. As the Director of the Naval Air Division subsequently remarked, "The results achieved by the small force of naval fighters are most outstanding."[95]

As the force reached the entrance to the Narrows at 2100, four Beaufighters from Malta arrived to relieve the hard-worked naval airmen: and at 2130 Vice-Admiral Curteis hauled round to the westward with Force "W", while the convoy stood on with Force "X" under Captain Hardy of the *Cairo*. The five remaining merchant ships formed single line ahead for the passage along the Tunisian coast with the men of war screening them: the *Cairo*, nine destroyers, four fleet sweepers and six motor launches. At 2205, as it was growing dark, eight Ju. 88s made a shallow dive-bombing attack, dropping down from 6,000 ft. to 3,000 ft. to release their bombs. They approached out of the dusk ahead and had the convoy clear against the western sky, but they were unsuccessful; they lost two aircraft, one shot down by a Beaufighter, the other by the ships' fire. This was the end of the day's fighting. Severe as had been the massed air attacks west of the Narrows, a greater trial and heavier losses awaited the convoy on the morrow.

Though up to time at noon, 14 June, the convoy was one and a half hours late on scheduled time for passing Cape Bon. This was due partly to delay caused by avoiding action and partly to the convoy's speed not being up to expectation[96] and was to have serious consequences, as it resulted in the convoy being one and a half hours further from Malta Spitfire protection at dawn on 15 June.

Movements of Italian Surface Forces

It will be remembered that the Italian plan provided for an attack on the convoy at dawn on 15 June by the cruisers and destroyers based on Cagliari. This force had accordingly sailed to the eastward in the evening of 13 June and put in to Palermo on 14 June, there to await news of the approach of the convoy.

The movement had not passed unnoticed by the British. The westernmost British submarine on patrol, *P.43*, attacked them at 1931/13, some 60 miles from Cagliari; she claimed to have hit a cruiser, but was mistaken. Two hours later the next submarine on the patrol line, *P.211*, sighted them also, but was too far off to attack.[97] On receiving the submarines' reports, Vice-Admiral Leatham at Malta arranged for a striking force of Wellington aircraft to intercept the enemy. These aircraft, or a reconnaissance aircraft, sighted the Italians north-west of Cape San Vito in Sicily at 0255/14, but lack of flares to light up the targets foiled attack. Two and a half hours later air reconnaissance showed the enemy to be off Palermo; at 1800 the two cruisers were reported in harbour there; and at 2125 (just when Admiral Curteis was parting company from the convoy) the two cruisers and four destroyers were sighted putting to sea, but the reconnoitring aircraft could not determine their subsequent course. Vice-Admiral Leatham judged that the enemy were bound eastward to join the Italian main fleet, which had sailed from Taranto the same evening, doubtless intending to intercept the convoy then on its way to Malta from Egypt (Operation "Vigorous"). Accordingly, he stationed a naval air patrol over the Strait of Messina, while a naval air striking force at Malta stood by to attack should the reconnaissance aircraft gain touch. The requirements of air support for the other operation – "Vigorous" – precluded further action.

Vice-Admiral Curteis, who was taking Force "W" westward, also received the report of the enemy's leaving Palermo, and had to decide whether to strengthen Force "X" with either or both of his cruisers, the *Kenya* and *Charybdis*. He was then, at 2315/14, in about 37° 30' N., 9° 30' E., over 50 miles from the convoy, which would be nearly 100 miles further on by dawn on 15 June.[98] He too judged that the Italians were unlikely to be a danger to the convoy, and that the escort was strong enough "to deter them from doing any harm" – especially as they would expect to be attacked by air from Malta. Apart from this, he was anxious for the safety of his aircraft carriers, which would need the cruisers' support while within striking distance of the air bases in Sardinia; furthermore, there was barely time to overtake the convoy by the morning. "With the force available," he said, "a decision either way was a gamble; if the *Liverpool* had been present, there would have been no doubt in my mind." He decided against sending either ship.[99]

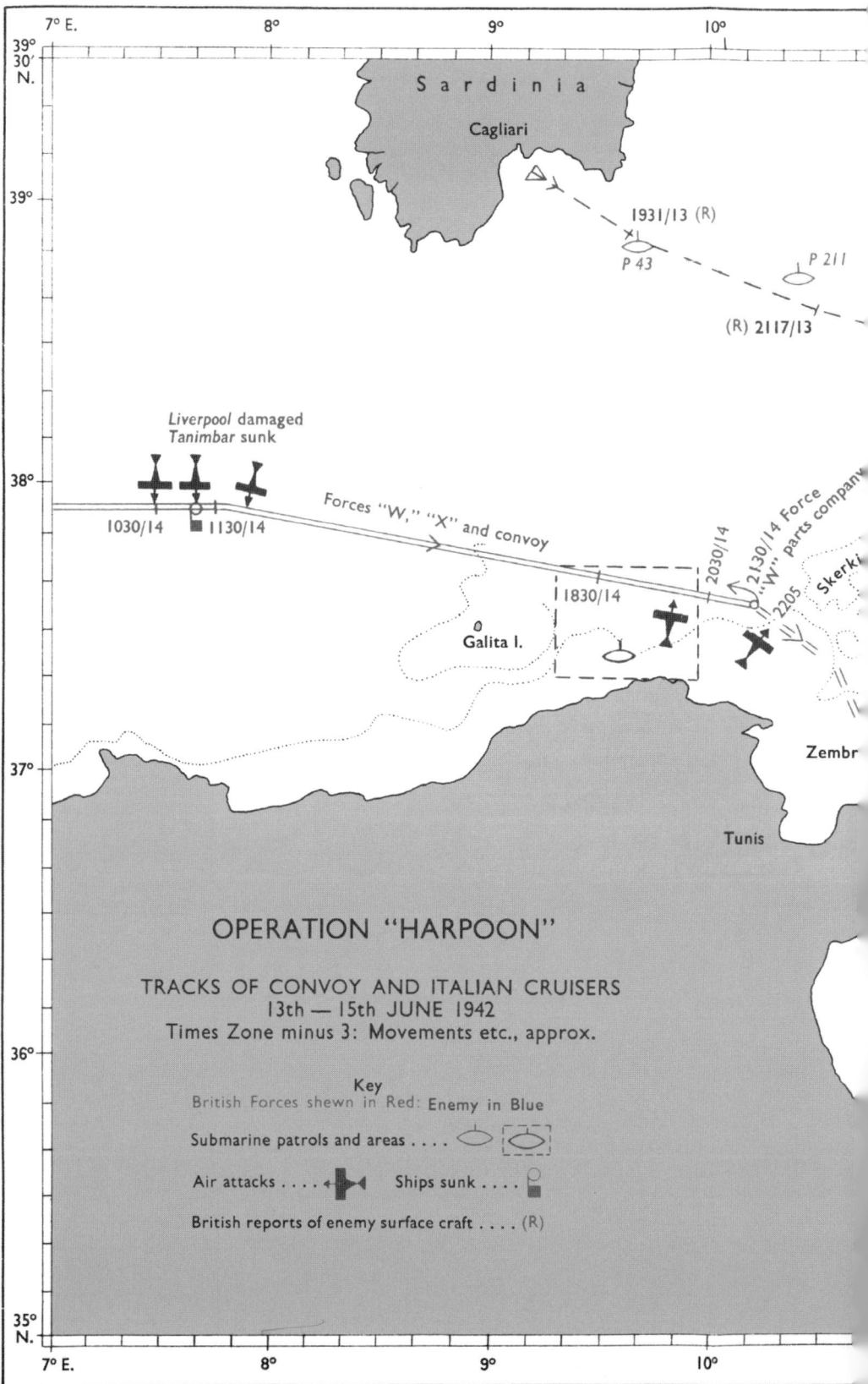

7° E.   8°   9°   10°

39° 30' N.

S a r d i n i a

Cagliari

39°

1931/13 (R)

P 43

P 211

(R) 2117/13

Liverpool damaged
Tanimbar sunk

38°

1030/14   1130/14

Forces "W," "X" and convoy

2030/14

2130/14 Force
"W" parts company

2205

Skerki

Galita I.

1830/14

Zembr

37°

Tunis

OPERATION "HARPOON"

TRACKS OF CONVOY AND ITALIAN CRUISERS
13th — 15th JUNE 1942
Times Zone minus 3: Movements etc., approx.

36°

Key
British Forces shewn in Red: Enemy in Blue

Submarine patrols and areas . . . . . ⌒ ⌐⌒¬

Air attacks . . . . ◄▬▶ Ships sunk . . . . ▯

British reports of enemy surface craft . . . . (R)

35° N.

7° E.   8°   9°   10°

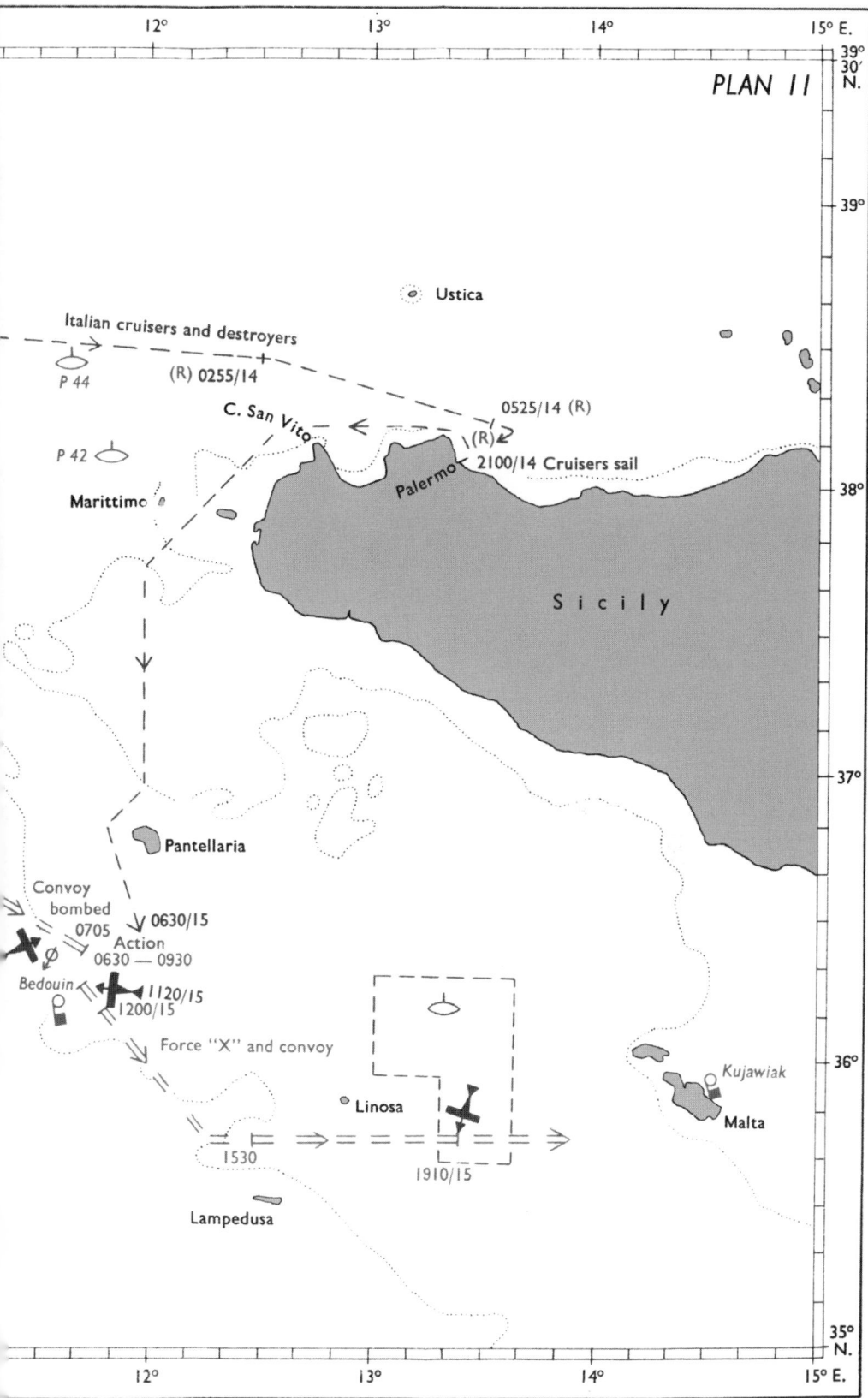

PLAN 11

Ustica

Italian cruisers and destroyers

P 44

(R) 0255/14

0525/14 (R)

C. San Vito

(R)

2100/14 Cruisers sail

P 42

Palermo

Marittimo

S i c i l y

Pantellaria

Convoy
bombed
0705

0630/15
Action
0630 — 0930

Bedouin

1120/15
1200/15

Force "X" and convoy

Linosa

Kujawiak

Malta

1530

1910/15

Lampedusa

Wind,
Force 2

0630
Convoy
(14 knots)

Cairo

Badsworth
Middleton
Kujawiak
Blankney

Matchless
Marne
Ithuriel
Partridge
Bedouin

0720
0705
0700

Chant sunk
Kentucky damd.

0930
0920
0930

0800

0710

0700

0830
0840
0840

0830

0920

0910

0900

PLAN 12

N (true)

0810
0720
0810
07:
0

08

0800

0740 x

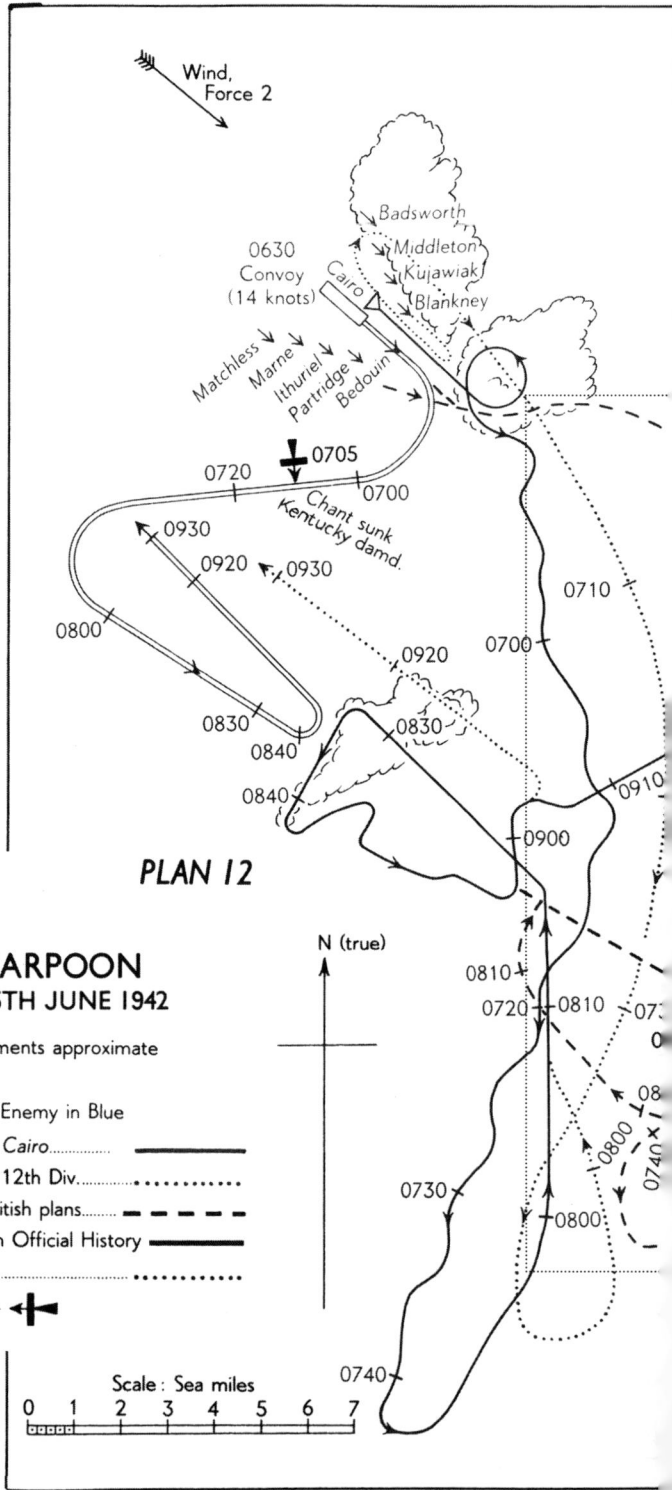

OPERATION HARPOON
SURFACE ACTION, 15TH JUNE 1942

Times Zone minus 3: movements approximate

Key

British Forces in Red : Enemy in Blue

Convoy	═══════	Cairo	────────
11th Div. (Marne)	▬ ▬ ▬ ▬	12th Div.	············
Italian cruisers from contemporary British plans	▬ ▬ ▬ ▬		
Italian cruisers after 0740 from Italian Official History	────────		
Italian Destroyers, Marne's plan	············		
Air Attack	◄┼		

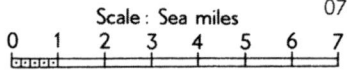

0730

0800

Scale : Sea miles

0 1 2 3 4 5 6 7

0740

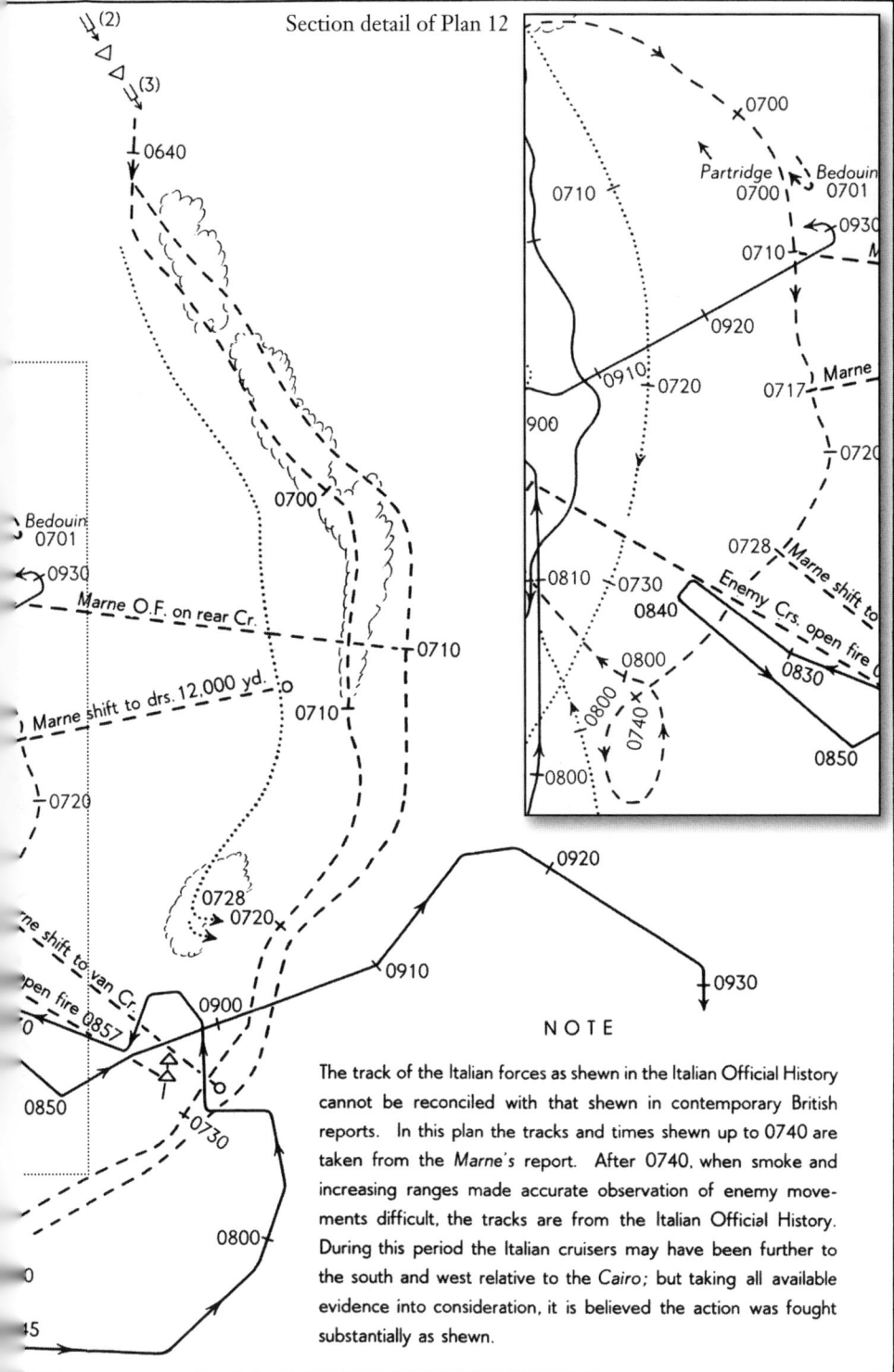

Section detail of Plan 12

NOTE

The track of the Italian forces as shewn in the Italian Official History cannot be reconciled with that shewn in contemporary British reports. In this plan the tracks and times shewn up to 0740 are taken from the *Marne's* report. After 0740, when smoke and increasing ranges made accurate observation of enemy movements difficult, the tracks are from the Italian Official History. During this period the Italian cruisers may have been further to the south and west relative to the *Cairo*; but taking all available evidence into consideration, it is believed the action was fought substantially as shewn.

Actually, the two cruisers with five destroyers, after rounding Cape San Vito, had steered for the area south of Pantellaria, with the intention of attacking the convoy at first light next day. Thus, in the early morning of 15 June, the convoy and its escort faced an enemy considerably superior in the range of its guns, if in nothing else.

Surface Action off Pantellaria

At daybreak on 15 June the convoy was through the Narrows and some 40 miles off the African coast, steering away to the east-south-eastward for its destination, when the Italian surface forces appeared on the scene.

Captain Hardy first knew of the enemy's presence through a Beaufighter which was on its way to patrol above the convoy, and which at 0620 reported two cruisers and four destroyers 15 miles on the port beam of the British force. The convoy was then steering south-east at 12 knots; and the merchantmen were formed in two columns again, with the *Cairo* ahead, five "Fleet" destroyers in the screen to starboard, four "Hunts" to port, and the mine-sweepers and motor launches astern. A few minutes later the Italians could be seen from on board ship, outlined hull down against the brightening sky to the eastward. They were broad on the port bow, steering a slightly converging course at high speed, and drawing ahead of the convoy; before long it was clear that they were two 6-inch cruisers with five destroyers (3 ahead and 2 astern), not four as was first reported.[100] Commander Scurfield in the *Bedouin* led out the "Fleets" to attack, while the *Cairo* and the rest of the escort started making smoke to cover the merchant ships, which were ordered to turn away to starboard and to seek shelter in Tunisian waters; for Captain Hardy's "immediate intention was to gain time and to fight a delaying action in the hope that an air striking force could be sent from Malta."

Despatches: Supplement to *The London Gazette*, Published by Authority
The following Despatch was submitted to the Lords Commissioners of the Admiralty on 24 June, 1942 by Vice-Admiral Sir Alban T. B. Curteis, K.C.B., Senior Officer, Force T.

Forces Employed

If further operations of this nature are undertaken, interference by surface craft must now be considered as probable between the time of the main force parting company and the arrival of the convoy at Malta.

On this assumption there should be sufficient ships in Force X to deal with surface attack, leaving the Fighter Directing Ship and some A.A. screen with the convoy. This will very materially increase the chances of success.

At 0640 the Italian cruisers opened fire at a range of over 20,000 yards; their second salvo straddled the *Cairo*, and others fell near the convoy before the smoke screen took effect. The British ships could not yet reply, the range being too great for their 4.7-inch and 4-inch guns; indeed, some never reached effective range, though "for moral effect" they fired a few rounds. As the 11th Division – "Fleets" – gathered way, they became strung out in a loose line of bearing, nearly line ahead, in the order, *Bedouin*, *Partridge*, *Ithuriel*, *Marne*, *Matchless*, though the last ship worked up to 32 knots in the endeavour to keep up. The first two ships opened fire on the cruisers at about 0645, with their guns at the maximum elevation; but in a quarter of an hour both ships, the *Bedouin* and the *Partridge*, were badly hit and stopped, and the fight passed them by. The *Ithuriel* held her fire till she got within 15,000 yards; then she engaged a cruiser, which she eventually hit at a range of 8,000 yards. The *Marne* also engaged a cruiser ahead, starting at over 18,000 yards. In the meantime, however, the Italian destroyers had fallen astern of the cruisers; three of them, in fact, soon left the line and disappeared to the northward, having apparently taken no part in the action.[101] The last two[102] opened fire on the *Marne* from her port beam at about 0700, and she and the *Matchless* astern of her replied. The British ships quickly found the range, hit one of the enemy (the *Ugolino Vivaldi)*, and drove them off. Then they pressed on to engage the cruisers, which were all the time keeping at a respectful distance, and zigzagging and making smoke to upset the aim of the British ships.[103]

As soon as the convoy was well behind its smoke screen and on its way to the westward, the *Cairo* and the 12th Division of destroyers – "Hunts" – steered south after the enemy as well, the destroyers firing on the two Italian destroyers engaged by the *Marne* and *Matchless* as they passed at extreme range. At about 0700, the *Cairo* again came under fire from the cruisers, which were each using two turrets against her and two against the ships of the 11th Division to port of her, and she received a hit from a 6-inch gun; she herself fired her 4-inch occasionally, though without much hope of harming the enemy. At 0715 Captain Hardy decided to concentrate his three remaining large destroyers on the *Cairo*, and he ordered the *Ithuriel* to join him.

According to her report, that ship was only 8,000 yards from the enemy when the signal reached her, and under heavy and accurate fire, though it was then that she scored her hit on the cruiser. The *Marne* and *Matchless* continued in action half an hour longer, and for a time the former was less than 10,000 yards from the enemy; the shooting on both sides was accurate, though neither succeeded in hitting. At 0745 the Italians turned away to port, on which Captain Hardy hauled round to the northward and ordered all the destroyers to rejoin.

The convoy 15 miles away in the north-west and hitherto steering westward turned south-east again at this time. At 0705, deprived of the support of the *Cairo* and destroyers and without air protection, the convoy had been attacked by eight Ju. 87 dive-bombers, which sank the *Chant* and disabled the *Kentucky* at a cost of one German aircraft shot down. The *Hebe* took the *Kentucky* in tow, and the convoy went on till 0745. Then, however, as the enemy had not sent ships to deal with the merchantmen, and the British force appeared to be holding its own, Commander Pilditch, commodore of the convoy, decided to return to his course for Malta in the hope of meeting fighter aircraft.[104] This course brought him back towards the main escort, and he could not continue on it long; for the Italians had turned northward soon after Captain Hardy, and were following the British ships – warily indeed, but keeping them under fire. At 0834, therefore, as he closed the convoy, Captain Hardy ordered it to reverse its course, while the *Cairo* and the destroyers laid a smoke screen across its track. This seems to have baffled the Italians, which first turned south-west and then at 0840 hauled round to the north-eastward and stood away. Sending the "Hunts" to the convoy, Captain Hardy led the "Fleets" after the enemy, the *Cairo* receiving a second hit at this time. For the time being, however, the Italians had given up the game; by 0930 they were out of sight, and the British ships turned back to meet the convoy.

An hour later the merchant ships were on their proper course, with the escort at full strength (except the *Bedouin* and *Partridge*, whose fortunes will be described later), and with long-range Spitfire aircraft from Malta overhead. But the convoy had not reached the end of its trials. At 1040 a few German bombers approached, but they were driven off before they could drop their bombs and the fighters shot one down. Unluckily, this exhausted the fuel and ammunition of the Spitfires, which were working at the limit of their range; and when another attack started, at 1120, the relief flight had not yet come. It was a combination of high-level and dive-bombing by Ju. 88 and Ju. 87 aircraft, ten all told. Gunfire destroyed one of the Germans, and one or two were shot down afterwards by the relieving Spitfires, which arrived during the attack; but the *Burdwan* was disabled.

There was still 150 miles to go, with the likelihood of further attacks from the air and with Italian ships not far away, so Captain Hardy resolved to sacrifice the damaged *Kentucky* and *Burdwan* as the best way to save the rest of the convoy, whose speed would be otherwise reduced to about 6 knots; he ordered the *Hebe* and *Badsworth* to sink the cripples, which enabled the two good ships remaining to go on at their best speed.[105] Dive-bombers attacked again at 1315, and again there happened to be no fighter aircraft in company; this time, however, the Germans were unsuccessful, and one bomber out of 12 attacking was shot down by the ships, while the relief flight of Spitfires came in time to destroy two more as they retired. That was the last attack from the air before the convoy arrived under the protection of short-range Spitfires in large numbers. The next threat of attack came from the Italian surface force, which appeared once more.

After the engagement in the morning the Italian cruisers had gone back to join the destroyers,[106] one of which (*Vivaldi*), as it turned out, had been badly damaged by the *Matchless* and *Marne*. While preparing to take her in tow, the Italians were disturbed by British aircraft; for, as Captain Hardy had hoped, Malta had been able to send a small torpedo striking force to attack them. Four naval Albacores under Lieutenant-Commander Roe, followed by two Beauforts, attacked about 12 miles south of Pantellaria at 1030, unluckily without success. The two cruisers and two destroyers afterwards went south again, doubtless learning from their allies in the air that there were stragglers from the convoy to pick up. They found the *Hebe*, which was on her way back to the convoy, having left the *Kentucky* sinking astern. The *Hebe* sighted the enemy a long way to the northward at 1255; in half an hour they had closed enough to open fire, and they eventually hit her. Receiving her report at 1341, Captain Hardy left the convoy and stood towards the Italians with the *Cairo* and his three large destroyers; besides the *Hebe* to protect, there were other ships coming back from the scuttled merchantmen, and the *Bedouin* and *Partridge*, which Captain Hardy believed to be following the convoy. At 1355 the Italians gave up the chase, presumably on sighting the *Cairo*, and turned to engage a target to the westward. This could only be the *Bedouin* and *Partridge*; but Captain Hardy felt bound to return to the convoy, then nearly 15 miles off, though it meant leaving the two damaged destroyers to their fate.

Loss of *Bedouin*

The *Bedouin* and *Partridge* meanwhile had been making strenuous efforts to overcome the damage they had received. The former had received at least a dozen 6-in. hits, and was completely disabled, though Commander Scurfield, hoping continually to be able to steam shortly, made a sanguine report to Captain Hardy as late as midday. The *Partridge* was ready to steam at 12 knots again by 0745, three quarters of an hour after being put out of action. She prepared to take the *Bedouin* in tow, but the preparations were interrupted by two Italian destroyers, which had to be driven away. By 1000, however, Lieutenant-Commander Hawkins had his consort in tow, and the two ships were proceeding slowly towards the convoy, which they had orders to join. They met it at 1145, still hoping to get one engine to work in the *Bedouin*; but later on this hope had to be abandoned, and Commander Scurfield then thought it best to make for Gibraltar. At 1320 the Italian squadron came in sight again, and two destroyers were apparently closing the British ships, while there were also dive-bombers about. The *Partridge* accordingly slipped the tow by order of Commander Scurfield and laid smoke round the *Bedouin*. As the cruisers approached, after their chase of the *Hebe*, the *Partridge* stood away to draw their fire, and in this she succeeded, being straddled at long range at 1400. But she was disappointed of her further intention of returning to her consort. At 1425 an Italian aircraft torpedoed the *Bedouin*, which sank within a few minutes, after managing first to shoot down her assailant.[107] Italian torpedo aircraft also sank the derelict *Kentucky* and *Burdwan* at about the same time.

The *Partridge* remained under fire from the Italian ships, which had an aircraft spotting for them, and whose shots fell close in spite of her smoke screen. After a while the enemy turned away, apparently under an air attack, which must have been made by their friends. Four German bombers, however, attacked the *Partridge* at 1530, and near misses jammed her rudder hard over. It took more than an hour to get it amidships, and during that time she had to lie stopped. She saw Italian ships approach the position where the *Bedouin* had sunk, some seven miles to the eastward, and thought they were picking up survivors. "It is deeply regretted," wrote Lieutenant-Commander Hawkins, "that, even if the ship could not be saved, the *Bedouin*'s commanding officer and her ship's company could not be rescued by a British warship."[108] When able to proceed, the *Partridge* went to the westward, intending to make good defects under shelter of the land; but a signal from Vice-Admiral Leatham at Malta ordered her back to Gibraltar, where she arrived without further incident on 17 June. The Italian ships made no effort to destroy the *Partridge*, but steered away to the northward,[109] and at 1700 on 15 June again encountered British naval aircraft near Pantellaria. These were three Albacores that Vice-Admiral Leatham had sent to attack with torpedoes in aid of the *Bedouin* and *Partridge*. The aircraft, not finding the enemy on the way out from Malta, sighted them by chance on the way back; but the attack did not succeed, and one Albacore was shot down by the swarm of fighter aircraft the enemy had then in company. The last news of the Italian ships came from Submarine *P.42* the same evening. At 2045/15, she sighted two cruisers and two destroyers steering north at high speed close to Marittimo and beyond her reach.

Arrival at Malta: Mine Damage

Captain Hardy rejoined the convoy at 1530/15 after the last encounter with the Italian squadron. At 1730 the *Welshman* joined south of Linosa, having reached Malta that morning and been sent out again by Vice-Admiral Leatham as soon as she had landed her cargo. Then, at 1910, there was another air attack. Up to that time radar warnings and fighter direction by the *Cairo* had enabled the strong escort of Spitfires to keep enemy aircraft at a safe distance and to frustrate two attempted attacks during the afternoon. At 1910, however, 12 German bombers managed to attack, and without doing actual harm they nearly hit the *Matchless*, *Troilus* and *Welshman*. A last attempt, at 2040, was foiled by the fighters and the ships' guns.

There remained one danger to overcome – the mines that the enemy had laid so industriously off Malta in the past few months; and they took their toll as the two merchant ships and their escort entered harbour that night. In the original plan it was hoped that the *Cairo* and the destroyers would not need to go into harbour; but the heavy fighting on 14/15 June required them to replenish with ammunition from the slender store at Malta. Owing to mistakes, the convoy and the main escort arrived at the entrance before the sweepers, which ought to have been sweeping ahead of them. The *Badsworth* and *Kujawiak* struck mines off Zonkor Point, a few miles short of Grand Harbour, and the *Orari*, *Matchless* and *Hebe* were mined just outside the breakwater. All except the *Kujawiak* reached harbour only slightly damaged, but the Polish destroyer was lost.[110]

Having arrived at Malta in the early morning of 16 June, the *Cairo* and the four undamaged destroyers sailed again for Gibraltar in the evening. On 17 June, as they skirted along the African coast, they were shadowed from sunrise onward, but not attacked until midday, when they were past the Galita Bank. From then until 2030 that evening German bombers pestered them continuously. The Germans came sometimes in flights of six, though generally in twos and threes, concentrating specially upon the *Ithuriel*, which reported the afternoon's progress as a "struggle for existence"; but apart from a few leaks caused by near misses no harm was done and the *Cairo* shot down a bomber. At 2017 they joined Vice-Admiral Curteis with the *Kenya* and *Charybdis* in 37° 30' N., 4° 30' E.

After leaving the convoy in the evening of 14 June the Vice-Admiral had taken Force "W" some 400 miles to the westward of Sardinia, in order to avoid observation and attack while awaiting the return of Force "X". His ships had been shadowed as a matter of course on 15 June, and two small groups of torpedo aircraft attacked that afternoon; but Hurricanes from the *Eagle* forced them to drop their torpedoes at long range and shot down one aircraft. From the morning of 16 June to 1200/17, he cruised with the *Kenya* and *Charybdis* on his rendezvous, sending his battleship, the two aircraft carriers and the destroyers to Gibraltar. Then he went east again to meet Captain Hardy, and after the junction had been made they returned to Gibraltar together.

This was the end of Operation "Harpoon". Out of six ships in the convoy, two reached their destination, the other four all being destroyed by air attack. But these two ships landed two months' supplies, enough to tide over the sorely-tried fortress till August. About 200 aircraft attacked the convoy and escort during the operation, losing 13 to the carrier-borne fighters and 16 to the ships' guns, besides several shot down by Royal Air Force fighters from Malta.[111] Of the escorting ships, two destroyers were lost, and a cruiser, three destroyers and a minesweeper damaged.

Operation "Vigorous"

Plan of Operation "Vigorous"

While the "Harpoon" forces were battling their way through to Malta from the west, operation "Vigorous" in the east was encountering even more formidable opposition, which eventually compelled the abandonment of the attempt.

The convoy from Egypt in March (or part of it) had succeeded in reaching Malta owing chiefly to the exertions of the slender force of cruisers and destroyers under Rear-Admiral Philip Vian. The same officer led the surface escort in the attempt in June that was complementary to Operation "Harpoon" from Gibraltar. For this occasion the strength of the Mediterranean Fleet was augmented by borrowing from the Eastern Fleet, so that Rear-Admiral Vian had seven cruisers, one anti-aircraft ship, and twenty-six destroyers as the main escort for eleven merchant ships.[112] There were also four motor torpedo boats, which were to be towed by merchantmen, ready to slip and attack should opportunity arise; four corvettes; two minesweepers, which were to sweep ahead of the convoy when approaching Malta; two unarmed rescue ships; and the former battleship *Centurion*, unarmed except against air attack, but masquerading as a capital ship.[113] In default of real battleships, however, the convoy was to depend for protection against the Italian main fleet rather on submarines and air striking forces than on its surface escort; for in midsummer an inferior force could not hope to gain as much by evasion and delay as it did in March. In these circumstances the general conduct of the operation rested directly with the Commander-in-Chief himself, and with the Air Officer Commanding-in-Chief, Air Marshal Sir Arthur Tedder, the two officers working together in "a special combined operations room" at the headquarters of the Naval Co-operation Group, Royal Air Force.

"In previous operations, available submarines had been disposed in the close approaches to Messina and Taranto. Apart from valuable early sighting reports and an occasional attack on returning enemy forces, these dispositions had produced little result."[114]

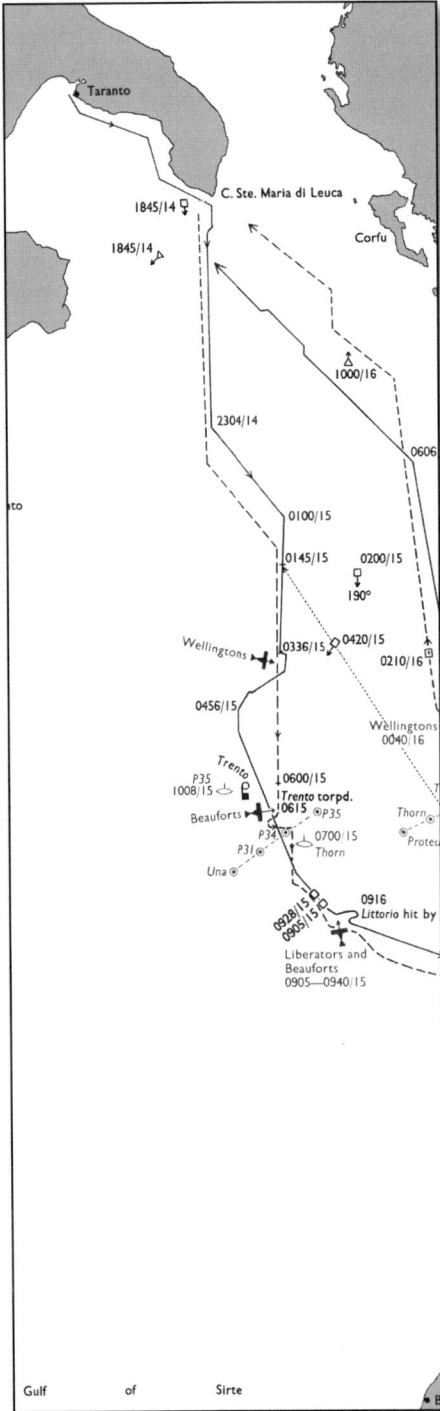

Section detail of Plan 13

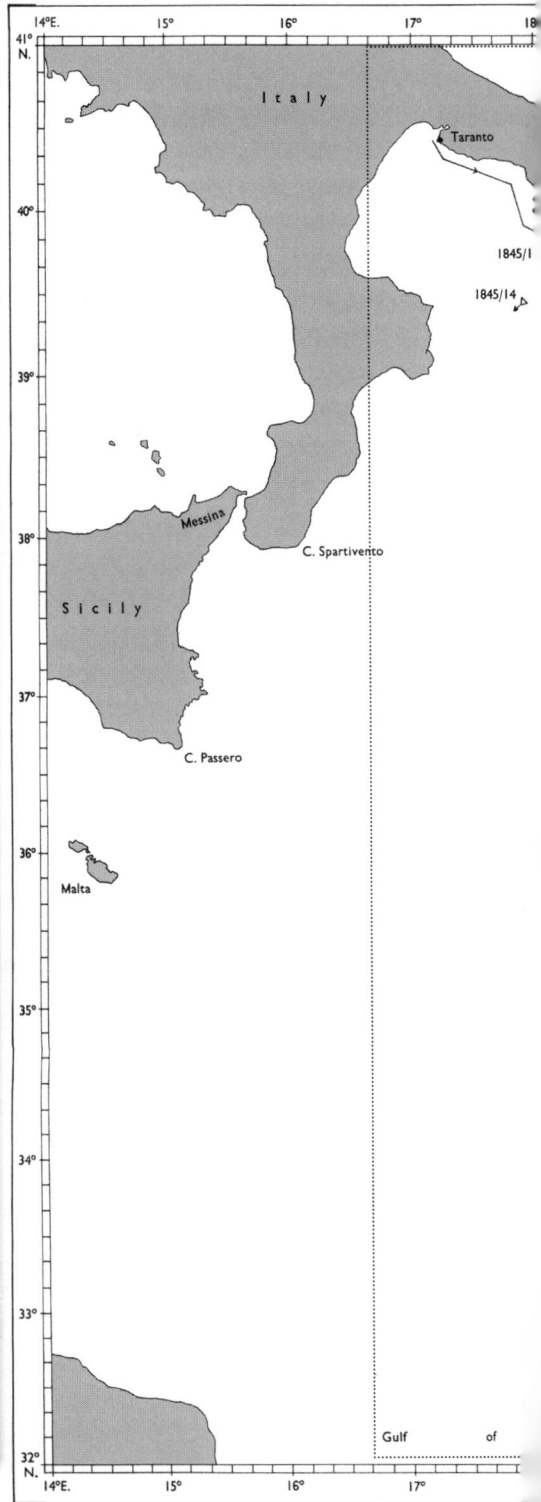

C.B.H. 22729

PLAN 13

OPERATION "VIGOROUS"

TRACKS OF CONVOY MW11, ESCORT AND ITALIAN FLEET
14th — 16th JUNE 1942
Times Zone minus 3: Movements and positions approximate
Based on plan in M.013471/42 and Italian official history.

Key
British forces shewn in Red: Enemy in Blue
Enemy reports received by C-in-C, Med. in Black
Convoy MW11 and escort . . . . ——— *Littorio* Group . . . . ——— Cruisers — — —
British Submarines, posn. on patrol, A.M. 15th, ⊕ posn. at time stated ⬦
Air attacks . . . . ✠ Ships sunk . . . .

Leuca

Corfu

1000/16

0606/16

Cephalonia

/15

Zante

/15 0200/15
190°

5 0420/15

0210/16

2250/15

Navarin

Wellingtons
0040/16 0040/16

2255/15 2100/15

C. Matapan

Porpoise

Thrasher

Kithera

5
torpd.
P35

Thorn Taku

700/15
horn

Proteus

Crete

0916
Littorio hit by bomb

ors and
rts
0940/15

235 miles

Gavdo

1330/15

1500/15

1500/15

0145/15 1510/15 0350/15 0940/15

M.T.B.'s
operating

Newcastle torpd. 0350

0655/15

Bhutan 1741/14

Hasty 0528/15

1500
Airedale
1525/15

Nestor bombed 1806/15

U205
Hermione 0127/16

0800/14 Convoy MW11 and escort

Aagtekirk
1220/14

Benghazi

Tobruk

143

This time, therefore, the submarines were to be used differently. From the point of view of surface attack, the critical day of the operation would be that on which the convoy passed through the "central basin" between Crete and Malta. Up to that morning nine submarines were to carry out normal diving patrols on lines north of the route, so placed as "to cover the enemy's most probable movements," but from which the submarines could reach the positions required on the critical day – the next stage of their task. On that day, they were to proceed on the surface formed as a screen, parallel to the convoy and between it and the enemy's line of approach from Taranto; and they were to have "complete freedom of action to intercept any enemy force which may be reported." The next day, when the convoy should have arrived in Malta, the submarines were to dive again, some on a line of stations from which they should help to cover the return of the surface escort to Alexandria, and the others in the Messina approaches, where they might have an opportunity of intercepting Italian ships returning through those waters.[115] As things turned out the plan was not fully carried out. The Italian fleet sailed earlier than the scheme allowed for, and the convoy was turned back by order of the Commander-in-Chief so as to avoid meeting the enemy. The moving screen of submarines thus became impracticable, and instead the patrol lines were adjusted according to the information received of the enemy's movements. Four submarines sighted the Italian fleet as it came south in the morning of 15 June, though one only was able to attack; and one sighted part of the fleet as it went north again that night, unfortunately outside her reach.

The air striking forces came from both Malta and Egypt. Some forty aircraft were employed: Wellingtons and Beauforts armed with torpedoes from Malta, torpedo Beauforts from a landing-ground in Egypt near the Libyan border, and United States Liberator bombers from as far away as the Suez Canal. It was intended to synchronize the bombing with the two main torpedo attacks by Beauforts, despite the long distances to be flown and the widely separated bases. But the plan proved too ambitious, though the Beauforts from Egypt managed to attack within a few minutes of the Liberators in the forenoon of 15 June. The Malta Beauforts had attacked three hours earlier, as the Italian fleet was crossing the submarine patrol line; and they disabled the cruiser *Trento*, which was sunk later by Submarine *P.35*. One bomb from the Liberators hit the battleship *Littorio*, which was hit again by a torpedo from a Wellington late that night when going back to

Taranto. But that was the sum of the airmen's success. The damage inflicted during their passage south did not deter the Italians. They continued on their course towards the convoy for six hours after the attack by the Liberators, and although they were never nearer than 100 miles they succeeded so far as to stop the convoy from finishing its voyage. For the convoy itself was heavily attacked by German aircraft that day and the day before; it lost time and distance by the diversion that the threatening approach of the Italian fleet imposed upon it; and when it might have retraced its course, in the evening of 15 June, it had not ammunition enough remaining for the air attacks it must still expect before reaching Malta.

Sailing of Convoys

In order to mislead the enemy and to deny them knowledge of the convoy for as long as possible, the ships were loaded at various ports between Beirut and Alexandria. Part of the convoy – M.W.11C – was to sail with a special escort from Port Said on 11 June, some thirty-six hours before the main body; it was to go as far west as 24° 50' E., nearly to Tobruk, arriving there at dusk on 12 June, and then to turn back to meet the rest of the convoy. Admiral Harwood hoped by this means to draw the Italian fleet to sea prematurely, "exposing them to attack and running them short of fuel" – but this ruse did not succeed. The rest of the convoy was to assemble at Haifa and Port Said in two parts, M.W.11A and M.W.11B, which were to join at sea and go to a rendezvous off Alexandria, where Convoy M.W.11C and part of the permanent escort were to join on 13 June. The remainder of the ships of war were to sail from Alexandria later with Rear-Admiral Vian and to overtake the convoy a little east of Tobruk in the morning of 14 June. For the first part of the passage, the route lay within the range of protection by shore-based aircraft against enemy submarines and air attack. Fighter protection was difficult to give, because the land battle in Libya demanded a share of the few aircraft available and because the enemy's advance had deprived the Royal Air Force of its airfields there; yet protection was given, by Hurricanes at first and then by longer-ranged Beaufighters and Kittihawks, to the limit of endurance.[116] As the course of the operation was governed largely by the movements of the Italian fleet, good air reconnaissance was essential, alike for the Allied submarines and air striking forces to fulfil their tasks and for enabling the convoy itself to evade attack; extensive searches were carried out accordingly from Malta and Egypt by day and by night, but the aircraft available for the purpose were too few to keep the enemy under continuous observation.

The four ships of Convoy M.W.11C, sailing on 11 June as arranged, escorted by the *Coventry* and eight destroyers, were found by German bombers in the evening of 12 June, when about to turn east again to rendezvous with the main body. A dozen Ju. 88 aircraft attacked, and one merchant ship was damaged by a near miss and had to be sent to Tobruk with two destroyers for escort. The rest of the force turned back at the appointed time and met the main convoy off Alexandria in the afternoon of 13 June. As another of the convoy had to return to harbour, being unable to maintain the speed of the convoy, 13 knots, only nine out of the original eleven ships left the rendezvous. They proceeded with the *Coventry*, ten destroyers and four corvettes, the *Centurion* and the two rescue ships, and the four motor torpedo boats; but the torpedo boats had to go back the same night, the weather being too rough for towing. In the morning of 14 June the force was completed by the junction of the two minesweepers and of Rear-Admiral Vian in the *Cleopatra*, with the cruisers *Dido*, *Hermione*, *Euryalus*, *Arethusa*, *Newcastle* (flag, Rear-Admiral Tennant) and *Birmingham* and fourteen more destroyers, and by the return of the two destroyers detached to Tobruk on 12 June – these last two ships had hunted an enemy submarine, till she was no longer a menace to the convoy, whilst rejoining. On the other hand, the corvettes *Erica* and *Primula* had to part company owing to defects; yet another merchant ship, the *Aagtekirk*, was found to be too slow, so was sent to Tobruk; and the destroyer *Tetcott* went with her. The *Aagtekirk* did not reach harbour.

About 40 German dive-bombers, Ju. 87 and Ju. 88, attacked at 1220[117] that day, when the merchantman and her escort were within a dozen miles of Tobruk, and the *Primula* was following them a few miles astern. The *Aagtekirk* was hit and sunk and the *Primula* was damaged by near misses. The two ships of war shot down three of the attacking aircraft between them.

Air, Submarine and M.T.B. Attacks

The main convoy had been threatened from the air the previous night. From sunset on 13 June to 0430/14, enemy aircraft had dropped flares almost continuously to guide attacks, while a few bombs were dropped near the screen. After 0430 the enemy had turned their attention to

Rear-Admiral Vian as he overhauled the convoy. One or two small bombs fell close to the flagship *Cleopatra* at that time, and the enemy went on dropping flares round the cruisers till daylight. Then, however, owing largely to the exertions of the fighter aircraft, there was no further sign of the enemy till the afternoon, though the convoy was well inside "Bomb Alley" between Crete and Cyrenaica; at least one strong formation of German bombers, escorted by fighters, was intercepted and dispersed by two squadrons of British fighters, which the Western Desert Command detached at a moment's notice from the land battle.[118] Even the afternoon attacks were individually less formidable than that which overwhelmed the *Aagtekirk*, though the enemy succeeded in sinking one merchant ship and damaging another at a cost of six bombers shot down by the escort and convoy out of 60 or 70 that attacked between 1630 and 2115. There were seven attacks, generally by 10 or 12 aircraft at a time, Ju. 87 and Ju. 88; they approached from astern or the quarter at a height of 10,000 ft., and dived in ones or twos to 3,000 or 4,000 ft. to release their bombs. The one attack that brought success to the enemy took place between 1730 and 1800. This time as many as 20 aircraft approached together on the beam and split into groups of three to attack. They hit and sank the *Bhutan*, sternmost ship of a wing column, and damaged the *Potaro* by near misses, but she was able to stay with the convoy. The rescue ships *Antwerp* and *Malines*, having picked up the survivors from the *Bhutan*, were detached to Tobruk.[119]

Towards the end of the air attacks, at 2000/14, a submarine appeared on the starboard bow of the force and nearly torpedoed the *Pakenham* in the outer screen; she was attacked with depth charges, but without success. A few minutes later, at sunset, the fighter patrol reported a flotilla of six motor torpedo craft – E-boats[120] – to the north-westward, and shortly afterwards the enemy were seen hull down from the *Euryalus* on the starboard bow of the convoy. The fighters were directed to attack; but the E-boats had an escort of German fighters, which held off the one British aircraft that complied, the others being engaged with enemy bombers. Accordingly, the E-boats remained undisturbed.

At 2115, by which time it was dark, Rear-Admiral Vian assumed his night disposition, in which he had a regular anti-submarine screen ahead and on the bows, a special "night screen" of two cruisers and four destroyers on each quarter, and single destroyers 5 miles out on either bow and quarter of the convoy. Enemy aircraft were dropping flares, evidently to assist submarines and E-boats as well as bombers, which still attacked sporadically; and Rear-Admiral Vian claimed that his force, thus disposed, "proved an unattractive proposition" to the E-boats, especially with the whole area lit up as it was by the flares. Certainly the *Airedale* and *Aldenham*, stationed out on either quarter, found little difficulty in driving off five boats that approached from astern at midnight. But Rear-Admiral Tennant, leading one of the night screens, remarked that "flares gave one a very naked feeling, when dropped overhead, and it is surprising that the E-boats did not achieve a great deal more success." For two successes they did achieve a few hours later.

This arose out of the convoy's reversing its course, which was an awkward manoeuvre at night in that formation and with ships out of position through turning to avoid bombs. At 2315, having learnt that an Italian force of two battleships and four cruisers had sailed from Taranto and would probably meet him on his present course at 0700 in the morning, Rear-Admiral Vian signalled to the Commander-in-Chief, "Do you wish me to retire?" For, with fine weather and a light north-westerly breeze, he could not hope "to hold off such a force from early morning to dusk." Admiral Harwood intended the convoy to make as much westing as possible, whilst leaving sea-room for the submarines and aircraft to attack the Italian fleet, and therefore ordered the Rear-Admiral to continue till 0200 and then to "turn back along the same track." The convoy turned accordingly at 0145/15. In carrying out the manoeuvre, Rear-Admiral Tennant's ships dropped several miles astern; and at 0350, while coming up to regain station, his flagship, the *Newcastle*, was torpedoed by an E-boat from 500 yards on the bow. The enemy was sighted in time for the *Newcastle* to avoid one torpedo and to receive the other well forward, and after shoring up the damaged compartments the ship was still capable of 24 knots' speed; in the meantime, Rear-Admiral Tennant sent his other cruiser and one destroyer to join the convoy, keeping three destroyers with the *Newcastle*. Before the *Newcastle* and her escort overtook the convoy they were attacked again and the *Hasty* was hit by one torpedo at 0528. She was so badly damaged that she had to be sunk by a consort.[121]

Movements of Italian Fleet: British Air and S/M Attacks: *Trento* Sunk

Meanwhile an Italian squadron consisting of the battleships *Littorio* and *Vittorio Veneto*, the cruisers *Gorizia*, *Trento*, *Garibaldi* and *Duca d'Aosta*, and 12 destroyers had left Taranto at 1430 on 14 June, with the intention of intercepting the convoy at dawn 15 June. When the convoy altered course to the east (0145/15) the Italian fleet was rather more than 230 miles away in the north-west, pressing south towards the line of passage to Malta.

The first news of them to reach the British came from a Malta aircraft, which sighted them clearing the Gulf of Taranto at 1845/14, and reported two battleships with four destroyers in company and four cruisers with four destroyers a few miles farther on. Photographic reconnaissance of Taranto by a Malta aircraft at 2000 showed that three *Cavour* class battleships still lay "in their nets" there, but that the two *Littorio* class ships, two 8-inch and two 6-inch cruisers and eleven destroyers had sailed. This information, however, did not reach Admiral Harwood until 0300/15, and at midnight he had only the first sighting at 1845 – signal received at 2230/14 – on which to base his reply to Rear-Admiral Vian's question whether to retire.[122] The next report of the Italians' progress came at 0224/15, but gave only a part of their force: one battleship, two cruisers and two destroyers in 37° 30' N., 19° 35' E., course 190°, speed 20 knots, at 0200. No further news arrived until 0630, except that the little torpedo striking force of Wellington aircraft had left Malta at midnight to attack; but at 0525 Admiral Harwood ordered the convoy to steer north-west again, for he considered its return into "Bomb Alley" more dangerous than an advance towards the Italian fleet. In compliance with this order Rear-Admiral Vian turned back towards Malta at 0655. The Italians had just crossed the submarine line, leaving behind them an 8-inch cruiser disabled by air attack, though neither the Commander-in-Chief nor Rear-Admiral Vian was to know of it for some time to come.

There had been two attempts upon the Italian fleet by aircraft from Malta. The Wellingtons were dispatched at midnight on the strength of the first sighting report and the photographic reconnaissance of Taranto. The aircraft found their target at 0340; but the Italian smoke screen was so effective that one only of the four was able to attack, and both its torpedoes missed. The nine Beauforts attacked at dawn, as the enemy were passing over the submarines. The Italians were steering south in two groups, disposed apparently as follows: two battleships and two cruisers, screened by five or six destroyers, with two cruisers and five or six destroyers several miles to the westward. According to the Italian report, the aircraft first attacked the cruiser group to the westward, approaching at 0610 and disabling the sternmost cruiser, *Trento*, which turned away and steamed slowly westward with two destroyers. Then the Beauforts attacked the battleships, but without success, though on their first return to Malta they claimed hits on both. The Italians avoided attack by making large alterations of course. Lieutenant Maydon, of Submarine *P.35*, who missed a chance of his own through their turning away, thus described what he saw. "*P.35* was in the unenviable position of being in the centre of a fantastic circus of wildly careering capital ships, cruisers, and destroyers ... of tracer-shell streaks and anti-aircraft bursts. At one period there was not a quadrant of the compass unoccupied by enemy vessels weaving continuously to and fro. It was only possible to count the big ships: destroyers seemed to be everywhere. It was essential to remain at periscope depth, for an opportunity to fire might come at any moment; one was in fact tempted to stand with periscope up and gaze in utter amazement."

The submarines, in accordance with the original plan of the operation, had left their stations on patrol during the night of 14/15 June to go south-west to their starting positions on the moving screen, parallel to the convoy, which they were to have formed on 15 June; but after the enemy's sailing was known (2230/14), they were ordered back to the previous patrol lines. The route of the Italian fleet crossed the western line of four U-class submarines of the Tenth Flotilla, three of which sighted the enemy. *P.35*, warned by the signal giving the enemy's position at 0200 and sighting aircraft flares to the northward soon after 0400, steered westward to intercept the Italians, which she expected to sight at dawn. She saw two battleships and two cruisers at 0545, and started to attack them. But a few seconds before she was due to fire (in the circumstances described in the last paragraph), the enemy turned away 90° under air attack, and the submarine lost her chance. The battleships circled round the damaged *Trento* to the westward (for they appeared beyond her), worked to the eastward again, and coming south gave Lieutenant Maydon another opportunity. At 0646, he fired his four torpedoes at the second battleship at a range of 5,000 to 6,000 yards, but without success. *P.34*, in her station at the patrol line, first sighted the fleet to the north-westward at 0615 during the Beauforts' attack. Lieutenant Harrison saw the battleships steering east after closing the *Trento*, while the three remaining cruisers screened by four destroyers came south towards *P.34*. He started an attack at 0622, arrived inside the screen and was about to fire, when the enemy turned 90° towards, passed over him and altered course to the southward again out of range. At 0700 the two battleships appeared once more, standing south with five destroyers, but *P.34* could not reach them. *P.31*, on the other side of the Italians' track, sighted them against the dawn sky at 0604, when she was already on their beam at extreme range.

Three submarines of the faster First Flotilla to the eastward also tried to intercept the Italian fleet. Receiving the 0200 sighting report, whilst going back north-eastward to their old positions under the new orders, they turned to head off the enemy, going at full speed on the surface. The *Thrasher* and *Taku* both gave up the attempt after some three hours, the latter misled by a second sighting report, timed 0420, which made the enemy's course southwesterly instead of southerly; otherwise, as her captain calculated, she would have met them about 0800. The *Thorn*, having started her westward stretch near the enemy, was able to dive in good time a little east of their line of advance. At 0700 she sighted a column of smoke in the north-west, which was evidently the *Trento* on fire, and at 0725 saw the masts of what proved to be the Italian battleships. She could not, however, approach nearer than 12,000 yards. There remained the disabled *Trento* for the three ships of the Tenth Flotilla, all of which closed her as soon as the main body of the fleet had passed. *P.31*, the farthest away, had begun to close at 0620; and according to Lieutenant Kershaw she was still "burning gloriously" three hours later, with her crew gathered on the quarterdeck and with two destroyers laying a smoke screen round her; but he had still an hour's diving before she would be within range. Lieutenant Harrison, of *P.34*, seeing her "definitely out of action and incapable of movement", decided that his first duty was to withdraw out of sight of the destroyers to signal the situation to the Commander-in-Chief "and to return later and sink the cruiser if still necessary". *P.35* forestalled both her consorts. Lieutenant Maydon hit the *Trento* with two torpedoes at 1006; her fore magazine blew up and she sank immediately.

Before this the main body of the Italian fleet, continuing southward towards the convoy, had been attacked by the torpedo and bombing air forces from Egypt. The eight Liberators arrived first, beginning their attack at 0905 after a flight of five and a half hours from their base.[123] The Italians were still steaming in two groups, battleships with a destroyer screen to the eastward, cruisers and destroyers 4 or 5 miles west of them. The American aircraft approached out of the sun on the bow of the battleships, and dropped their bombs from an average height of 14,000 ft. They claimed half a dozen hits on each battleship; but the Italians admit only one hit on the *Littorio*, though many bombs fell around them. Four German fighters had joined the Italians at 0800, but they do not seem to have been in company during this attack, for the Liberators report "erratic" gunfire from the ships to be the only opposition they met with until they were many miles on their way home. The Beauforts were not so fortunate. Twelve aircraft set out at 0625, but five Messerschmitt 109 fighters intercepted them half-way to the target; two Beauforts were shot down, while five more had to turn back owing to damage received in the encounter or to excessive fuel consumption, and one of them never arrived. The remaining Beauforts reached the enemy at about 0940 under the eyes of the Americans, who saw the torpedo aircraft flying close to the water below them as they finished their own attack. The Italians met the British attack with a heavy fire at long range, damaging two Beauforts. On the other hand, by altering course 90° when they were bows on to the aircraft, they helped the attack. The British airmen believed that at least one of their torpedoes hit a battleship, while the watching Americans reported hits on a cruiser and a destroyer, but in fact not a ship was touched. And all the gallantry of the airmen, all the skilful leading that enabled the little striking forces to find their targets on each occasion, had not availed: the Italian fleet stood on.

C–in–C. Mediterranean's Instructions

Admiral Harwood had already decided to turn the convoy east once more until he should learn the results of the air attacks. Finding from an air reconnaissance report, timed 0828, that both battleships, three cruisers and nine destroyers were within 150 miles of the convoy and steering south-east, he ordered Rear-Admiral Vian to steer 105°; and the convoy altered round at 0940. Then came the claim of the Malta Beauforts to have hit both Italian battleships. On this, at 1151, Admiral Harwood ordered the convoy to resume its course for Malta; and giving the Rear-Admiral the supposed result of the Beauforts' attack, he told him that an 8-inch cruiser was believed to be also damaged and retiring, and that a further attack by British aircraft was intended in the afternoon. Lastly, he repeated an order he had given early in the morning (0705/15): "Avoid contact until aircraft have attacked, which should be by 1030. If air attack fails, every effort must be made to get convoy through to Malta by adopting offensive attitude. Should this fail, and convoy be cornered, it is to be sacrificed and you are to extricate your forces, proceeding to the eastward or westward." Meanwhile, however, the air reconnaissance had stopped, the latest report being timed 0944. The Commander-in-Chief began to suspect that the cruiser might be the only Italian ship seriously damaged; he did not know whether the convoy had suffered attack and damage, nor how it stood for fuel and ammunition. At 1245, therefore, he signalled to the Rear-Admiral, "I must leave decision to you whether to comply with my 0705/15, or whether to again retire with hope of carrying out a night destroyer attack, if enemy stand on."[124]

Threat of Italian Fleet: Further Air Attacks on Convoy

Rear-Admiral Vian received the signal to turn again for Malta at 1345. By that time a fresh reconnaissance aircraft was shadowing the Italian fleet. He soon had its first report, which showed that the enemy were standing on, whereas his two best ships, the *Newcastle* and *Birmingham*, were damaged.

"My heavy striking force, the Fourth Cruiser Squadron, being somewhat under the weather, I held on to the eastward awaiting the Commander-in-Chief's reactions to Aircraft T's report." At 1420 he received Admiral Harwood's discretionary signal, timed 1245, which confirmed his decision to continue eastward.

The *Newcastle*, it will be remembered, had been hit by an E-boat's torpedo early that morning and had her speed reduced. The *Birmingham*'s injuries (she had two 6-inch guns out of action) were the result of an air attack at midday – for the convoy was back in "Bomb Alley". About 20 German dive-bombers (Ju. 87) had attacked from the quarters at 1150, and six of them concentrated upon the *Birmingham*, which was stationed on the port side ahead of the merchant ships, scoring a near miss; the convoy suffered no other damage, and one of the attackers was brought down by the ships' fire. A further attack took place at 1525, when between 30 and 40 dive-bombers, escorted by Messerschmitts, approached from astern. A dozen aircraft attacked the *Airedale*, stationed in the air-warning screen on the starboard quarter; she was smothered with hits and near misses and completely disabled, and another destroyer had to sink her. The other aircraft, generally in groups of three, attacked the convoy itself, but without success, except that nine aircraft concentrating upon the *Centurion* inflicted slight damage from near misses. Four of the enemy were shot down, one falling to the guns of the *Centurion*, and others may have been destroyed by British fighters after the attack.

Meanwhile, the general situation had changed; for the Italians had given up the chase. At 1515, when rather more than 100 miles astern of the convoy, they hauled round to the north-westward, and at 1605 the shadowing aircraft reported them well away on the course for Taranto. The moment Admiral Harwood was waiting for had come, and as soon as the position was clear he made the following signal to Rear-Admiral Vian (1625/15): "Now is golden opportunity to get convoy to Malta. Have Hunts, *Coventry*, minesweepers and corvettes enough fuel and ammunition for one-way trip? If so, I would like to turn convoy now, cruisers and destroyers parting company after dark and returning to Alexandria." Two hours later, having had no reply from the Rear-Admiral, he modified the plan, intending to send to Malta only the four fastest merchant ships of the seven remaining in the convoy, and adding the *Arethusa* and two large destroyers to their escort. But the first signal reached Rear-Admiral Vian during the most trying air attack of the day, under conditions that precluded his reversing the course of forty ships. Moreover, it was an hour before he could ascertain the quantity of high-angle ammunition still on board the destroyers; and upon that the decision rested.

The attack lasted two hours, beginning at 1720. "All known forms of attack were employed," said Rear-Admiral Vian, "the fire of the fleet being fully extended." The Germans and Italians evidently tried to synchronize high-level and shallow dive-bombing with torpedo attack – on a scale somewhat larger than that which the British and Americans had achieved against the Italian fleet in the morning. Nearly 30 bombers took part, while 10 Italian torpedo aircraft arrived towards the end of the attack. The high-level bombers came first, approaching from the western sun, unseen until they were nearly overhead; "without blind radar-controlled fire, many unopposed attacks would have been made." The bombing was accurate, from a height of 16,000 ft., and three ships had narrow escapes. Shallow-diving Ju. 88 aircraft followed at about 1800, as the high-level bombers were finishing. They attacked both screen and convoy from several directions, diving to 5,000 ft. The *Arethusa* and the *Centurion* suffered slightly, and the Australian destroyer *Nestor* was badly holed, all from near misses. Lastly, the Savoia 79s came in on both quarters at about 1900, attacking independently and dropping their torpedoes at long range to no purpose. The two Beaufighters on patrol with the convoy had intercepted four Savoias half an hour earlier and destroyed one. The ships' guns accounted for three Savoias and two bombers.

Convoy Recalled to Alexandria: *Hermione* Sunk by U–Boat

Rear-Admiral Vian answered Admiral Harwood's signal at 1842, during the dive-bombing attack. Exact figures were still impossible to get from the hard-pressed destroyers, but he estimated from their reports that they had under 30 per cent of ammunition left; it was being used fast, and he considered it insufficient for the passage to Malta. This crossed Admiral Harwood's second signal, ordering the four best ships to turn back for Malta with a strengthened escort. When it reached him the Commander-in-Chief decided that he must abandon the attempt; he signalled to the Rear-Admiral at 2053, "Return to Alexandria with your whole force."

The unhappy ending of the enterprise was made worse by the loss of two more ships of the escort. A last attempt from the air at dusk on 15 June did no harm, though bombs fell all round the convoy; but the *Hermione* was torpedoed and sunk in the night, and next morning the damaged *Nestor* had to be scuttled. The *Hermione* was on the starboard quarter of the convoy, which was zigzagging at 13 knots, when at 0127/16 one or perhaps two torpedoes hit her and she sank in twenty minutes; there was no sign of the enemy, which was probably a submarine.[125] The *Nestor*, having been disabled in the dive-bombing attack at about 1800/15, was taken in tow by the *Javelin* and escorted by three more destroyers. That evening they were twice attacked unsuccessfully by small numbers of aircraft, and on each occasion they shot down one of the enemy. But the *Nestor* yawed badly through being down by the bow, and towing was difficult; at 0430/16 the tow parted for the second time, soon after which a flotilla of E-boats was sighted. The British ships were still more than 200 miles from port, with their position known to the enemy, and they could only crawl through a long summer's day exposed to submarine and air attack, so Commander Rosenthal decided that to go on was to invite the loss of the *Javelin* as well as of his own ship, the *Nestor*, and at 0700 he scuttled her. The other four destroyers overtook the convoy late in the afternoon. Rear-Admiral Vian had had several submarine contacts in the early afternoon (position about 31° 30' N., 28° E.), but had avoided attack. He arrived at Alexandria in the evening, sending on part of the convoy to Port Said.

Return Passage of Italian Fleet

The Italian fleet arrived at Taranto the same day, having narrowly escaped attack by submarines the previous evening and having suffered one torpedo hit from an aircraft in the night. Captain Ruck-Keene, commander of the First Flotilla, who was directing the submarines under the Commander-in-Chief, gave various orders on 15 June with a view to placing the submarines in the path of the fleet when it should go north again, so far as his scanty information allowed. But signals took so long to get through on that day (sometimes above four hours) that as Lieutenant Mackenzie of the *Thrasher* said, "The only possible course was to remain on the surface, and by the use of reports of the enemy from aircraft and other sources keep on the direct line between him and Taranto." Unfortunately, reports ceased at 1625, the aircraft then shadowing the Italians being apparently shot down after making one signal, while its relief was chased and engaged by German aircraft on the way out from Egypt, and it did not find the Italian fleet. The small and slow submarines of the Tenth Flotilla were far to the westward of the Italians' return route – they had had their chance in the morning. So was the *Thorn*, which had then tried to intercept the enemy; but she did her best by going north at full speed in the hope of reaching ahead of the fleet next morning. The other four large ships of the First Flotilla, "all bristling with torpedoes", as Lieutenant Bennington, the captain of the *Porpoise*, put it, made their way towards the enemy; and with a little more information they should have been able to attack. The *Thrasher* actually sighted the three Italian cruisers at sunset. The *Porpoise*, farther south, very likely missed seeing them only through being forced to dive by their escorting aircraft.

The *Porpoise* was well placed originally, for her position on the patrol line was the easternmost of all, and she had stayed near her station all the morning. Lieutenant Bennington shared Lieutenant Mackenzie's opinion that to stay on the surface was essential in order to ensure receiving all reports made and to be made ready to act on them at once.[126] "The all-important factor was to avoid being left in a position through which the enemy would pass in dark hours." At 1535, receiving the air report of the Italians' turn-back north-westward, he steered away at full speed to the southward to meet them. At 1935 he had to dive and go deep on sighting an aircraft which bombed him; it is most probable that the enemy passed him unseen at that time. The *Thrasher* had tried to intercept the Italian fleet on its way south in the morning. Working eastward again, she crossed ahead of its track on return at 2000, as Lieutenant Mackenzie thought, and he stood on some miles, hoping to put the enemy against the lighter sky to the westward. Then he too had to dive to avoid being seen by a patrolling aircraft. At 2038 he sighted through the periscope the masts and funnel-tops of three large ships nine or ten miles south-eastward, and closed to attack; but the enemy passed seven miles off about twenty minutes later.

There was still a chance of striking at the enemy from the air, and Malta sent out a reconnaissance aircraft and five torpedo Wellingtons that night. The reconnaissance aircraft found the Italian fleet at 2255 – six and a half hours since the last air sighting report. The Wellingtons sighted the battleship division an hour later, but were baffled by the enemy's smoke screen. One aircraft persisted, however, and at 0040/16 hit the *Littorio* forward with one torpedo. Thus the Italians lost a cruiser in the operation and had a battleship twice hit and put out of action for several months. Had the Allied submarines and aircraft really disabled the Italian fleet, it would have made all the difference to future operations for supplying Malta that summer. Later convoys would have been spared the diversion of course to avoid the surface threat, which added so much to the difficulty of fighting the way past Cyrenaica under air attack. As it was, no further convoy from Egypt sailed for Malta till November, and by then the German and Italian forces were in full retreat out of Libya.

In this unsuccessful Operation "Vigorous" a cruiser, three destroyers and two merchant ships were lost, and three cruisers, the special service ship *Centurion*, a corvette and two merchantmen were damaged. The Royal Air Force suffered considerable losses of fighter aircraft, though the fighters prevented several attempts upon the convoy and destroyed a number of enemy aircraft. The ships shot down 21 out of some 220 aircraft that attacked them during the operation.

"Events proved with painful clarity," wrote Admiral Harwood, "that our air striking force had nothing like the weight required to stop a fast and powerful enemy force, and in no way compensated for our lack of heavy ships." [127]

Operation "Pedestal"

Strategical Situation

Operation "Pedestal" was the culmination of the series of convoys to Malta. On its success or failure the fate of Malta may well have hinged. Both sides fully appreciated its importance, and both sides put all their previous experience into their offensive or defensive efforts. Probably no convoy in history has ever been subjected to such a scale and diversity of attack. In the event, though sorely mauled, sufficient ships got through to Malta to tide the island over until the great events of the autumn finally brought relief. But it was a near thing, and had the Italians used their surface forces as they had originally intended, they might well have prevented a single merchant ship from getting through.

For these reasons, this operation will be dealt with in greater detail than those previously described.

Strategically, the position in the Mediterranean was more difficult than at any other time. It was indeed the darkest hour before the dawn – though at the time few would have predicted how soon the dawn would come. In North Africa Field-Marshal Rommel's May offensive had brought the German and Italian forces as far as El Alamein – only 90 miles from Alexandria – by the beginning of July. There he was held. Fierce fighting throughout July, with local gains and losses on both sides, was followed by siege warfare which continued for some weeks in August. With all the Libyan airfields in the hands of the enemy and the powerful Italian fleet based on Taranto, the eastern Mediterranean route to Malta was practically closed to the Allies.

Meanwhile, Malta's situation as regards supplies was critical. After the "Harpoon"–"Vigorous" operations the Commander-in-Chief, Mediterranean, though fully appreciating the gravity of the situation, was doubtful whether it was worth even attempting to run in another convoy.[128] The question really was whether the island could hold out on the supplies brought by the two survivors of "Harpoon" until another convoy could be run from the west during the next moonless period. At home, owing to the partial failure of the last three convoys, there was general depression.

The Governor of Malta, Field-Marshal Lord Gort, v.c., however, took a more cheerful view.[129] He reported on 20 June that the unloading of the two "Harpoon" ships was almost completed, and that he was actively examining how best to eke out Malta's supplies till late in September.

Planning and Plan of Operation "Pedestal"

Under these difficult conditions the decision was taken to make another attempt from the west in August. No time was lost in commencing preparations. Acting Vice-Admiral Syfret, then on his way home after his successful occupation of Diego Suarez (in May), was chosen to command the operation and was ordered to disembark at Takoradi and fly to the United Kingdom. Accompanied by his S.O.O., he arrived home on 13 July and meetings between himself, the two flag officers who were to take part in the operation – Rear-Admirals Lyster, R.A.(A), Home Fleet, and Burrough, R.A. 10th C.S. – and the Naval Staff were at once started at the Admiralty, at which the details were carefully planned.[130]

Operation "Pedestal" was "Harpoon" over again on a larger scale, but without the corresponding operation from Egypt. The principal feature of the operation was the increased strength of carrier-borne air protection for the convoy. There were three "Fleet" carriers – the *Victorious* (flag, Rear-Admiral Lyster), *Indomitable* and *Eagle* – each with her attendant cruiser for anti-aircraft defence, and altogether 72 fighter aircraft – Hurricanes, Martlets and Fulmars – and 28 Albacores.

The full escort consisted of Force "Z", comprising two battleships, the *Nelson* (flag, Vice-Admiral Syfret) and *Rodney*, the three carriers, three cruisers, *Sirius*, *Phoebe* and *Charybdis*, and twelve destroyers; and Force "X", comprising three cruisers, *Nigeria* (flag, Rear-Admiral Burrough), *Kenya* and *Manchester*, the A.A. ship *Cairo* and twelve destroyers.[131]

On arrival at Skerki Bank at dusk on D3, the main force was as usual to withdraw to the westward, while Rear-Admiral Burrough with three cruisers, the *Cairo* and twelve destroyers (Force "X") proceeded through the Sicilian Narrows as far as the approaches to Malta, where he would meet the Malta minesweeping flotilla, which would sweep the convoy into harbour. An ocean tug was to have accompanied the convoy (an innovation due to the experiences of Operation "Harpoon"); but, as things turned out, she was diverted early in the operation to assist a damaged ship (the *Eagle)* and had not sufficient speed to catch up again. There was the usual provision for fuelling the escort during the passage: two fleet oilers and a tug with their own escort of corvettes, known as Force "R". There were also eight spare destroyers, additional to the main escort; they were used to strengthen force "R" whilst it cruised alone on its rendezvous, for other incidental duties, and to screen the *Furious*, which had to be included in the operation at a late stage in the planning, on her return to Gibraltar after carrying out a special service. This (Operation "Bellows") consisted of flying off 36 spitfires to Malta, as it was realized that those already in the island would be quite inadequate to cover the convoy for the last stage of its voyage.

Another subsidiary operation (Operation "Ascendant") was planned to take place under cover of the main operation – the passage of the two surviving ships of "Harpoon" which had reached

Malta in June back to Gibraltar. Escorted by two destroyers, they sailed on 10 August and arrived safely on 14 August, undisturbed by the enemy.

Eight submarines took part in the operation. Two carried out normal diving patrols north of Sicily, one off Palermo, the other off Milazzo, farther east. The other six were given alternative patrol lines south of Pantellaria, one of which they were to take up at dawn on 13 August, according to the movements of enemy surface ships that might threaten the convoy from the westward. When the convoy had passed the patrol line, which it should have done by that time, the submarines were to proceed on the surface parallel to the convoy as a screen, as had been intended in Operation "Vigorous", and to dive away clear of the convoy at noon. It was expressly intended that they should be seen on the surface and reported by enemy aircraft in order to deter enemy ships from attacking the convoy. "Therefore," ran the order, "the line is to be maintained so far as air activity allows; but submarines have complete freedom of action on sighting any enemy ships, and should endeavour to attack cruisers or battleships." Actually, though Italian cruisers and destroyers put to sea from Cagliari and other ports, they did not come south of Sicily; and as soon as it was evident that the enemy could not reach the convoy the submarines were ordered to dive and retire, "thus concluding," said one of them, "two hours very intense hide-and-seek" with enemy aircraft. These submarines had no other contact with the enemy; but one off the north coast of Sicily torpedoed and severely damaged two Italian cruisers near Stromboli in the morning of 13 August.[132]

The Royal Air Force at Malta under Air Vice-Marshal Sir Keith Park was cast for an important part.[133] The strong torpedo striking force was kept in readiness to deal with a possible attack by the heavy ships from Taranto after the convoy had passed the Narrows. Attack by cruisers stationed at Cagliari, Naples and Messina had also to be considered; and it was anticipated – as turned out to be the case – that the enemy would strengthen his air forces in Sardinia, Pantellaria and Sicily. It was decided to use all the air striking forces of the island (except torpedo aircraft) to minimise this latter threat, and the plan eventually worked out defined the role of the air forces as: –

(a) to locate, report and shadow all enemy surface forces, in order to warn the convoy and escort;
(b) to protect "Pedestal" from air-borne attack;
(c) to destroy enemy surface forces which might jeopardise the safe passage of "Pedestal";
(d) to dislocate the enemy's air forces on the ground, by means of low flying attacks by Beaufighters, night bombing attacks on Sardinia by R.A.F. Liberators based on Malta, and by large scale night bombing attacks by U.S. Liberators based on the Middle East.

How these arrangements worked out will emerge in the course of the narrative, but it may be mentioned here that an attack on two stations near Cagliari in the night of 11/12 August proved particularly useful; according to the Italian report, six aircraft were destroyed on the ground and others put out of action – whilst the wakeful night ("notte de veglia") passed by the aircrews handicapped them in their action against the convoy next day.[134]

In the eastern Mediterranean, the fleet carried out a diversion as another aid to the safe passage of the convoy from the westward. Though it was not possible to send supplies to Malta from Egypt at this time, Admiral Harwood sent a dummy convoy – M.W.12 – to sea "with the object of preventing the enemy's directing the full weight of surface and air forces against the convoy being run from Gibraltar." Three cruisers and ten destroyers with three merchant ships sailed from Port Said in the evening of 10 August, and Rear-Admiral Vian with two cruisers, five destroyers, and one merchant ship sailed from Haifa next morning. The two forces joined that day, proceeded in company as far west as the longitude of Alexandria, where they arrived at dusk, on 11 August, and then turned back, dispersing during the night. At the same time, to profit by possible movements of the Italian fleet, one submarine was stationed off Navarino, where the Italians had three cruisers, and two more were ordered to a position 100 miles west-south-west of

Crete, where the dummy convoy should have arrived in the afternoon of 13 August, had it gone on. But the Italians stayed in harbour. "The only point of interest in this little operation," remarked Admiral Harwood, "was that considerable disappointment was expressed by the merchant ships taking part, when they found they were not going through to Malta."

Actually, this operation had an important effect on the fortunes of the convoy, since according to the Italian official history it was partly anxiety about this diversion which caused the enemy to call off a projected attack by a strong cruiser force, which would have found "Pedestal" in a state of considerable disorganisation after serious losses by air and E-boat attack the night before.

Preparations: Passage, U.K. to Gibraltar

Operation "Pedestal" may be said to have started with the arrival of Vice-Admiral Syfret at Scapa Flow, where he joined the *Nelson* on 27 July. Most of the ships taking part were assembled there, and on 29 July he held a conference with the Flag and Commanding Officers concerned, at which the orders for the operation were gone through in detail.

On 31 July Rear-Admiral Lyster in the *Victorious*, with the *Argus*,[135] *Sirius* and four destroyers sailed to rendezvous with the *Eagle* and *Charybdis* from Gibraltar and the *Indomitable* and *Phoebe* from Freetown for exercises in the Atlantic (Operation "Berserk") before joining Admiral Syfret's force west of the Strait of Gibraltar. Of this operation Admiral Syfret subsequently wrote that it was "of the utmost benefit in exercising fighter direction and co-operation between the three carriers."

Admiral Syfret himself left Scapa in the *Nelson* with the *Rodney* and six destroyers in the afternoon of 2 August, and was joined next morning by the convoy – fourteen merchant ships, known as W.S.21.S – escorted by the *Nigeria* (flag, Rear-Admiral Burrough), *Kenya* and destroyers which had sailed from the Clyde during the night. Just prior to sailing, but after the "normal" convoy conference, Admiral Burrough had held a meeting in his flagship with the masters of the merchant ships, at which the whole plan was explained to them in detail. A meeting with their radio operators was also held and all details regarding fleet communications and procedure were fully explained. "These two meetings were invaluable."[136]

The passage of the convoy from the United Kingdom to the rendezvous with the carriers west of the Strait of Gibraltar passed without incident, apart from many U-boat alarms. The convoy was repeatedly exercised in emergency turns and in changing from one cruising disposition to another, using both flags and short range wireless. The risk to security in breaking W/T silence was accepted and "as a result of these exercises the convoy attained an efficiency in manoeuvring comparable to a fleet unit."[137]

On 7 August the *Manchester* with the *Furious*, which owing to technical difficulties in connection with her aircraft had been delayed in sailing from the Clyde, joined Admiral Syfret's flag; and the next day Admiral Lyster's carrier force also joined, except the *Indomitable* and screen, which had been detached to Gibraltar for fuel. She joined on 9 August, and that afternoon dummy air attacks were carried out on the force, which proved to be of the utmost benefit for exercising the radar reporting and fighter-direction organisation. The "attacks" were followed by a fly-past for identification purposes, which was of great value in giving everyone an opportunity for studying the characteristics and marking of the F.A.A. aircraft.[138] It is believed that this was the first occasion on which as many as five of H.M. aircraft carriers operated in company at sea simultaneously.

Operation "Bellows": Loss of *Eagle*: First Air Attack

Convoy WS.21.S. entered the Strait of Gibraltar in dense fog in the early hours of 10 August. The fog cleared at 0500[139] and by 0800 the convoy was clear of the Strait and making to the eastward at 13½ knots. This was the time appointed for the master of each merchant ship to open an envelope which had been handed to him before leaving the Clyde and which contained a personal message of good cheer signed by the First Lord of the Admiralty. Admiral Syfret subsequently remarked that this act of courtesy and encouragement was very highly appreciated.

Since 5 August various ships of the escort had been sent into Gibraltar to fuel during the nights, the last of them going there while passing through the Strait.[140] These ships rejoined the convoy at intervals during 10 August, the last two destroyers arriving at 1600.[141]

At 0645, 11 August, there commenced an elaborate fuelling programme from Force "R", which was finished by 2030 that evening, when "thanks very largely to the extreme efficiency"[142] shown by R.F.A.s *Dingledale* and *Brown Ranger*, three cruisers and 26 destroyers had completed with fuel. This evolution was helped by the weather, which was calm with a light easterly breeze.

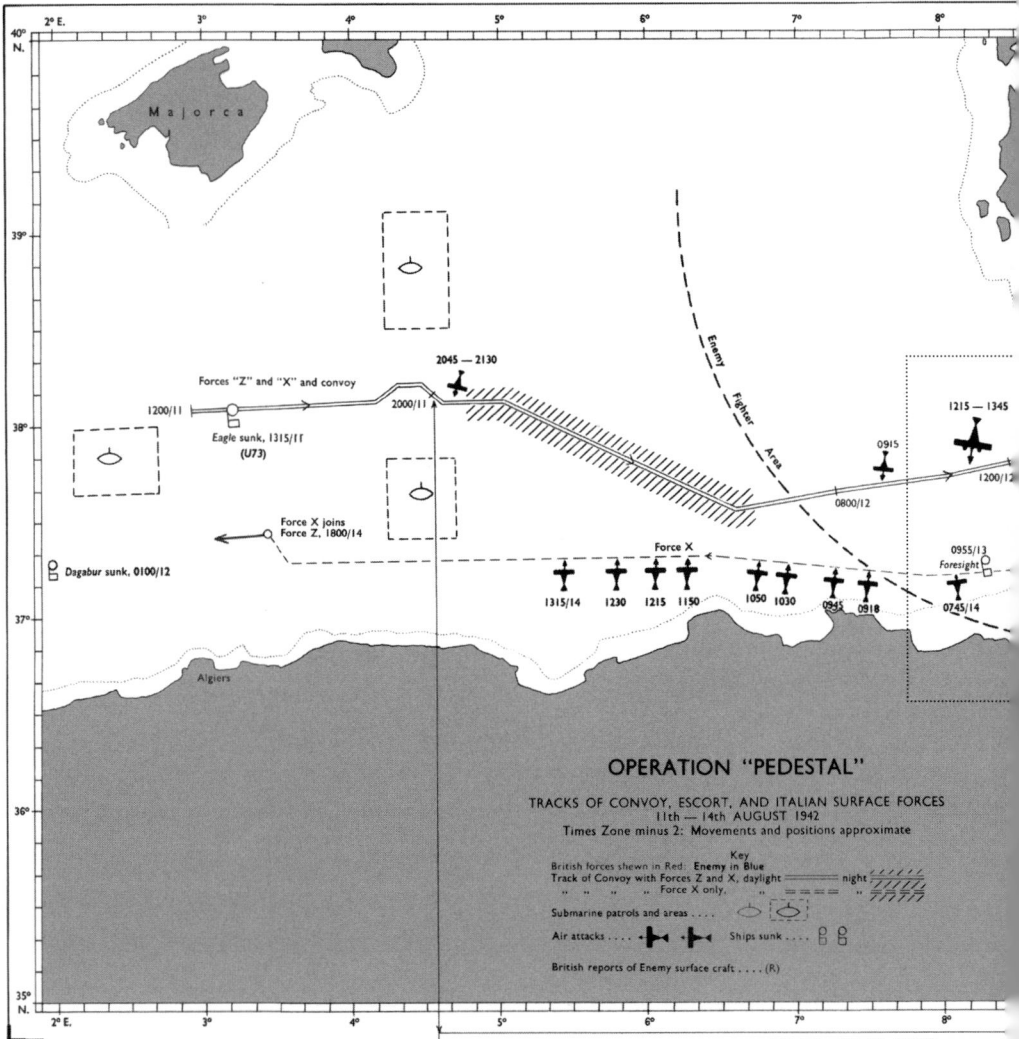

OPERATION "PEDESTAL"

TRACKS OF CONVOY, ESCORT, AND ITALIAN SURFACE FORCES
11th — 14th AUGUST 1942
Times Zone minus 2: Movements and positions approximate

Key
British forces shewn in Red: Enemy in Blue
Track of Convoy with Forces Z and X, daylight ——— night
" " " " " Force X only, ‒ ‒ ‒ "
Submarine patrols and areas . . . .
Air attacks . . . . Ships sunk . . . .
British reports of Enemy surface craft . . . . (R)

Majorca

2045 — 2130

Forces "Z" and "X" and convoy
1200/11   2000/11   1215 — 1345
Eagle sunk, 1315/11   0915
(U73)   1200/12
                        0800/12
Force X joins
Force Z, 1800/14   0955/13
                        Foresight
Dagabur sunk, 0100/12   Force X
                        0745/14
1315/14 1230 1215 1150   1050 1030 0945 0918

Enemy Fighter Area

Algiers

SHIPPING CASUALTIES	FIGHTER PROTECTION	2000, 11th — 1900, 12th AUGUST
		CARRIER BORNE (60) (Casualties 13)
	AIR ATTACK	DAMAGED Foresight (sunk 13th Aug.) Indomitable Deucalion (later sunk while detached)
2000, 11th — 2000, 13th AUGUST	SUBMARINES	
	M.T.B'S.	

PLAN 14

(R) 1854/12
(R) 1918/12
R.V. 1900/12 3rd and 7th Divs.
(R) 2305/12
(R) 2345/11   (R) 0120/12
0130/12
Div.
(R) 2330/12 (R)
Ustica
0806/13 P42 attack
Stromboli
Bolzano Attendazo torpd.
0140/13 (R)   0230/13 (R)   0230/13 (R)
3rd Div.
P42
0051/13   0130/13   P211
C. San Vito
Milazzo
Palermo
Messina
Indomitable Foresight Deucalion damaged
1835 — 1850
(12)
Force Z parts company 1900/12
Nigeria, Cairo, Ohio torpd. 2000/12
(S/m Axum)
Maritimo
Sicily
Cobalto sunk 1616/12
2030
Skerki Bank
sunk
Kenya torpd. 2111/12
(S/m Alagi)
Cairo
Deucalion
Fratelli ocks
Cani Rocks
Catania
Zembri
Tunis
C. Bon
M.T.B.
Sta. Elisa
Pantellaria
Manchester Kelibia Glenorchy
Attacks
Almeria Lykes
Wairangi
P44 P222 P31 P34 P46   Utmost
0810   1015
0800/13   1050   Ohio disabled   1125
Waimarama   Dorset   1200/13
Gulf of   Hammamet
Brisbane Star
1930/13
0925 Linosa
Total sorties 414 (1 Beaufighter, 4 Spitfires lost)
Malta
Monastir
Force X
Force X parts Co. 1600/13
Lampedusa

	1900 — 2130	2130, 12th — 0600, 13th	0600 — 1200, 13th	1200 — 2000, 13th
	6 BEAUFTERS	SHORE-BASED	BEAUFTERS: LR. SPITFIRES	SHORT RANGE SPITFIRES
		NO FIGHTER DIRECTION		

SUNK Empire Hope Clan Ferguson DAMAGED Brisbane Star	SUNK Santa Elisa	SUNK Waimarama DAMAGED Dorset (later sunk) Ohio	
SUNK Cairo DAMAGED Nigeria Ohio			
	SUNK Manchester Glenorchy Almeria Lykes Wairongi DAMAGED Santa Elisa Rochester Castle		

Section detail of Plan 14

1215 — 1345
Indomit Fores Deuca dama
1835
(12)
1200/12
1600/12
Cobalto sunk 1616/12
Cairo
Galita I.
Fratelli Rocks
Deucalion
0955/13 Foresight
Force X 0450/14
0745/14
Tunis

German reconnaissance aircraft started shadowing soon after daylight, and thereafter they or Italian aircraft kept the convoy under continuous observation, despite the efforts of the fighters from the carriers. But the speed and the height of the Ju. 88s made the fighters' task a hopeless one. "It will be a happy day," wrote Admiral Syfret, "when the Fleet is equipped with modern fighter aircraft." There were also a large number of sightings and reports of torpedoes and U-boats in the course of the day, "a proportion of which may well have been actualities."[143] At noon, 11 August, the convoy was about 75 miles south of Majorca, zigzagging on a mean course 090°, and shortly afterwards the *Furious* (Captain Bulteel) hauled out on the port quarter and at 1229 started flying off her Spitfires to Malta from a position 584 miles from the island. After two flights of eight Spitfires had been flown off, the programme was rudely interrupted.

The convoy was in four columns at the time, on the starboard leg of the zigzag, with the heavy ships stationed close round it and a destroyer screen ahead; there were only 13 ships in the screen, however, the rest being engaged in screening the *Furious* or with Force "R" several miles away. Suddenly, without warning, at 1315 the *Eagle* (Captain Mackintosh) – on the starboard quarter of the convoy – was hit by four torpedoes from the German submarine *U.73*, which had dived through the screen and convoy columns undetected. All four torpedoes hit her port side within about 10 seconds; she heeled over sharply to port and sank in eight minutes.[144] The *Laforey* and *Lookout*, which were screening the *Furious*, were at once ordered to her assistance and with the tug *Jaunty* picked up 927 of her ship's company, including Captain Mackintosh.

This was a severe blow. Not only was the Royal Navy deprived of a well-tried and valuable carrier, but Admiral Syfret's force was bereft of 25 per cent of its fighter strength. Four of her aircraft then on patrol were subsequently landed on the other carriers.

After this unfortunate occurrence, the *Furious* completed Operation "Bellows", flying off the remainder of the Spitfires by 1450. In all 38 were flown off; one developed a defect and landed on the *Indomitable*, and the remaining 37 arrived safely at Malta.[145] In the evening the *Furious* was detached to Gibraltar, escorted by a division of spare destroyers which had joined the force during the afternoon. The passage was fortunate, for at 0100/12, the *Wolverine* (Lieut.-Commander Gretton) rammed and sank the Italian submarine *Dagabur* in 37° 18' N., 1° 55' E.

Late in the afternoon of 11 August Admiral Syfret received warning from the Flag Officer, North Atlantic, that aircraft might attack the convoy at dusk, so he extended the destroyers to form an all-round screen. All this time the force was being shadowed by three or more aircraft and our fighters were kept extremely busy. At 2030 radar indicated that the attack was imminent, and not many minutes later reports of enemy aircraft were received from the screen. The last destroyers to oil opportunely rejoined at this time, thus bringing the force to full strength.

The attack began at 2056, a quarter of an hour after sunset. The enemy were 36 German bombers and torpedo aircraft, Junkers 88 and Heinkel 111, most of which attacked the convoy, while a few went on to attack Force "R" to the southward. The Junkers arrived first, diving down from 8,000 ft. to 2,000–3,000 ft. to drop their bombs, and subsequently claiming hits on an aircraft carrier and a merchantman; the Heinkels also claimed to have torpedoed a cruiser, but in fact no ship was touched. On the other hand, the ships shot down three bombers, one of which fell to the tug *Jaunty* (Lieut.-Commander Osburn, R.N.R.), then on her way to Force "R". Admiral Syfret described the barrage put up as "most spectacular." The attack lasted till about 2130; just before the end the *Quentin* confirmed an asdic contact and carried out three depth charge attacks. The British fighters which were up were unable to find the enemy in the failing light. They had to land on after dark, and in doing so some were fired on by our own ships.

No further incidents occurred during the night and the force continued its voyage unmolested. But dawn would find it within 150 miles of Cagliari; the whole day would be spent well within fighter-escorted range of the Sardinian airfields, and air attack on a very heavy scale was certain. There we will leave it for the present, and see how the enemy proposed to deal with the situation.

Enemy Intentions

The first news of the "Pedestal" forces to reach the Italian Naval Staff had come from Ceuta early in the morning of 9 August. Definite confirmation of their having entered the Mediterranean, however, did not reach them till the afternoon of 10 August. The presence of the three carriers together with the battleships indicated a determination to fight the convoy through in the teeth of the heavy air attacks to be expected from Sardinia, and surface attack by their own main naval forces, should they be employed in the Western Mediterranean.

Previous experience enabled them to forecast the plan with considerable accuracy. They expected the heavy ships and carriers to turn to the westward on reaching the Sicilian Narrows, leaving a strong force of cruisers and destroyers to see the convoy through the remainder of the passage. They estimated that Cape Bon would be passed late in the afternoon of 12 August and Pantellaria during hours of darkness. There was no indication as yet that a complementary convoy from the eastern Mediterranean was contemplated, as in June.

Their plan followed much the same lines as that employed against "Halberd". Special air reconnaissance in the Western Mediterranean was arranged in collaboration with the German Air Force for 11 and 12 August. Submarines, of which there were available 18 Italian and two German, were disposed in five areas at intervals along the estimated convoy track from south of the Balearics to just west of Malta.[146] Twenty-three motor torpedo boats (five of them German) were stationed off Cape Bon, Pantellaria and south of Marittimo; and a destroyer was detailed to augment the minefields in the Narrows during the night of 12 August.

As regards surface forces, an acute oil fuel shortage prohibited the use of their battleships. On the assumption that the convoy would be accompanied through the Sicilian narrows by stronger forces than in June, but without battleships, it was arranged that the 3rd division – the 8-inch cruisers *Gorizia*, *Bolzano* and *Trieste* – and the 7th division – the 6-inch cruisers *Savoia*, *Montecuccoli* and *Attendolo* – with 11 destroyers should rendezvous about 100 miles north of Marittimo in the evening of 12 August, and intercept the convoy in the region of Pantellaria in the morning of 13 August; but this was subject to effective fighter protection being available in view of the increased number of aircraft in Malta. Any convoy from Egypt was to be dealt with by the 8th division (three 6-inch cruisers), based at Navarino. Some modifications were made to these plans during 12 August, especially as a result of a report which came in that morning of Admiral Harwood's dummy convoy.

So much for the naval part of the Axis plan. But their great effort was to come from the air. For this purpose they had concentrated about six hundred aircraft, bombers and fighters, on the Sardinian and Sicilian airfields of which about 200[147] were German, specially reinforced for the occasion from Crete and North Africa. The main attacks, which were carefully co-ordinated, were naturally planned for 12 August, when the convoy would be passing to the southward of Sardinia and fighter protection could be given to the bombers all day.

Air Attacks

To return to the British forces: at first light[148], 12 August, radar reports of enemy shadowing aircraft began to come in and all ships went to the first degree of readiness for H.A. and L.A. guns. Twelve fighters were flown off at 0610, and this number was maintained in the air throughout the day, being reinforced when necessary. From then onwards "there were few moments" – to quote Admiral Syfret – "when neither aircraft, submarines, torpedoes nor asdic contacts were being reported."

The first air attack of the day took place at about 0915. Some twenty or more Ju. 88s, approaching out of the sun ahead, were intercepted by fighters 25 miles off. Only a dozen got through to the convoy, making high-level or shallow dive-bombing attacks individually without result. Eight Germans were believed to be shot down by fighters, who had also shot down three shadowers before the attack, and two by the ships' guns. All this time, too, there were submarine alarms. Destroyers dropped depth charges on obtaining asdic contacts and probably foiled attempts during the air attack and again at about 1130.

But the enemy's great effort from the Sardinian airfields came at midday, 12 August. It was to be a combined attack by some 70 aircraft, heavily escorted by fighters, carried out in stages and employing new methods. First, ten Italian torpedo-bombers were each to drop a "motobomba FF" (apparently a circling torpedo or mine, used for the first time in this attack) a few hundred yards ahead of the British force, while eight fighter-bombers made dive-bombing and machine-gun attacks; and the object at this stage was to dislocate the formation of the force and to draw anti-aircraft fire, making the ships more vulnerable to a torpedo attack, which was to follow in five minutes, though the Italians hoped also that the "motobomba" would do underwater damage – indeed, they claimed mistakenly to have sunk a merchant ship. The torpedo aircraft, 42 all told, were to attack in two groups, one on either bow of the convoy. The next stage was a shallow dive-bombing attack by German aircraft, after which two Reggiane 2001 fighters, each with a single heavy armour-piercing bomb, were to dive-bomb one of the aircraft carriers, whilst yet another new form of attack was to be employed against the other carrier, but defects in the weapon prevented this last attack from taking place.[149]

The enemy's plan was carried out in the main, though the normal torpedo attack was made half an hour instead of five minutes after the special mines had been dropped. British fighters met the minelaying aircraft, and shot down one of them as they approached; the other nine dropped their mines at 1215 in the path of the force, which turned at right-angles to avoid the danger, and heard the mines exploding harmlessly some minutes later. Only three of the fighter-bombers at this stage of the attack appear to have reached as far as the screen, but the *Lightning* (Commander Walters) had a narrow escape from their bombs. The torpedo aircraft arrived at 1245, likewise reduced from their original strength to 25 or 30, some being destroyed and others driven off by the British fighters. They attacked the convoy from the port bow, port beam, and starboard quarter, but dropped their torpedoes well outside the screen, 8,000 yards from the merchant ships they had been ordered to make their targets; the force turned 45° to port and back to starboard to avoid the attack, and the *Rodney* (Captain Rivett-Carnac), on the port quarter of the convoy, joined her 16-inch guns to the barrage fire with which the enemy were received. In the next stage, the German bombing attack, the enemy scored their one success. These aircraft, too, were intercepted on their way in; but about 12 out of perhaps 20 persevered, and, crossing the convoy from starboard to port, they dived to 3,000 ft. and damaged the *Deucalion*, leading the port wing column, while bombs fell close to several other ships. This was at 1318. Finally, at 1345, the two Reggiane fighters approached the *Victorious* (Captain Bovell), flagship of Rear-Admiral Lyster, "as if to land on." They looked like Hurricanes, and the ship was engaged in landing on fighters of her own; they dropped their bombs, one of which hit the flight deck amidships, fortunately breaking up without exploding; they then made off out of range before the *Victorious* could open fire. Altogether, nine enemy aircraft were credited to fighters in these attacks, and two to ships' fire.

The *Deucalion*, unable to keep up with the convoy, was ordered to follow the inshore route along the Tunisian coast accompanied by the *Bramham* (Lieutenant Baines). Two bombers found these ships late in the afternoon, but their bombs missed. At 1940, however, near the Cani Rocks, two torpedo aircraft attacked; and a torpedo hitting the *Deucalion*, she caught fire and eventually blew up.

The convoy, passing some 20 miles north of Galita Island, spent the afternoon avoiding submarines, which were known to be concentrated in these waters. There were "innumerable reports" of sightings and asdic contacts, said Vice-Admiral Syfret, and at least two submarines proved dangerous. At 1616 the *Pathfinder* (Commander Gibbs) and *Zetland* (Lieutenant Wilkinson) attacked one on the port bow, and hunted her till the convoy was out of her reach. The *Ithuriel* (Lieut.-Commander Maitland-Makgill-Crichton) stationed on the quarter, then attacked, brought the enemy to the surface, and finally rammed her; she proved to be the Italian submarine *Cobalto*. Meanwhile the *Tartar*, on the starboard quarter, saw six torpedoes[150] fired at close range at 1640, and the next ship in the screen, the *Lookout* (Commander Brown), sighted a periscope; together they attacked the submarine, continuing until she was no longer dangerous, but without gaining definite evidence of success. The Vice-Admiral commended "the constant anti-submarine vigilance" shown by the destroyers throughout the operation. "It is true," he wrote, "that the submarine which sank H.M.S. *Eagle* was undetected, but I am very sure that their watchfulness foiled many another attack." And as an illustration of the value of their work he remarked that the convoy made forty-eight emergency turns during 10–12 August in consequence of warnings of submarines given by the screen.

At 1750, on her way to rejoin after sinking the *Cobalto*, the *Ithuriel* was unsuccessfully attacked by a few dive-bombers when a dozen miles astern of the convoy. This attack may have been made as a last attempt by the air forces in Sardinia or by part of the force from Sicily, which was then gathering to attack the convoy and with which the British fighters were already in touch. This force numbered nearly 100 aircraft – Ju. 87 and Ju. 88 bombers and S.79 torpedo aircraft, with a strong escort of fighters.[151] The enemy arrived at 1835, the bombers attacking both from ahead and astern (the direction of the sun), while the torpedo aircraft came from ahead to attack on the starboard bow and beam of the convoy. Vice-Admiral Syfret called their timing excellent, the result of careful position-taking as they approached the convoy; many aircraft must have waited some 25 miles away for nearly an hour before the moment came to fly in. As at midday, the Savoias dropped their torpedoes about 3,000 yards outside the screen, and once again the convoy was turned away to avoid them; but this time the destroyer *Foresight* (Lieut.-Commander Fell) was hit and disabled. The bombers made their chief effort against the *Indomitable* (Captain Troubridge), which was astern of the *Rodney* on the port quarter of the convoy. Four Ju. 88s and eight Ju. 87s, "appearing suddenly from up sun out of the smoky blue sky," said Captain Troubridge, dived steeply on the *Indomitable* from astern, some of the Ju. 87s coming down to 1,000 ft.; the carrier received three hits, her flight deck was put out of action, and her fighters had to return to the *Victorious*. Captain Frend of the *Phoebe*, astern of the *Indomitable*, said that his attention was mainly directed to the Savoias on the starboard bow, which appeared to be working aft, when the Junkers came down from 9,000 ft. almost overhead out of the shell-bursts to attack the carrier he was attending. The *Rodney* also had a narrow escape from a bomber that attacked her from ahead a few minutes before the attack on the *Indomitable*. The ships shot down one enemy aircraft; and the twenty or so Hurricanes, Martlets and Fulmars in the air destroyed seven more, though the enemy's fighters were probably twice as numerous as the British.

Altogether, the 60 British fighters available since the loss of the *Eagle* claimed 39 enemy aircraft of all sorts, at a cost of 13 British aircraft, whilst on 11 and 12 August the ships shot down nine of the enemy.[152]

The *Tartar* (Commander St. J. Tyrwhitt) took the damaged *Foresight* in tow and proceeded westward for Gibraltar; but next day, as they were persistently shadowed by enemy aircraft and submarines were about, it was decided to sink the cripple, lest both ships should be lost, and the *Tartar* torpedoed her a few miles from Galita Island.

This last air attack took place about 20 miles west of the Skerki Channel; and at 1900, when it was clearly over, Admiral Syfret turned away with Force "Z" and proceeded to the westward, leaving Rear-Admiral Burrough with Force "X" to take the convoy on.

S/M Attack in Narrows: *Nigeria, Cairo, Kenya, Ohio* Torpedoed: Dusk Air Attack

So far, apart from the loss of the *Eagle*, things had gone well. The massed air attacks south of Sardinia had succeeded in damaging only the *Indomitable* and *Foresight*, and the 14 merchant ships, save for the *Deucalion*, were still intact. But an hour after parting from Force "Z" its previous good fortune deserted the convoy. Thrown into disorder by submarine and air attacks, which inflicted serious damage and losses on both convoy and escorts, the straggling ships offered an easy prey later in the night for the motor torpedo boats awaiting them south of Cape Bon. The trouble started with a remarkably effective submarine attack. The convoy was just changing its formation from four into two columns at the entrance to Skerki Channel when at 1956 the *Nigeria* (Captain Paton) and *Cairo* (Captain Hardy) – leading the columns – and the tanker *Ohio* were all damaged by under-water explosions practically simultaneously – whether from mines or torpedoes was not known. Actually, the Italian submarine *Axum* fired four torpedoes, which were responsible for the damage. The *Nigeria* turned back for Gibraltar, escorted by two destroyers (afterwards joined by a third), and Rear-Admiral Burrough shifted his flag to the *Ashanti* (Captain Onslow). The *Cairo*, with her stern blown off, had to be sunk. The *Ohio* struggled on. As all three ships had been damaged on the port side, the convoy, then led by the *Kenya* (Captain Russell) and *Manchester* (Captain Drew), altered course to the southward to avoid the danger, and in the process became "scrummed up" or "a heterogeneous mass" – as naval liaison officers in the merchant ships afterwards described it. Most of the ten destroyers[153] were standing by the damaged ships, and two of the cruisers had gone; most unfortunate of all, these two cruisers were the only ships fitted for fighter direction. The convoy was, moreover, deprived of the leadership of Admiral Burrough, while he was shifting his flag.

In these conditions, while trying to form the two columns previously ordered, the convoy was attacked from the air at 2030, half an hour after its earlier misfortune. Six Beaufighters from Malta were patrolling overhead, but – bereft of fighter direction and, incidentally, frequently fired on by our own ships – they were unable to see much in the growing dusk[154] and soon withdrew to Malta.[155] The enemy had an easy task. About 20 German aircraft, Ju. 88s, made dive-bombing and torpedo attacks, hitting the *Empire Hope* with a bomb and the *Clan Ferguson* and *Brisbane Star* with torpedoes. The first of these ships had to be sunk (by the *Penn*, which rescued her survivors); the second blew up – it was thought with the loss of all hands, but some reached the Tunisian coast; the last eventually arrived at Malta. The *Ashanti*, which with the *Penn* had been laying a smoke-screen between the convoy and the light western horizon to prevent the ships being silhouetted, was very narrowly missed by a torpedo. Soon after this attack, at 2111, the *Kenya* was torpedoed by the Italian submarine *Alagi*, which fired four torpedoes at her. She fortunately saw the enemy in time to avoid all of them but one, which hit her on the forefoot; her speed was reduced to 25 knots, but she was able to stay with the convoy.

The situation was then as follows. The *Kenya* and *Manchester*, with two merchant ships and with the minesweeping destroyers *Intrepid*, *Icarus* and *Fury* sweeping ahead, had passed the Skerki Channel and were steering to pass inshore of Zembra Island on the way to Cape Bon. The *Ashanti*, with Admiral Burrough on board, was fast overhauling this main body. The destroyers *Pathfinder*, *Penn* and *Ledbury* were rounding up the remaining nine merchant ships, which, having separated during the air attack, were following along the route spread out over several miles to the north-westward. The *Deucalion* having sunk, the *Bramham* was returning from the vicinity of the Cani Rocks, and the *Nigeria* with the other three destroyers was well to the westward on her way to Gibraltar.

On learning of the fate of the *Nigeria* and *Cairo*, Admiral Syfret had detached the *Charybdis*, *Eskimo* and *Somali* to reinforce Admiral Burrough, but it would take them several hours to catch up with the convoy. "By this time," wrote Admiral Burrough, "the situation was becoming rather critical, as there was still a possibility of the Italian surface forces coming south to attack the convoy at dawn." Four cruisers and six destroyers steering to the southward had in fact been reported by Malta reconnaissance aircraft at 1922, in a position some 90 miles north of Marittimo.

M.T.B. Attacks: Loss of *Manchester* and 4 M.S.

The main body of the convoy, led by Admiral Burrough in the *Ashanti*, passed Cape Bon at midnight, 12/13 August. Forty minutes later E-boats were detected to port, and soon afterwards to starboard, by Type 285 radar. "They used smoke cover and were extremely difficult to engage";[156] and they took a heavy toll in a series of attacks that lasted until the convoy was well past Kelibia and on the course for Malta. Their first victim was the *Manchester*, torpedoed by two Italian E-boats at 0120/13, a few miles short of Kelibia. The *Pathfinder* (Commander Gibbs), detached to stand by her, went alongside twenty minutes later and took off about 150 of her ship's company, then rejoined Admiral Burrough in accordance with his orders. Subsequently, Captain Drew decided that the *Manchester* must be abandoned and scuttled.[157] This was done and she sank at 0500; most of the crew, including the captain, reached the shore and were interned by the French; but some were picked up later by destroyers sent to her assistance.

The other ships hit were all stragglers – the *Glenorchy*,[158] *Wairangi*, *Almeria Lykes*, *Rochester Castle* and *Santa Elisa*; they were attacked between 0215 and 0500 to the south-eastward of Kelibia, whilst taking a short cut to overhaul the main body. The *Wairangi* and *Almeria Lykes* were abandoned in a sinking condition, but the *Rochester Castle* survived and, "merrily doing 13 knots", she caught up the main body about 0530, two hours after being torpedoed. The *Santa Elisa*, the last to be torpedoed (about 0500), was also abandoned, her crew being rescued by the *Penn* and *Bramham*, who arrived on the scene with the *Port Chalmers*; at early dawn she was bombed by a lone Ju. 88 and sank in five minutes. All this damage was the work of about a dozen E-boats, and was inflicted without loss to themselves.

Meanwhile, the *Charybdis* (Captain Voelcker), *Somali* (Commander

Currey) and *Eskimo* (Commander le Geyt) had joined Admiral Burrough's flag at 0330, just in time to take part in another running fight with several E-boats. It was in the course of this attack that the *Rochester Castle* was hit; the *Ashanti* was again narrowly missed.

At dawn[159], 13 August, the situation was as follows. In company with Admiral Burrough in the *Ashanti* were H.M. ships *Charybdis, Kenya, Intrepid, Icarus, Fury, Pathfinder, Somali* and *Eskimo* and M.T. ships *Rochester Castle, Waimarama* and *Melbourne Star*. As it became lighter the *Ledbury*, with the *Ohio* in company, was seen about five miles astern, overtaking the convoy rapidly. Some ten miles away to the north-west the *Port Chalmers* with the *Penn* and *Bramham* was in sight; and the *Santa Elisa* could be seen stopped and on fire. The *Dorset* was following alone. Lastly, the *Brisbane Star*, torpedoed the evening before, was hugging the Tunisian coast independently, intending to steer for Malta at nightfall. From signals received during the night the danger of attack by heavy Italian surface forces appeared to have abated. This must have been a relief to Admiral Burrough, for with his reduced escort and scattered charges a resolute attack ought to have had very serious consequences. It will therefore be of interest at this stage to see what the enemy cruisers had been about.

Movements of Italian Cruisers: *Bolzano* and *Attendolo* Torpedoed

The first move of the Italian cruisers to carry out their part in the plan had been the departure of the 7th Division from Cagliari in the evening of the 11 August. As it chanced they were sighted leaving harbour by Beaufighters returning from attacks on neighbouring airfields, and subsequently shadowed while steering easterly in the Tyrrhenian Sea by a Wellington till 0130/12, when, having dropped its bombs without effect, it returned to Malta. That forenoon the *Gorizia* and *Bolzano* left Messina and joined the 7th Division and *Trieste*, which had come from the north, at 1900/12, at the rendezvous north of Marittimo, setting course to the southward. As already mentioned, they were located soon after this and reported at 1922. When just north of Cape San Vito, orders were received for the 7th Division to proceed to Naples and the 3rd Division to Messina and course was altered to the eastward accordingly.

The reason given in the Italian Official Naval History for this change of plan is that a report of Admiral Vian's force as four cruisers and ten destroyers in the eastern Mediterranean with the diversionary convoy was received from a German submarine, and it was decided that the 8-in. cruisers must reinforce the 6-in. cruisers at Navarino to counter this force. It will be remembered, too, that the attack on "Pedestal" off Pantellaria was subject to air protection for the cruisers being available, and actually there was a shortage of fighters to accompany the bombers for the attacks planned for next day. According to one version, the matter was referred to Mussolini himself, who gave precedence to the claims of the aircraft. Probably both considerations had their effect on the Naval Staff in coming to the decision; in any case, it was a welcome one for the British, to whom the cruiser force had become a keen anxiety.

The receipt in Malta of the sighting report at 1922/12, had caused no perturbation. In the words of Vice-Admiral Sir Ralph Leatham, "all appeared to be going well with the convoy, and I felt that Force 'X' would be more than a match for the Italian cruiser force ..." But before long the picture changed. Reports of the dusk air attack came in, followed by news of the damage to the *Nigeria*, *Cairo* and *Kenya*, and it became clear that a dawn attack by the Italian cruisers when the convoy was scattered, with its much reduced escort, might well be disastrous. The shadowing aircraft, therefore, was ordered in plain language to illuminate and attack, which it did without causing damage at 0140 on 13 August, soon after the cruisers had turned to the eastward. Similar orders were signalled to relief shadowers including an order to report the position for the benefit of imaginary Liberator bombers, lest the Italians should change their minds and turn back.[160]

But they held their easterly course – and ran into trouble. Submarine *P.42* (Lieutenant Mars), which had moved out from her inshore station off Cape Milazzo after being discovered and heavily attacked on 10 August, sighted them a few miles south-westward of Stromboli, steaming about 25 knots. At 0806 she fired her four torpedoes, claiming two hits; she was then attacked by destroyers for more than eight hours, and counted 105 depth charges. She had hit the *Bolzano*, which went north for repairs, and the *Muzio Attendolo*[161] which reached Messina with her bows blown off. The *Gorizia* returned to Messina later in the day and the other cruisers put in to Naples.

Air Attacks on Force "X" and Convoy: Further Damage

At 0800 on 13 August, just as Lieutenant Mars was having his eminently satisfactory encounter with the Italian cruisers, some two hundred miles to the south-westward Admiral Burrough and the convoy were facing up to the first air attack of the day. About half an hour previously the Rear-Admiral had sent back the *Eskimo* and *Somali* to stand by the *Manchester*[162], of whose sinking he was unaware; he then had left with him the *Kenya* and *Charybdis* and five destroyers, with the merchant ships *Rochester Castle*, *Waimarama*, *Melbourne Star* and *Ohio* formed in line ahead, and the *Port Chalmers* and *Dorset* about to rejoin.

The events of the night had delayed the passage, and the force was only a little over 30 miles S.S.E. of Pantellaria, barely within range of the Malta long-range fighters; but the Beaufighters and Spitfires played up magnificently in the fighting which ensued – the latter patrolling above 170 miles from the island[163] – and, despite the serious handicap of lacking fighter direction, inflicted considerable losses on the enemy aircraft, though at times outnumbered by enemy fighters, as was admitted by the Italians.

The attack came in at 0810, when about twelve Ju. 88s made a shallow diving attack, coming down from about 6,000 to 2,000 ft. to drop their bombs. Two dived on the *Waimarama*, making several hits, and she blew up immediately, one of the bombers being destroyed in the explosion. Her next astern, the *Melbourne Star*, could not avoid passing through the flames which immediately blazed up; this she did at full speed and escaped unscathed. The *Ledbury* (Lieutenant-Commander Hill) was ordered to pick up survivors, though it seemed unlikely that there could be any. Skilfully handled, she rescued no fewer than 45 men from the water which, in the words of Admiral Burrough, "must have entailed great gallantry on the part of all concerned as the sea for some distance round was a blazing inferno".[164]

Soon after this attack the *Port Chalmers* and *Dorset* joined up and the convoy was then formed in two columns. The next attack came at 0925. It was carried out by Stuka dive-bombers and described by Admiral Burrough as "of a most determined nature." Diving to 1,500 or 1,000 ft., they concentrated on the *Ohio*, the last ship but one in the starboard column, which received several near misses. One Stuka failed to pull out of his dive and, damaged by the *Ohio*'s guns and those of the *Ashanti*, actually hit the side of the ship; but its bombs fell short and did little damage. The *Ohio*'s main steering gear was put out of action, however. The *Kenya*, leading the port column, was "near-missed." The Malta fighters brought down a bomber in this attack, but lost a Spitfire, possibly by the ships' gunfire.

At 1017, and again at 1050, further dive-bombing attacks were made, accompanied by Italian aircraft which dropped parachute mines or circling torpedoes ahead and on the flanks of the convoy. In the latter attack, carried out by about 20 bombers (mostly Ju. 88s, with a few Ju. 87s), the *Ohio* suffered again from four or five near misses and her engines were disabled. At the same time the *Rochester Castle* in the other column was near-missed and set on fire but continued with the convoy; and the *Dorset* astern of her was hit and brought to a standstill.

The convoy went on, leaving the *Penn* and *Bramham* with the cripples. They were joined by the *Ledbury*, overtaking with the *Waimarama*'s survivors on board, but shortly afterwards, as the result of a signal from the Vice-Admiral, Malta, she proceeded to look for the *Manchester*[165], believed to be moving south along the Tunisian coast.

At 1125 the main body suffered its last air attack. This was a torpedo attack by five S.79s, accompanied by more parachute mine dropping by other aircraft. The torpedoes were dropped at long range and no tracks were observed; but the *Port Chalmers*, which so far had "experienced extraordinary good fortune in just missing the bombs time after time,"[166] had a narrow escape, a torpedo being caught by her paravane.[167]

During these attacks the Beaufighters and Spitfires had been seen to shoot down at least four enemy aircraft in the distance; and at about 1240 the convoy came within range of the short-range Spitfires, which, flying up to 70 or 80 miles from their base, provided "such excellent protection"[168] that no further attacks against it developed, though large formations were frequently detected coming in, only to be dispersed and driven off.

At 1430/13, the Malta escort force – four minesweepers and seven motor launches under Commander Jerome – joined the convoy. He had swept the approach channel in the morning, and then prepared to take over the three merchant vessels remaining in company, sending on the *Rye* and two motor launches to assist the disabled tanker *Ohio*, whose cargo of 12,000 tons of oil was "vital to Malta".[169] After an exchange of signals with Commander Jerome, Admiral Burrough decided to withdraw to the westward and with his two cruisers and five remaining destroyers parted company at 1600, signalling a rendezvous at which the *Penn*, *Bramham* and *Ledbury* were to rejoin him at 2030 that evening.[170]

Arrival at Malta

After the departure of Force "X", the *Port Chalmers*, *Melbourne Star* and *Rochester Castle* – the last ship "lying very low in the water" – stood on with Commander Jerome, arriving in Grand Harbour two hours or so later, 13 August.

There were still the *Dorset*, *Ohio* and *Brisbane Star*. But the *Dorset* was lost the same evening. After being disabled in the morning, she and the *Ohio* had been lying helpless, with the *Penn* and *Bramham* standing by, the destroyers having found them unmanageable in tow. When the *Rye* arrived at 1730, she and the *Penn* got the *Ohio* in tow, while the *Bramham* remained with the *Dorset*. Then German bombers came again, and the ships were attacked repeatedly till dark; both merchantmen were hit at about 1900 and the *Dorset* sank. Strenuous efforts to tow the *Ohio* throughout the night produced little result.

At daylight, 14 August, the *Ledbury* arrived, after a fruitless search in the Gulf of Hammamet for the *Manchester*. She had, however, shot down two Italian torpedo bombers which had attacked her the previous afternoon.[171] Attempts to tow the *Ohio* by the three destroyers and the *Rye*, later directed by Commander Jerome who arrived in the *Speedy*, with two motor launches, continued throughout the forenoon. At 1045 enemy aircraft made their last attack, near-missing the *Ledbury* and causing the tow to part, while protecting Spitfires shot down a bomber and one of the many fighters escorting them. Once again the tow was passed. The slow procession went on, with the *Ohio* becoming ever more unwieldy. At last the endeavours of those tired men were rewarded; in the morning of 15 August the "vital" tanker reached Malta.

"Even though the *Ledbury* was leading her," wrote Admiral Leatham, "the passage of *Ohio* through Tunisian waters at high speed without a compass, with extensive damage to the ship and in hand steering, was a remarkable feat of seamanship and tenacity on the part of Captain Mason and his officers and crew .... The towage of this unwieldy ship for a distance of nearly 100 miles from a position in sight of an Italian island and within easy range of his aerodromes was a feat of seamanship, courage and endurance of the highest order ... In particular, the highest praise is due to the Master of the *Ohio*[172] for his courageous handling of the ship until she was immobilised, the Captain of H.M.S. *Penn*, who bore the responsibility during the first desperate day and night, and to Commander M/S, who brought her safely to port through many difficulties."[173]

Meanwhile the *Brisbane Star* had arrived at Malta the day before. After being torpedoed in the dusk air attack on 12 August, she could not make more than 10 knots. Rather than saddle Force "X" with a lame duck, Captain Riley decided to leave the convoy and hug the Tunisian coast till off Monastir, striking across to Malta during the night of 13/14 August. 13 August was spent fencing with French signal stations and French boarding officers; the latter he handled so firmly and tactfully that they (somewhat reluctantly) allowed the ship to proceed, and were helpful in landing a seriously wounded man for him at Susa. The *Brisbane Star* shaped course for Malta at dusk, 13 August; soon after daylight, 14 August, she was twice attacked by single aircraft, one of which was damaged by her gunfire and the other shot down by a Beaufighter. She reached harbour without further incident at 1530 that afternoon.

Return Passage of Forces to Gibraltar

After leaving the convoy off Malta, Rear-Admiral Burrough with his depleted Force "X" steered to pass 12 miles south of Linosa, and thence for position "R", about seven miles south of Kelibia. Led by the *Intrepid* – the only destroyer with a T.S.D. sweep remaining, the others having parted theirs on the outward passage – the force passed through position "R" at 0012, 14 August. A few minutes later an E-boat was sighted to seaward; the *Kenya* opened fire very promptly and, it was thought, blew her up.[174]

At 0450, near the Fratelli Rocks, the Italian submarine *Granito* fired five torpedoes at the *Ashanti* from the surface, and was nearly rammed by the *Kenya*, next astern of the flagship.

By daylight Force "X" had reached a position S.S.E. of Galita, and soon afterwards the inevitable shadowers appeared, heralding air attacks that began at 0730 and continued till 1315. German bombers started the business with three attacks by a few Ju. 88s, followed by a severe attack by 30 aircraft – Ju. 88 and Ju. 87 – between 1030 and 1050. An hour later, 15 Savoia high-level bombers attacked, and from then until 1315 the force was vexed by torpedo-carrying Savoias, about 20 aircraft attacking in ones and twos, while others flying very low dropped mines ahead. Several ships were nearly hit in these attacks, both by bombs and torpedoes, but none was seriously damaged. Three aircraft were shot down.

After this, Force "X" was left alone. At 1530 a Catalina flying-boat made contact as A/S escort, and at 1800 Force "X" joined Vice-Admiral Syfret's flag in position 37° 29' N., 3° 25' E.

The Vice-Admiral, after parting company with the convoy in the evening of 12 August, had continued to the westward, apparently unobserved by the enemy, till 2300/13, when, having detached the damaged *Indomitable* with the *Rodney* and five destroyers to Gibraltar, he altered course to the eastward and cruised to the northward of Algiers in order to be in a position to support

Force "X" should that prove necessary. After effecting their junction, the two forces headed for Gibraltar, arriving 1800/15.

Most of the remainder of Force "X", proceeding independently, had already arrived. The *Nigeria*, down about 11 ft. by the head, with the *Derwent*, *Bicester*, *Wilton* and latterly the *Tartar* (after sinking the *Foresight)* had been able to steam from 14 to 16 knots and reached harbour at 0010/15. She was fortunate in experiencing calm weather the whole way, and apart from an ineffective attack by three torpedo bombers on 13 August and a couple of submarine alarms, the passage was uneventful. Some hours later the *Eskimo* and *Somali* arrived. After leaving Force "X" in the morning of 13 August to succour the *Manchester*, they fell in with the sinking *Almeria Lykes* and *Wairangi*, whose survivors they picked up from their boats. During the forenoon they recovered about 150 of the *Manchester*'s survivors from Carley floats. They were only about half a mile from the coast and were able to see the melancholy spectacle of several hundreds of her ship's company, who had reached the shore, being marched away for internment. They then shaped course for Gibraltar in accordance with their orders, and except for an attack by a single Ju. 88 which narrowly missed the *Somali*, their passage was without incident.

Force "R" (the fuelling force), which had remained cruising in the western basin till it was certain none of Force "X"'s destroyers would require oil arrived back at Gibraltar on 16 August; and the *Penn*, *Ledbury* and *Bramham*, which had put in to Malta after their fine efforts on the *Ohio*'s behalf, reached Gibraltar safely on 21 August.

Conclusion

Such was Operation "Pedestal". Five arrivals out of a convoy of fourteen ships with a powerful escort is not a high score, especially at the cost to the escort of an aircraft carrier, a cruiser, an anti-aircraft ship, and a destroyer lost, besides a carrier and two cruisers damaged. But they had to meet attacks by some 240 bombers and 90 torpedo aircraft, all in the space of three days, with the enemy supported by fighters in much greater strength than those which the carriers and Malta could provide; magnificent as the naval and Royal Air Force fighters were, the scales were too heavily weighted. The convoy had also to contend with 20 submarines which had the aid of air reconnaissance, and with minefields and E-boats during the passage at night along the Tunisian coast. Despite the losses, 15,000 tons of fuel and 32,000 tons of general cargo were delivered to Malta.

The spirit in which the operation was carried out appears in Vice-Admiral Syfret's report.

"Tribute has been paid to the personnel of His Majesty's ships; but both officers and men will desire to give first place to the conduct, courage and determination of the masters, officers and men of the merchant ships. The steadfast manner in which these ships pressed on their way to Malta through all attacks, answering every manoeuvring order like a well-trained fleet unit, was a most inspiring sight. Many of these fine men and their ships were lost. But the memory of their conduct will remain an inspiration to all who were privileged to sail with them."

Despatches: Supplement to *The London Gazette*, Published by Authority
The following Despatch was submitted to the Lords Commissioners of the Admiralty on 25 August, 1942 by Vice-Admiral E. N. Syfret, C.B., Flag Officer Commanding, Force F.

General Remarks
Planning and Assembly
It was a great advantage that the planning could be done at the Admiralty for the following reasons:
 a) Early decisions could be obtained and questions answered, thus saving signals.
 b) Communications were better and there was less chance of loss of security.
 c) General views on policy could be obtained.
 d) Experts in all branches were readily available.
 e) The advice and help of the Naval Staff was always at hand.

Assembling and sailing of ships at Scapa Flow not only enabled me to discuss the operation with the majority of Commanding Officers of ships taking part, but also gave many advantages from the security point of view. The use of a telephone, fitted with a scrambler, was invaluable as it enabled many points of detail to be cleared up, up to the moment of sailing. I am sure that the decision to bring *Nelson* and *Rodney* from Freetown to Scapa was fully justified.

It was some disadvantage from the cooperation point of view that *Indomitable* and *Eagle* and their attendant ships should have had to start from Freetown and Gibraltar respectively; from the security point of view, however, this was probably advantageous.

The work of the aircraft carriers (H.M.S. *Indomitable*, Captain T. H. Troubridge, and H.M.S. *Victorious*, Captain H. C. Bovell) under the command of Rear-Admiral Lyster, was excellently performed, while that of their fighters was magnificent; flying at great heights, constantly chasing the faster Ju. 88s, warning the fleet of approaching formations, breaking up the latter, and in the later stages doing their work in the face of superior enemy forces, they were grand.

Comment and Reflections

Strategical Conditions

The convoys to Malta in 1941 and 1942 had to face a heavier scale of attack under conditions more favourable to the enemy than was ever before developed in history. The geographical position of Malta – roughly a thousand miles alike from Alexandria and Gibraltar, and within 50 miles of Sicily – conferred on the enemy immeasurable advantage. Whether the convoy came from the east or from the west, it had to pass through waters where the enemy held all the cards.

To recapitulate, the convoys were liable to attack by submarines (of which in 1942 the enemy were always able to dispose at least 20 against them) throughout the length of their routes, which for geographical and other reasons allowed of little variation. In any case, air reconnaissance invariably gave the enemy early intelligence of their movements. The efforts of the U-boats were reinforced by M.T.B.s, based in Crete and Pantellaria, which on more than one occasion were used with considerable effect. The powerful Italian fleet, with its bases situated within a few hundred miles of the convoy routes, was a constant menace. Lack of sea-room and the danger of mines in the Sicilian Narrows made it imprudent for capital ships to accompany the convoys from Gibraltar beyond Skerki Bank, and for the last 250 miles of the passage they had to rely on relatively weak forces of cruisers and destroyers for protection. In the eastern Mediterranean there were no British capital ships during the critical first nine months of 1942. Though no Italian heavy ship ever actually got within sight of a convoy, on two occasions its intervention was sufficient to render abortive operations to replenish Malta from the east, and it was the existence of this fleet "in being" which put an end to such attempts after the failure of operation "Vigorous" in June 1942.

But the chief danger came from the air. Convoys from Gibraltar had to spend the last 400 miles (26 hours at 15 knots) of their passage within 150 miles of the Sardinian and Sicilian airfields, exposed to air attack of every variety covered by enemy shore-based fighters. Convoys from Alexandria had to pass through the 300-mile stretch known as "Bomb Alley" between Cyrenaica[175] and Crete, only 180 miles apart, a few hours after putting to sea, and again had to face heavy attack from Tripoli and Sicily as they neared Malta. The fighters to counter these air attacks either had to accompany the convoys in carriers or to come from Malta, where they were urgently needed for the defence of the island itself, or from distant bases in Egypt.

Comparison with Arctic Convoys

A comparison with the convoys to North Russia[176] is of interest. The weather conditions which in the Arctic imposed such a prolonged and unique strain on ships and crews were of course entirely different; nor were the complications due to perpetual daylight in summer and perpetual darkness in winter present in the Mediterranean. The Arctic passage was about twice as long as the passages to Malta; in each case the routes were severely restricted by land (in the Arctic by ice as well); in each case, too, the convoys were liable to submarine attack throughout their whole voyages, and to a heavy scale of both surface and air attack at a considerable distance from their own bases by forces conveniently placed on the flank of the route. But in the Arctic attacking aircraft had much further to fly to reach their targets, and so lacked the support of the fighter escorts which usually accompanied the enemy striking forces in the Mediterranean. True, the Malta convoys had some air protection, whereas in 1942, except on one occasion, the Arctic convoys had none; but the carrier-borne aircraft were inferior in performance to the enemy's aircraft, and our shore-based fighters from Malta, Libya or Egypt often had to work at their extreme range. It is remarkable that in the circumstances the Fleet Air Arm and Royal Air Force fighters accomplished as much as they did,

As regards heavy surface forces, both the Germans in the Arctic and the Italians[177] in the Mediterranean showed extreme discretion in their employment, and though opportunity offered more than once, they never really pressed home an attack on a convoy; but in both cases (for somewhat different reasons) their potentiality presented the defence with a well-nigh insoluble problem. Their mere existence led to the virtual annihilation of Convoy PQ 17 in the Barents Sea (though they were never within 300 miles of the convoy), and if no comparable disaster occurred in the Mediterranean, it frustrated the attempts to replenish Malta on certainly two occasions.

Two forms of attack not practised against the Arctic convoys had to be met in the Mediterranean, viz. M.T.B.s and minefields laid in the easily mineable waters of the Sicilian Narrows and approaches to Malta.

The Mediterranean convoys enjoyed certain advantages over those in the Arctic. Only ships of 13–15 knots were included, as against the 8–9 knot ships of the latter; the convoys were much smaller and therefore handier; and the comparative shortness of sea time, the generally better weather conditions and absence of the bitter cold and ice left the crews of both merchant ships and escorts fresher when called upon to face attack. But the risks from enemy action – owing mainly to the weight and variety of the attacks which geographical features enabled them to stage at times and places where they would be most effective – were even greater than in the Arctic. Figures not fully qualified by *all* the factors governing them are apt to be misleading; the following percentages are, however, of interest.

In the four operations in 1942 (M.G.I., "Harpoon", "Vigorous" and "Pedestal") 35 merchant ships sailed. Of these 45 per cent were sunk on passage, 25 per cent were obliged to turn back,[178] and 30 per cent – more or less damaged – arrived at Malta.[179] During the corresponding period (March – September, 1942), which also happened to be the peak period of the attacks in the Arctic, out of 179 ships which sailed in six convoys to North Russia 29 per cent were sunk on passage, 11 per cent turned back,[180] and 60 per cent duly completed their voyage.[181] Air attack proved most deadly in both theatres, 55 per cent of those sunk being from this cause in the Arctic and 81 per cent in the Mediterranean. Submarines sank 33 per cent in the Arctic and none in the Mediterranean, the remaining 19 per cent there falling to M.T.B.s. Escorting craft during this period, too, suffered more heavily in the Mediterranean; many more ships were damaged than in the Arctic, and one carrier, two cruisers, one A.A. ship and eight destroyers[182] were sunk as against two cruisers, two destroyers and two minesweepers.

Planning and Preparation: Security

Naturally, these Mediterranean convoys were carefully studied and analysed as they occurred, and the reports teem with recommendations and suggestions. Many of these were of a topical or technical nature, e.g. the best disposition of escorting vessels to meet the weapons of the day and tactics employed by the enemy in the various forms of attack, suggestions for improvement of the primitive radar and fighter direction organisation, etc. No attempt is made here to comment on such points; actually, with the march of time, many of them are already out-dated.

But certain broad conclusions emerge from the story which are of more permanent value. The following remarks are mainly based on Operation "Pedestal", because on that occasion – the last seriously contested passage – the experience gained in the previous similar operations had been digested and made use of by both sides.

In the first place, the necessity for the most careful planning and preparation to meet every eventuality that could be foreseen is to be stressed. Early planning *at the Admiralty* by the Commanders concerned was found to be most satisfactory; and verbal explanation of the plan to commanding officers of escorting vessels and the masters of the merchant ships (in addition to the usual "Convoy Conference"), special instruction to the signal ratings in the merchant ships, and the exercising of the convoy in manoeuvres, aircraft recognition, etc. before called upon to face the enemy were considered of great importance.

These measures in different ways might compromise security to some extent, but in the opinion of Admiral Syfret the objections to this were outweighed by the advantages. Intelligence of the passage of these particular convoys through the Strait of Gibraltar, no matter what ruses and precautions were employed, was almost certain to reach the enemy from his efficient organisation on shore in plenty of time for him to organise his attacks for the most vulnerable periods of the passage. But that did not mean that security in the early stages could be dispensed with, and it was with concern that several officers, on joining the merchant ships before the convoy had left the Clyde, discovered that knowledge of their destination was common property, owing to loose talk, the careless labelling of certain stores, etc. The last-minute issue of Mediterranean charts to certain ships hithereto unprovided with them also gave a pointer to where they were going.

Tactical Aspect

As regards the tactical aspect, nothing particularly new emerged: but two great lessons – already in course of assimilation – received ample confirmation:

1. The necessity to keep ships in convoy and the escort in formation and closed up for mutual support. Stragglers and detached ships presented all forms of attack with their opportunities.

2. The necessity for fighter protection and *fighter direction* (it must be remembered that in 1942 few ships were fitted for the latter) against shore-based air attack.

Provided these two conditions could be maintained, the risks from submarines, M.T.B.s, mines and air were acceptable.

Submarines did not accomplish so much against the merchant ships as might have been expected, only hitting one ship in the four convoys in 1942, though the prowess of the German *U.73* in her bold attack on the *Eagle* and of the Italian *Axum* in hitting three ships with a salvo of four torpedoes shews that resolute and skilful commanders were not lacking. M.T.B.s were difficult to see and harder to hit, but they only once managed to damage a ship in convoy, though they had their successes against escorting craft. The five merchant ships they hit in operation "Pedestal" were all stragglers. Mines, though a constant anxiety at certain stages of the passage, were mainly of nuisance value and could be dealt with by destroyers' T.S.D. sweeps and the minesweeping forces.[183]

Air attack on the scale the enemy was able to lay it on was by far the greatest danger that had to be faced, and, combined with the threat of the Italian battle fleet, compelled the cessation of the convoys in the eastern basin, where neither British capital ships nor carriers were available, during the most critical months of 1942. In the western basin it was largely countered by the inclusion of as many carriers as possible in the escort; and in this connection may be noted the great value of carriers for the provision of fighter protection in areas inaccessible to friendly shore-based fighters.

Operation "Pedestal" provides an example of the effectiveness of the fighter protection so provided, and also of the disastrous results accruing from lack of it and the break up of the convoy formation. The very heavy air attacks from Sardinia by over 100 escorted bombers throughout daylight hours of 12 August, when the convoy was protected by a total of 60 carrier-borne fighters, only succeeded in damaging one merchant ship and two of the escorting ships. The fighters attacking at a distance from the convoy were usually able to break up the enemy formations sufficiently for the A.A. guns of escort and convoy to be able to deal with those that got through. That evening, after the carriers had withdrawn and when the convoy, in some disorder after the submarine attack which robbed it of both its fighter direction ships (one of them its A.A. ship), was protected in the air by only six Beaufighters, about 20 Ju. 88s hit three merchant ships with bombs or torpedoes. The convoy then became completely disorganised; five stragglers (in addition to H.M.S. *Manchester)* fell victims to M.T.B.s. Three merchant ships in convoy were hit by bombs next morning while there was still no fighter direction; and ships which had become detached suffered further damage in the course of day (see Plan 14).

No mention has been made of the Italian heavy surface forces, but in fact they exercised a preponderating influence on the conduct of these operations. It may well be considered that for the furtherance of an object of such supreme importance as was the reduction of Malta, and in view of their numerical superiority, they might have been used with more resolution: unlike a lonely raider far from home in the open ocean, or even the German fleet in the Arctic, which lacked repair facilities in their poorly equipped Norwegian bases, they were operating on the threshold of their homeland with all their metropolitan resources near at hand at their disposal.

In the western basin, their potentiality could be largely offset by the loan of forces from other stations to accompany the convoys as far as the Narrows: thereafter navigational difficulties and the expedient of doing this part of the passage at night were likely to deter them from attack; and the formation of a respectable air striking force at Malta was an insurance for the last stages of the passage. They could never be discounted, however, and their existence on more than one occasion influenced the decision to scuttle damaged ships, which otherwise might perhaps have been saved.

But in the eastern basin the Italian fleet in 1942 tipped the scale. Admiral Vian's brilliant action in March held their superior force off the convoy, but the delay – as the Italian commander had foreseen – enabled the enemy air forces to cut it up before it reached its destination. Operation "Vigorous" proved that "our air striking force had nothing like the weight required to stop a fast and powerful enemy force, and in no way compensated for our lack of heavy ships".[184] The efficiency of a submarine screen keeping pace with the convoy was never put to the test. No doubt the knowledge that half a dozen submarines were between them and the convoy would have had considerable moral effect on the enemy; but the relatively slow speed of the submarines, especially when submerged, would militate against their doing more than possibly delay a determined attack.

The lesson, of course, is that for all such operations as those under consideration it is essential to be able to confront the heaviest surface force the enemy can muster with a force that can fight it with at least some chance of defeating it.

"By-products"

Though perhaps not strictly part of the story of the Malta convoys, it is of interest to note some of their unplanned effects on the general strategical situation in the Mediterranean, as illustrating the inter-reaction between the operations of one Service and those of others under the conditions of modern warfare.

The immediate object of these convoys was to succour Malta, the key to the whole strategical position in the Mediterranean. Enough – but only just enough – was run into Malta to enable the island to hold out and – except for intervals – to stage serious attacks on the Axis vital supply route to North Africa; but the very fact of running even the least successful (from that point of view) of these convoys carried with it most important "by-products".

For example, the convoys in June 1942 ("Harpoon" and "Vigorous"), which between them succeeded in getting only two merchant ships to their destination, had a fortuitous but far-reaching effect on the operations on shore in North Africa. The convoys had originally been planned by the War Cabinet and the Middle East Defence Council to coincide with an offensive by the Eighth Army. This was forestalled by the German Field-Marshal Rommel, who launched his own attack on Bir Hakeim on 26 May, 1942. By 14 June he had destroyed a high proportion of the British armour, and the retreat of the Eighth Army from Gazala had already begun. Hundreds of Eighth Army vehicles, packed nose to tail along the coast road during the critical days between 14–16 June, presented ideal targets for enemy air attack, which might well have turned the well-ordered retreat into a rout. But, in view of the importance attached to Convoy "Harpoon", the Panzer Army was informed in the morning of 14 June by General von Waldau, A.O.C., Africa, that air support to the *Afrika Corps* "would have to wait". Actually, on that day a total of 166 German aircraft, bombers and fighters, were diverted from the land targets presented by the retreating Eighth Army against the British shipping. There was a comparable situation the next day; and these intensive operations against the convoy had a marked effect on the general serviceability of the German air force, which, in conjunction with other factors – e.g. the orderly retreat of the British Western Desert Air Force, which left airfields stripped of useful stores and equipment and yet managed to maintain a high level of aggressive operations – resulted in the Panzer Army being forced to advance into Egypt without adequate air support.

The arrival of the *Welshman* and the two ships from the "Harpoon" Convoy at Malta enabled Malta to recommence offensive operations, and on 24 June Mussolini informed the German Army General Staff that difficulties after the collapse of the Eighth Army lay less in the battle on the ground than in the transport situation at sea. "Owing to Malta's active revival, supply of the Panzer Army in Africa has once more entered a critical phase . . ."

A further interesting side-issue of the June convoys to Malta is provided by the German Admiral Weichold, which shows how intricate and unexpected the effects of an apparently straightforward operation can be under the conditions of modern warfare. In these operations the Italian Fleet expended 15,000 tons of fuel, and this left them with insufficient to maintain their extensive convoy protection commitments. This contributed to a further drop in supplies to North Africa, at a time when extra quantities were urgently required to make good the heavy drain on stocks caused by the fighting.

Much the same, though not so important, were the repercussions of "Pedestal" on the operations on shore. This convoy coincided with a period when the strength, and especially the serviceability, of the German Air Force were being rigidly conserved in preparation for Rommel's last attempt to break through the El Alamein positions and to proceed with the occupation of Egypt. In order to deal with the convoy, about 220 German bombers and fighters were detailed to reinforce the Italian air forces. The result of these operations was to reduce the potentiality of the enemy air force to such an extent that it was unable to provide effective escort for their convoys, and this at a time when the replenishment of the island's fuel made possible a resumption of air strikes from Malta.

As for the fighting on shore, at the Battle of Alam el Halfa (31 August – 4 September) – according to the enemy commander – "The R.A.F.'s command of the air had been virtually complete." This was undoubtedly due in part to the fact that the enemy air force had been stretched to the limit for some time, and the additional burden on both crews and machines demanded by the heavy attacks on "Pedestal" had a directly adverse effect on the efficiency of the air force.

Viewed from this angle, the whole story of the Malta convoys is a good illustration of the inexorable effect of sea power.[185] Sea power enabled the aircraft on which Malta so largely depended to be flown in from carriers. Sea power provided fuel for these aircraft, and the munitions which sustained the island itself, and made possible the attacks thence which so seriously disturbed the Axis line of communications with North Africa. Sea power, too, frequently compelled the diversion of the enemy air effort from the tactical support of their army in North Africa to the paramount need of denying supplies to Malta, and thereby exercised an important influence on the operations ashore at critical periods; and finally, before the end of 1942, sea power made possible the Allied landings in Algeria, which, combined with the advance of the Eighth Army (itself dependent on sea power for its supplies by the Cape of Good Hope route) transformed the whole situation in the Mediterranean in favour of the Allies. The most conspicuous contribution of sea power in the Mediterranean, perhaps, was the periodical reinforcement of Malta by the convoys, in the teeth of all that the Italian Navy and the apparently overwhelming shore-based air forces of the Axis could do to prevent it.

The story of the Malta convoys may well be regarded with pride by the Royal Navy and the Mercantile Marines which took part. As in all operations of war, their success ultimately hinged on the human element. This never faltered; grievous though the losses were; and thanks to the morale engendered and nourished by the leaders, they won through in the end. Heavy though the strain was on capital ships, carriers and cruisers, it was even heavier on the destroyers – often steaming for days on end, with no let-up on the necessity for their vigilance and with frequent encounters with the enemy – on the F.A.A., both ship-borne and shore-based, pitted against aircraft superior in performance and numbers, and on the R.A.F., working often at extreme range in support of the operations.

But to the merchant ships must go the highest credit, as was stressed in the reports of the Flag Officers conducting the operations. As another admiral wrote about this time in connection with the Arctic convoys, "We in the Navy are paid to do this sort of job, but it is beginning to ask too much of the men of the Merchant Navy. We may be able to avoid bombs and torpedoes with our speed . . ."[186]

But in the Mediterranean, as in the Arctic, it was *not* asking too much; and it is good to read the comments of those best able to judge on the skill and determination of the masters and officers and the fortitude of the ships' companies of those sorely-tried ships. Nor must the work of the Naval Liaison Officers and guns' crews embarked in them be forgotten.

The disappointment of the masters of the ships in the diversionary convoy from the east when they found they were not actually going through to Malta, as noted by Admiral Harwood, will be remembered; and the spirit in which these dangerous ventures were carried through may well be epitomised in the last sentence of Admiral Syfret's report on "Pedestal":–

"In conclusion I think I am speaking for all in saying that we are disappointed at not doing better, but we should like to try again." Without that spirit, it is hardly possible that the Malta convoys could have succeeded against the material forces arrayed against them: with such spirit, it is difficult to set a limit to the operations of war which can be undertaken with success.

Epilogue

On 20 June, 1943 – a year almost to the day after the arrival of the battle-scarred remnant of the "Harpoon" convoy – Malta, her sore ordeal now a thing of the past, was en fête. The Baraccas and all other vantage-points were thick with cheering people, as the *Aurora*, flying the Royal Standard, passed through the breakwater and took up her buoys.

On a special platform in front of the bridge stood His Majesty King George VI, come from a visit to the fighting men in North Africa, to mark his admiration for the achievement of the island.

"I have witnessed many memorable spectacles," writes Admiral of the Fleet Lord Cunningham of Hyndhope, "but this was the most impressive of them all. The dense throngs of loyal Maltese, men, women and children, were wild with enthusiasm. I have never heard such cheering and all the bells in the many churches started ringing when he landed.

"The King made an extensive tour of the island . . . and the effect on the inhabitants was tremendous."[187]

The Malta convoys had been justified.

Appendix A

Forces : Operation "Excess", January 1941

Notes – 1. The "Forces" are shown in the order in which they appear in the text, which is not always in the alphabetical order of their distinguishing letters.

2. Group II consisted of the *Bonaventure*, *Duncan*, *Hasty*, *Hero* and *Hereward* and the four escorted ships. The remainder of Forces "H" and "F" formed Group I.

Name	Type	Armament	Commanding Officer
I. From Gibraltar			
Force "H"			
Renown	Battle cruiser	Six 15-in. Twenty 4.5-in.	Captain C. E. B. Simeon (flag of Vice-Admiral Sir J. F. Somerville, K.C.B., D.S.O.)
Malaya	Battleship	Eight 15-in. Twelve 6-in. Eight 4-in.	Captain A. F. E. Palliser, D.S.C.
Ark Royal	Aircraft carrier (30 Swordfish aircraft, 24 Fulmar aircraft)	Sixteen 4.5-in.	Captain C. S. Holland
Sheffield	Cruiser	Twelve 6-in. Eight 4-in.	Captain C. A. A. Larcom
Faulknor	Destroyer	Five 4.7-in. One 3-in.	Captain A. F. De Salis
Forester	Destroyer	Four 4.7-in.	Lieut-Cdr. E. B. Tancock, D.S.C.

Fury	Destroyer	Four 4.7-in. One 3-in.	Lieut-Cdr. T. C. Robinson
Foxhound	Destroyer	Four 4.7-in. One 3-in.	Cdr. G. H. Peters, D.S.C.
Firedrake	Destroyer	Four 4.7-in. One 3-in.	Lieut-Cdr. S. H. Norris, D.S.O., D.S.C.
Fortune	Destroyer	Four 4.7-in. One 3-in.	Lieut.-Cdr. E. N. Sinclair
Duncan	Destroyer	Four 4.7-in. One 3-in.	Captain F. S. W. de Winton
		Force "F"	
Bonaventure	Cruiser	Eight 5.25-in.	Captain H. J. Egerton
Hasty	Destroyer	Four 4.7-in.	Lieut-Cdr. L. R. K. Tyrwhitt
Hero	Destroyer	Four 4.7-in.	Cdr. H. W. Biggs, D.S.O.
Hereward	Destroyer	Four 4.7-in.	Cdr. C. W. Greening
Jaguar	Destroyer	Six 4.7-in. One 4-in.	Lieut-Cdr. J. F. W. Hine
		Force "G": Submarines	
Triumph	Submarine	Eight torp. tubes	Lieut-Cdr. W. J. W. Woods
Upholder	Submarine	Four torp. tubes	Lieut. M. D. Wanklyn

II. Mediterranean Fleet
Force "B"

Gloucester[188]	Cruiser	Twelve 6-in. Eight 4-in.	Captain H. A. Rowley (flag of Rear-Admiral E. de F. Renouf, C.V.O.)
Southampton[189]	Cruiser	Twelve 6-in. Eight 4-in.	Captain B. C. B. Brooke
Ilex	Destroyer	Four 4.7-in.	Captain H. St. L. Nicolson, D.S.O.

Force "A"

Warspite	Battleship	Eight 15-in. Eight 6-in. Eight 4-in.	Captain D. B. Fisher, C.B.E. (flag of C.-in-C., Admiral Sir A. B. Cunningham, K.C.B., D.S.O.)
Valiant	Battleship	Eight 15-in. Twenty 4.5-in.	Captain C. E. Morgan, D.S.O.
Illustrious[190]	Aircraft carrier (21 Swordfish aircraft, 12 Fulmar aircraft)	Sixteen 4.5-in.	Captain D. W. Boyd, C.B.E., D.S.C. (flag of Rear-Admiral A. L. St. G. Lyster, C.B., C.V.O., D.S.O.)
Jervis	Destroyer	Six 4.7-in. One 4-in.	Captain P. J. Mack, D.S.O.
Juno	Destroyer	Six 4.7-in.	Cdr. St. J. R. J. Tyrwhitt
Janus	Destroyer	Six 4.7-in.	Cdr. J. A. W. Tothill
Nubian	Destroyer	Eight 4.7-in.	Cdr. R. W. Ravenhill
Mohawk	Destroyer	Eight 4.7-in.	Cdr. J. W. M. Eaton
Greyhound	Destroyer	Four 4.7-in. One 3-in.	Cdr. W. R. Marshall-A'Deane, D.S.C.
Gallant[191]	Destroyer	Four 4.7-in. One 3-in.	Lieut.-Cdr. C. P. F. Brown, D.S.C.
Griffin	Destroyer	Four 4.7-in. One 3-in.	Cdr. J. Lee-Barber, D.S.O.
Dainty	Destroyer	Four 4.7-in. One 3-in.	Cdr. M. S. Thomas, D.S.O.

Force "C": Convoy Escorts

Calcutta	Anti-aircraft ship	Eight 4-in.	Captain D. M. Lees, D.S.O.
Diamond	Destroyer	Four 4.7-in. One 3-in.	Lieut.-Cdr. P. A. Cartwright
Defender	Destroyer	Four 4.7-in. One 3-in.	Lieut.-Cdr. G. L. Farnfield
Peony	Corvette	One 4-in.	Lieut.-Cdr. M. B. Sherwood, D.S.O.

Salvia	Corvette	One 4-in.	Lieut.-Cdr. J. I. Miller, D.S.O., R.D., R.N.R.
Hyacinth	Corvette	One 4-in.	Lieut.-Cdr. F. C. Hopkins, R.N.R.
Gloxinia	Corvette	One 4-in.	Lieut.-Cdr. A. J. C. Pomeroy, R.N.V.R.

Force "D"

Orion	Cruiser	Eight 6-in. Eight 4-in.	Captain G. R. B. Back (flag of Vice-Admiral H. D. Pridham-Wippell, C.B., C.V.O.)
Ajax	Cruiser	Eight 6-in. Eight 4-in.	Captain E. D. B. McCarthy.
Perth	Cruiser	Eight 6-in. Eight 4-in.	Captain Sir P. W. Bowyer-Smyth, Bt.
York	Cruiser	Six 8-in. Four 4-in.	Captain R. H. Portal, D.S.C.
Pandora	Submarine	Eight torp. tubes	Lieut-Cdr. J. W. Linton

III. Convoys

Name	Tonnage	Destination
	"Excess" (16 knots)	
Clan Cumming	7,500	
Clan Macdonald	9,500	Piraeus
Empire Song	9,000	
Essex	13,500	Malta
	M.W.5½ (15 knots)	
H.M.S. *Breconshire*	10,000	Malta
Clan Macaulay	10,500	
	M.E.5½ (15 knots)	
Lanarkshire	10,000	Alexandria
Waiwera	12,500	

	M.E.6 (11 knots)	
Volo	1,500	
Pontfield	8,500	
Rodi	3,500	Port Said
Trocas	7,500	
Hoegh Hood	9,500	
Devis	6,000	Alexandria

Note. Tonnage is "gross registered tonnage," shown to the nearest 500 tons.

Speeds of convoys are those given in the operation orders.

H.M.S. *Breconshire* was a commissioned auxiliary supply ship.

All ships arrived safely.

Appendix B

Particulars of Attacks from the Air

Extract from a signal from the Commander-in-Chief, Mediterranean, to the Admiralty, 1916 of 8 February 1941:

1. Torpedo-bomber attack at 1223 was of usual Italian type with steady level approach from six miles on a bearing abaft destroyer screen at height 150 ft. to drop torpedoes at 2,500 yd. from battle fleet.

   Fighters gave chase, damaging one aircraft: no apparent damage from gunfire.

2. Relief fighters were being flown off at 1235, when dive-bombing aircraft were sighted at long range at height 12,000 ft. in two very loose and flexible formations. On being engaged they worked round into positions on each quarter of battle fleet, where they circled while waiting their turn to attack.

   Dive attack started at 1240, concentrated mainly on *Illustrious* (18 to 24 aircraft); but *Warspite* and *Valiant* were also attacked (3 to 6 aircraft each); both Junkers 87B and Junkers 88 were employed.

   The attack on *Illustrious* developed in three main waves, in each of which at least two sub-flights of three each carried out synchronised attacks in different sectors. Aircraft of each sub-flight attacked in succession from bearings 5 to 10 degrees apart. The main weight of the attack came from astern; and it appeared that in each wave one or two sub-flights attacked from astern and one from either beam. Each wave lasted about a minute and a half, and the interval between waves about thirty seconds.

   Some aircraft dived straight from 12,000 ft. to release bombs at 1,500 ft., but most spiralled down to about 5,000 ft. before turning into aiming dive; bomb release in some cases was as low as 800 ft. Many aircraft continued their dive across the ship to flatten out at

100 ft. and zigzag away, flying low. Angle of dive varied between 50 and 80 degrees.

Confirmed three aircraft shot down and two damaged by gunfire, and three unconfirmed. Fulmars, engaging retiring aircraft, shot down five certain, two probable, and damaged two.

3. High-level bombing at 1330 by seven aircraft each on *Illustrious* and battle fleet and three on Convoy "Excess" was ineffectual. Aircraft variously reported as Savoia 79, Heinkel III, and Junkers 88. One damaged by gunfire from *Calcutta*, escorting convoy.

4. Dive-bombing attacks at 1615 on *Illustrious* and at 1715 on battle fleet were small-scale repetitions of 1240 attack. That on *Illustrious* was markedly less determined and less synchronised: that on battle fleet was comparable in skill and determination, but bomb release was at or above 1,500 ft.

At least one aircraft in each attack was damaged by gunfire, and three by Fulmars, which intercepted after the attack.

5. Probable moonlight torpedo-bomber attack on *Illustrious* in Malta searched channel by two aircraft, which were heard and seen. No torpedoes or tracks observed.

Appendix C

Remarks on Operation "Excess", January 1941, by Admiral Sir Andrew Cunningham, Commander–in–Chief, Mediterranean

"These operations marked the advent of the German Air Force in strength in the Mediterranean, and included the damaging of H.M.S. *Illustrious* on 10 January and the loss of H.M.S. *Southampton* on 11 January . . .

"The dive-bombing attacks by German aircraft were most efficiently performed, and came as an unpleasant surprise. The results of short-range anti-aircraft fire were disappointing, though it has been subsequently learned that this fire was in fact more effective than it appeared, and the Germans suffered considerable loss. Nevertheless, it is a potent new factor in Mediterranean war, and will undoubtedly deny us that free access to the waters immediately surrounding Malta and Sicily which we have previously enjoyed, until our own air forces have been built up to a scale adequate to meet it.

"The dive-bombing attacks on the 3rd Cruiser Squadron in the afternoon of 11 January – resulting in the loss of the *Southampton* – were a complete surprise, delivered at a time when the ships concerned believed themselves to have drawn clear of the threat of air attack, and when officers and men were doubtless relaxing the vigilance to some extent after a very strenuous four days. This damaging attack served to emphasize the importance of including a radio-direction-finder in detached units whenever possible.

"The remarks of the commanding officer, H.M.S. *Jaguar*[192], are of considerable interest, in particular his practice of firing 4.7-inch barrage over the stern of a ship attacked by dive-bombers. The idea is now under development in the Mediterranean Fleet with a view to the destroyer screen's putting an umbrella barrage over the fleet . . .

"It is satisfactory to record that convoy 'Excess', whose safe passage had been the main object of the operation, reached its destination safely."

From the Mediterranean War Diary for January, 1941: Part of the General Summary of the Month's Work

"The arrival of German air units in the central Mediterranean early in January had a profound effect upon the whole strategical position. By the end of December, 1940, the fleet had achieved a degree of supremacy over the large-scale Italian air attacks sufficient to give it complete freedom of movement in the eastern Mediterranean and a large measure of immunity in the central Mediterranean. But the disablement of the *Illustrious*, the loss of the *Southampton*, and the heavy air attacks on Malta quickly made it clear that until adequate fighter protection was available not only must the through-Mediterranean convoys be suspended, but the fleet itself would operate by day within range of the dive-bombers only at considerable risk. In the absence of a modern aircraft carrier, it therefore became necessary to abandon any idea of offensive operations against the enemy's coasts. It seemed, however, that the acquisition of aerodromes in Libya would enable the Royal Air Force to provide a high degree of immunity to shipping all along the Libyan coast. This would simplify the running of convoys to Malta and the Aegean, and enable light forces to operate from these advanced bases; but in spite of the rapid advance of the army to beyond Derna by the end of the month there was still little security gained to compensate for the enormously increased supply requirements. Previously, a fair proportion of supplies could reach the advanced units of the army and air force by road and rail; but now, owing to the rapidly lengthening lines of communication, everything had to be transported by sea. The air force was fully extended in maintaining pressure on the retreating enemy, and had no fighters to spare for protection of shipping.

"In these circumstances, it was to be expected that the enemy light forces known to be based at Brindisi and Taranto would attempt to interfere with our extended lines of communication in the Aegean and along the Libyan coast; but apparently the German influence had not yet reached the Italian Navy, for no attacks developed ...

"There was a decided slowing up in the rate of advance of the Greek Army. At the beginning of the month, it seemed that Valona and the line of high land to the eastward would fall into Greek hands; but the advance was checked by the arrival of heavy Italian reinforcements and the difficulties of mountain transport in winter. The Greek supply problems were eased by the arrival at Piraeus of the three remaining ships of 'Excess' convoy; but the most important of all, the *Northern Prince*, with ammunition and essential supplies for the Greek powder factories, had been left at Gibraltar, having grounded there."

Appendix D

Forces: Operation "Substance", July 1941

Name	Type	Armament	Commanding Officer
		Force "H"	
Renown	Battle-cruiser	Six 15-in. Twenty 4.5-in.	Rear-Admiral R. R. McGrigor (as Captain) (flag of Vice-Admiral Sir J. F. Somerville, K.C.B., D.S.O.)
Nelson	Battleship	Nine 16-in. Twelve 6-in. Six 4.7-in.	Captain T. H. Troubridge
Ark Royal	Aircraft carrier (30 Swordfish aircraft, 24 Fulmar aircraft)	Sixteen 4.5-in.	Captain L. E. H. Maund
Hermione	Cruiser	Ten 5.25-in.	Captain G. N. Oliver
Faulknor	Destroyer	Five 4.7-in. One 3-in.	Captain A. F. De Salis
Foresight	Destroyer	Four 4.7-in. One 3-in.	Commander J. S. C. Salter
Forester	Destroyer	Four 4.7-in.	Lieut.-Cdr. E. B. Tancock, D.S.C.
Fury	Destroyer	Four 4.7-in. One 3-in.	Lieut.-Cdr. T. C. Robinson

Lightning	Destroyer	Six 4.7-in. One 4-in.	Cdr. R. G. Stewart
Duncan	Destroyer	Four 4.7-in. One 3-in.	Lieut.-Cdr. A. N. Rowell

Force "X"

Edinburgh	Cruiser	Twelve 6-in. Twelve 4-in.	Captain H. W. Faulkner (flag of Rear-Admiral E. N. Syfret)
Manchester[193]	Cruiser	Twelve 6-in. Eight 4-in.	Captain H. Drew, D.S.C.
Arethusa	Cruiser	Six 6-in. Four 4-in.	Captain A. C. Chapman
Manxman	Minelayer	Six 4-in.	Captain R. K. Dickson
Cossack	Destroyer	Six 4.7-in. Two 4-in.	Captain E. L. Berthon, D.S.C.
Maori	Destroyer	Six 4.7-in. Two 4-in.	Cdr. R. E. Courage, D.S.O., D.S.C.
Sikh	Destroyer	Six 4.7-in. Two 4-in.	Cdr. G. H. Stokes
Nestor	Destroyer	Six 4.7-in. One 4-in.	Cdr. A. S. Rosenthal, R.A.N.
Fearless[194]	Destroyer	Four 4.7-in.	Cdr. A. F. Pugsley
Foxhound	Destroyer	Four 4.7-in. One 3-in.	Cdr. G. H. Peters, D.S.O.
Firedrake[195]	Destroyer	Four 4.7-in. One 3-in.	Lieut.-Cdr. S. H. Norris, D.S.O., D.S.C.
Farndale	Destroyer	Six 4-in.	Cdr. S. H. Carlill
Avon Vale	Destroyer	Six 4-in.	Lieut. R. G. Dreyer
Eridge	Destroyer	Six 4-in.	Lieut.-Cdr. W. F. N. Gregory-Smith

Force "S"

Brown Ranger	Oiler

Beverley	Destroyer	Three 4-in. One 12-pdr.	Lieut.-Cdr. J. Grant

Submarines

0.21 (Dutch)	Submarine	8 torp. tubes	Lieut.-Cdr. J. F. van Dulm, R.N.N.
Olympus	Submarine	8 torp. tubes	Lieut.-Cdr. H. G. Dymott
P.32	Submarine	4 torp. tubes	Lieut. D. A. B. Abdy
Unique	Submarine	4 torp. tubes	Lieut. A. F. Collett
Upholder	Submarine	4 torp. tubes	Lieut.-Cdr. M. D. Wanklyn, D.S.O.
Upright	Submarine	4 torp. tubes	Lieut. J. S. Wraith, D.S.C.
Urge	Submarine	4 torp. tubes	Lieut. E. P. Tomkinson
Utmost	Submarine	4 torp. tubes	Lieut.-Cdr. R. D. Cayley, D.S.O.

Escort Convoy M.G.1

Encounter	Destroyer	Four 4.7-in. One 3-in.	Lieut.-Cdr. E. V. St. J. Morgan

Convoys

Name	Tonnage	Remarks
Gibraltar to Malta (G.M.1)		
Melbourne Star	11,000	
Sydney Star[196]	12,500	
City of Pretoria	8,000	Speed of convoy:
Port of Chalmers	8,500	14 knots
Durham	13,000	
Deucalion	7,500	

Name	Tonnage	Remarks
Malta to Gibraltar (M.G.1)		
H.M.S. *Breconshire*	10,000	Speed of group: 17
Talabot	7,000	knots

Thermopylae	6,500	Speed of group: 14 knots
Amerika	10,000	
Settler	6,000	Speed of group: 12 knots
Svenor	7,500	
Hoegh Hood[197]	9,500	

Appendix E

Forces: Operation "Halberd", September 1941

Name	Type	Armament	Commanding Officer
		Force "A"	
Nelson[198]	Battleship	Nine 16-in. Twelve 6-in. Six 4.7-in.	Captain T. H. Troubridge (flag of Vice-Admiral Sir J. F. Somerville, K.C.B., D.S.O.)
Rodney	Battleship	Nine 16-in. Twelve 6-in. Six 4.7-in.	Captain J. W. Rivett-Carnac, D.S.O.
Prince of Wales	Battleship	Ten 14-in. Sixteen 4.25-in.	Captain J. C. Leach, M.V.O. (flag of Vice-Admiral A. T. B. Curteis, C.B.)
Ark Royal	Aircraft Carrier	Sixteen 4.5-in. (30 Swordfish aircraft, 24 Fulmar aircraft)	Captain L. E. H. Maund
Duncan	Destroyer	Four 4.7-in. One 3-in.	Captain H. W. Williams
Gurkha	Destroyer	Eight 4-in.	Cdr. C. N. Lentaigne
Legion	Destroyer	Eight 4-in.	Cdr. R. F. Jessel
Lance	Destroyer	Eight 4-in.	Lieut-Cdr. R. W. F. Northcott
Lively	Destroyer	Eight 4-in.	Lieut-Cdr. W. F. E. Hussey, D.S.C.
Fury	Destroyer	Four 4.7-in. One 3-in.	Lieut-Cdr. T. C. Robinson

Isaac Sweers (Dutch)	Destroyer	Six 4-in.	Cdr. J. Houtsmuller, R.N.N.
Piorun (Polish)	Destroyer	Six 4.7-in. One 4-in.	
Garland (Polish)	Destroyer	Four 4.7-in. One 3-in.	

Force "X"

Kenya	Cruiser	Twelve 6-in. Twelve 4-in.	Captain M. M. Denny, C.B. (flag of Rear-Admiral H. M. Burrough, C.B.)
Edinburgh	Cruiser	Twelve 6-in. Twelve 4-in.	Captain H. W. Faulkner (flag of Rear-Admiral E. N. Syfret)
Sheffield	Cruiser	Twelve 6-in. Eight 4-in.	Captain A. W. Clarke
Hermione	Cruiser	Ten 5.25-in.	Captain G. N. Oliver
Euryalus	Cruiser	Ten 5.25-in.	Captain E. W. Bush, D.S.O., D.S.C.
Cossack	Destroyer	Six 4.7-in. Two 4-in.	Captain E. L. Berthon, D.S.C.
Zulu	Destroyer	Six 4.7-in. Two 4-in.	Commander H. R. Graham, D.S.O.
Foresight	Destroyer	Four 4.7-in. One 3-in.	Commander J. S. C. Salter
Forester	Destroyer	Four 4.7-in.	Lieut-Cdr. E. B. Tancock, D.S.C.
Farndale	Destroyer	Six 4-in.	Cdr. S. H. Carlill
Heythrop	Destroyer	Six 4-in.	Lieut-Cdr. R. S. Stafford
Laforey	Destroyer	Six 4.7-in. One 4-in.	Captain R. M. J. Hutton
Lightning	Destroyer	Six 4.7-in. One 4-in.	Cdr. R. G. Stewart

Oribi	Destroyer	Four 4.7-in. One 4-in.	Lieut-Cdr. J. E. H. McBeath, D.S.O.

FORCE "S"

Brown Ranger	Oiler		
Fleur de Lys	Corvette	One 4-in.	Lieut. A. Collins, R.N.R.

Submarines

0.21 (Dutch)	Submarine	8 torp. tubes	Lieut.-Cdr. J. F. van Dulm, R.N.N.
Upholder	Submarine	4 torp. tubes	Lieut.-Cdr. M. D. Wanklyn, D.S.O.
Trusty	Submarine	10 torp. tubes	Lieut.-Cdr. W. D. A. King, D.S.O., D.S.C.
Sokol (Polish)	Submarine	4 torp. tubes	Lieut.-Cdr. B. Karnicki, Polish Navy
Urge	Submarine	4 torp. tubes	Lieut.-Cdr. E. P. Tomkinson
Upright	Submarine	4 torp. tubes	Lieut.-Cdr. J. S. Wraith, D.S.C.
Utmost	Submarine	4 torp. tubes	Lieut.-Cdr. R. D. Cayley, D.S.O
Ursula	Submarine	6 torp. tubes	Lieut. I. L. M. McGeoch
Unbeaten	Submarine	4 torp. tubes	Lieut. C. P. Norman

CONVOYS

Name	Tonnage	Remarks
Gibraltar to Malta (G.M.2)		
Clan Macdonald	9,500	
Clan Ferguson	7,500	
Ajax	7,500	Speed of convoy: 15
Imperial Star[199]	12,500	knots
City of Lincoln	8,000	
Rowallan Castle	8,000	

Dunedin Star	14,000	Speed of convoy: 15 knots
City of Calcutta	8,000	
H.M.S. *Breconshire*	10,000	

Malta to Gibraltar (M.G.2)

Melbourne Star	11,000	Part 1
City of Pretoria	8,000	Part 2
Port Chalmers	8,500	

Appendix F

Remarks on Operation "Halberd", September 1941
(From M.016621/41 and M.04385/42)

By Vice-Admiral Somerville

"The rough handling which the enemy torpedo aircraft received whilst passing over the destroyer screen may have accounted for the tendency of the later attacks to be delivered from abaft the beam. Should this direction of attack be adopted, it will be necessary to station additional destroyers on after bearings at the expense of anti-submarine protection. Deliberate attacks by torpedo aircraft against destroyers on the screen may force the latter to take drastic avoiding action; this will have the effect of disturbing gunfire and distracting attention, thereby opening a gap in the screen through which successive attackers could pass. Destroyers on the screen adjacent to the vessel attacked, and close escorts on the threatened bearing, must maintain a careful watch in order to frustrate such manoeuvres.

"Cruising Disposition No. 17, adopted for the passage of the Narrows, was a compromise designed to give protection against E-Boat and torpedo-bomber attack at night. It did not prove satisfactory, and amendments are under consideration."

(The need was to increase arcs of fire.)

By Rear-Admiral Burrough

"The air torpedo attack at dusk in bright moonlight presented a most difficult problem. With the exception of one or two individuals in *Kenya*, the aircraft were neither seen nor heard, and it was only by alarm signals from the destroyers on the flank and on one occasion by *Kenya*'s [radio direction-finder] that the direction of attack could be gauged; in spite of this, ships put up a very good anti-aircraft barrage on the three occasions that the attack appeared to be pressed home.

"I feel very strongly that in any future operation of this nature success will be gravely jeopardized unless a moonless night is selected for the passage through the Sicilian Channel. The final air torpedo attack took place thirty minutes after official dusk, and the invisible enemy had the whole convoy clearly silhouetted against a bright moon in a cloudless sky. Had the enemy sent reconnaissance machines, they would have had no difficulty in maintaining touch until moonset at 0010, thus enabling continuous attacks to be carried out up to this hour, by which time the evasive route of the convoy would have been entirely compromised and air and surface attacks could have been planned for dawn. I do not consider that this unseen attack could have taken place on a moonless night, and am strongly of the opinion that, had the night [of 27–28] been moonless, the convoy would have reached Malta intact. The cruising disposition adopted under these circumstances proved its efficiency."

By Rear–Admiral Syfret

"It is easy to criticize the disposition of our own forces, both before and after Force "X" parted company, if only one form of attack by the enemy is envisaged. But regarded from all points of view, viz., evasion, attack by surface vessels or submarines or E-Boats, various forms of attack by aircraft, and protection against mines, I find it difficult to suggest any improvements on the disposition used.

"Every commanding officer would like his ship stationed so that its clear arcs for gunfire were the maximum possible. Unfortunately, the greater the number of escorting ships, the less the clear arcs; and a particularly strong escort was provided. In my view, a 'square' formation provides the best all-round defence; and I can find no fault in the dispositions adopted for heavy ships, cruisers, and ships of the convoy, except that I think it would have been better if the heavy ships had kept abaft the beam of the cruisers leading the convoy columns.

"I consider the positioning of the destroyers both by day and night to have been the best possible, except that I think it would have been better to station the destroyers at night so that they were abaft the beam of the leading escorting cruisers and before the beam of the rear escorting cruisers."[200]

By Captain Troubridge, H.M.S. *Nelson*

"Italian tactics have hitherto been the same. The formations approach within about 20 to 30 miles at heights up to 5,000 ft., and then commence to lose height, being usually lost on the radio-direction-finder screen at about 15 miles. Shortly afterwards the machines are sighted low over the water on relative bearings of Red or Green 70 degrees to the mean line of advance, when they maintain a steady course and a height of approximately 100 ft., coming on until they either fire, are shot down, or turn away without attacking – a few press on with commendable gallantry.

"To counter those tactics, it has been the practice in Force 'H' to fire two barrages successively, long at 4,000 yd. and short at 2,000 yd. In order that this may be done without endangering our own ships, the destroyer screen is moved out with the wings thrown back at such an angle that there is a distance of 6,000 yd. clear space for big ships to fire the long barrage. In both operations [July and September] there were sufficient destroyers to ensure that the attacks caused through the wings of the screen, where the destroyers' fire and the long barrage caused the faint-hearted (some 50 per cent or more) to turn away.

"It seems probable that these tactics are forced on the enemy for two reasons: (1) because the large machines they use are not so manoeuvrable as Swordfish or Albacores, and hence are committed to a long straight approach; (2) the low height at the early stages of the approach is probably accounted for by the need for security from our fighters. In future attacks the enemy may well come in from further aft with a view to avoiding the fire of the screen.

"The chief difficulty, in firing both long and short barrages, encountered in the *Nelson* has been target selection. This is due principally to the smoke of bursting shell from the destroyer screen intermittently obscuring the enemy planes; and [in September] some interference in addition was caused by the *Ark Royal* and her cruiser escort, at the critical moment, fouling the range.

"It is emphasized that the above is the experience of action in Mediterranean summer visibility. In thick weather, target selection for the long barrage would be very much more difficult, and barrage would in all probability be confined to the short variety, possibly even fired in sectors."

Appendix G

Vice-Admiral Sir James Somerville's orders for action against enemy surface ships

Note. The paragraph numbers are those in the respective operation orders, of which these are extracts.

The Orders for January, 1941

"The enemy may attempt to interfere with the passage of the convoy by (i) a concentration of force superior to the British forces with the object of direct attack on the escort and convoy, (ii) a feint with a smaller force to draw off the escort from the convoy and thus provide an opportunity for attack on the latter by cruiser and destroyer forces."

"To deal with (i): If air reconnaissance indicates that the enemy is concentrated, and there is a prospect of engaging him within a reasonable distance, i.e. about 30–40 miles, it is my intention to move out and attack with all forces, less *Bonaventure* and two destroyers, who will remain as anti-aircraft and anti-submarine escort for the convoy. Early disablement and if possible destruction of enemy vessels at this stage may exercise a deterrent effect to further attempts by the enemy to interfere with the passage of the convoy."

"To deal with (ii): It is my intention to act as in paragraph 55, but to maintain a position on interior lines, from which I can frustrate any such attempts."

"Should there be reasonable prospects of destroying one or more enemy capital ships, it is my intention to accept a certain degree of risk to the convoy: but unless I am satisfied that the destruction of enemy capital ships can probably be effected, the safety of the convoy will remain my primary object."

"I intend that capital ships, cruisers, and destroyers shall remain in close support of one another during the approach with a view to bringing concentrated fire to bear on any enemy encountered within range."

Ships to follow the Admiral's motions "should communications fail or be delayed."

Two destroyers to screen the *Ark Royal*, when she is detached, the remaining destroyers screening the *Renown* and *Malaya* until required "for attack or counter-attack."

Ships "may be ordered to make smoke" to cover movements or to hide the convoy.

The *Bonaventure* and the convoy to endeavour to go on to the eastward. Should this prove impossible, the convoy "may be ordered to retire to the west." The convoy would then separate, if necessary, to give the escort freedom of action to engage the enemy.

The Orders for July, 1941

Similar to paragraph 57 in the January orders.

Action by day. The *Manxman* and the three *Hunt* class destroyers to stay with the convoy.

The *Ark Royal* and two destroyers "to operate under cover of our main force, remaining as close to the convoy as is practicable."

Other ships "to concentrate on *Renown*. If effective air reconnaissance is available, cruisers should normally remain close to *Renown*, and destroyers continue to screen *Renown* and *Nelson* until contact with the enemy is made."

The *Ark Royal* to provide spotting aircraft for the capital ships and a torpedo striking force – both to be flown off when ordered by the Admiral.

Action by night. The capital ships, and the destroyers on the disengaged side of the screen, to turn away until the nature of the enemy is determined.

Cruisers and destroyers on the side making contact to close and engage.

"As our policy is evasion," searchlight rather than star-shell to be used.

The Orders for September, 1941

"To judge from previous experience, it is unlikely that the enemy will seek action with his main fleet. He may, however, arrange a concentration of his main units to the south of Sardinia, but under cover of his shore-based aircraft, with a view to drawing off our escorting forces and thus opening the way for attack on the convoy by light surface forces and aircraft.

"Our primary object is the safe passage of the convoy to its destination. This object must be constantly borne in mind; and action taken by our escorting forces must in consequence be related to the achievement of this object."

"Unless the enemy main forces close the convoy, or the speed of an enemy capital ship is reduced materially as the result of torpedo attack, and in a position which renders interception by our forces practicable, or some other very favourable opportunity arises to bring the enemy's main forces to action, it is not my intention to part company from the convoy until forced to do so by near approach to the Skerki Channel."

"Should I decide to engage the enemy": –

The *Hermione, Euryalus,* and four destroyers to stay with the convoy.

The *Ark Royal* and two destroyers to work independently near the convoy – the convoy to have first claim on fighter protection.

Other ships "to join my flag as ordered, *Prince of Wales* and cruisers in the van, destroyers screening the capital ships until ordered otherwise" – five destroyers to screen the *Prince of Wales,* seven to screen the *Nelson* and *Rodney.*

The ships in the van (under the Vice-Admiral in the *Prince of Wales)* "are to be manoeuvred so that, if the enemy continues to close, fire can be opened by the van and main body simultaneously. The van must be prepared to fall back on the main body immediately, should the situation become obscure by reason of smoke, and a danger arise of the van's becoming heavily engaged without the support of the main body."

Note. An Appendix contains the orders for action against surface ships after the convoy parted company with the capital ships, and proceeded with an escort of cruisers and destroyers only. The escort was to be organized in three divisions as follows: –

1st Division: *Kenya, Sheffield,* and four destroyers.
2nd Division: *Edinburgh, Hermione, Euryalus,* and four destroyers.
3rd Division: Two destroyers.

When ordered to engage the enemy, "the 1st and 2nd Divisions will move out as necessary to interpose themselves between the convoy and the enemy, and will attack the enemy from either bow with torpedoes, making the fullest use of smoke for this purpose." The 3rd Division was to take charge of the convoy, and both escort and convoy were to make smoke. "The convoy should not be diverged from its direct course for Malta until ordered to do so: in the last resort, the convoy should be ordered to scatter."

Appendix H

Vice-Admiral Somerville's Orders for Action During Air Attacks

The Orders for January, 1941

"When air attack is expected, the screen may be ordered to close by the signal flag 9. If an attack develops without warning, destroyers are to close the battle fleet without further orders during day or night.

"A good look-out for torpedo-bomber attacks is to be maintained, particularly at dusk, during moonlight, and during high-level bombing attacks. Experience in the eastern Mediterranean indicates that high-level bombing, especially at or after dusk, is used to provide cover for torpedo-bomber attack.

"Reliance is placed on the destroyers to protect the fleet from torpedo-bomber attack over the arcs covered by the destroyer screen."[201]

The Orders for July, 1941

"If our fighters are in hot pursuit of any enemy who is under fire from the fleet, or is about to come under fire from the fleet, *Ark Royal* may order 'Cease fire...' On receipt of this signal, which is to remain operative for one minute, all ships are immediately to check fire on the bearing ordered. The order to cease fire is only to be given when there is a good chance of our fighters either destroying the enemy or preventing an attack on the fleet: it is not to be given while dive-bombers are in the near vicinity of the ships.

"It must be borne in mind that all forces may be engaged with enemy aircraft throughout Day 3, Day 4, and a part of Day 5; and a careful control must therefore be kept on the expenditure of anti-aircraft ammunition. A heavy concentration is required against the first bombing attack, as this will probably affect the morale of the enemy in subsequent attacks – in subsequent attacks, fire should not be opened until the target is within range, and should cease when the target passes overhead."

The Orders for September, 1941

"The best defence against enemy air attack is (a) interception by our fighters before the enemy can reach their target; and subsequently (b) the development of the maximum volume of anti-aircraft fire.

"(b) requires that ships shall not become scattered, but keep locked up in their assigned stations, except when torpedo-bomber attack renders it desirable to increase speed to obtain greater manoeuvrability.

"Synchronized high-level bombing and torpedo-bomber attack must be expected. Of these, the latter is the more serious danger.

"Destroyers on the screen must consider it their first duty to sight, report and ward off such attacks by opening fire on the approaching low-flying aircraft directly they are within range. Destroyers must also be careful not to drop inside their assigned distance from the fleet, in order that the latter can develop barrage fire to the fullest extent, if the torpedo aircraft succeed in passing the destroyer screen.

"A careful watch must be maintained by all ships for torpedo tracks, and immediate action taken to comb, if these approach on bearings which may result in a hit."

Appendix I

Forces and Convoy: Operation M.G.1, March 1942

Name	Type	Armament	Commanding Officer
		Force "B" (From Alexandria)	

15th Cruiser Squadron

Name	Type	Armament	Commanding Officer
Cleopatra	Cruiser	Ten 5.25-in. 6 torp. tubes	Captain G. Grantham, D.S.O. (flag of Rear-Admiral P. L. Vian, D.S.O.)
Dido	Cruiser	Eight 5.25-in. One 4-in. 6 torp. tubes	Captain H. W. U. McCall
Euryalus	Cruiser	As *Cleopatra*	Captain E. W. Bush, D.S.O., D.S.C.

14th Destroyer Flotilla

Name	Type	Armament	Commanding Officer
Jervis	Destroyer	Six 4.7-in 9 torp. tubes	Captain A. L. Poland, D.S.O., D.S.C.
Kipling	Destroyer	Six 4.7-in. One 4-in. 5 torp. tubes	Cdr. A. St. Clair-Ford, D.S.O.
Kelvin	Destroyer	As *Kipling*	Cdr. J. H. Allison, D.S.O.
Kingston	Destroyer	As *Kipling*	Cdr. P. Somerville, D.S.O., D.S.C.

22nd Destroyer Flotilla

Name	Type	Armament	Commanding Officer
Sikh	Destroyer	Six 4.7-in. Two 4-in. 4 torp. tubes	Captain St. J. A. Micklethwait, D.S.O.
Lively	Destroyer	Eight 4-in. 8 torp. tubes	Lieut.-Cdr. W. F. E. Hussey, D.S.O., D.S.C.

Hero	Destroyer	Four 4.7-in. 8 torp. tubes	Cdr. R. L. Fisher, D.S.O., O.B.E.
Havock	Destroyer	Four 4.7-in. One 3-in. 4 torp. tubes	Lieut.-Cdr. G. R. G. Watkins, D.S.C.
Zulu	Destroyer	As *Sikh*	Cdr. H. R. Graham, D.S.O., D.S.C.
Hasty	Destroyer	As *Havock*	Lieut.-Cdr. N. H. G. Austen

Force "K" (from Malta)

Penelope	Cruiser	Six 6-in. Eight 4-in. 6 torp. tubes	Captain A. D. Nicholl, D.S.O.
Legion	Destroyer	Eight 4-in. 8 torp. tubes	Cdr. R. F. Jessel

Close Escort for Convoy

Carlisle	Anti-aircraft Ship	Eight 4-in.	Captain D. M. L. Neame, D.S.O.

5th Destroyer Flotilla

Southwold	Destroyer	Six 4-in.	Cdr. C. T. Jellicoe, D.S.C.
Beaufort	Destroyer	As *Southwold*	Lieut.-Cdr. Sir. O. G. Roche, Bart.
Dulverton	Destroyer	do.	Lieut.-Cdr. W. N. Petch, O.B.E.
Hurworth	Destroyer	do.	Lieut.-Cdr. P. A. R. Withers, D.S.C.
Avon Vale	Destroyer	do.	Lieut.-Cdr W. F. N. Gregory-Smith, D.S.C.
Heythrop[202]	Destroyer	do.	Lieut.-Cdr. R. S. Stafford

Submarines

In Southern Approaches to Messina

Unbeaten	Submarine	4 torp. tubes	Lieut.-Cdr. E. A. Woodward, D.S.O.
P.34	Submarine	4 torp. tubes	Lieut. P. D. R. Harrison, D.S.C.

In Approaches to Taranto

Proteus	Submarine	8 torp. tubes	Lieut.-Cdr. P. S. Francis
Upholder	Submarine	4 torp. tubes	Lieut.-Cdr. M. D. Wanklyn, V.C., D.S.O.
P.36	Submarine	4 torp. tubes	Lieut. H. N. Edmonds, D.S.C.

Convoy M.W. 10

Name	Tonnage[203]	Remarks
H.M.S. *Breconshire*[204]	10,000	Captain C. A. G. Hutchison (Commodore). Disabled by bombs 23 March, and anchored outside Malta; towed into Marsaxlokk, 25 March; damaged again by bombs, 26 March; and sank, 27 March.
Clan Campbell	7,500	Sunk by bombs on way into Malta, 23 March.
Pampas	5,500	Arrived Malta, 23 March; damaged by bombs and aground with all holds except two flooded, 26 March.
Talabot (Norwegian)	7,000	Arrived Malta, 23 March; damaged by bombs, 26 March, and had to be scuttled.

Appendix J

Forces and Convoys: June 1942

1. Operation "Harpoon"

Name	Type	Armament	Commanding Officer
		Force "W"	
Malaya	Battleship	Eight 15-in. Twelve 6-in. Eight 4-in.	Captain J. W. A. Waller
Eagle	Aircraft Carrier	Nine 6-in. Four 4-in. (16 Hurricane and 4 Fulmar aircraft)	Captain E. G. N. Rushbrooke, D.S.C.
Argus	Aircraft Carrier	Four 4-in. (2 Fulmar and 18 Swordfish aircraft)	Captain G. T. Philip, D.S.C.
Kenya	Cruiser	Twelve 6-in.	Captain A. S. Russell (flag of Vice-Admiral A. T. B. Curteis, C.B.)
Liverpool	Cruiser	Twelve 6-in. Eight 4-in.	Captain W. R. Slayter, D.S.C.
Charybdis	Cruiser	Eight 4.5-in.	Captain L. D. Mackintosh, D.S.C.
Onslow	Destroyer	Four 4.7-in. One 4-in.	Captain H. T. Armstrong, D.S.C.
Icarus	Destroyer	Four 4.7-in. One 3-in.	Lieut.-Cdr. C. D. Maud, D.S.C.
Escapade	Destroyer	As *Icarus*	Lieut.-Cdr. E. N. V. Currey, D.S.C.

Wishart	Destroyer	Three 4.7-in. One 12-pdr.	Cdr. H. G. Scott
Westcott	Destroyer	Four 4-in. One 12-pdr.	Cdr. I. H. Bockett-Pugh, D.S.O.
Wrestler	Destroyer	Three 4-in. One 12-pdr.	Lieut. R. W. B. Lacon
Vidette	Destroyer	As *Wrestler*	Lieut.-Cdr. E. N. Walmsley
Antelope	Destroyer	Three 4.7-in. One 3-in.	Lieut.-Cdr. E. N. Sinclair

Force "X"

Cairo	Anti-aircraft ship	Eight 4-in.	Act. Captain C. C. Hardy, D.S.O.
Bedouin	Destroyer	Six 4.7-in. Two 4-in.	Cdr. B. G. Scurfield, O.B.E., A.M.
Marne	Destroyer	Six 4.7-in.	Lieut.-Cdr. N. H. A. Richardson, D.S.C.
Matchless	Destroyer	As *Marne*	Lieut.-Cdr. J. Mowlam
Ithuriel	Destroyer	Four 4.7-in.	Lieut.-Cdr. D. H. Maitland-Makgill-Crichton, D.S.C.
Partridge	Destroyer	Five 4-in.	Lieut.-Cdr. W. A. F. Hawkins, O.B.E., D.S.C.
Blankney	Destroyer	Six 4-in.	Lieut.-Cdr. P. F. Powlett, D.S.C.
Middleton	Destroyer	As *Blankney*	Lieut.-Cdr. D. C. Kinloch
Badsworth	Destroyer	do.	Lieut. G. T. S. Gray, D.S.C.
Kujawiak (Polish)	Destroyer	do.	Cdr. L. Lichodziejewski
Speedy	Minesweeper	One 4-in.	Lieut.-Cdr. A. E. Doran
Hebe	Minesweeper	As *Speedy*	Lieut.-Cdr. G. Mowatt, R.D., R.N.R.
Rye	Minesweeper	One 3-in.	Lieut. J. A. Pearson, R.N.R.
Hythe	Minesweeper	One 3-in.	Lieut.-Cdr. L. B. Miller

No. 121		One 12-pdr.	
134		One 3-pdr.	
135		One 2-pdr.	
168	Motor Launch	or	Lieut.-Cdr. E. J. Strowlger,
459		Two 2-pdr.	R.N.V.R. in No. 121, S.O.
462		Two 0.5-in.	
		2 Lewis	

Force "Y"

Geranium	Corvette	On 4-in.	Lieut.-Cdr. A. Foxall, R.N.R.
Coltsfoot	Corvette	As *Geranium*	Lieut. Hon. W. K. Rous, R.N.V.R.
Brown Ranger	Oiler		

Special Service

Welshman	Minelayer	Six 4-in.	Captain W. H. D. Friedberger

Submarines

P.211	Submarine	7 torpedo tubes	Cdr. B. Bryant, D.S.C.
P.42	Submarine	4 do.	Lieut. A. C. G. Mars
P.43	Submarine	4 do.	Lieut. A. C. Halliday
P.44	Submarine	4 do.	Lieut. T. E. Barlow

Convoy
Commodore: Commander J. P. W. Pilditch, O.B.E.

Name	Tonnage	Remarks
Troilus	7,500	Arrived Malta, 16 June.
Burdwan	6,000	Damaged by near miss, 15 June; torpedoed and sunk by aircraft later same day.
Chant (U.S.)	5,500	Sunk by bombs, 15 June.

Orari	10,500	Damaged by mine, 16 June; arrived Malta same day.
Tanimbar (Dutch)	8,000	Torpedoed and sunk by aircraft, 14 June.
Kentucky (U.S.)	5,500	As *Burdwan*.

2. Operation "Vigorous"

(*Note*. The 4th Cruiser Squadron and the 7th, 12th and 2nd Destroyer Flotillas and *Centurion* were lent from the Eastern Fleet for the occasion.)

Name	Type	Armament	Commanding Officer
15th Cruiser Squadron			
Cleopatra	Cruiser	Ten 5.25-in.	Captain G. Grantham, D.S.O. (flag of Rear-Admiral P. L. Vian, K.B.E. D.S.O.)
Dido	Cruiser	As *Cleopatra*	Captain H. W. U. McCall
Hermione	Cruiser	do.	Captain G. N. Oliver, D.S.O.
Euryalus	Cruiser	do.	Captain E. W. Bush, D.S.O., D.S.C.
Arethusa	Cruiser	Six 6-in. Four 4-in.	Captain A. C. Chapman
Coventry	Anti-aircraft Ship	Eight 4-in.	Captain R. J. R. Dendy
4th Cruiser Squadron			
Newcastle	Cruiser	Twelve 6-in Eight 4-in.	Captain P. B. R. W. William-Powlett, D.S.O. (flag of Rear-Admiral W. G. Tennant, C.B., M.V.O.)
Birmingham	Cruiser	As *Newcastle*	Captain H. B. Crane
7th Destroyer Flotilla			
Napier	Destroyer	Six 4.7-in. One 4-in.	Captain S. H. T. Arliss, D.S.O.
Nestor	Destroyer	As *Napier*	Cdr. A. S. Rosenthal, D.S.O., R.A.N.

Norman	Destroyer	do.	Cdr. H. M. Burrell, R.A.N.
Nizam	Destroyer	do.	Lieut.-Cdr. M. J. Clark, D.S.C., R.A.N.

14th Destroyer Flotilla

Jervis	Destroyer	As *Napier*	Captain A. L. Poland, D.S.O., D.S.C.
Kelvin	Destroyer	do.	Cdr. M. S. Townsend, O.B.E., D.S.C.
Javelin	Destroyer	do.	Lieut.-Cdr. H. C. Simms, D.S.O.

12th Destroyer Flotilla

Pakenham	Destroyer	Five 4-in.	Captain E. B. K. Stevens, D.S.O., D.S.C.
Paladin	Destroyer	As *Pakenham*	Cdr. A. F. Pugsley
Inconstant	Destroyer	Four 4.7-in.	Lieut.-Cdr. W. S. Clouston

22nd Destroyer Flotilla

Sikh	Destroyer	Six 4.7-in. Two 4-in.	Captain St. J. A. Micklethwait, D.S.O.
Zulu	Destroyer	As *Sikh*	Cdr. R. T. White, D.S.O.
Hasty	Destroyer	Four 4.7-in. One 3-in.	Lieut.-Cdr. N. H. G. Austen
Hero	Destroyer	Four 4.7-in.	Lieut. W. Scott

5th Destroyer Flotilla

Dulverton	Destroyer	Six 4.7-in.	Lieut.-Cdr. W. N. Petch, O.B.E.
Exmoor	Destroyer	As *Dulverton*	Lieut.-Cdr. L. St. G. Rich
Croome	Destroyer	do.	Lieut.-Cdr. J. D. Hayes, D.S.O.

Eridge	Destroyer	do.	Lieut.-Cdr. W. F. N. Gregory-Smith, D.S.C.
Airedale	Destroyer	Four 4-in.	Lieut.-Cdr. A. G. Forman
Beaufort	Destroyer	As *Dulverton*	Lieut.-Cdr. Sir S. O'G. Roche, Bart.
Hurworth	Destroyer	do.	Lieut.-Cdr. J. T. B. Birch
Tetcott	Destroyer	do.	Lieut. H. R. Rycroft
Aldenham	Destroyer	Four 4-in.	Lieut. H. A. Stuart-Menteth

2ⁿᵈ Destroyer Flotilla

Fortune	Destroyer	Three 4.7-in. One 3-in.	Lieut.-Cdr. R. D. H. S. Pankhurst
Griffin	Destroyer	Four 4.7-in. One 3-in.	Lieut.-Cdr. A. N. Rowell
Hotspur	Destroyer	As *Griffin*	Lieut. T. D. Herrick, D.S.C.

Other Vessels[205] in Company

Delphinium	Corvette	One 4-in.	Cdr. R. L. Spalding
Primula	Corvette	As *Delphinium*	Lieut.-Cdr. J. H. Fuller, R.N.R.
Erica	Corvette	do.	Lieut.-Cdr. W. C. Riley, R.N.V.R.
Snapdragon	Corvette	do.	Lieut. P. H. Potter, R.N.R.
Boston	Minesweeper	One 3-in.	Lieut. D. H. G. Coughlan, R.N.R.
Seaham	Minesweeper	As *Boston*	Lieut. R. E. Brett, R.N.R.
Centurion	Unarmed special service		Cdr. A. H. Alexander
Antwerp	Unarmed rescue ship		Lieut.-Cdr. J. N. Hulse, R.N.R.
Malines	do.	do.	Lieut. J. R. Freeman, R.N.R.

Submarines

Proteus	Submarine	8 torp. tubes	Lieut.-Cdr. P. S. Francis
Thorn	do.	11 do.	Lieut.-Cdr. R. G. Norfolk
Taku	do.	11 do.	Lieut.-Cdr. J. G. Hopkins
Thrasher	do.	11 do.	Lieut. H. S. Mackenzie
Porpoise	do.	6 do.	Lieut. L. W. A. Bennignton, D.S.C.
Una	do.	4 do.	Lieut. C. P. Norman
P.31	do.	4 do.	Lieut. J. B. Kershaw
P.34	do.	4 do.	Lieut. P. R. Harrison, D.S.C.
P.35	do.	4 do.	Lieut. S. L. C. Maydon

Convoy M.W.11
Commodore: Rear-Admiral H. T. England (Ret.)

Name	Tonnage	Remarks
City of Pretoria	8,000	
City of Calcutta	8,000	Damage by near miss, 12 June; detached to Tobruk.
Bhutan	6,000	Sunk by bombs, 14 June.
Potaro	5,500	Damaged by near miss, 14 June; returned to Alexandria with the convoy.
Bulkoil	8,000	
Rembrandt (Dutch)	8,000	
Aagetekirk (Dutch)	7,000	Detached to Tobruk, 14 June, being too slow; sunk by bombs the same day.
City of Edinburgh	8,000	
City of Lincoln	8,000	
Elizabeth Bakke (Norwegian)	5,500	Detached to Alexandria, 13 June, being too slow.
Ajax	7,500	

Appendix K

Forces and Convoys: August 1942
Operation "Pedestal"

Name	Type	Armament	Commanding Officer
		Force "Z"	
Nelson	Battleship	Nine 16-in. Twelve 6-in. Six 4.7-in.	Captain H. B. Jacomb (Flag Of Acting Vice-Admiral E. N. Syfret, C.B.)
Rodney	Battleship	As *Nelson*	Captain J. W. Rivett-Carnac, D.S.C.
Victorious	Aircraft Carrier	Sixteen 4.5-in. (6 Hurricane, 16 Fulmar and 12 Albacore aircraft)	Captain H. C. Bovell, C.B.E. (flag of Rear-Admiral A. L. St. G. Lyster, C.B., C.V.O., D.S.O.)
Indomitable	Aircraft Carrier	As *Victorious* (10 Martlet, 24 Hurricane and 16 Albacore aircraft)	Captain T. H. Troubridge
Eagle[206]	Aircraft Carrier	Nine 6-in. Four 4-in. (16 Hurricane aircraft)	Captain L. D. Mackintosh, D.S.C.
Sirius	Cruiser	Ten 5.25-in.	Captain P. W. B. Brooking
Phoebe	Cruiser	Eight 5.25-in. One 4-in.	Captain C. P. Frend
Charybdis	Cruiser	Eight 4.5-in.	Captain G. A. W. Voelcker

Laforey	Destroyer	Six 4.7-in. One 4-in.	Captain R. M. J. Hutton
Lightning	Destroyer	As *Laforey*	Cdr. H. G. Walters, D.S.C.
Lookout	Destroyer	do.	Cdr. C. P. F. Brown, D.S.C.
Quentin	Destroyer	Four 4.7-in.	Lieut.-Cdr. A. H. P. Noble, D.S.C.
Tartar	Destroyer	Six 4.7-in. Two 4-in.	Cdr. St. J. R. J. Tyrwhitt, D.S.C.
Eskimo	Destroyer	As *Tartar*	Cdr. E. G. Le Geyt
Somali	Destroyer	do.	Cdr. E. N. V. Currey, D.S.C.
Wishart	Destroyer	Three 4.7-in One 12-pdr.	Cdr. H. G. Scott
Zetland	Destroyer	Six 4-in.	Lieut. J. V. Wilkinson
Ithuriel	Destroyer	Four 4.7-in.	Lieut.-Cdr. D. H. Maitland-Makgill-Crichton, D.S.C.
Antelope	Destroyer	Three 4.7-in One 3-in.	Lieut.-Cdr. E. N. Sinclair
Vansittart	Destroyer	As *Wishart*	Lieut.-Cdr. T. Johnston, D.S.C.

Additional Ships for Detached Escorts

Keppel	Destroyer	Two 4.7-in. One 3-in.	Cdr J. E. Broome
Westcott	Destroyer	Four 4-in. One 12-pdr.	Cdr. I. H. Bockett-Pugh, D.S.O.
Venomous	Destroyer	As *Wishart*	Cdr H. W. Falcon-Steward
Malcolm	Destroyer	As *Keppel*	Acting Cdr. A. B. Russell
Wolverine	Destroyer	Two 4.7-in. One 12-pdr.	Lieut.-Cdr. P. W. Gretton, O.B.E., D.S.C.
Amazon	Destroyer	As *Keppel*	Lieut.-Cdr. Lord Teynham

Wrestler	Destroyer	Three 4-in.	Lieut. R. W. B. Lacon, D.S.C.
Vidette	Destroyer	As *Wrestler*	Lieut.-Cdr. E. N. Walmsley, D.S.C.

Force "R"

Jonquil	Corvette	One 4-in.	Lieut.-Cdr. R. E. H. Partington, R.D., R.N.R.
Spirea	Corvette	As *Jonquil*	Lieut.-Cdr. R. S. Miller, D.S.C., R.D., R.N.R.
Geranium	Corvette	do.	Lieut.-Cdr. A. Foxhall, R.N.R.
Coltsfoot	Corvette	do.	Lieut. the Hon. W. K. Rouse, R.N.V.R.
Salvonia	Tug		
Brown Ranger	Fleet Oiler		
Dingledale	Fleet Oiler		

Force "X"

Nigeria	Cruiser	Twelve 6-in. Eight 4-in.	Captain S. H. Paton (flag of Rear-Admiral H. M. Burrough, C.B., D.S.O.)
Kenya	Cruiser	As *Nigeria*	Captain A. S. Russell
Manchester	Cruiser	do.	Captain H. Drew, D.S.C.
Cairo	Anti-aircraft Ship	Eight 4-in.	Acting Captain C. C. Hardy, D.S.O.
Ashanti	Destroyer	Eight 4.7-in. Two 4-in.	Acting Captain R. G. Onslow, D.S.O.
Intrepid	Destroyer	Four 4.7-in. One 3-in.	Commander C. A. De W. Kitcat
Icarus	Destroyer	As *Intrepid*	Lieut.-Cdr. C. D. Maud, D.S.C.
Foresight[207]	Destroyer	do.	Lieut.-Cdr. R. A. Fell

Fury	Destroyer	do.	Lieut.-Cdr. C. H. Campbell, D.S.C.
Derwent	Destroyer	Four 4-in.	Cdr. R. H. Wright, D.S.C.
Bramham	Destroyer	Six 4-in.	Lieut. E. F. Baines
Bicester	Destroyer	As *Bramham*	Lieut.-Cdr. S. W. F. Bennetts
Ledbury	Destroyer	do.	Lieut.-Cdr. R. P. Hill
Pathfinder	Destroyer	Five 4-in.	Cdr. E. A. Gibbs, D.S.O.
Penn	Destroyer	As *Pathfinder*	Lieut.-Cdr. J. H. Swain
Wilton	Destroyer	As *Bramham*	Lieut. A. P. Northey, D.S.C.
Jaunty	Tug	One 12-pdr.	Lieut.-Cdr. H. Osburn, O.B.E., R.N.R.

Malta Escort Force
(Acting Commander H. J. A. S. Jerome, Senior Officer, in *Speedy*)

Speedy	Minesweeper	One 4-in.	Lieut.-Cdr. A. E. Doran
Hebe	Minesweeper	As *Speedy*	Lieut.-Cdr. G. Mowatt, R.D., R.N.R.
Hythe	Minesweeper	One 3-in. One 12-pdr.	Lieut.-Cdr. L. B. Miller
Rye	Minesweeper	One 3-in.	Lieut. J. A. Pearson, D.S.C., R.N.R.
No. *121*			
126		One 3-pdr.	
134	Motor Launch	One 2-pdr.	
135		or	Lieut.-Cdr. E. J. Strowlger, R.N.V.R., in No. 121, S.O.
168		Two 2-pdr.	
459		Two 0.5-in.	
462		2 Lewis	

Operation "Bellows"

Furious	Aircraft Carrier	Twelve 4-in. (4 Albacore aircraft); 40 Spitfires for Malta	Captain T. O. Bulteel

Force "Y" (Operation "Ascendant")

Matchless	Destroyer	Six 4.7-in. One 4-in.	Lieut.-Cdr. J. Mowlam
Badsworth	Destroyer	Six 4-in.	Lieut. G. T. S. Gray, D.S.C.

Submarines

North of Sicily

P.211	Submarine	7 torp. tubes	Cdr. B. Bryant, D.S.C.
P.42	Submarine	4 do.	Lieut. A. C. G. Mars

Between Malta and Tunisia

P.44	Submarine	4 torp. tubes	Lieut. T. E. Barlow
P.222	Submarine	7 do.	Lieut.-Cdr. A. J. Mackenzie
P.31	Submarine	4 do.	Lieut. J. B. Kershaw, D.S.O.
P.34	Submarine	4 do.	Lieut. P. R. Harrison, D.S.C.
P.46	Submarine	4 do.	Lieut. J. Stevens
Utmost	Submarine	4 do.	Lieut. A. W. Langridge

Convoys

Convoy W.S.21.S: to Malta

Commodore: Commander A. G. Venables

Name	Tonnage	Remarks
Port Chalmers	8,500	Arrived Malta, 13 August.
Clan Ferguson	7,500	Sunk by air torpedo, 12 August.

Melbourne Star	11,000	Arrived Malta, 13 August.
Brisbane Star	13,000	Damaged by air torpedo, 12 August; arrived Malta 14 August.
Almeria Lykes (U.S.)	8,000	Torpedoed by motor torpedo boat, 13 August, and abandoned.
Santa Elisa (U.S.)	8,500	Torpedoed by motor torpedo boat, 13 August, and abandoned; sunk by bombs later same day.
Rochester Castle	8,000	Torpedoed by motor torpedo boat, 13 August; arrived Malta with the convoy same day.
Empire Hope	12,500	Disabled by bombs, 12 August; sunk by *Penn*.
Glenorchy	9,000	Sunk 13 August; cause uncertain.
Dorset	13,000	Disabled by bombs, 13 August; sunk by bombs later same day.
Deucalion	7,500	Damaged by near misses, 12 August; sunk by air torpedo later same day.
Wairangi	12,500	Torpedoed by motor torpedo boat and abandoned, 13 August.
Waimarama	13,000	Sunk by bombs, 13 August.
Ohio	10,000	Torpedoed by submarine, 12 August; disabled by near misses, 13 August, and damaged again by bombs that day; towed to Malta, arriving 15 August.

Convoy "Ascendant": Malta to Gibraltar

Troilus	7,500	Sailed 10 August; arrived at
Otari	10,500	Gibraltar 14 August.

Appendix L

Report on Planning Operation "Pedestal"
(R.O. Case W.H.S.8268)
The following recommendations with regard to planning an operation similar to "Pedestal" in the future were made: –

"We understand that the planning of this operation was far better than in any of its predecessors, because it was started earlier and was done more thoroughly because the facilities at, and the resources of, the Admiralty were placed at the disposal of the Flag Officer concerned.

"We strongly recommend that a similar procedure should be carried out in future operations, with certain modifications as suggested below:–

(A) It would greatly assist the officers who carry out the planning if there was a permanent officer appointed to Operations Division who would attend during the planning of all such operations and would analyse the results, in the same manner as we are doing now. This officer would know all the Admiralty Departments, and he would insure that details, which are liable to be overlooked by the planning officers and their operational staffs, are raised at an early stage, and that lessons learnt are not forgotten. It is understood that the present staff of Operations Division does not allow of one officer specialising in this duty.

(B) We strongly recommend that where possible a Senior Officer, or officers, as representatives from the place or station affected should be sent home by air to take part in the planning. In this operation certainly the Malta Command, and also possibly Gibraltar, should have been represented, thereby making for closer contact and obviating excessive signalling.

(C) In a 'Fleet' the various communication orders are cut-and-dried, and are continually being used and exercised, but this is not the case with a Command, as was Force 'F' on this occasion. Therefore for any special operation of this nature we recommend that the Senior Officer, or Officers, conducting the operation should bring their Signal Officers as well as their Operations Officers to the Admiralty during the planning stage."[208]

Appendix M

Operations "M.G.1","Harpoon", "Vigorous", "Pedestal": Analysis of Ships Lost and Damaged

(Ships sunk are shown in capitals)

I. Warships

Method of Attack	Name	Class	Remarks	Operation
Aircraft (bombs)	*Indomitable*	Carrier	Damaged	"Pedestal"
	Victorious	Carrier	Slightly damaged	"Pedestal"
	Birmingham	Cruiser	Damaged	"Vigorous"
	Arethusa	Cruiser	Damaged	"Vigorous"
	LEGION	Destroyer	Damaged: later sunk, Malta	"M.G.1"
	KINGSTON	Destroyer	Sunk, Malta	"M.G.1"
	AIREDALE	Destroyer	Damaged: sunk by own forces	"Vigorous"
	NESTOR	Destroyer	Damaged: sunk by own forces	"Vigorous"
	Primula	Corvette	Damaged	"Vigorous"
	P.36	S/M	Sunk, Malta	"M.G.1"
	Centurion	Sp. Service	Slightly damaged	"Vigorous"

Aircraft (torpedoes)	*Liverpool*	Cruiser	Damaged	"Harpoon"
	BEDOUIN	Destroyer	Sunk	"Harpoon"
	FORESIGHT	Destroyer	Damaged: sunk by own forces	"Pedestal"
Surface Ships	*Cleopatra*	Cruiser	Damaged	"M.G.1"
	Havock	Destroyer	Damaged	"M.G.1"
	Kingston	Destroyer	Damaged	"M.G.1"
	Lively	Destroyer	Damaged	"M.G.1"
	Bedouin	Destroyer	Damaged	"Harpoon"
	Partridge	Destroyer	Damaged	"Harpoon"
	Hebe	Minesweeper	Damaged	"Harpoon"
Motor Torpedo Boats	MANCHESTER	Cruiser	Damaged: scuttled	"Pedestal"
	Newcastle	Cruiser	Damaged	"Vigorous"
	HASTY	Destroyer	Damaged: sunk by own forces	"Vigorous"
Submarines	EAGLE	Carrier	Sunk	"Pedestal"
	Nigeria	Cruiser	Damaged	"Pedestal"
	HERMIONE	Cruiser	Sunk	"Vigorous"
	Kenya	Cruiser	Damaged	"Pedestal"
	CAIRO	A.A. Ship	Damaged: sunk by own forces	"Pedestal"
Mines	HEYTHROP	Destroyer	Sunk	"M.G.1"
	SOUTHWOLD	Destroyer	Sunk	"M.G.1"
	KUJAWIAK	Destroyer	Sunk	"Harpoon"
	Badsworth	Destroyer	Damaged	"Harpoon"
	Matchless	Destroyer	Damaged	"Harpoon"
	Hebe	Minesweeper	Damaged	"Harpoon"

II. Merchant Ships

Method of Attack	Name	Tonnage	Remarks	Operation
Aircraft (bombs)	H.M.S. BRECONSHIRE	10,000	Damaged: later sunk, Malta	"M.G.1"
	CLAN CAMPBELL	7,500	Sunk	"M.G.1"
	TALABOT	7,000	Sunk, Malta	"M.G.1"
	PAMPAS	5,500	Damaged: later sunk, Malta	"M.G.1"
	CHANT	5,500	Sunk	"Harpoon"
	KENTUCKY	5,500	Damaged: sunk by own forces	"Harpoon"
	BURDWAN	6,000	Damaged: sunk by own forces	"Harpoon"
	City of Calcutta	8,000	Damaged	"Vigorous"
	AAGTEKIRK[209]	7,000	Sunk	"Vigorous"
	BHUTAN	6,000	Sunk	"Vigorous"
	Potaro	5,500	Damaged	"Vigorous"
	Deucalion	7,500	Damaged	"Pedestal"
	EMPIRE HOPE	12,500	Damaged: sunk by own forces	"Pedestal"
	WAIMARAMA	13,000	Sunk	"Pedestal"
	Rochester Castle	8,000	Damaged	"Pedestal"
	SANTA ELISA[209]	8,500	Sunk	"Pedestal"
	Ohio[209]	10,000	Damaged	"Pedestal"
	DORSET[209]	13,000	Sunk	"Pedestal"

Aircraft (torpedoes)	*TANIMBAR*	8,000	Sunk	"Harpoon"
	CLAN FERGUSON	7,500	Sunk	"Pedestal"
	Brisbane Star	13,000	Damaged	"Pedestal"
	DEUCALION[209]	7,500	Sunk	"Pedestal"
Surface ships	–		–	
Motor torpedo boats	*GLENORCHY*[209]	9,000	Sunk	"Pedestal"
	WAIRANGI[209]	12,500	Sunk	"Pedestal"
	ALMERIA LYKES[209]	8,000	Sunk	"Pedestal"
	Rochester Castle[209]	8,000	Damaged	"Pedestal"
	Santa Elisa[209]	8,500	Damaged	"Pedestal"
Submarines	*Ohio*	10,000	Damaged	"Pedestal"
Mines	*Orari*	10,500	Damaged	"Harpoon"

Abstract

Method of Attack	Warships		Merchant Ships		Total
	Sunk	Damaged	Sunk	Damaged	
Aircraft, bombs	5	6	13	5	29
Aircraft, torpedoes	2	1	3	1	7
Surface ships		7			7
Motor torpedo boats	2	1	3	2	8
Submarines	4	2		1	6
Mines	2	3		1	6

Appendix N

Strengths in Operations and Numbers Sunk or Damaged

1941

Type	January "Excess"			July "Substance"			September "Halberd"		
	No.	S.	D.	No.	S.	D.	No.	S.	D.
Capital Ships	4			2			3		1
Aircraft Carriers	2		1	1			1		
Cruisers	8	1	1	4		1	5		
Anti-aircraft Ship	1								
Minelayer				1					
Destroyers	23		1	18	1	1	18		
Corvettes	4						1		
Submarines	3			8			9		
Merchant Ships	14			13		1	12	1	

1942

Note. These figures do not necessarily agree with those given in the abstract in Appendix M, since in Appendix M the same ship may appear more than once, e.g. *Bedouin* damaged by *surface craft*, sunk by *A/C torpedoes; Ohio* damaged by *submarine*, and again by *A/C bombs.*

Type	March "M.G.1"			June "Harpoon"			June "Vigorous"			August "Pedestal"		
	No.	S.	D.	No.	S.	D.	No.	S.	D.	No.	S.	D.
Capital Ships				1						2		
Aircraft Carriers				2						3	1	1
Cruisers	4		2	3		1	7	1	3	6	1	2
Anti-aircraft Ships	1			1			1			1	1	

Minelayers				1								
Destroyers	18	2	3[210]	17	2	3	26	3		34	1	
Corvettes				2			4		1	4		
Submarines	5	1		4			9			8		
Minesweepers				4		1	2			4		
Motor Launches				6						7		
Merchant Ships[213]	4[211]	1	1	6	4	1	11[212]	2	2	14	9	3

Appendix O

Table of Performance of British Aircraft, 1941–1942

(a) Fighter Aircraft Capable of Deck Landing

	British Naval[214]			R.A.F.	
	Sea Hurricane	Martlet	Fulmar	Hurricane	Spitfire
Crew	1	1	2	1	1
Armament	8 Browning	4 Colt 0.5	8 .303F[215] One 500-lb or One 250-lb bomb	8 .303F	8 .303F
Whether dive-bomber	No	No	No	No	No
Whether fitted for observer navigation, W/T, and folding	No[216]	No[216]	Yes	No[216]	No[216]
Maximum speed (knots)	250	260	230	No	No
Endurance at maximum speed (approx.)	¾ hr	1½ hr	2 hr	1 hr	¾ hr
Maximum endurance at economical speed	2¾ hr (420 miles approx.)	4½ hr (720 miles approx.)	6 hr[217] (750 miles approx.)	4¼ hr	3½ hr

(b) Reconnaissance and Strike Aircraft

	British Naval			R.A.F.
	Swordfish	Albacore	Walrus[218]	Battle
Crew	3 Recce. 2 for strike	3 Recce. 2 for strike	3 Recce.	2 or 3
Armament	Torpedo[219] or bombs: 1,500 lb	Torpedo[219] or bombs: 1,500 lb	Bombs[219]: 500 lb	Bombs[219]: 1,000 lb plus 500 at expense of range
Whether capable of dive-bombing	Yes	Yes	Limited	No
Whether capable of torpedo attack	Yes	Yes	No	No
Maximum speed (knots)	125	155	110	220
Maximum endurance and range without extra tankage:				
(i) Recce.	5½ hr	6 hr	3½ hr	8 hr
(ii) Strike force	550 miles	650 miles	300 miles	1,200 miles
Whether extra tankage	Yes	Yes	No	No

Appendix P

Performance Table – German and Italian Aircraft, 1940 – 1942

(All figures approximate)

	Fighters			Bombers	
	German		Italian	German	
	Me. 109	Me. 110	C.R. 42	Ju. 87D	Ju. 88
Description	Single-engine monoplane	Twin-engine monoplane	Single-engine biplane; open cockpit	Single-engine monoplane	T/B. recce. fighter; twin-engine monoplane
Crew	1	2	1	2	4
Armament	One 7.9 mm., Two 20mm., (occasionally) in wings	Four 7.9 mm., One 20 mm.; Dorsal – two or twin 7.9 mm.	No provision for wing guns; Two 12.7 mm.	One 2,000 lb bomb; Wing gun – two 2.79 mm.; Dorsal – 7.9 mm.	Typical bomb or torpedo load two 2,000-lb and two 500-lb; For'd – 7.9 mm. and 20 mm.; Dorsal – two 7.9 mm.; Ventral – twin 7.9 mm.
Capable of Dive Bombing	In some forms Glide Bomber	In some forms Glide Bomber	No	Yes	No
Capable of Torpedo Attack	No	No	No	No	Yes
Maximum Speed	317 knots	328 knots	262 knots	204 knots	249 knots
Maximum Range	655 miles	1,200 miles	690 miles	670 miles	1,900 miles
Endurance at	3.3 hours	7.5 hours	4.5 hours	3.7 hours	10.7 hours
Speed	178 knots	160 knots	132 knots	159 knots	180 knots

	Bombers			Naval Reconnaissance		
	German		Italian	German		Italian
	He. 111	F.W. 200[220]	S. 79	Do. 18	Ar. 196	Cant. 501
	T.B.R. twin-engine monoplane	T.B.R. four-engine monoplane	T.B.R. three-engine monoplane	Twin-engine monoplane, flying boat	Fighter-bomber, single-engine, monoplane, twin floats	Recce. and light bombing single-engine monoplane flying boat
	5 – 6	5 – 7	4 – 5	4	2	4 – 5
	For'd. – One or two 7.9 mm.; One 20 mm.; Dorsal – one 7.9 mm.; Lateral – two 7.9 mm.; Ventral – twin 7.9 mm. or one 20 mm.	Three 300-lb (mixed) bombs; Mixed 20 mm. turret and 7.9 mm. in dorsal, lateral and ventral positions (variable)	Five 500-lb bombs; For'd. – one 12.7 mm.; Dorsal – one 12.7 mm.; Lateral – one or two 7.7 mm.; Ventral – one 12.7 mm.	440-lb bomb; One dorsal turret gun 7.9 20 mm.; One for'd. 7.9 13 mm.	Two 112-lb bombs; For'd. – one 7.9 mm.; Wings – two 20 mm.; Dorsal – twin 7.9 mm.	For'd. – one 7.7 mm.; Dorsal – three 7.7 mm.
	No	No	No	Yes (Glide only)	Yes	No
	Yes	Yes (Not so used)	Yes	No	No	No
	218 knots	213 knots	227 knots	130 knots	172 knots	134 knots
	1,930 miles	2,700 miles	1,700 miles	2,640 miles	600 miles	2,700 miles
	10 hours	16.5 hours	11 hours	24 hours	5.2 hours	38 hours
	166 knots	147 knots	136 knots	97 knots	105 knots	72 knots

Appendix Q

Italian Surface Ships in 1942

Name	Armament	Remarks
	Battleships (6)	
Littorio *Vittorio Veneto*	Nine 15-in. Twelve 6-in. Twelve 3.5-in.	
Andrea Doria *Caio Duilio*	Ten 12.6-in. Twelve 5.3-in. Ten 3.5-in.	
Giulio Cesare *Conte di Cavour*	Ten 12.6-in. Twelve 4-7-in. Eight 4-in.	*Cavour* under repair.
	8-in. Cruisers (4)	
Gorizia *Bolzano* *Trieste*	Eight 8-in. Twelve 4-in.	
Trento		*Trento* disabled by air torpedo and sunk by *P.35* on 15 June.
	6-in. Cruisers (8)	
Luigi de Savoia, Duca degli Abruzzi *Giuseppe Garibaldi*	Ten 6-in. Eight 4-in.	

Raimondo Montecuccoli		
Muzio Attendolo		
Eugenio di Savoia	Eight 6-in.	
Emanuele Filiberto,	Six 4-in.	
Duca d'Aosta		
Luigi Cadorna		
Giovanni delle Bande		*Bande Nere* sunk by *Urge* on 1
Nere		April.

	"Fleet" Destroyers (30)
Twenty-one	Four 4.7-in.
	6 torpedo tubes
Nine	Six 4.7-in.
	4 torpedo tubes

Notes.

(1) There were ten old destroyers and about 40 torpedo boats, mostly armed with three or four 4-in. guns and four torpedo tubes.

(2) " E-boats" *(motoscafi anti-sommergibili)*: there were 40 to 50 with four 21-in. torpedo tubes, and about 35 with two 18-in. tubes.

Endnotes

1. See N.S.H., *Battle Summary No. 8* and *Mediterranean, Vol. I.*
2. See N.S.H., *Battle Summary No. 9* and *Mediterranean, Vol. II.*
3. The *Barham* was sunk by a submarine on 25 November, 1941. In December the *Prince of Wales* and *Repulse* were sunk off Malaya, and the *Queen Elizabeth* and *Valiant* seriously damaged by Italian midget submarines at Alexandria.
4. Besides the 8 destroyers mentioned as lost in the following account, the *Gurkha* was sunk by a submarine on 17 January, when with Convoy MW 8 from Egypt.
5. *Battle Summary No. 11* (revised).
6. *Battle Summary No. 32* (revised).
7. See Appendix A. There should have been another ship for Greece, the *Northern Prince*, but she drove on shore in a gale a few days before the convoy sailed from Gibraltar.
8. See Appendices G and H.
9. The battleship *Malaya* had joined Force "H" from the eastern Mediterranean towards the end of December 1940. Besides the ships employed with the convoys, there was another battleship (*Barham*) and another aircraft carrier (*Eagle*) with a destroyer screen in the eastern Mediterranean. These ships were earmarked for an attack on enemy shipping that was to start whilst the convoys were still at sea.
10. This was an over-estimate. Flieger Corps X, based in Sicily, by mid-January 1941 comprised 120 long-range bombers, 150 dive-bombers, 40 twin-engined fighters and 20 reconnaissance aircraft.
11. At 1630 on 8 January the convoy was some 30 miles south-westward of the *Renown*.
12. Zone Time minus 2 is used throughout.
13. Admiral Somerville remarked that the aircraft were aware that Force "B" would be encountered and that more care should have been taken in establishing identity.
14. See Appendix A.
15. 640 tons, three 4-in. guns, four 18-in. torpedo tubes.
16. In this action and her previous action with a raider in the Atlantic on 25 December, 1940, the *Bonaventure* expended 75 per cent of her low-angle outfit of ammunition. On this occasion she had one man killed and four wounded.
17. The *Bonaventure* was destined for Malta in any case, having embarked passengers from the *Northern Prince*, the transport that could not sail from Gibraltar with Convoy "Excess".
18. The *Calcutta* had arrived off Malta that morning, 10 January, with Convoy MW.5½. She then joined ME.6, on its sailing, but was soon called away to join Convoy "Excess" presumably to replace the *Bonaventure*.
19. Appendix B gives further details of the attack. The *Illustrious* had 13 officers and 113 men killed or missing, and 7 officers and 84 men wounded.
20. Captain Boyd remarked that there "may have been" some Hurricane fighters from Malta present during this attack.
21. The *Janus* had joined the fleet screen only that afternoon, having come from Malta, where she had been docking.
22. The *Illustrious* left Malta on 23 January, arrived at Alexandria on 25 January, and later proceeded to Durban and on to Norfolk (U.S.A.) for repairs, which were completed on 29 November, 1941.

23. The *Diamond* then joined the crippled *Gallant*, and later proceeded in company with Admiral Renouf's cruisers.

24. The *Ajax* had parted company soon after joining on 10 January with orders to fuel at Suda Bay and then to join Rear-Admiral Rawlings, who was due to leave Alexandria on 11 January in the *Barham*, with the *Eagle, Wryneck* and four destroyers, for operations in the eastern Mediterranean,

25. "*Diamond* was most skilfully handled throughout and her assistance was invaluable, many more lives being saved than would otherwise have been possible."– Rear-Admiral Renouf's report.

26. The *Gloucester* embarked 33 officers and 678 ratings, of whom 4 officers and 58 ratings were wounded: the *Diamond* retained 16 wounded ratings. The *Gloucester*'s own casualties amounted to 1 officer and 8 ratings killed, and 10 officers and 13 ratings wounded.

27. See Appendix C.

28. See Appendix D.

29. Zone Time minus 2 is used throughout this chapter.

30. The *Manchester* had 750 troops for Malta on board.

31. The *Edinburgh* and *Firedrake* both sighted tracks of torpedoes during the air attack by the bombers, perhaps fired by a submarine.

32. Captain Chapman remarked: "It was most noticeable from H.M.S. *Arethusa* that when destroyers ahead of the convoy exposed searchlights, the ships of the convoy stood out clearly in the silhouette, so much so that E-boats in a position to benefit would have been greatly assisted in finding and attacking targets. It was appreciated that waiting E-boats were probably ahead of the convoy, and for this reason it was decided not to expose a searchlight in H.M.S. *Arethusa*."

33. The *Nestor* took nearly 500 people from the *Sydney Star*. She had already nearly 300 on board of her own ship's company and passengers.

34. Details of Forces "A" and "X" and the Convoys are shown in Appendix E. Only the *Nelson, Ark Royal, Hermione* and ten destroyers belonged to Force "H" proper.

35. Zone Time minus 2 is used throughout.

36. "During the 26th," says an Italian account, "the English ships divided into various groups on different courses and adopted other methods to confound our reconnaissance. The enemy's ruses were successful – the Naval Staff was induced to think that the English force included only one, or at most two, battleships."

37. It was thought at the time that damage might have been inflicted, but it is now known that this was not the case.

38. The *Rodney, Prince of Wales, Lively, Heythrop* and s.s. *Rowallan Castle* seem to have had the chief share in destroying the Italian aircraft shot down by the fleet.

39. The hit was abreast 60 Station, 10 ft. below the waterline. Admiral Somerville remarked that *Nelson*'s lack of anti-aircraft guns which will bear on fine bow bearings was possibly the cause of her being torpedoed; "she has not a single anti-aircraft gun which will train across the bow at low elevation."

40. This second signal was received in the *Prince of Wales* about 1412.

41. Appendix G shows Admiral Somerville's previous instructions. See also Plans 5 and 6.

42. This signal was received by the *Nelson* at 1506 and by the *Ark Royal* at 1510.

43. See Plan 6. A third signal, made by the R.A.F. shadower at 1515, reported that the enemy had altered course "to the north"; it was not received by Malta or by any ship. (Force "H" Report, paragraph 103).

44. This signal stated that the British had only one battleship and one cruiser, and reported that Italian aircraft had sunk a cruiser and hit two more cruisers and possibly a battleship.

45. The following are the position of the submarine attacks:–

Date	Position	
1942/28	37° 30' N., 3° 45' E.	(*Duncan*)
0612/29	37° 30' N., 6° 25' E.	(*Gurkha* and *Isaac Sweers*)

0810/29	37° 26' N., 7° 14' E.	(*Gurkha*)
1645/29	37° 26' N., 4° 37' E.	(*Legion* and *Lively*)
0930/30	37° 10' N., 0° 56' E.	(*Gurkha* and *Legion*)

46. M.020005/41. H.M.S/M. *Unbeaten*'s Report.
47. See also Appendix F.
48. A Battle Honour – "Sirte" – was subsequently awarded for this action. The Italians refer to it as the *Second* Battle of Sirte, and to the action fought on 17 December 1941 (see *N.S.H., Mediterranean*, Vol. II) as the *First* Battle of Sirte.
49. The *Vide* [see] Kempenfelt to Middleton, July 1779: "Much, I may say almost all, depends upon this fleet; 'tis an inferior against a superior fleet; therefore the greatest skill and address is requisite to counteract the designs of the enemy, to watch and seize the favourable opportunity for action ... to hover near the enemy, keep him at bay, and prevent his attempting to execute anything but at risk and hazard, to command their attention and oblige them to think of nothing but being on their guard against your attack." (*The Barham Papers*, I, p. 292.)
50. See Appendix I.
51. No. 826 Naval Air Squadron, working with the Royal Air Force, bombed targets at Derna on the nights of 20/21 and 21/22 March, "to assist in creating a diversion while a convoy was on passage to Malta" (A.0991/42).
52. Zone Time minus 2 is used throughout this chapter.
53. The *Cleopatra*'s group had also been reported by submarines off Cyrenaica on 21 March.
54. Actually, two 8-inch, one 6-inch and destroyers – Admiral Parona's force from Messina. The *Gorizia* sighted Admiral Vian's ships at 1425.
55. Lieutenant Edmonds remarks that "it was not feasible either in this case" – at 0330 – "or at 0131 to fire by asdic, as the hydrophone effect was of more than one ship and was spread over a large area."
56. "As soon as our ships were sighted by the enemy ... he spread a smoke cloud which after only 40 seconds completely covered the convoy and blotted out a large area of the surrounding sea."– Admiral Iachino's report.
57. According to the Italian account, the cruisers did not turn to the south-east, but stood on to S.S.W. and W.S.W. till 1429 (see Plan 10). Possibly the movements of his destroyers, at least one of which was taken for a cruiser, may have given rise to this impression.
58. This movement of the *Bande Nere* is not shown in the Italian plan, and there is no mention of the incident in their report.
59. Admiral Parona's instructions confined him to a reconnaisance role until after junction with the C.-in-C., which he was then steering to effect.
60. As a result of her movements to avoid the bombs, the *Carlisle* came into collision with the *Avondale* in the thick smoke at 1505. Only superficial damage was sustained.
61. The *Legion* had attached herself to this division during the surface engagement.
62. Admiral Iachino's report.
63. Actually two 8-in., one 6-in. cruisers.
64. Actually 1 battleship, 2 destroyers.
65. The shell hit the starboard side of the Air Defence position, putting it out of action, also W/T and radar. One officer and 14 ratings were killed; one officer and four ratings were seriously wounded. Splinters from near misses killed one rating and caused superficial damage.
66. This alteration of course by the *Littorio* is not mentioned in the Italian account.
67. The three cruisers reported by the *Dido* as in line ahead at 1703 were probably in a loose line abreast about a mile apart. The distances of the enemy reported by Captain Micklethwait at 1649 and 1659 are considerably less than those shown on the combined track chart in M.08720/42.
68. According to the Italian account, no hits were scored at this time.
69. No. 3 boiler-room was flooded and the boiler damaged. Structural strength members

were cut. Two officers and five ratings were killed; one officer and eight ratings were wounded.

70. Captain Micklethwait commended these two ships for "following astern of *Sikh* through salvoes of large and small shell fire" when not "even in a position to see what was going on."

71. According to the Italian report, this alteration was made in an attempt to clear the smoke and not on account of the *Cleopatra*'s torpedoes, which they had not seen fired.

72. There is doubt as to the *Sikh*'s position relative to the *Littorio* at this time. The plan accompanying the report of the action places her about 19,000 yards from the battleship (see Plan 10); but Captain (D) 22nd Flotilla's report, Gunnery Notes, states:—

> "Towards the end of the battleship engagement when the range had closed to about 6,000 yards, nearly all salvoes, except overs, could be seen. This period was not of long duration, but the target was definitely found and a straddle observed at about 1820 at a range of 6,000 yards"

– a discrepancy of 13,000 yards. Errors in dead reckoning during an engagement of this nature in heavy weather and thick smoke are inevitable. It seems probable that in fighting the *Littorio* off, the *Sikh* was actually steering considerably farther to the westward and northward than shown in Plan 10 from about 1800 till her turn to the northward at 1820; but if this was the case she must have altered course to the south-westward earlier than shown for the *Lively* to have fired torpedoes at 7,000 yards range at 1851.

73. This was an under-estimate; actually they were about 11 miles apart.

74. This turn is not shown on the Italian plan.

75. The shell passed through the ship and exploded beyond. Fires broke out in the engine-room and boiler-room, which were quickly extinguished: upper deck suffered serious damage, impairing structural strength, and pom-pom, Oerlikon and searchlight supports were extensively damaged. One officer and 12 ratings were killed, and 21 ratings were wounded.

76. The details of torpedoes fired by the 1st Division are as follows:–

Ship	No. of Torpedoes Fired	Remarks
Jervis	5 out of 9	"Owing to difficulty in controlling the swing in the prevailing bad weather, was able to fire only five torpedoes."
Kipling	All 5	
Kelvin	4 out of 5	Fired two prematurely at 1835, having mistaken the signal to turn to run in for a signal to fire.
Kingston	3 out of 5	Two torpedo-tubes damaged by gunfire.
Legion	All 8	

All ships aimed at the battleship except the *Jervis*, which chose the third ship in the enemy's line for her target.

Commander Jessel of the *Legion* steered a south-westerly course on the run-in, instead of west, because he thought the ships too much bunched together, and because he did not wish to lose bearing on the enemy. Owing to shell splashes he did not see the signal to turn to starboard to fire; but he had already trained his tubes to starboard, i.e. for a turn to port, for the reasons that led him to hold away south-westward on the run-in, so he turned to port.

77. The base of the shell entered the fore lower mess deck, which flooded, and passed through the bulkhead to the after lower mess deck, which partially flooded later. There were no casualties.

78. The ammunition expended by individual ships varied greatly, depending on how often they were clear of the smoke. The expenditure by British and Italians was as follows: –

	BRITISH					ITALIAN					
	6 in.	5.25 in.	4.7 in.	4 in.		15 in.	8 in.	6 in.	4.7 in.	4 in.	3.5 in.
Cleopatra	–	868	–	–	Littorio	181	–	445	–	–	21
Dido	–	200	–	–	Gorizia	–	226	–	–	67	–
Euryalus	–	421	–	–	Trento	–	355	–	–	20	–
Penelope	64	–	–	–	Bande Nere	–	–	112	–	–	–
Jervis	–	–	106	–	Aviere	–	–	–	84	–	–
Kipling	–	–	110	–	Ascari	–	–	–	0	–	–
Kelvin	–	–	73	–	Oriani	–	–	–	0	–	–
Kingston	–	–	56	–	Alpino	–	–	–	0	–	–
Sikh	–	–	450	–	Bersagliere	–	–	–	0	–	–
Lively	–	–	–	275	Fuciliero	–	–	–	0	–	–
Havock	–	–	92	–	Lanciere	–	–	–	0	–	–
Hero	–	–	88	–							
Zulu	–	–	0	–							
Hasty	–	–	4	–							
Legion	–	–	–	?							
	64	1,489	979	275		181	581	557	84	87	21

79. According to Commander Jellicoe of the *Southwold*, about 60 bombers and at least nine torpedo aircraft attacked during the afternoon and evening.

80. The *Bande Nere* reached Messina on 24 March, but was sunk on 1 April to the southeast of Stromboli by the *Urge* (Lieut.-Commander Tomkinson).

81. On 9 May, 60 Spitfires reached Malta from U.S.S. *Wasp* and H.M.S. *Eagle*. They destroyed or damaged 30 enemy aircraft the same day and 60 the following day. "Daylight raiding was brought to an abrupt end." – Malta War Diary.

82. Actually, the mining was even more serious than was known at the time.

83. Some ships from other commands were attached for the occasion.

84. See Appendix J.

85. The Admiralty subsequently took up with D. of S.T. the question of checking actual speeds of merchant ships during the planning stage.

86. Zone Time minus 3 is used throughout this chapter.

87. Admiral Curteis recommended that in future the refuelling force should if possible accompany the remainder.

88. Force "Y" remained cruising ready to oil ships of Force "X" on their return passage. On this Captain Russell, of the *Kenya*, remarked – "That the oiler *Brown Ranger* was allowed to cruise for some six days or more unmolested across the enemy submarine areas appears to be the fault of the enemy."

89. According to the Italian report, the submarine *Uarsciek* attacked the formation at 0245, 14 June, and claimed to have hit one vessel, and the *Giada*, attacking a few hours later, claimed to have scored two torpedo hits on the *Eagle* (or another unit near her) at 0605, after which she was subjected to prolonged hunting. There is no mention of these attacks in the British reports.

90. Under the daytime cruising disposition the carriers and their attendant ships formed one group stationed on the weather quarter of the convoy; but they seem to have worked in two separate groups on 14 June, though generally on the same side of the convoy.

91. See Appendix J for the original equipment of the two ships. The *Argus* carried Swordfish aircraft as a torpedo striking force and for anti-submarine work.

92. The number of aircraft shot down by ships' fire, seven in all, is the assessment by the Gunnery and Anti-aircraft Warfare Division, Naval Staff. Individual claims amounted to 28, not including those made by merchantmen (the *Troilus* claimed two); it is impossible, therefore, to identify the successful ships.

93. The *Welshman* had replaced the *Liverpool* as guide of the starboard column in the convoy; but the *Welshman* parted company at 2000 and went to Malta alone, the Polish destroyer *Kujawiak* taking her station in the convoy.

94. This is not confirmed by Italian sources.

95. Staff Minute on M.08465/42 (Record Office, Case 8285).

96. See page 116.

97. See Plan 11.

98. Dawn was about 0630, Zone Time minus 3.

99. This difficult decision was subsequently approved by the Admiralty.

100. See Plan 12 for ensuing action.

101. This is how it appeared to the British. The Italian account states that these destroyers "brilliantly withstood the encounter with the cruisers and the many similar enemy units" till at 0809 they were detached to the assistance of the damaged *Vivaldi*.

102. According to the Italian report these two destroyers, *Vivaldi* and *Malocello*, had been detached to attack the merchant ships.

103. The track marked "11th Division" on Plan 12 is that of the *Marne*. The courses and times for the *Ithuriel* ahead and the *Matchless* astern were slightly different.

104. The Beaufighter that originally sighted the Italian ships seems to have gone back to Malta at once to report in full. No other aircraft made contact with the convoy till 0930.

105. This decision was subsequently approved by the Admiralty.

106. The decision of the Italian admiral to withdraw his whole force on account of one damaged destroyer seems rather to have lost sight of his object. The *Vivaldi*, towed by the *Premula*, reached Pantellaria at 1530.

107. Approximate position: 36° 12' N., 11° 37' E.

108. Actually, the Italians made no attempt at rescue work at this time, and it was not till 2000 that an Italian rescue plane picked up a few. An hour later an Italian hospital ship arrived and picked up the remainder (208 out of a total crew of 241), being bombed by her own aircraft during the rescue.

109. They received orders from the Naval High Command at 1520 to return to harbour.

110. The report of the Board of Inquiry held upon this matter is in M.010042/42. Subsequent sweeping by the newly-arrived flotilla showed that the minefield was even more extensive and more thickly sown than was appreciated before the convoy arrived. The *Matchless* and *Badsworth* escorted the *Troilus* and *Orari* to Gibraltar in August during Operation "Pedestal".

111. From the time the convoy came within range of Malta-based aircraft until the surviving ships reached harbour, the R.A.F. flew 414 sorties in support of the convoy – 292 by short-range Spitfires, 97 by long-range Spitfires and 25 by Beaufighters.

112. See Appendix J.

113. The Italians were not seriously perturbed by this ruse, having assessed her as "probably another unit camouflaged" as early as 13 June.

114. Commander-in-Chief, Mediterranean, report in M. 013471/42.

115. The positions marked on Plan 13 are those on the first patrol lines, the only lines actually occupied. The choice of further positions to which submarines could be moved was limited by the speed of submarines; and this presumably accounts for the Messina approaches patrol, to which the slow U-class vessels were to go. The scheme may be compared with that adopted for the Russian convoys in July and September the same year. Instead of

forming a moving screen, the submarines in the northern theatre occupied successive patrol lines according to the progress of the convoy. (See Naval Staff History, Battle Summary No. 22, *Arctic Convoys*, 1942–45.)

116. To lessen the weight of enemy air attack from Crete, parties were landed there before and during the operation to raid air stations. For instance, Captain Lord Jellicoe with some French soldiers landed from the Greek submarine *Triton* in the night of 13/14 June, and did some damage at Maleme, though not so much as was believed at the time.

117. Zone Time minus 3 is used throughout this chapter.

118. "R.A.F., Middle East" (H.M. Stationery Office, 1945), p. 57. See also the report of No. 201 (Naval Co-operation) Group, R.A.F., in M.013471/42.

119. The eight merchant ships and the *Centurion* were formed in four columns, with the two rescue ships between the inner columns. The seven cruisers and the *Coventry* were disposed as a screen round the convoy 1,200 yards out. There was an all-round air-warning screen of Hunt class destroyers and smaller vessels, 1,600 yards outside the cruisers; and an antisubmarine screen of Fleet destroyers, from ahead to either quarter, 2,500 yards beyond the air-warning screen.

120. These were German E-boats, based on Crete.

121. On this occasion the E-boat was not seen, and it was thought that the torpedo came from a submarine. It has since been confirmed by German sources that it was E-boat *S55*.

122. The reported positions of the Italian fleet are marked on Plan 13.

123. A ninth Liberator had to abandon the attack and return, owing to defective engines.

124. Air Vice-Marshal Sir Leonard Slatter, commanding No. 201 (Naval Co-operation) Group, who wrote the Air report of the operation, commented on Admiral Harwood's difficulties "on account of the very meagre information provided by air reports" both in the night of 14/15 and in the forenoon of 15 June. "Striking forces and shadowers," he said, "should report at once any results observed from attacks. This is of the greatest value to the Commander-in-Chief, and was not done in this operation." Again, "During the whole of the morning the Commander-in-Chief, Mediterranean, was greatly hampered in making a decision as to whether to turn the convoy towards Malta, as no results of our air attacks on the enemy had been received, and it was not known whether Malta had attacked or not." (M.013471/42).

Admiral Harwood said he received the results of the Malta Beauforts' attack at 1115. His belief that a cruiser was retiring damaged was presumably founded on an air reconnaissance report timed 0810 and received about 0830.

125. It is now known that it was the German submarine *U.205*.

126. A signal from Captain Ruck-Keene, timed 1315, ordered all submarines to remain on the surface, but it did not reach any of them till after 1700.

127. Commander-in-Chief, Mediterranean, report in M.013471/42.

128. Commander-in-Chief, Mediterranean, to Prime Minister, 18 June 1942 (P.M.'s files).

129. Colonel Hollis to General Ismay, 20 June 1942 (P.M.'s files).

130. The planning of this operation was considered far better than that of any of its predecessors, because it was started earlier and was done more thoroughly, and because the resources and facilities at the Admiralty were placed at the disposal of the Flag Officer concerned. After the operation was over a small Committee was set up at the Admiralty to consider whether any improvements in the planning arrangements for future operations of this sort could be made. Extracts from the report of this Committee which are considered of permanent value will be found in Appendix L. The whole report is contained in Record Office Case War History 8268.

131. See Appendix K.

132. See Plan 14 for the positions of the submarines on patrol.

133. The air forces at Malta were strongly reinforced from the United Kingdom and Egypt. The maximum numbers of aircraft serviceable at any one time during the operation were

100 Spitfires, 36 Beaufighters, 30 Beauforts, 3 Wellingtons, 2 Liberators, 2 Baltimores, 3 F.A.A. Albacores and Swordfish. In addition reconnaissance aircraft consisted of 5 Baltimores, 6 P.R.U. Spitfires and 5 Wellington VIIIs.

134. N.I.D. 06680/44. In addition to the air attacks on Italian airfields, a party was landed from the submarine *Una* to raid Catania airfield in the night of 11/12 August; but the attempt was unsuccessful. (Mediterranean War Diary and M.052185/42).

135. The *Argus* took part in Operation "Berserk", but then went to Gibraltar and had no share in the main operation.

136. Vice-Admiral Syfret's report (in R.O. Case W.H.S. 8268).

137. Idem.

138. These exercises, of course, entailed "a great volume of W/T and R/T traffic, which must have been very apparent to enemy or enemy-controlled listening stations. This risk to security was considered acceptable when balanced against the benefit to be derived from the practices." – Vice-Admiral Syfret's report.

139. Zone Time minus 2 is used throughout this chapter.

140. This inevitably gave warning to the enemy, but owing to the fog the first definite report reached the Italians from a passenger aircraft which sighted the British force in the afternoon of 10 August.

141. Except the *Wrestler*, which was detained by defects. Her place was later filled by the *Amazon*, by direction of the Flag Officer, North Atlantic, at Gibraltar.

142. Vice-Admiral Syfret's report. The Vice-Admiral remarked, "In previous operations it has not been necessary to provide for so large an oiling programme since ships going to Malta have been able to fuel there. In this case Malta had no oil to spare. The problem of oiling cruisers and 26 destroyers at sea, under enemy observation and in U-boat-infested waters was an anxious one, failure of which could have seriously upset the whole plan."

143. Vice-Admiral Syfret's report.

144. Lat. 38° 05' N., Long. 3° 02' E.

145. Admiral Syfret in his report stated that he was informed later in the day by Vice-Admiral, Malta, that 36 only had arrived, but the Vice-Admiral, Malta, writing on 26 August, gave 37 as the number.

146. See Plan 14.

147. Discrepancies as to these numbers occur in the German and Italian accounts, ranging from 480 as given by the German Admiral Weichold to 784 as given in the Italian Official Naval History. After examining various sources the British Air Ministry Historical Branch came to the conclusion that the probable numbers were:– *Bombers*, 334 (148 German, 186 Italian): *Fighters*, 273 (72 German, 201 Italian) – a total of 607 aircraft. Of these 90 were torpedo-bombers. These figures take no account of a force earmarked to bomb Malta, reconnaissance, escort and transport aircraft, rescue planes, etc.

148. Sunrise 0653, Zone minus 2: beginning of Civil Twilight (sun 6° below horizon), 0615.

149. This account of the Italian plan comes from N.I.D.06680/44; but the Italian report does not mention the attack by German bombers that followed the torpedo attack.

150. According to the Italian report, the submarine *Emo* fired *four* torpedoes at this time. The *Emo* survived the counter-attack.

151. Vice-Admiral Syfret reported the strength as 12 Ju. 87s, 30 Ju. 88s, and 40 S.79 and other torpedo aircraft, besides fighters. The Italian account in N.I.D.06680/44 mentions only 8 Ju. 87s, 14 S.79s, and 28 fighters.

152. According to Italian sources only 17 aircraft were lost on 12 August. Total of aircraft lost throughout the operation is given as 42 (21 German, 21 Italian).

153. Of the original twelve destroyers the *Bramham* had parted company in the afternoon to escort the *Deucalion*, and the *Foresight* had been disabled.

154. Sunset was 2016, Zone minus 2: end of Civil Twilight, 2044.

155. Air Vice-Marshal Park, referring to this incident in his report, remarked, "it is considered

essential that as many as possible (up to 100 per cent) of warships should be capable of giving V.H.F. fighter direction." With this opinion Vice-Admiral Leatham, V.A., Malta, concurred. – V.A. Malta's report and enclosure in R.O. Case W.H.S.8269.

156. Rear-Admiral Burrough's report, in R.O. Case W.H.S. 8269.

157. The sinking of the *Manchester* was subsequently the subject of a Court Martial and is dealt with in Naval Staff History, Mediterranean, Vol. II.

158. The fate of the *Glenorchy* was unknown at the time, but from Italian sources it seems she was torpedoed off Kelibia at 0215, about an hour after the *Manchester*. As in the case of the *Clan Ferguson*, it was feared for some time that there were no survivors, but a telegram from the U.S. Consul at Tunis on 17 August reported that 130 survivors from these two ships were safe in Tunis.

159. Sunrise 0628, Zone minus 2: Civil Twilight commenced 0601.

160. The torpedo striking force was held back in case the Italian battleships should leave Taranto.

161. It is not clear why the *Attendolo*, which had been ordered to Naples with the 7th Division, was with the *Bolzano* at this time.

162. See page 165.

163. As opposed to 120 miles for which they had planned.

164. Lieut.-Commander Hill in his report remarked, "I cannot speak too highly of the sheer guts of these men. They were singing and encouraging each other, and as I went through them explaining . . . that I must get the ones nearest the flames first, I received cheerful answers of 'That's all right, Sir. Go and get the other chaps.' The flames were spreading outward all the time . . ." Some time later it was discovered that 23 of the survivors came from the *Melbourne Star*. As she steamed through the flames, those aft – "quite understandably," said Lieut-Commander Hill, who had seen what it looked like – thought their own ship had blown up and jumped over the side.

165. Actually, it was the *Brisbane Star*, using a peculiar call-sign.

166. Report by Commander Venables, in R.O. Case W.H.S. 8269.

167. "... The first torpedo passed underneath and the second passed close along the starboard side. Later starboard paravane wire commenced to vibrate violently; ship was stopped and on paravane being hoisted out of water, the torpedo was found fixed firmly along the paravane body, the fins of the torpedo having caught in the guard of the paravane tail. The clump chain forward was unshackled and let go, and the derrick purchase holding paravane was then let go. The torpedo exploded on bottom in 400 fathoms, but the uplift was tremendous, though the ship was clear." – Commander Venables' report.

168. Rear-Admiral Burrough's report.

169. Signal, Commander Jerome to Rear-Admiral Burrough.

170. Owing to the urgency of the duty on which they were employed and further directions from the Vice-Admiral, Malta, these three destroyers did not keep the rendezvous.

171. "Two three-engined Italian bombers approached on the port beam. Four-inch Cease Fire bells were rung in order not to discourage them, and short bursts from Oerlikon and pom-pom shot them both down in flames . . . This success came at a very apt time, as the ship's company were showing signs of great fatigue, and the survivors were, most understandably, jumpy. The whole ship was cheering hard and everything after this went with a swing." – Lieutenant-Commander Hill's report.

172. H.M. The King approved the award of the George Cross to Captain D. W. Mason for his conduct on this occasion.

173. Vice-Admiral Sir R. Leatham's report.

174. This is not substantiated by Italian sources.

175. Conditions in this area varied with the fighting on shore in North Africa; but during most of the period under consideration, Cyrenaica was in the hands of the enemy.

176. See Naval Staff History, Battle Summary No. 22: *Arctic Convoys*.

177. The Italian heavy ships laboured under the disadvantage that they had not been trained in night fighting, and they were determined (especially after the Battle of Matapan) to give no opportunity of being brought to action after sunset.
178. Owing to enemy action.
179. Of those which arrived at Malta about 30 per cent were destroyed after arrival.
180. Owing to weather, etc.
181. The losses in convoys to North Russia for the whole period over which they were running (1941–1945) amounted to 7.2 per cent. For comparison, the losses in the Atlantic convoys from all causes amounted to 0.7 per cent.
182. These figures include those sunk by own forces on account of damage, but do not include those sunk after arrival in harbour.
183. In 1942 the "Oyster" mine and such types were not yet in use.
184. C.-in-C., Mediterranean, report in M.013471/42.
185. The term "sea power" of course includes the air component, without which sea power cannot be efficiently exercised in modern warfare.
186. Rear-Admiral Bonham-Carter.
187. *A Sailor's Odyssey*, pp. 544–545 (English edition).
188. Hit by bomb, 11 January – damaged.
189. Hit by bombs, 11 January – caught fire, sunk by own forces.
190. Hit by bombs, 10 January – severely damaged.
191. Hit by mine, 10 January – damaged.
192. The following is an extract from the report of Lieutenant-Commander Hine, H.M.S. *Jaguar:–*

"In the first attack [1240 on 10 January] *Jaguar*, which was on port side of screen, commenced in controlled fire, and later fired barrage abaft *Illustrious* with 4.7-inch and 4-inch. Aircraft were engaged when pulling out of dive or retiring within range of pom-pom, 0.5-inch, and military Bren . . .

"In waters where dive-bombing is likely, it is suggested that modern destroyers with six guns . . . should be put on the wings of the screen. It is the German practice to dive-bomb from astern; and the controlled fire from these destroyers could be employed on formation as it prepares to attack, shifting to long-range barrage over carrier's stern as dive-bombing developed, and employing close-range armament on them as they pull out and retire."

(The *Jaguar* had on board her some soldier passengers who engaged the enemy aircraft with their Bren guns.)
193. Torpedoed by aircraft, 23 July – damaged.
194. Torpedoed by aircraft, 23 July – sunk.
195. Damaged by near miss, 23 July.
196. Torpedoed by motor torpedo-boat, 24 July – reached Malta.
197. Torpedoed by aircraft, 24 July – reached Gibraltar.
198. Torpedoed by aircraft, 27 September – damaged.
199. Torpedoed by aircraft, 27 September – sunk.
200. In another letter, Admiral Syfret said that the *Rodney* and *Nelson* sometimes fouled the lines of fire of the *Kenya* and *Edinburgh* respectively, and that at night the *Edinburgh's* line of fire was "severely restricted" by the positions of the *Cossack* and *Laforey*.
201. Compare Admiral Cunningham's remarks and the report of the *Jaguar* in Appendix C.
202. Torpedoed by submarine and later sank, 20 March.
203. Tonnage is gross registered tonnage to the nearest 500 tons.
204. H.M.S. *Breconshire* was a commissioned auxilliary supply ship.
205. Four motor torpedo boats were to have accompanied the convoy for its protection. They joined p.m. 13 June and were taken in tow by merchant ships. Owing to the bad weather, they had to be sent back the same night, and M.T.B. No. 259 was so much damaged that

she foundered; the rest arrived at Alexandria again on 14 June.

206. The *Eagle* was sunk on 11 August, before the convoy came under air attack.

207. The *Foresight* was disabled before the sepaeration on 12 August, and did not continue with Force "X".

208. These recommendations were approved in principle by the Board, but events in North Africa rendered the further running of convoys to Malta under such adverse conditions unnecessary.

209. Straggling or detached from convoy.

210. Two sunk in harbour after arrival at Malta.

211. Three sunk in harbour after arrival.

212. Survivors returned to Egypt: none arrived at Malta.

213. Including H.M.S. *Breconshire*.

214. The climb of these aircraft varied from 3½ to 4½ minutes to 10,000 ft.

215. F = fixed gun front.

216. But with R/T.

217. With extra tank; 8 hours equal about 1,100 miles.

218. Catapault ship aircraft.

219. With one .303-in. (.3-in.) front gun, and one .303-in. (or .3-in.) rear gun.

220. Extra fuel in drums for replenishment in flight in early type.

Part III

BR 1886 (1) A

DAMAGES AND PLANS

REVIEW OF DAMAGE TO HIS MAJESTY'S SHIPS

3 September 1941 – 2 September 1942
With accounts to H.M. Ships Nelson, Queen Elizabeth, Indomitable and Liverpool

N.I.D. 06702/42
Naval Construction Department,
Admiralty, S.W.1

This book has been prepared in accordance with Board instructions promulgated in Office Acquaint BDX/42. The contents have been prepared by D.N.C. in close conjunction with E.-in-C., D.E.E., D.N.O., D.T.M., and D.N.E. (D.C.). The sections relating to Damage Control, Damage to Machinery and Damage to Electrical Equipment were prepared by the Departments primarily concerned.

Contents

Introduction 264

General
Watertight Integrity 266
Underwater Protection 267
Counter Flooding 267
Shock 268
Splinter Protection 268

Damage Control
Instruction and Training of Ratings 271
Special Ratings for Damage Control 272
Watertight Integrity 272
Damage Control Section of D.N.E. Department, Admiralty 272
Position of Damage Control Headquarters 272
Arrangement of Damage Control Room 273
Sectional Headquarters 273
Materials for Repair of Damage 273

Damage Reports
H.M.S. *Nelson* 274
H.M.S. *Queen Elizabeth* 292
H.M.S. *Indomitable* 306
H.M.S. *Liverpool* 330

Introduction

This book, which is a review of damage caused by enemy action during the third year of the war, is a continuation of C.Bs. 4107 and 4168A and B which dealt similarly with the first and second years of the war.

A large number of the incidents referred to herein have occurred in the Mediterranean and for most of them it has not been possible for representatives of the Admiralty Technical Departments to inspect the damage. In these circumstances the data have been obtained to a large extent from reports forwarded in compliance with Admiralty Fleet Orders, by the Commanding Officers of the ships concerned. It is perhaps not inapt in this introduction to emphasize the need for compliance with these orders to the maximum extent possible as it is only by this means that the Admiralty Technical Departments can obtain full and complete knowledge of the behaviour of the material for which they are responsible and so be able to incorporate improvements and take full advantage of the invaluable experiences of actual action conditions. The orders in question are C.A.F.Os.3833/39, 3967/39, 889/40, 21/42, and 965/42. These are now superseded by C.A.F.O. 2489/42.

This Review contains, in addition to general remarks summarising the more important lessons learned during the third year of war, Damage Reports for the following incidents which have been selected as affording representative examples of the damage received by various classes of ships under attack by various weapons:–

H.M.S. *Nelson* damaged by torpedo on 27.9.41
H.M.S. *Queen Elizabeth* damaged by mine on 19.12.41.
H.M.S. *Indomitable* damaged by bombs on 12.8.42.
H.M.S. *Liverpool* damaged by torpedo on 14.6.42.

During the period under review two major incidents which have occurred have been the subject of special investigation by the Admiralty Technical

Departments. The reports of damage drawn up as a result of these investigations have been considered to be of special interest and they have been issued as confidential books. They are:–

(1) H.M.S. *Ark Royal*, sunk by torpedo in the Mediterranean, C.B.04188.
(2) H.M.S. *Prince of Wales*, sunk by torpedoes and bombs off Malayan Peninsula, C.B.04237.

Also a Committee was appointed "To review the circumstances attending the loss by enemy action of capital and other heavy ships since the beginning of the war, and to consider whether there are any specific material measures or lines of investigation which might profitably be adopted or pursued, with intent to improve the defence of British warships against existing or anticipated enemy weapons." This Committee, presided over by Mr. Justice Bucknill, gave early attention to the circumstances and lessons of the loss of H.M.S. *Prince of Wales*. They considered the matter sufficiently pressing to issue an interim report and this is included in C.B.04237 dealing with the loss of *Prince of Wales*. They put forward a number of recommendations many of which have already been adopted.

In their final report the Bucknill Committee deal with the loss of H.M.S. *Ark Royal*. They state "We think that there is not sufficient evidence to prove conclusively whether it was a contact torpedo or a non-contact torpedo just under the turn of bilge. For reasons which are set out hereafter in this report, our conclusion is that it was not a non-contact torpedo exploding under the flat of the bottom. Without coming to any definite decision as to whether the damage was done by a contact or non-contact torpedo near the turn of the bilge, we think it very probable that it was a contact torpedo."

General

Watertight Integrity

Experience has confirmed the importance of the maintenance of a high degree of watertight integrity. It has been established that some sacrifice in habitability and in convenience of access must be accepted in order that the watertight subdivision of ships may be preserved in a high state of efficiency, not only at sea, but also in harbour where sudden air or other attack is possible. Measures for the improvement of watertight integrity have been put into force as outlined in the following paragraphs.

C.A.F.O. 1144/42 provided for a series of modifications to ventilation systems. Permanent ventilation trunks are to be removed from spaces such as store rooms except those containing perishable food stuffs and those in which personnel require to be employed for long periods. All spaces should be ventilated, by hose, before being entered. Locally worked watertight slide valves are to be fitted in ventilation trunks at the weather and armour decks wherever practicable. Watertight ventilation trunks below the weather deck are to be of plating not less than ⅛" thick and are to be tested to the same head of water as the compartments through which they pass.

Trunked access is being fitted to all important action spaces. These trunks are carried up at least to the datum deck and, where possible, to the deck above with access doors between these decks. Reliable watertight hatches at the lower ends of the trunks are essential. Armour decks are not pierced in satisfaction of this requirement because of the necessity for maintaining protection at the highest possible standard.

Some watertight doors have been blanked. Others have been reduced in size by fitting sills 3 feet high in battleships, 2 ft. 6 ins. in cruisers.

Some watertight hatches have been blanked. Others have been surrounded by coamings 2 feet to 3 feet high.

A series of experiments has been in hand for many months with the object of making watertight doors, hatches and coamings appreciably stronger than at present. The results are being applied in New Construction.

C.A.F.O. 1505/42 and A.F.O. 4304/42 ordered the permanent blanking of all side scuttles below the weather decks leaving only one escape scuttle each side in each main compartment. To this can be fitted discharge hose connections for electric portable pumps.

A.F.O. 4299/42 made provision for reduction of flooding hazards through air escapes. In particular, in capital ships and aircraft carriers plug cocks are to be fitted in air escape pipes except those from oil fuel and petrol tanks. The cocks are to be fitted below amour decks and below junctions of pipes. They are normally to be kept shut except those from magazines and fresh water tanks.

Weather-deck scupper drain pipes are to be removed, and the holes in the ships' sides blanked. Screw down storm valves are to be fitted to W.C. discharges.

It has been approved to provide separate access to ring main spaces in battleships in which such a facility does not involve cutting additional holes in armour decks.

Underwater Protection

The compartments immediately above the air and liquid spaces of modern underwater protection systems are intended to form a venting space. Heavy fittings must not be fitted or stowed in these compartments as they may, by projectile effect, pierce the surrounding watertight structure.

Experience has confirmed the need for the protective bulkhead to be continued as high as possible and for the provision of cofferdam bulkheads inboard of the protective bulkhead in order to limit slow flooding; these are features which are provided as far as other design requirements allow.

Counter Flooding

Experience indicates that under certain circumstances the instructions issued to ships fitted with the "sandwich" construction of underwater protection need revision. If a greater correcting moment is given to the ship by flooding the outer wing compartments than by flooding the inner wing compartments then counterflooding <u>when urgently necessary</u> should be carried out in the following order:–

    (i) Outer wing W.T. compartments
    (ii) Alternate or all inner wing W.T. compartments, according to urgency.
    iii) Spaces above the sandwich protection if essential.

Flooding the outer wing compartments reduces the protection afforded against torpedo hits and therefore as soon as possible these compartments should be pumped out and the desired righting moment obtained by alternative means such as transference of oil fuel or flooding inner wing watertight compartments.

For rapid correction of heel and trim it would be desirable to fit a separate sea-cock in each air space of the underwater protection system, each sea-cock having its own gearing carried at least to main deck level. However, the additional weight, number of holes in bottom and amount of rod gearing involved are prohibitive.

Shock

A Committee (known as the Admiralty Shock Committee) was formed in December 1941 to study the effects of shock in ships due to non-contact explosions and to make recommendations for the protection of items of machinery and equipment from the effect of shock. The ex-American destroyer *Cameron* has been allocated to this Committee for full scale trials, after receiving extensive damage due to enemy action whilst in dry dock. These trials have been continued during the year and are still in progress. Many valuable lessons have already been learnt and have been incorporated in the new designs of auxiliary machinery and equipment and in instructions issued for the protection of existing machinery and equipment.

In *Queen Elizabeth* class battleships forged steel collars have been fitted to the rudder posts to prevent the yokes moving due to the shock of underwater explosions.

War experience has confirmed that clips of watertight doors do not jump off or slack back provided they are put on in a downward direction and made reasonably tight. Arrangements have been made to provide levers for tightening the clips. One lever is to be fitted each side of each door.

A.F.O. 4422/41 extended to store rooms the requirements of A.F.O. 4584/40 concerning stowage battens in magazines, namely, that the battens should be provided with fittings to prevent them jumping from their sockets under shock.

Splinter Protection

Experience during the third year of war has confirmed previous experience of the damaging effect of splinters of bombs and shell. In the first year of war an outstanding example of such damage was that suffered by H.M.S. *Mohawk* when a bomb burst on the surface of the water close alongside and riddled the ship with splinters. In the third year of war an outstanding example of such damage was that suffered by O.R.P. *Garland* when one of a stick of four bombs burst abreast the bridge before impact with the water and riddled the ship's side with splinters causing very severe casualties, starting fires, cutting the steampipe from one boiler and putting half the main and secondary armament out of action.

A lesson from the loss of H.M.S. *Hood* was that at fine inclinations and at certain ranges it is possible for a projectile to avoid the main protection of some of our capital ships and burst within the ship so close to the magazines that splinters may enter them. The protection of all these ships has been closely re-examined from this point of view and wherever necessary additional splinter protection to, or in the neighbourhood of, the magazine has been fitted or will be fitted as opportunity offers.

C.A.F.O. 322/42 stated that protection from splinters from bombs and shell must be afforded as far as possible to all important circuits and lines of communications in destroyers and larger ships. In armoured ships protection from shell and bombs penetrating the ship and bursting on or above the armoured deck must be afforded to important circuits and lines of communications which are necessarily run outside the armour protection. This protection should be on a scale comparable with that afforded to the positions that they serve outside the main armour. In existing ships any general scheme of increased protection involves a large amount of re-wiring and can only be undertaken during a long refit or reconstruction. Also, weight and stability conditions in most ships prohibit substantial additions and each ship needs individual consideration.

In New Construction the thickness of main bulkheads is being increased to limit the destructive power of splinters and to afford increased resistance to blast damage.

Damage Control

An essential requirement is a wide knowledge of this diverse subject by Officers and men and for practical training as far as it can be carried out.

The experiences of the third year of war have again shown the vital importance of the efficiency of the Damage Control Organisation. The Damage Control communication system has several times failed completely due to the centralisation of the system at the D.C. headquarters and these headquarters being themselves damaged. This is being remedied by fitting independent secondary D.C. headquarters and linking the whole system by sound powered telephones. A Wa/t system from the primary D.C.H.Q. is also being fitted. Otherwise the material arrangements, though capable of improvements which are in hand, have proved fairly adequate.

Damage Control Handbook. A revised book (C.B. 4198R) was issued in July, 1942. Chapter 1 embodies the main lessons of recent war experience. New chapters have been added on fire-fighting and medical organisation. The advance in Damage Control arrangements is rapid and it is expected that anothe revision will be required within a year or so.

Stability of Ships. A book under this title was issued in March, 1942 (B.R. 298/42). It explains in a simple manner the broad principles of this complex subject.

Damage Control School. A Damage Control School for Officers was opened in London at the end of August, 1942. All branches and ranks are eligible to take the course which lasts for the inside of a week. Commanding Officers of ships can arrange direct with the school for any of their Officers to attend so as to fit in satisfactorily with leave arrangements, refitting, and so on. The syllabus covers the following:–

Stability of ships.
Armour and underwater protection.

Water-tight integrity, marking of doors, etc.
Ships' services, pumping, fire-main, ventilation, etc.
Damage control organisation.
Training.
Dealing with damage – underwater.
                             above-water.
                             fire-fighting.
Electrical – organisation, emergency arrangements, etc.
Engine room and boiler room – dealing with damage.
Destroyers and small craft.
Damage reports – typical cases, *Prince of Wales*, *Ark Royal* etc.

To illustrate problems of stability and underwater damage, large-scale models are being provided of *King George V*, *Illustrious*, *London* and *Sirius*. These will float in tanks. The principal compartments of each ship are floodable. C.A.F.O. 2497/42 gives full particulars of the school.

Reports of Damage to Ships, after analysis by Admiralty, are being issued on a wider basis than formerly. In the case of Cruisers and larger ships a copy is issued to each ship of the type concerned so that it shall be available for study and to help in framing exercises. Destroyer reports can only be issued to Captains (D) for circulation in flotillas. By the courtesy of the American Naval Authorities some reports of damage to U.S. ships are also being issued to the Fleet.

Instruction and Training of Ratings

This is a difficult matter. No realistic practice is obtained till the day of battle when damage actually occurs. Repair parties have a great deal to learn and it is difficult to get down to satisfactory simulation of the practical side of the work in their own ships.

Consideration is being given to the establishment of small scale Damage Control Schools at various bases at which Repair Parties can do practical drill in shoring, plugging shot holes, etc. Other aspects of damage control will be taught as far as possible. These schools would meet the need of Destroyers and small craft.

Large Fire-fighting Schools are being built at the Home Ports. The existing schools at Rosyth and Lyness are being enlarged. New schools are being started in the Eastern Mediterranean and East Indies Stations.

Special Ratings for Damage Control

Consideration is being given to the addition to each ship of some Petty Officers and men specially trained in Damage Control. They would be permanent members of the Damage Control Party and would be employed in giving instructions to Repair Parties and in taking care of the fire-fighting and repair gear.

Watertight Integrity

A new system of marking watertight doors, etc., referred to in C.B. 4198R, paragraph 230, as XYZ System (1940), has been under trial in several ships. Although this is an improvement on the 1938 system in its endeavour to keep doors closed below the datum deck, it has not proved possible to meet clearly the varied requirements with the two letters X and Y. A new system is under consideration using two colours and three letters which should be easier for the sailor to understand.

Damage Control Section of D.N.E. Department, Admiralty

In March, 1942, a new section of the D.N.E. Department was instituted to deal with Damage Control matters. This organization is known as the Damage Control Section (short title D.N.E. (D.C.)) and its primary function is to study all information and experience available about Damage Control and keep the Fleet fully informed and instructed on the subject. The Section also collaborates with the Department of the Director of Naval Construction and the Engineer-in-Chief in the matter of fire-fighting.

The duties of D.N.E. (D.C.) include:–

(i) Revision of the D.C. Handbook.
(ii) Issue of Damage Reports to the Fleet.
(iii) Co-ordination of damage control arrangements in New Construction.
(iv) Study of methods employed in ships available and the making of recommendations for improvement where thought necessary.
(v) Maintenance of records of available information on Damage Control.

Position of Damage Control Headquarters

The Staff Requirements for Damage Control Headquarters in future construction are:–

(a) The Damage Control Room should be sited amidships behind and below protection and be easy of access. It should not be so low down as to be flooded <u>quickly</u> by underwater explosion and should be well separated from the Secondary Damage Control Headquarters, (i.e. Machinery Control Room or Controlling Engine Room).

(b) Since electrical damage control is an integral part of damage control, the Damage Control Room should be adjacent to and interconnect with the Main controlling switchboard. Similarly, the secondary Damage Control Headquarters should be fitted to contain the secondary electrical control position.

Recent experience has shown that in cruisers the Damage Control Headquarters on the platform deck is likely to be flooded by underwater damage in the vicinity. In new cruisers the Damage Control Headquarters is being sited on the lower deck. In existing cruisers it will be brought up to a deck above the platform deck if space can be found.

Arrangement of Damage Control Room

It has been found that the requirements of the Damage Control Officer are best met by placing him and his crew at a table in the centre of the room where he can face and direct them and at the same time see the diagrams and indicators on the bulkheads which are kept free for this purpose. The sound-power telephone control boxes are let in to the table.

W.T. door and hatch boards, and fire main, main suction, and oil fuel suction boards, mounted on bakelite to take coloured pegs, are being supplied to ships.

Sectional Headquarters

In New Construction the sectional headquarters will consist of built in cabooses which will contain two or three telephone control boxes and operators and a desk for the sectional officer. It is proposed that 50% of the Section's repair gear should be stowed in lockers near to the sectional headquarters and that the remainder of the gear should be distributed in other compartments of that section's area.

Materials for Repair of Damage

Hitherto ships have filled their repair lockers as they think best without having access to the action experience of ships of their class. The outfit of stores required for Damage Control is under review and a list of stores for each class of ship will be issued. It is also intended to design standard patterns of repair party lockers.

Damage Reports
H.M.S. *Nelson*

Torpedo Damage

<u>Type of Ship</u>	Battleship, completed 1927	
<u>Principal Dimensions</u>	Length	710 ft. 0 ins.
	Breadth	106 ft. 0 ins.
	Displacement	33,500 tons – standard
	Draught (mean)	28 ft. 3 ins. – standard

On Saturday, 27 September, 1941, H.M.S. *Nelson* was operating with Force H on convoy duties in the Western Mediterranean.

Weather conditions were:– Sea 00; Wind, N.N.E.1; Visibility, 8.
Speed of ship, 15 ½ knots. Depth of Water, 100 fathoms.
Draught of ship:– 35' 3" forward; 34' 6" aft.

The convoy was subjected to attacks by torpedo carrying enemy aircraft and at 1337 *Nelson* was torpedoed on the port side. The attacking aircraft was believed to be Italian and the torpedo to have been Italian, type S.L. 170/450 x 5.25, 18" with a charge of 170 kgms. (375 lbs.) T.N.T. Parts of its air vessel were found in the starboard after corner of the torpedo body room and the tail was found in the port forward corner of the port cold room.

The centre of the explosion was at 59 station, port, and at platform deck level, i.e. about 16 ft. 6 ins. below the waterline.

The immediate effect of the explosion was to hole the bottom plating, approximately 30 ft. long x 15 ft. deep extending from lower deck edge to just below the platform deck, between stations 50 and 65, and to cause extensive flooding of compartments in the vicinity. About 29 compartments were affected, the total weight of flood water was approximately 3,700 tons.

Before the explosion the vessel was trimming 9 inches by the bow but by 1800/27 the flooding referred to in the previous paragraph increased the mean draught by just over 3 feet with a trim of 12 feet by the bow and a heel of about

1½°, the draughts of the vessel were 44 feet, forward and 32 feet aft.

Course was set for Gibraltar at speeds varying between 17 and 10 knots until 1800/27 after which a speed of 12 to 14 knots was maintained until the arrival at Gibraltar at 1045 on 30 September. Pumping operations had been put into effect and on entering Gibraltar the draught of the vessel was 39 ft. 6 ins. forward; 32 ft. 3 ins. aft.

While berthed alongside, 1130 tons of oil fuel were discharged and vessel was de-ammunitioned.

On 2 October, *Nelson* was docked in No.1 dock; her draught was 35 ft. 9 ins. forward; 33 ft. 6 ins. aft.

Temporary repairs to enable the ship to proceed to the refitting Yard (Rosyth) were carried out and vessel undocked on 7 November, the draught was 28 ft. 5 ins. forward; 31 ft. 11 ins. aft.

Structural Damage

Outer Bottom

On the port side, the main hole extended from the edge of the lower deck to half way across "H" strake and between 50 and 65 stations, about 15 ft. in depth, by 30 ft. in length. Long, jagged, fractures occurred upwards across "N" and "O" strakes between 52 and 54 stations; across "N" strake between 58 and 60 stations, and across "N", "O" and 12 ins. into "P" strake between 64 and 66 stations. Downwards, fractures occurred diagonally forward across "H" strake between 55 and 58 stations and to the lower edge of "C" strake between 60 and 62 stations. The jagged edges of plating were turned in sharply at the forward and after ends and along the bottom of the hole and considerable distortion of plating around the hole was caused over an area extending from middle deck to the bottom of "C" strake and from about 48 to 70 stations, approximately 40 ft. by 40 ft.

All outer bottom plating was 20 lbs. D. except "M" strake, immediately below the lower deck, which was 20 lbs. D. before and 25 lbs. D. abaft 61 station.

On the starboard side the outer bottom was pierced by three splinters in "M" and "L" strakes between 56 and 60 stations.

Framing

The main frames (6 ins. x 3 ins. x 3 ins. x 14 lbs. channel bar) were completely destroyed in way of the hole and were severely distorted and torn from beam arm brackets in way of the damaged bottom plating.

Middle Deck

A hole, approximately 3 ft. x 2 ft. situated about 2 ft. 6 ins. before 60 bulkhead and 20 ft. to port of middle line, was caused by an armoured manhole cover blown up from the lower deck. The deck plating (12 lbs. D. with 14 lbs. stringer) was bulged upwards, maximum 9 ins. over an area extending from 48 to 60 stations in a fore and aft direction, and from the ship's side to within 4 ft. of the middle line athwartships, i.e. approximately 23 ft. in length by 21 ft. in width. Abaft 60 bulkhead the deck was bulged upward, slightly between 60½ and 69 stations and from 17 ft. to 29 ft. to port of the middle line, i.e. about 17 ft. in length by 12 ft. in width. Except for the hole referred to above there were no holes or fractures in this deck. Slight leaks occurred along plate edges, boundary angle at side, and through screw-holes to corticene strips which were broken by the bulged plating.

Lower Deck

The deck plating (10 lbs. 14 lbs. stringer, 100 – 120 lbs. N.C. armour) was forced upwards over an area extending from the ship's side to within 6 ft. of the middle line between 50 and 60 stations and to about 20 ft. from the middle line between 60 and 70 stations. The 10 lbs. and 14 lbs. plating was severely distorted, perforated by splinters and torn.

The 100 lb. armour plate adjacent to the ship's side, 48 to 52 stations was forced upwards, maximum 4½ ins. along the butt at 52 station. This plate was not distorted.

The 120 lbs. armour plate, 52 to 60, was forced upward 9 ins. at the forward butt and 19 ins. at the after butt. The plate was distorted but not fractured.

The adjacent armour plate (120 lbs.) abaft 60 station, and also next toward the middle line, 52 to 60, were disturbed upward, maximum 3½ ins. No distortion occurred.

The deck beams (7 ins. x 3 ins. x 14.6 lb. bulb angle) on the port side in way of the explosion were destroyed and the deep girder at 52 station (14 lb. x 24 ins. plate, with 9 ins. x 3½ ins. x 3½ ins. x 25 lbs. channel bar to deck and 3½ x 3 x 8 lbs. double angle stiffeners on the lower edge) was severely distorted.

Platform Deck

In the torpedo body room, 43 to 60 stations, the deck plating (14 lbs. chequered) was distorted over an area extending 12 ins. from ship's side at

43 station to within 6 ft. of the middle line at 60 station.

In the E.A. plant room, 60 to 80 stations, the deck plating (25 lbs. and 14 lbs.) was distorted between 60 and 72 stations.

The plating adjacent to the ship's side was destroyed between 57 and 62 stations and jagged edges were turned down over the bottom plating which had been blown inwards. The hatch between 62 and 63 stations, leading to the air compressor room (under) was destroyed.

Hold

The plating in the air compressor room and air bottle compartment, 52 to 70, was slightly distorted,

Bulkheads

No. 43 bulkhead was slightly distorted near the ship's side between lower and platform decks.

No. 60 bulkhead. The scantlings of this bulkhead were, 12 lbs. D. plating between main and platform decks, 14 lbs. D. below the platform deck. Stiffeners, 4 ins. x 2½ ins. x 6.5 lbs. D. bulb angles between middle and lower decks; 6 ins. x 3 ins. x 3 ins. x 14 lbs. D. channels (continuous) between lower deck and inner bottom.

Below the lower deck the bulkhead was destroyed from ship's side to the longitudinal bulkhead of the cold room, i.e. a distance of 9 ft. 6 ins. from the ship's side at platform deck level. The remainder of the bulkhead was distorted to within 4 ft. of the middle line. Between the lower and middle decks the bulkhead was distorted over an area extending from the ship's side to the port longitudinal bulkhead of the provision room, i.e. about 13 ft. from the ship's side.

Below the platform deck the port longitudinal bulkhead to central store, 60 to 80, M.L., was distorted between 60 and 70 stations and torn from the boundary angle at 60 transverse bulkhead. The vertical stiffeners, 8 ins. x 3½ ins. x 3½ ins. x 20 lbs. channels at 62 to 65 and 67 stations were distorted and fractured across the standing flanges. The divisional watertight bulkhead at 70 station was bulged aft, maximum 12 ins. The door at the middle line of this bulkhead, hinged on the fore side, remained watertight. Slight distortion occurred to the inner bottom in the vicinity of 60 bulkhead.

On the platform deck, the port longitudinal bulkhead of the torpedo body room, 43 to 60, was torn from 60 bulkhead and from its deck connections. The bulkhead was blown inboard and severely distorted. The starboard longitudinal bulkhead was holed by splinters, about 20 No., maximum size 8 ins. by 6 ins. between 50 and 60 stations. Three of the splinters perforated the outer bottom on the starboard side in "M" and "L" strakes, between 50 and 60 stations. A splinter perforated the cover of the hatch leading to the lobby under.

The outer longitudinal bulkhead of the cold room, 60 to 80, port, was severely distorted between 60 and 72 stations; stiffeners and brackets were torn from the bulkhead and decks. The lower forward portion of the bulkhead was crushed and a hole about 2 ft. 6 ins. square led directly into the cold room. The after bulkhead at 76 station was demolished and blown into the lobby between 76 and 80 stations.

On the lower deck the minor bulkheads to lobby and prisons, 50 to 60 stations, and to Canvas Room, 60 to 70 stations, were buckled and distorted.

Machinery Damage

Main

No damage was caused to main machinery. The water level in the boilers was not affected.

Auxiliary

All auxiliary machinery outside the flooded area continued to operate normally with the exception of the electrical generators which slowed up due to sudden overloads caused by earths in the circuits. The overloading was momentary, power breakers operated immediately and reduced the load. The overspeed trip gear was gagged. The threee hydraulic engines which were on pressure at the time, were undamaged and continued to function normally.

The plating adjacent to the ship's side was destroyed between 57 and 62 stations and jagged edges were turned down over the bottom plating which had been blown inwards. The hatch between 62 and 63 stations leading to the air compressor room (under) was destroyed.

The refrigerating machinery was put out of action due to flooding of the compartment.

The B.A. plant, except motors, compressors and starters, caustic columns and starters was destroyed.

Diagram of ring main

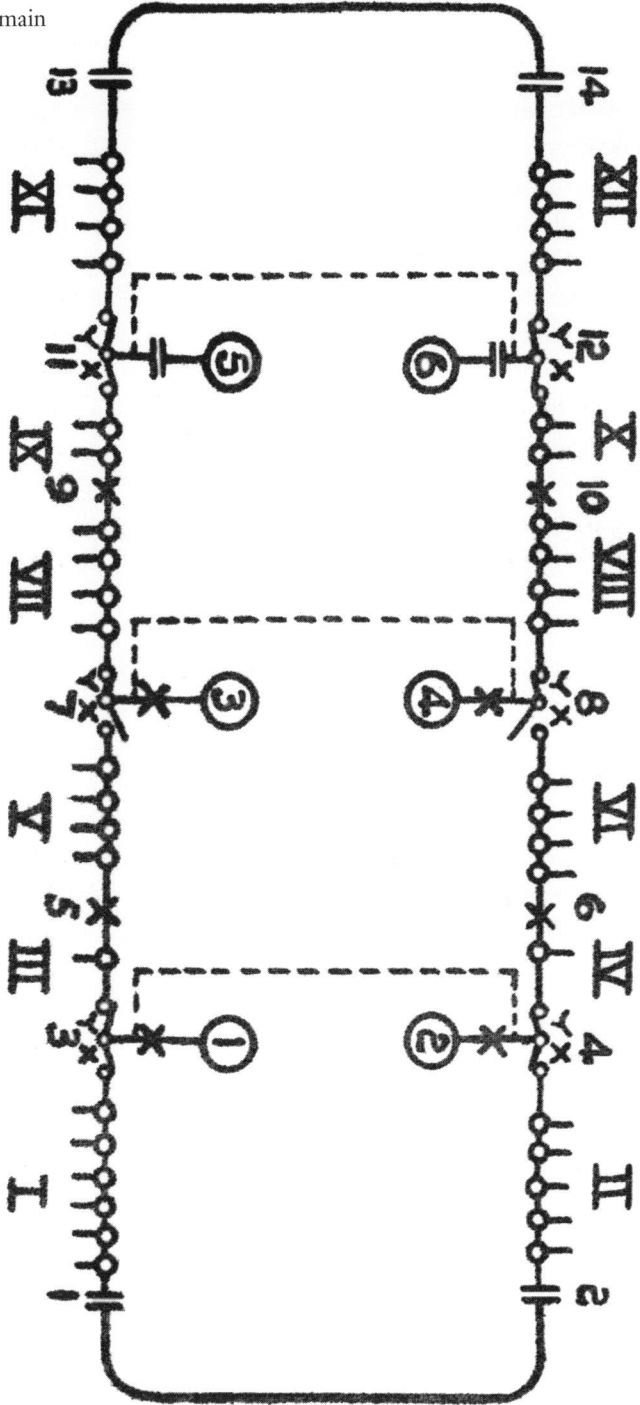

Electrical Report

<u>State of Ring Main</u>

The state of the ring main when *Nelson* was struck on Saturday, 27 September, was Nos. 1, 2, 3 and 4 dynamos running, numbers 1, 2, 13 and 14 ring main breakers open, the forward end of Nos. 7 and 8 ring main switches open. Numbers 1 and 2 dynamos each had a load of 900 amps.

At 1331 the shock of the torpedo hitting abreast 60 station port was not greatly felt at the main switchboard, and there is no evidence to show that any electrical gear in the ship not in damaged compartments was affected by shock.

(a) At 1335 there were intermittent overloads on Nos. 1 and 2 dynamos, shown by their ammeters swinging between zero and maximum and breakers IC3 – lighting and power stem to 84, IIC3 – lighting and power stem to 84, ID1-1A CO_2 machine and IID1-1B CO_2 machine opened within short intervals of one another. These four breakers are in the forward ring main space.

(b) After these breakers opened Nos. 1 and 2 dynamos settled down and no further overloads were experienced.

(c) Dynamo watchkeepers noted the ammeter fluctuations and heard the complaining of the machinery at such unusal demands but did well not to trip their machines.

At 1340 the electrical artificer in charge of the forward repair party, whose station is in the forward ring main space, reported to the main switchboard that the four breakers mentioned had blown their main fuses and opened. All lighting in the sick bay flat and forward therefrom along the main deck was reported out by exchange telephone, and numbers 1, 3 and 4 electrical repair parties were ordered to provide and run emergency cables. The assistant torpedo officer left the main switchboard to go forward and take charge. The commissioned electrician remained in charge at the main switchboard. Communication between repair parties and main switchboard was maintained through sound powered telephone at "F" D/G generator.

It was ascertained that all lighting and power services forward of 84 bulkhead were off due to flooding of compartments between 43 and 80 bulkheads, and especially the flooding of the junction boxes in the refrigerator flat, fed from breakers IC3 and IIC3. At 1350 the main switchboard opened the breakers for A, B and C, 50 ton pumps, numbers 1, 2, and 3, 350 ton pumps and the E.A. plant, as a precaution.

Restoration of Lighting and Power

"F" D/G motor generator panel just abaft 95 station port, was used for supplying temporary leads to all compartments where lighting was required, and for supplying power to the shipwrights' workshop machinery.

Two portable pump starters were supplied from No.2 deck winch change-over switch (IID3). Additional portable pump supplies were required. Continual shorts were experienced on the temporary lighting leads due to salt water and the disrespect of men struggling with shores, pumps, and hoses. A better supply was rigged from No.2 dynamo change-over switch 500 amp. emergency terminals to the shore blocks in No.2 dynamo shore supply panel, and from thence by the permanent leads to the shore connection box on the main deck. From this box the emergency ring, rigged along the main deck forward, was fed, and tappings taken from bulkhead terminals where needed. All leads passing through doors were thereby eliminated.

Final consolidation of lighting and minor power circuits in all compartments which could be reached was achieved by taking out the links in section and distribution boxes on the main and middle decks, and feeding the boxes from temporary runs direct from bulkhead terminals or from bulkhead terminals through six way fuse boards. As soon as the full extent of the flooding was known the fusible links in the following breakers were taken out:– IC1, IC2, ID2, IE1, IE3, IIC1, IIC2, IID2. Blown fusible links in IC3, IIC3, ID1 and IID1 had previously been taken out.

The pitometer log below No.3 naval store worked until 0345 Sunday, 28 September, when flooding of the store affected the speed unit.

On Sunday, 28 September, the door in bulkhead 43 middle deck could be opened owing to the lowering of the water level on the communication mess deck, and lighting was restored in compartments thus made accessible. "A" 50 ton and No.1 350 ton pump starters were supplied from the centre line capstan starter on the foc'sle and down through the sheet navel pipe. Capstan and cable holder motors were run for test.

Telephones

Many of the forward telephones failed due to the flooding of compartments where they or their junction boxes were situated. Most of these 'phones were isolated by their fuses blowing or their fuses being removed when it was obvious there was a fault on.

At 1600 on Saturday, 27 September, the main supply fuse for the underwater control 'phones blew due to shorts on No.5 and 24 'phones. Ship's staff had, however, fitted a change-over switch in the damage control headquarters, and change-over was made from D panel to B.

General Conclusions

(a) So little shock was felt at the main switchboard that the explosion was thought to be a near miss. Gags on dynamo over speed trips, bulkhead through terminals on the main deck and fusible links in branch breakers proved their worth. The necessity for vertical permanent emergency cables through decks, already authorised, was again demonstrated. All electrical gear between bulkheads 43 to 84 below the main deck had flooded with salt water but there appeared to be no electrical gear not salvable.

(b) 350 ton submersible pump starters are below the L.W.L. and are not watertight, although the pump itself is designed to work underwater. So far as is known the sole reason why No.3 pump could not be used was due to flooding of the starter.

Armament

The two torpedoes which were loaded in the tubes were undamaged. Of the ten torpedoes in the torpedo body room, all warheads were dented, all after bodies and tails were smashed and holed, mostly beyond repair; no air vessel was damaged; two water chambers were dented and one was cut open at the after dome; the balance chambers on four of the air vessels were intact.

All fittings in the torpedo body room were destroyed or distorted except the rear door of the port tube, the two foremost charging columns, the starboard de-hydrator, and the two warhead lifting winches. It was considered that much of the damage was caused by the torpedoes being thrown about. As a point of interest it was noted that a barrel (wood) of methylated spirit was undamaged.

Flooding

As a result of the explosion all compartments on the lower deck between 43 and 85 bulkheads, on the platform deck between 43 and 84 and below the platform deck between 43 and 80 were flooded. The port torpedo tube room was flooded from the torpedo body room through a multiple electric cable gland in No.43 bulkhead. The drain valves to the drain tank from the tube rooms had been left open and resulted in the drain tank and starboard torpedo tube room being flooded. This flooding may have been accentuated by leakage past the rear door of the starboard tube which was found to have been damaged. Both tubes were loaded, with bow and rear doors closed and drain valves open.

The middle deck was flooded to a depth of 2 ft. between 43 and 60 bulkheads through the hole caused by the armoured manhole cover blown up from the lower deck, and through the ventilation supply trunk to the prison flat below.

The compartments affected were as follows:–

Lower Deck

Prisons, lobby and music room	43 – 60
Canvas room	60 – 70, Port
Awning room	60 – 70, Std.
Provision room	60 – 78, M.L.
Provision room	70 – 80, Port
Canteen store	70 – 80, Std.
Flour Store	80 – 85, Port
Flour Store	80 – 85, Std.
Lobby	78 – 85, M.L.

Platform Deck

Torpedo tube rooms	28 – 43, Pt. & Std.
W.T. compartment	43 – 60, Port
Torpedo body room	43 – 60, M.L.
W.T. compartment	43 – 60, Std.
Refrigerating machinery room	60 – 80, Std.
Cold room and lobby	60 – 76, M.L.
E.A. plant room	60 – 80, Port

Hold

"A" pump room drain tank	23 – 28
Torpedo tube drain tank	28 – 31
Warhead magazine	43 – 52, Port
Torpedo gunner's store	47 – 60, M.L.
Warhead magazine	43 – 52, Std.
Air bottle compartment	52 – 60, Pt & Std.
No. 3 central store (forward)	60 – 70, M.L.
No. 3 central store (aft.)	70 – 80, M.L.

Double Bottoms

W. T. compartment		43 – 60
W. T. compartment		60 – 80

It was thought that the entry of about 3,700 tons of water as the result of a hit with one aircraft torpedo was excessive. A study has been made of the details of the flooding.

The torpedo struck forward clear of the bulge and in a position where watertight subdivision was the only protection against underwater attack. The centre of the explosion was just forward of a main transverse bulkhead (No.60) and at platform deck level. The minimum flooding which would be expected was as follows:–

	Stations	Compartment	Capacity in Tons
Hold			
	43 to 52 P.	Torpedo head magazine	47
	52 to 60 P.	Air bottle compt.	56
	47 to 60 M.L.	Torp. gunner's store and lobby	71
	70 to 80 P.	W.T. compartment	95
	60 to 70 M.L.	Central store	128
Platform Deck			
	43 to 60 P.	W.T. compartment	80
	43 to 60 M.L.	Torpedo body room	321
	60 to 70 P.	Enriched air room	209
	60 to 80 M.L.	Cold and cool room	221
Lower Deck			
	43 to 80	Prisons, sentry walk, lobby, etc.	440
	60 to 70 P.	Canvas room	110

60 to 78 M.L.	Provision room	360
		2138

The following additional flooding occurred:–

<u>Double Bottoms</u>

43 to 60		43	Damage to 60
60 to 80		105	Blkd, below Hold. Vertical keel between 60 and 80 is non-watertight.

<u>Hold</u>

23 to 28 M.L.	"A" Pump room drain tank	62	
28 to 31 M.L.	Torpedo tube drain tank	41	Drain valves had been left open
43 to 52 P.	Warhead magazine	47	
43 to 52 S.	Warhead magazine	47	Hatches damaged by blast and splinters
52 to 60 S.	Air bottle compt.	56	
70 to 80 M.L.	Central store	126	Damage to No.70 bulkhead

Platform Deck

28 to 43 P. & S.	Torpedo tube rooms	155	Leaking multiple gland in No. 43 bulkhead, leakage past rear door of starboard tube, and flooding up from drain tanks through drain valves which were open.
43 to 60 S.	W.T. compartment	80	Through longitudinal bulkhead, 43 to 60 which was holed by splinters.
60 to 80 S.	Refrigerating machinery room	156	Through W.T. door, which was closed but clipped only on the hinged side. The door opened inward.

Lower Deck

60 to 70 S.	Awning room	110	
70 to 80 S.	Canteen store	156	Not known.
80 to 85 S.	Flour store	67	Probably through doors insecurely closed.
78 to 85 M.L.	Lobby	106	
70 to 80 P.	Canteen store	156	
80 to 85 S.	Flour store	67	

<u>Middle Deck</u>

43 to 60	Mess deck	80	Through splinter hole and through leaking edges of plating due to distortion of deck.
	Total	1660	

The situation was aggravated because the manhole in the armoured hatch on lower deck, in the lobby 78 to 85 was left open, and all five 350 ton pumps and two 50 ton pumps were out of action due to flooded starters.

Damage Control

<u>Shoring</u>

Some time elapsed before the forward boundary of the flooded area was established, due to the flooding of the middle deck, but it was quickly ascertained that no flooding had occurred forward of 23 bulkhead.

At the after boundary of the flooded area, the watchkeeper escaped from the refrigerating machinery room and closed the watertight door, but only clipped it on the side nearest the hinge (this door opens into the compartment and is hinged on the fore side).

The hole in the middle deck was plugged by hammocks shored from the deck over. Shores, closely spaced, were erected between main and middle decks throughout the flooded area, the work being continued incessantly for 48 hours.

More than 24 hours after the explosion, when the ship had been lightened sufficiently to partially empty the lower deck compartments (43 to 60) which were open to the sea, the surge of water caused the middle deck to bulge upwards about 9 inches in the vicinity of the hole and further shoring was carried out overhead between main and upper decks. Shores were erected between main and middle decks in way of the bulged plating on the middle deck, port side, 60 to 70 stations. Small leaks were plugged and shored and leaks in the boundary angle were stopped with cement.

The armoured hatch and manhole cover on the lower deck, 78 to 80 M.L. were shored down but it was not possible completely to stop the leakage around the cover and manhole.

There was no sign of strain in No. 43 bulkhead and shoring was not considered necessary. Leakage occurred through a cable gland into the torpedo tube compartment but was controlled.

No. 84 bulkhead, at the after end of the flooded area, is well stiffened by armour. No shoring was necessary and some leakage through the watertight trunk for electric cables was effectively overcome with wood plugs.

Pumping

All compartments in the flooded area are serviced by Nos. 1, 2, 3, 4 and 5 submersible 350 ton pumps which are cross-connected, and by "A" and "B" 50 ton pumps. All these pumps were put out of action due to flooding which prevented the operation of suction and discharge valves from upper control positions and by flooding of non-watertight starters fitted below the L.W.L. Immediate pumping operations were, therefore, carried out by five 75 ton portable pumps. (Six of these pumps were carried but one was sited in the prison flat, lower deck 43 to 60).

The flooding of the middle deck was first dealt with. About 6 hours after the explosion the water level was reduced below the sill of the W.T. door in No. 43 bulkhead and access was obtained to No.1 350 ton pump, "A" 50 ton pump, and compartments forward of No. 43 bulkhead. Temporary electric leads were rigged to these pumps which were used to pump out the torpedo rooms and drain tanks.

No. 3 central store, 70 to 80, hold, was pumped out by No.4 350 ton pump and leakage into the store was kept under control until the suction strainer became choked. No other flooded compartments could be opened up due to the speed of the ship maintaining the water level above the middle deck. Consequently, all buoyancy compartments forward were pumped out and certain rapid flooding compartments aft were flooded. The resultant change of trim lowered the water level below the middle deck, and the awning room (lower deck, 60 to 70 stard.) was pumped out by two 75 ton portable pumps.

Before access could be gained to the remaining flooded compartments which were thought to be intact it was necessary to close the armoured manhole cover to the armoured hatchway in the lobby, 78 to 85, lower deck. The manhole was 13 ft. below the water level. Two divers, equipped with Salvus breathing apparatus succeeded in closing the cover but were unable to operate the clips. The cover was shored down and the lobby pumped out;

four 75 ton portable pumps were required to overcome the leakage from the armoured hatch and manhole cover. The canteen store, 70 to 80 stard., and the flour stores, 80 to 85, port and stard. were drained into the lobby and pumped out.

The provision room, 60 to 78 was not drained into the lobby as it was not deemed advisable to ease the clips of the watertight door which opened outwards into the lobby.

In all, 29 compartments, (including the partial flooding of middle deck) were flooded and, of these, 10 were pumped out and the remainder were drained out in dock.

General

There were no incendiary effects or subsequent explosions. A few of the damage control personnel who were working in compartments in the vicinity of the explosion were affected by poisonous fumes. The nature of the fumes was not diagnosed as no special measures were necessary to dissipate them and conditions were normal within a few minutes.

Effect on Fighting Efficiency

Torpedo tubes were out of action and of 12 torpedoes carried 10 were destroyed or rendered unfit for service.

Speed of ship was reduced on account of the amount of water in the flooded compartments and the risk of undue strain on structure in the immediate vicinity of compartments open to the sea.

Except for the possibility that firing the 16 inch guns would have disturbed the shoring of the middle deck the fighting equipment was not affected.

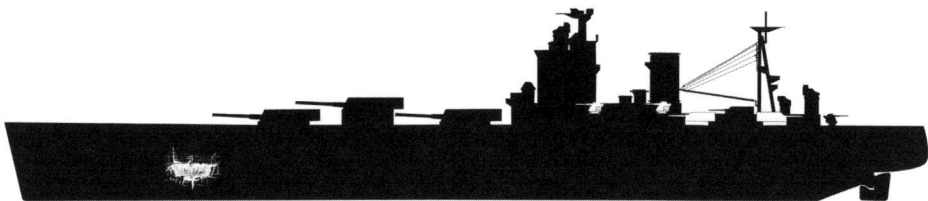

H.M.S. NELSON
TORPEDO DAMAGE 27-9-41

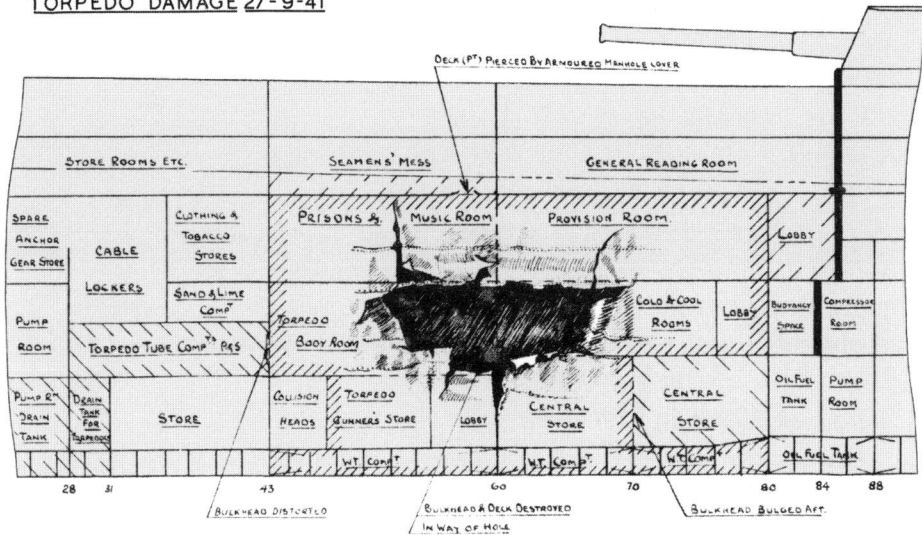

DECK (PT) PIERCED BY ARMOURED MANHOLE COVER

STORE ROOMS ETC.   SEAMENS' MESS   GENERAL READING ROOM

SPARE ANCHOR GEAR STORE   CABLE   CLOTHING & TOBACCO STORES   PRISONS & MUSIC ROOM   PROVISION ROOM   LOBBY

LOCKERS   SAND & LIME COMP

PUMP ROOM   TORPEDO TUBE COMP PRS   TORPEDO BODY ROOM   COLD & COOL ROOMS   LOBBY   BUOYANCY SPACE   COMPRESSOR ROOM

PUMP R DRAIN TANK   DRAIN TANK FOR TORPEDO   STORE   COLLISION HEADS   TORPEDO GUNNERS STORE   LOBBY   CENTRAL STORE   CENTRAL STORE   OIL FUEL TANK   PUMP ROOM

W.T. COMP   W.T. COMP   W.T. COMP   OIL FUEL TANK

28   31   43   60   70   80   84   88

BULKHEAD DISTORTED   BULKHEAD & DECK DESTROYED IN WAY OF HOLE   BULKHEAD BULGED AFT.

UPPER PLATFORM

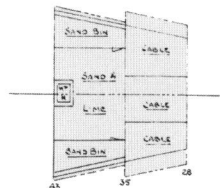

SAND BIN   CABLE
SAND &   LIME   CABLE
SAND BIN   CABLE

43   35   28

PLATFORM DECK

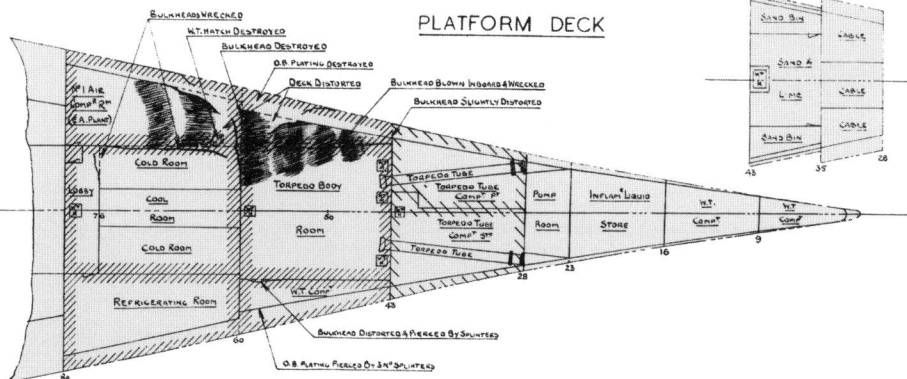

BULKHEADS WRECKED
W.T. HATCH DESTROYED
BULKHEAD DESTROYED
O.B. PLATING DESTROYED
DECK DISTORTED
BULKHEAD BLOWN INBOARD & WRECKED
BULKHEAD SLIGHTLY DISTORTED

N°I AIR COMP R°2 (E.A. PLANT)   COLD ROOM   TORPEDO BODY   TORPEDO TUBE COMP° P°

LOBBY   COOL ROOM   ROOM   TORPEDO TUBE COMP° 3°°   PUMP ROOM   INFLAM LIQUID STORE   W.T. COMP   W.T. COMP

COLD ROOM   TORPEDO TUBE

REFRIGERATING ROOM   W.T. COMP

BULKHEAD DISTORTED & PIERCED BY SPLINTERS
O.B. PLATING PIERCED BY 34" SPLINTERS

28   23   16   9

MIDDLE DECK

LOWER DECK

HOLD

Damage Reports
H.M.S. *Queen Elizabeth*

Mine Damage

<u>Type of Ship</u>	Battleship, completed 1915	
<u>Principal Dimensions</u>	Length (B.P.)	601 ft. 4 ins.
	Breadth	104 ft. 0 ins.
	Displacement	30,600 tons – standard
	Draught (mean)	28 ft. 0 ins. – standard

Circumstances

On 19 December, 1941, *Queen Elizabeth* was moored at 'S' berth in Alexandria Harbour, in water 8 fathoms deep. The weather was calm.

Attack

An Italian two-man submarine passed under the ship's protective net. The crew slung a mine under the bottom of the ship at about 109 station, that is under 'B' boiler room, by means of lines secured to the bilge keels. At 0615 the mine exploded, blowing a large hole in the ship's bottom. The charge was variously reported as being 1000 lb. T.N.T. lying on the bottom of the harbour, i.e. 14 ft. below the keel and as 500 lb. T.N.T. charge having positive buoyancy, and therefore possibly in contact with ship's bottom.

Other reports give the charge weight carried by Italian 2 man submarine as 300, 400 and 500 Kilos, of "Tritualite fusa".

Heel and Trim

	Forward	Aft.
Draughts of ship before damage were	33 ft. 5 ins.	32 ft. 7 ins.
Draughts of ship after damage were	41 ft. 10 ins.	33 ft. 10 ins.

Heel due to damage was 4½° to starboard and was corrected by counter-flooding as stated in paragraph headed "Liquid Conditions".

Shoring

The forward side of No. 81 Bulkhead was shored in the following compartments:– 4.5" L.A. magazine (Hold M.L.), Pitometer Log Compartment, port and starboard 4.5" magazines (Lower Deck), Second W/T Office. The after side of No. 136 Bulkhead was shored inside 'Y' Boiler Room.

Hatches to the following compartments were shored:– 'A' Boiler Room, 'B' Boiler Room and Nos. 3 and 5 Kit Locker Rooms.

Liquid Conditions

Compartment		Position		Capacity in Tons	Condition before damage	Liquid in compartment after damage	Estimated weight of water entry in Tons
Immediate Uncontrolled Flooding							
'A' Boiler Room		80–100 Hold		739	Empty	Full	739
'B' Boiler Room		100–118 Hold		751			751
'X' Boiler Room		118–136 Hold		751			751
Air Space		81–82 Hold		42			42
'B' Hydraulic Room		100–118 Hold		126	Empty	Full	126
No. 1 Turbo Generator Room		82–100 Hold	S	128			128
No. 2 Turbo Generator Room		100–118 Hold	P	122			122
Pitometer Log Compartment		80–81 Hold		6			6
Oil Fuel Tanks	B1	82–100 D.B.	S	57	95%		3
	B2	82–100 D.B.	P	57	95%		3
	B3	100–118 D.B.	S	58	95%		3
	B4	100–118 D.B.	P	58	95%		3
	B5	118–136 D.B.	S	57	95%		3
	B6	118–136 D.B.	P	57	95%		3
	B7	136–154 D.B.	S	55	95%	Oil Fuel	3
	B8	136–154 D.B.	P	55	95%		3
	C1	83–91 I.B. to Mid.Dk.	S	59	95%		3
	C3	91–100 "	S	79	27%		58

Compartment	Position			Capacity in Tons	Condition before damage	Liquid in compartment after damage	Estimated weight of water entry in Tons
Oil Fuel Tanks	C5	100-109 "	S	81	53%		38
	C8	109-118 "	P	82	95%		4
	D1	82-91 "	S	36	95%	Oil Fuel	2
	D3	91-100 "	S	39	95%		2
	D5	100-109 "	S	49	95%		3
	D8	109-118 "	P	58	95%		3
Lower Bulge Compartments	79½-89½		S	79			79
	89½-99½		S	80			80
	99½-109½		S	80			80
	109½-119½		P	79			79
Wing D.B. Compartments	91-100		S	35		Full	5
	100-109		S	37			37
	109-118		S	38			38
	109-118		P	38	Empty		38
D.B.C. 3rd longl. P)							
to 3rd longl. S)	68-82 D.B.	ML		89			89
3rd longl. S)	82-100 D.B.	ML		118			118
3rd longl. S)	100-118 D.B.	ML		118			118
Steam Drain Tank	118-122 D.B.	P		10			10
Steam Drain Tank	118-122 D.B.	S		10			10
D.B.C. 3rd longl. P)	118-136			100			100
to 3rd longl. S)	136-154			120			120
							3933

Flooding Arrested by Pumps

Compartment	Position		Capacity in Tons	Condition before damage	Liquid in compartment after damage	Estimated weight of water entry in Tons
'Y' Boiler Room	136-154 Hold		757		12' deep	336
No. 3 Turbo Generator Room	118-136 Hold	S	122		Full	122
No. 4 Diesel Generator Room	118-136 Hold	P	122		50% full	61
No. 5 Diesel Generator Room	136-154 Hold	S	115		Full	115
'A' Hydraulic Room	82-100 Hold	P	21	Empty		21
4.5" H.A. Magazine	68-81 Hold	ML	160			160
Searchlight Stabilising Room	82-100 Plat. Dk.	P	74		Full	74
Boiler Spare Gear Store	100-118 L. Dk.	S	69			69
No. 1 4.5" H.A. Magazine	68-82 plat. Dk.	S	106			106

Compartment	Position		Capacity in Tons	Condition before damage	Liquid in compartment after damage	Estimated weight of water entry in Tons
No. 2 4.5" Magazine	68-82 Plat. Dk.	P	106	Empty	Full	106
No. 3 4.5" Magazine	68-81 Plat. Dk.	ML	166			166
D.B.C's 3rd - 6th longls.	68-82	P	43			43
		S	43			43
Oil Fuel Tanks C2	83-91 I.B. to Mid. Dk.	P	59	95%	Full	3
C4	91-100 "	P	79	95%		4
C9	118-127 "	S	82	95%		4
C12	127-136 "	P	82	95%	Oil Fuel	4
D2	82-91 "	P	36	95%		2
D4	91-100 "	P	39	95%		2
D9	118-127 "	S	60	95%		3
D12	127-136 "	P	61	95%		3
No. 1 Oil Fuel Working Space	89-93 Mid. Dk.	S	19		Flooded to W.L.	18
No. 3 Oil Fuel Working Space	107-111 "	S	18			15
No. 5 Oil Fuel Working Space	125-129 "	S	18			14
No. 2 Hammock & K.L. Space	68-82 "	S	66			66
No. 3 Hammock & K.L. Space	82-100 "	S	159			145
No. 4 Hammock & K.L. Space	82-100 "	P	159			145
No. 5 Hammock & K.L. Space	100-118 "	S	115			92
No. 6 Hammock & K.L. Space	100-118 "	P	115			92
No. 7 Hammock & K.L. Space	118-136 "	S	115	Empty		92
Medical Store	68-82 "	S	66		Full	62
Medical Distg. Station	68-82 "	ML	122			115
Protected Navigation Plot	75-80 Lower Dk.	P	115			115
Main Switchboard Room	68-80 "	P	115			115
Lower Conning Tower	77-81 "	ML	23		Full	23
L.P. Machinery Room	68-82 "	S	77			77
No.2	68-82 "	P	85			85
W/T Transmitting Room	100-118 "	P & S	30			30
Cable Passage	118-136 "	P & S	30			30

Net amount of water entered due to damage   6496

Compartment	Position		Capacity in Tons	Condition before damage	Liquid in compartment after damage	Estimated weight of water entry in Tons
Counterflooding to Correct Heel						
Lower Bulge Compartments	139½-149½	P	80	⊤	⊤	80
	149½-159½	P	83	Empty	Full	83
	159½-169½	P	85			85
	169½-179½	P	89	⊥	⊥	89
						257
Condition of Tanks Unaffected by Flooding						
Oil Fuel Tanks						
A1 & A2				95%		
B9 to B12				95%		
C6				95%		
C7				78%		
C10 & C11				95%		
C13 to C18				95%		
D6, D7, D10				95%		
D11				78%		
D13 to D24				95%		
X1 to X3				95%		
Water Protection Compts.	31½-52	P		⊤		
	52-82	P & S				
	33½-52	S		Empty Flooded		
	196-220	P				
	196-232	S				
Bulges						
W/T Compts.						
D.B. Compts.				⊥		
Drain Tanks.	118-122	P & S		25%		

The net amount of water entered due to damage as calculated above would necessitate a slightly greater sinkage than actually occurred. This discrepancy is due to the fact that in some cases pumping arrested flooding before compartments were completely full.

Structural Damage

The whole bottom structure over the area of "B" Boiler Room was blown up into the ship. Similar damage occurred in "A" and "X" Boiler Rooms but to a lesser degree owing to the support given by No,s.100 and 118 bulkheads.

The Outer Bottom plating (40 lbs.) in the area bounded by 100 and 118 bulkheads and "C" strakes port and starboard was badly ruptured and set up to a maximum of 16 feet above the keel. Outside this area the plating was distorted and ruptured in several places between 65 and 154 stations and strake port to "H" strake starboard.

The Inner Bottom plating (20 lbs.) was buckled and ruptured in several places between 79 and 135 stations from the 5th longitudinal port to 5th longitudinal starboard and particularly between 100 and 118 stations from 3rd longitudinal port to the 3rd longitudinal starboard where the Inner Bottom was badly ruptured and set up to a maximum height of 23 feet above the keel.

The Vertical Keel (40 lbs.) was distorted and ruptured between 82 and 126 stations and destroyed between 100 and 118 stations.

The 1st, 2nd and 3rd longitudinals port and starboard (each 20 lbs.) were badly buckled and ruptured where they passed through the damaged area.

The 4th (20 lbs.) and 5th (30 lbs.) longitudinals port and starboard were distorted in the damaged region.

Floor plates, W.T. frames and angle frames within the region 100–118 stations and inboard of the 4th longitudinals were badly distorted where not actually destroyed. Outside of this region to the 6th longitudinals and 98 to 122 stations the floor plates were distorted.

Bulge plating (22.5 lbs.) was corrugated from 81½ to 126 stations port and 80½ to 139½ stations starboard on A, B and C strakes. The areas most affected were between 99½ to 109½ bulkheads port and 97½ to 109½ stations starboard where the maximum depth of the corrugations was 4½ inches. The bulge bulkheads at 99½, 109½ and 119½ stations starboard were buckled at the bottom.

Nos. 81 and 82 bulkheads (each 20 lbs.) including vertical stiffening plates and angles in the Air Space 81–82 were buckled (max. 2") from the Inner Bottom to Middle Deck between the 3rd longitudinal bulkheads.

No. 100 bulkhead (17 and 20 lbs.) including the stiffeners (8 x 6 x 6 x 35 lbs. I bar each side of bulkhead) and brackets was badly buckled and ruptured at the bottom to a height of about 8 feet above the Inner Bottom between the 3rd longitudinal port and the 5th longitudinal bulkhead starboard.

No. 118 bulkhead (17 and 20 lbs.) was distorted and ruptured at the bottom to a height of about 6 feet above the Inner Bottom between the 3rd longitudinal bulkhead port and 5th longitudinal bulkhead starboard.

3rd longitudinal bulkhead, port (17 and 20 lbs. and 6 x 3 x 3 x 13.6 lbs. stiffeners) was buckled (maximum 3 inches) between the Inner Bottom and Platform Deck from 82 to 103 stations, and between Inner Bottom and Middle Deck 103–118 stations. The bottom angle was broken away from the bulkhead between 110 and 116 stations and the connecting brackets on the stiffeners distorted.

3rd longitudinal bulkhead, starboard sustained similar but rather more extensive damage.

5th longitudinal bulkhead, port (17 and 20 lbs. and 6 x 3 x 3½ x 14 lbs. stiffeners) was buckled (max. 3" at 96 station) between the Inner Bottom and Platform Deck from 82 to 118 stations.

5th longitudinal bulkhead, starboard, was similarly buckled (max. 4" at 98 station) from 82 to 126 stations.

Platform Deck plating (10 lbs.) between 102–107 in W.T. compartment starboard was buckled.

Electrical Report

The electrical repair parties were closed up in Electrical Organisation No. 1, an "alert" having been promulgated earlier. Nos 2, 3, 6 and 7 turbo-dynamos were on load and the ring main split into four quarters as laid down in BR.268(6). The electrical separation was, in fact, illusory as all dynamos derived their steam supply from "A" boiler room. No. 4 diesel dynamo had been reported as ready for starting and No. 5 diesel dynamo was out of action owing to a defective engine.

The shock of the explosion on the main switchboard was not unduly severe. Nos. 2, 6 and 7 dynamos failed immediately due to loss of steam. The voltage of No. 3 dynamo dropped, but it did not come off load and it was thought that it would keep running. No ring main switchgear appears to have come off due to shock.

An attempt to complete the ring main was made. Nos. 9 and 13 ring main breakers were closed (the latter had presumably opened with the opening of No. 7 supply breaker) but it was then evident that No. 3 dynamo was failing, the supply breaker opened and the blackout was complete. The time elapsing between the explosion and the blackout was 20 seconds. All steam had failed, "A" boiler room having flooded completely in 30 seconds.

The low power batteries took over the low power supply and communications having been established, instructions to start up No. 4 diesel dynamo were given from the main switchboard. Trouble was experienced with the spindle of the circulating pump and about three minutes elapsed before the machine was running. Three attempts were made to close No. 4 supply breaker, but these were unsuccessful, an overload causing the supply breaker to open on each occasion, due to the flooding of the starboard electric cable passage abreast "B" boiler room.

The port ring main was shorted by this flooding via the group change-over switches VIIA and VIIAA and the cross-connecting cables between group change-over switches VA and VIA, in the flooded boiler room were also damaged. It was found that of the 4 – 600 amp. fuses in the group changeover switches VIIIA and VIIIAA, one had been blown and the others had been very hot.

The 1000 ton pump in "X" boiler room was urgently required and emergency cables were run from No. 4 dynamo room, and also the cross-connecting links between Nos. 3 and 4 dynamos' main supply switchgear units were changed over to feed No. 4 dynamo into the starboard side of the ring main. Unfortunately, before either of these operations was complete the circulating pump spindle of No. 4 dynamo fractured and the machine stopped after only 20 minutes running.

At 0750, two submarines secured alongside and at 0830 a supply was arranged from one submarine through No. 8 shore connection box. The ring main was then made up on both sides as far forward as Nos. 9 and 10 ring main breakers; the closing of either of these produced a short circuit and therefore the forward sections of the ring main had to be left "dead". The blackout had lasted two hours.

The emergency supply system on the port side of the main deck was run and used to supply the ring main as far aft as No. 6 ring main breaker via the group change-over switch IIA. Attempts to close Nos. 1 and 2 ring main breakers resulted in short circuits, so these were left open, group change-over switches on section I were put to "emergency" and lighting forward was restored. At this time all ring main switchgear, except No. 17 ring main breaker, was operative in switchboard control.

Subsequently the second submarine gave a supply through No. 7 shore connection box, the main deck emergency supply system on the starboard side was energised and group change-over switches on section I were used to feed from this source. The ring main was then split so that each submarine supplied its own side.

Diagram of ring main

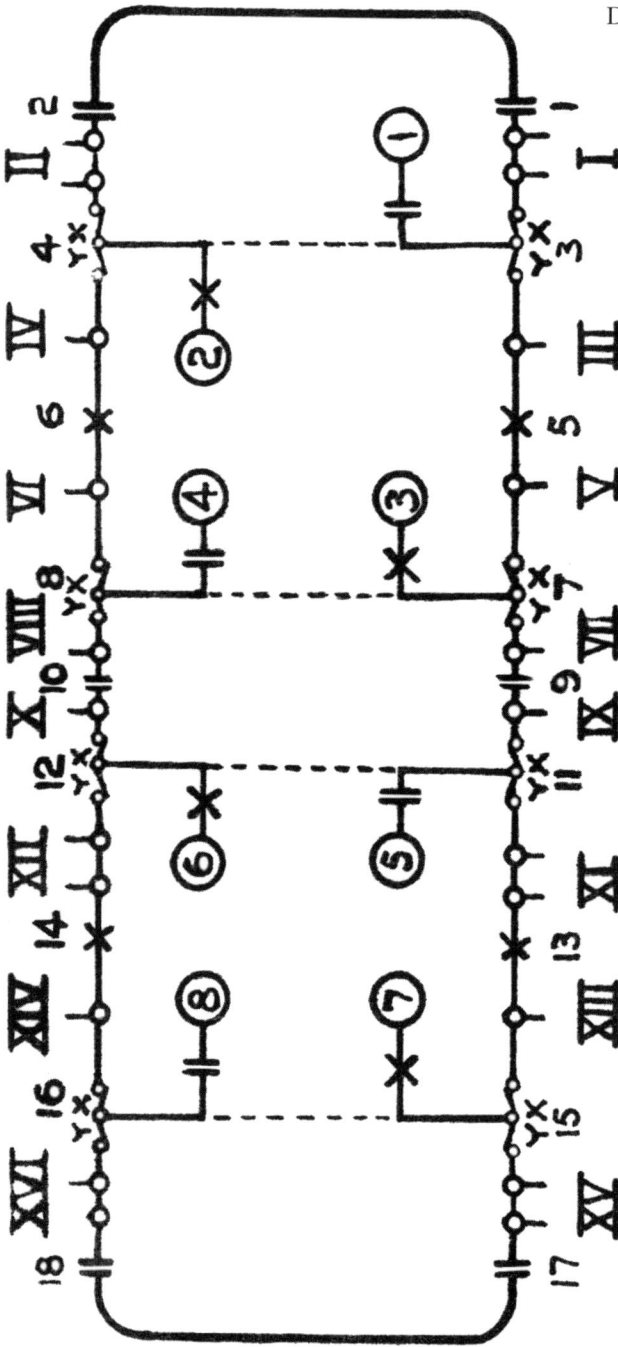

As it was known that there was a short on the starboard ring main forward of No. 9 ring main breaker, and the ship had a list to starboard, the fuse release switches feeding group change-over switches IA, IAA and IB were opened, when supply to them was arranged as described in the preceding para. The reason for the short circuit on the starboard ring main was eventually traced to the failure of No. 3 dynamo fuse release switch to open, which left a dead short on the ring main, the dynamo itself being flooded.

Power was supplied by emergency cables to the pom pom motors, type 279 R.D.F., the 10" signalling projectors and temporary lighting between 82 and 154 stations. During the afternoon, winches and 4.5" ammunition hoists were used for de-ammunitioning.

At 1435, one submarine cast off and separate supplies were arranged from the other submarine to Nos. 7 and 8 shore connection boxes with the ring main split in order to localise any further breakdown.

About 1600 on 19 December, 82 bulkhead began leak into the lower steering position, this compartment was abandoned and the door shored up. At about the same time, oil fuel and water began to leak into the main switchboard and No. 1 low power room.

At 1630 the passage abreast "X" boiler room, port side, flooded sufficiently to cause fuse release switch No. X to open. By 2100 the lower steering position had failed completely and water and oil fuel were leaking into the main switchboard room through fan trunking. Constant baling, however, enabled the danger of flooding to be kept in check. During the night of 19/20 December, the electric cable passage on the starboard side of "X" boiler room flooded sufficiently to operate No. IX fuse release switch and branch breaker groups 9A and 9AA dropped off.

20 December, 1941

By 0400, the lower steering position had been emptied by allowing the water to flood into the flat, from whence it was baled out and the leakage was eventually got under control. During this day de-ammunitioning was continued, portable pumps were in use in various compartments and adequate lighting was provided.

21 December, 1941

During the forenoon, the 500 amp. fuses in No. 8 supply breaker feeding the port emergency run blew. Fuse release switch 2A was opened and group change-over switch 2B was first put to emergency to feed from the starboard side, and later replaced in normal with a feed from the bulkhead terminals at 68 port lower deck. The reason is not clear.

An emergency feed from bulkhead terminals at 154 starboard main deck was arranged to "Y" boiler room to enable the boiler room fans to be started, lighting provided, and steam raised. At this time the ring main was alive fed from the submarine, from Nos. 17 to 9 and from Nos. 18 to 10 ring main breakers on the starboard and port sides respectively.

At 1400, No. 7 turbo dynamo was run up, tested in switchboard control and put on load on the starboard side. At 1600, it also took over the port side, and the submarine shoved off.

During the afternoon ring main breaker No. 14 opened and could not be re-closed in either "switchboard" or "local". Hand switch 12X was opened and ring main breaker No. 14 was then re-closed in local control. No reason for this fault was discovered. The branch breakers on section 12 were closed normally in switchboard control.

At 1800 No. 8 turbo dynamo was run up, tried in parallel with No. 7 satisfactorily, and the ring main was then re-arranged, each machine feeding its own side as far forward as No.9 ring main breaker and hand switch 12X.

Hand switch 11X was opened with Nos. 7 and 8 dynamos feeding their respective sides of the ring main.

22 December, 1941

Water leaked into the main switchboard and damaged control junction boxes for 1A, 1AA, 1B, 2A, 2AA and 2B sections and the branch breakers for these sections were put into local control.

General Remarks

When eventually opened up several weeks later watertight boxes on the ring main, which had been under water, were found to have leaked, due in the main to leakage through the sealing ends. In some cases they had been exposed to pressures up to 7 lbs. per square inch for a period of several weeks.

The automatic emergency lanterns functioned correctly and were of great value providing the sole lighting during the blackout. Bucket type flood lights pattern 17022 later proved extremely valuable.

Communications remained good until the forenoon of 20 December when shorts and earths due to flooded telephones caused trouble on the main and engine room exchanges. Faulty telephones were cut out and communications restored.

All H.P. supplies to the forward L.P. board were lost due to flooding, and the automatic selector switch was covered with oil fuel due to a leak in the bulkhead, as were several L.P. panels. The L.P. supply was taken from the aft L.P. room via the cable linking the auxiliary boards, on the forenoon of 19 December.

Nos. 1, 2 and 3 dynamos all flooded rapidly and Nos. 4 and 5 eventually during the same day.

Armament Damage

Forward 4.5 inch turrets, with the exception of S3 were out of action through flooded pumps and distorted roller path bearings.

Effect on Fighting Efficiency

The ship was rendered unseaworthy and immobilised.

The Forward section of the ring main, Nos. 1 to 5 Dynamos, No. 2 Transmitting Room, and both automatic plots were put out of action.

H.M.S. QUEEN ELIZABETH.
MINE DAMAGE. 19-12-41.

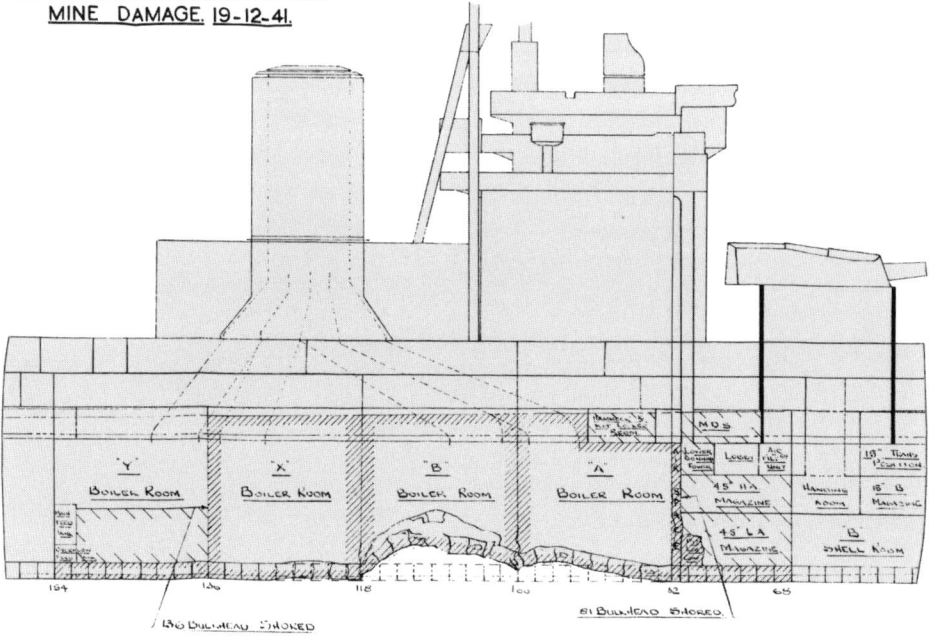

(LOOKING AFT)

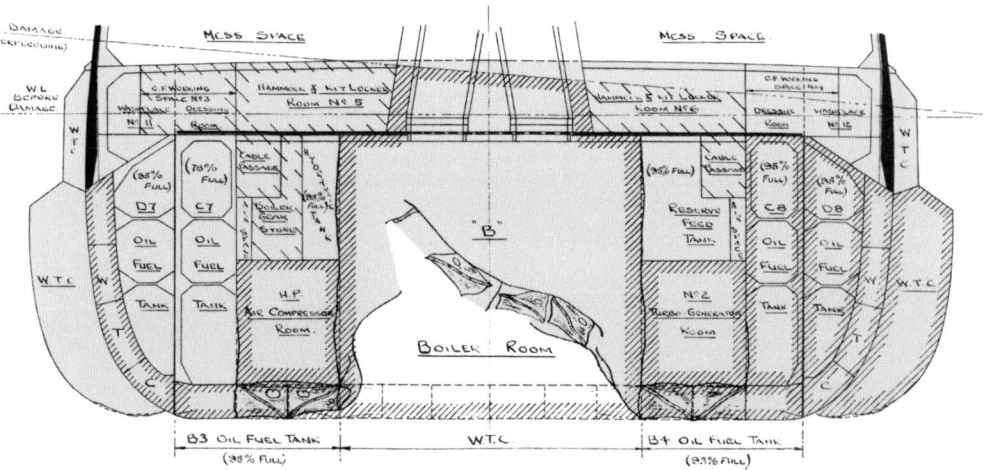

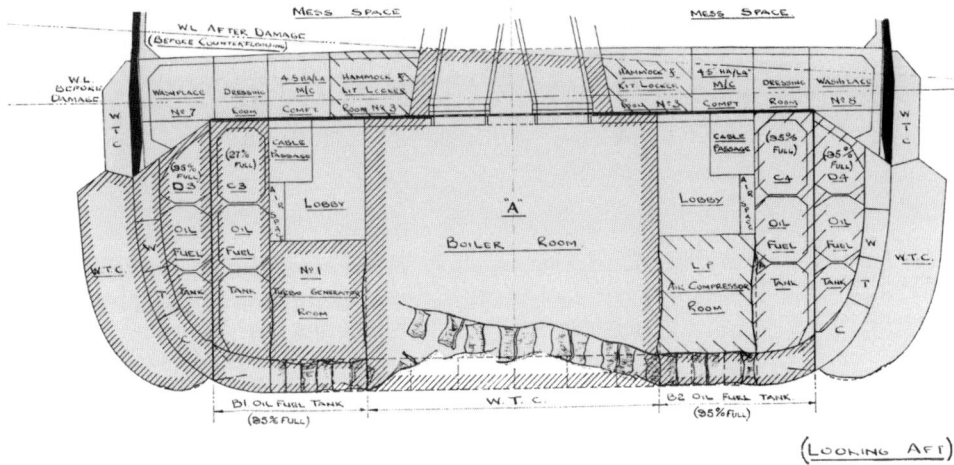

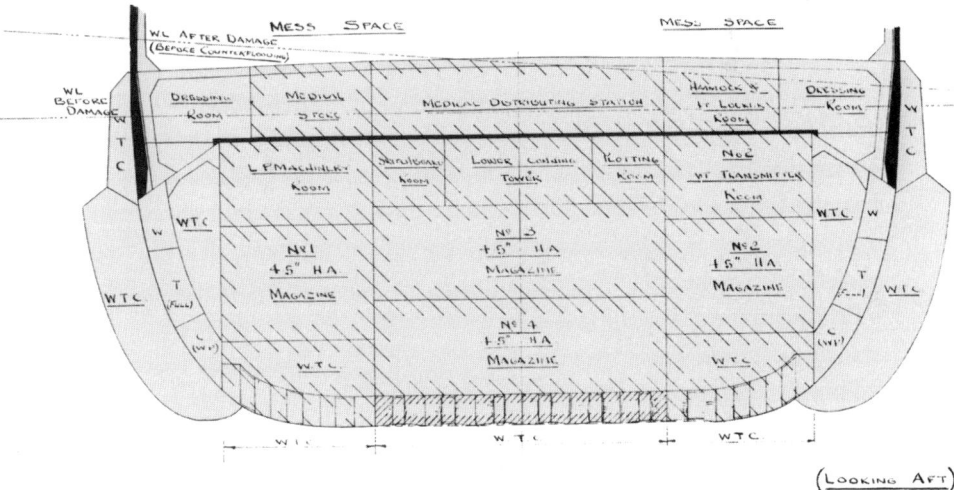

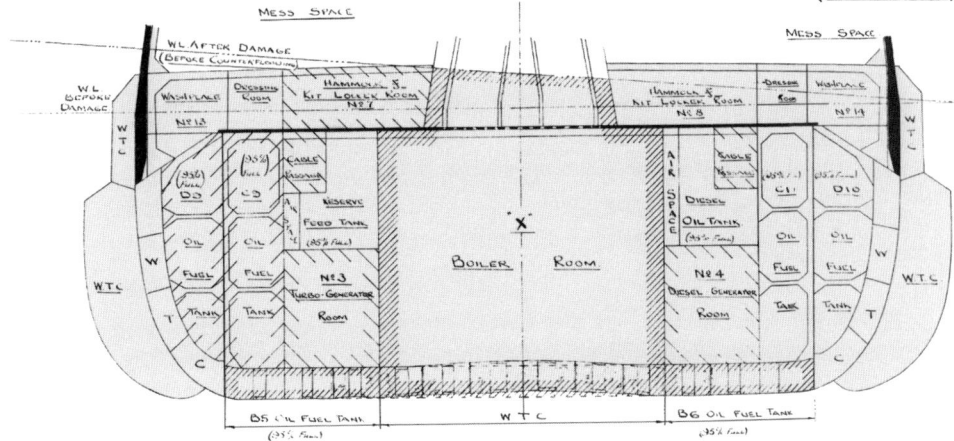

Damage Reports
H.M.S. *Indomitable*

Bomb Damage

Type of Ship	Aircraft Carrier, completed 1941	
Principal Dimensions	Length overall	745 ft. 0 ins.
	Breadth on waterline (deep)	95 ft. 0 ins.
	Displacement	29,084 tons – deep condition
	Draught (mean)	28 ft. 5 ins. – deep condition

Circumstances

At 1845B on 12 August 1942 the ship was south west of Sicily escorting a convoy towards Malta and was steaming at 22 knots. Periodic air attacks had been experienced since leaving Gibraltar.

Weather – fine, intensity of light – strong, sea – calm, wind – nil, cloud – nil, visibility 15.

Attack

Seven aircraft, of which at least five were Stukas approached from astern at 15,000 feet. Each aircraft released a bomb in a 70° dive – the first aircraft at 1,500 feet, the others at lower heights – and then passed over the ship at heights of 500 to 1,000 feet without firing machine guns. The ship was damaged by 2 hits and 3 near-misses. No identifiable fragments were recovered. Detonation of each bomb was judged complete.

Hit No. 1 struck the flight deck at 30 station 6 feet to starboard of the forward edge of the forward lift, made a hole 14-inch diameter in the 60-lbs. flight deck, perforated the 10-lbs. upper gallery deck and detonated just above the upper hangar deck after a travel of 16 feet from the point of first impact. Fire broke out, including a petrol fire at the forward end of the hangar, but was under control after 40 minutes. The fire was below and slightly forward of A1 turret and no great heat reached A2. "Clearing charges" in A2 were undamaged, being in a closed locker. In A1, the cordite exploded and split the cylinders. Some shell then fell through the damaged deck into the fire and eventually exploded. A number of large shell fragments were found in the wreckage and landed at Gibraltar. Bomb was judged to be 250 Kgm. S.C. type.

Hit No. 2 struck the flight deck on the middle line at 164 station abaft the after lift, perforated the 14-lbs. flight deck and the 10-lbs. upper gallery deck and detonated just above the upper hangar deck, after a travel of 16 feet from the point of first impact, in the cabins adjacent to the No. 2 torpedo body room. Fire broke out without igniting the torpedo warheads in their mantlet stowages. Bomb was judged to be 250 Kgm. S.C. type.

Near-miss No.1 carved a groove in the lower edge of the pom-pom director bulwark at 63 station, port side, and detonated in air 5 feet from the ship's side at the level of the upper hangar deck after a travel of 16 feet from the point of impact. Bomb was judged to be 250 Kgm. S.C. type.

Near Miss No. 2. A fragment of a bomb has been recovered in No. 2 naval store and identified as part of a 250 Kgm. S.C. type. Evidently the bomb burst very near the ship's side.

Near-miss No. 3 struck the sea off the port quarter and detonated under water with no serious effect on the ship. About a dozen splinters entered the Captain's apartments. Bomb was judged to be 250 Kgm. S.C. type.

Structural Damage

Hit No. 1 The 12 and 14-lbs. ship's side plating was blown out between 21 and 30 stations, lower gallery deck to upper gallery deck. The flight deck was set up 2 feet from 22 station to 34 station, a length of 48 feet.

A hole 20 feet by 12 feet was blown upwards in the upper gallery deck (10-lbs.)

A hole 20 feet by 28 feet was blown downwards in the upper hangar deck (14-lbs.).

Lower Gallery deck broke from its connection at 28 bulkhead starboard for a distance of about 2 feet.

The 14-ins. bulkhead 21 on upper hangar deck was bulged forward a few inches over the whole width of the ship.

The 14-lbs. bulkhead 28 was destroyed above the upper hangar deck, and bent forward 6 feet at upper hangar deck level between the lift well and the ship's side.

The 14-lbs. longitudinal bulkhead bounding the starboard side of the lift well was destroyed between 28 and 30 stations, upper hangar deck to upper gallery deck.

Splinters were evenly and closely distributed around the point of burst, travelling effectively a maximum of 30 feet.

The forward lift was canted upwards 5 feet on the starboard side. This was soon afterwards reduced to a 2-ft. 6-in. arch at the middle line in order to allow aircraft to fly off.

Hit No. 2. A large hole was blown upwards in the 14-lbs. flight deck, length unknown. The plating was soon afterwards burnt off by the ship's staff in order to remove the obstacle to aircraft landing on, leaving a hole 56 feet long and 40 feet wide between longitudinal bulkheads.

The 10-lbs. upper gallery deck was destroyed between 160½ and 165 stations, a length of 12 feet, over a width of 20 feet.

The 14-lbs. upper hangar deck was destroyed between 161 and 165½ stations, a length of 18 feet, over a width of 16 feet.

The 14-lbs. lower gallery deck was dished slightly downwards.

158 bulkhead (14-lbs.) between upper gallery deck and upper hangar deck was buckled and distorted over the whole width of the ship.

The after lift sides were set down about 6 inches but the lift was only out of action until ship's staff faired parts of the platform.

Splinters were evenly distributed about the point of burst, travelling effectively a maximum of 16 feet forward through 158 bulkhead (14-lbs.).

Near-miss No. 1 destroyed 17 and 14-lbs. ship's side plating between 59 and 63 stations, a length of 16 feet, over a height of 12 feet, between lower gallery deck and upper gallery deck.

The 10-lbs, longitudinal bulkhead of the wardroom was torn from its welded heel connection between 58 and 71 stations, a length of 52 feet.

Splinters reached a maximum of 52 feet within the ship, that is, about 57 feet from the point of burst, perforating the 14-lbs. ship's side and the 10-lbs. wardroom bulkhead.

Near-miss No. 2 was opposite the after lower corner of the side were few and travelled a maximum of 20 feet inside the ship.

Damage to Lifts
Forward Lift
The platform located at flight deck level but still suspended on the sprocket chains was badly buckled longitudinally, having apparently been forced

upwards by blast.

The operating gear, including electrical equipment, on the starboard side was badly damaged and required almost complete renewal.

The differential gear was also damaged.

Transmission gearing on the port side was left in fairly good order except for minor defects but required to be closely overhauled.

The suspension chains on the port side appeared in good condition but may have been strained as the platform was jerked bodily upwards and subsequently dropped. Thus the chains have borne a suddenly applied over-load of considerable magnitude.

After Lift

The after lift, although slightly distorted, was soon restored to operation at half speed by means of the starboard motor.

The platform was slightly distorted having developed an athwartships sag of a few inches mid length.

The operating gear was damaged at the port after corner of the lift where the length of shafting connecting the port side transmission to the differential box was slightly bent and the mitre gearing distorted. This length of shafting was removed to facilitate operation of the platform.

Comment by D.N.C. Department

In the design of these lifts provision had been made for operation under conditions which might produce a considerable degree of misalignment of the transmission gear. This feature, although involving considerable cost, proved to be of great advantage in the case of the after lift as it rendered possible its continued use after damage was sustained.

Regarding the position in which the platforms should be kept during a bombing attack, experience both in *Illustrious* and *Indomitable* indicates no technical reason for restricting operation in action.

The utility of keeps in electrically operated lifts in the light of their assistance in removing strains from the operating gear under conditions such as those recently experienced does not appear to be well supported observing that in the case of the forward lift the distortion of the platform was such that the keeps would not have registered and in the after lift that the excessive stresses resulting in the distortion of the platform would probably have jammed the keeps and rendered the lift inoperable. Keeps are being abolished for electrically operated lifts.

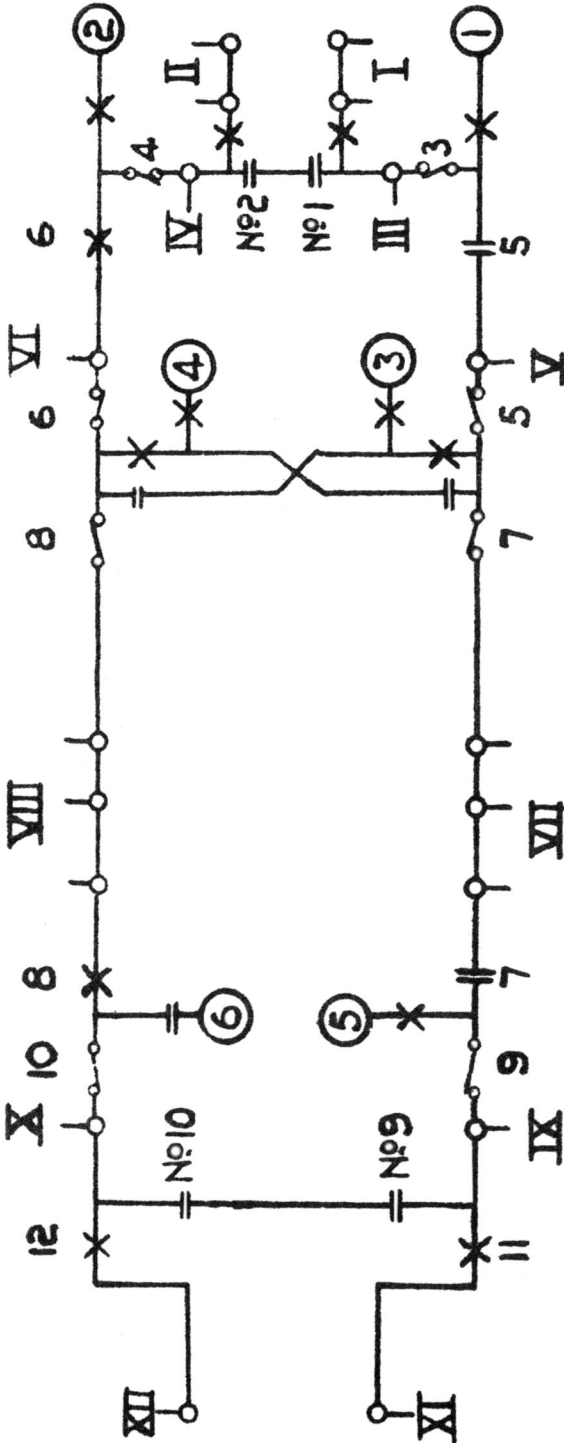

Diagram of ring main

Electrical Report

Electrical organisation No. 1 was in force and all electrical repair parties were closed up. The main supply system was under the control of the Commissioned Electrician at the main switchboard, while the three electrical repair parties received their orders from the Assistant Torpedo Officer at the damage control headquarters. This arrangement was decided on because of the communication system fitted.

Five dynamos were running and on the board. The starboard ring main was split into three parts, viz:–

No. 1 dynamo feeding sections I and III
No. 3 dynamo feeding sections V and VII
No. 5 dynamo feeding sections IX and XI

The port side was not split, Nos. 2 and 4 dynamos feeding this side in parallel.

No. 6 dynamo was out of action due to a burst turbine. This damage was sustained some weeks before the action, due to overspeeding.

The electrical system generally remained unaffected by the bombing. Nothing came off due to shock except some Mark VI telephones which jumped off their hooks. The ring main was undamaged and main dynamos unaffected and all damaged branch circuits were correctly isolated by their respective protective devices.

The cordite fire, caused by the bomb hit to starboard of the forward lift well, bared electric cables in its vicinity. The turret pump machinery of A1 was a total wreck but that of A2 escaped damage. The feeds to A1 and A2 were damaged by fire and splinters, but were correctly isolated by their respective branch breakers.

The bomb hit abaft the after lift well, although causing great structural damage and a fire, did not damage the electrical gear in the well.

The hit on the pom pom director platform caused extensive splinter damage, the most important circuits damaged being those from "B" director, which were cut where they enter the tower. The cables from the port forward pom pom director were also cut, but this director was not in use as remote power control was not fitted. Splinters also passed across the ship and cut the control cables from No. 1 bomb lift motor on the starboard side. The D/G S.W.A. cables were so torn that the cores were exposed, some of these being cut and the broken armouring wires were, in some cases, wrapped round the cores.

The bomb which exploded in the sea abreast 125 station did not cause any electrical damage.

No major electrical action was necessary other than the precautionary isolation of some circuits feeding the damaged parts of the ship to avoid electrical fires.

A small fire in the C.C.O. annexe caused unnecessary alarm and led to all three C.W.S. alternators being stopped by the C.C.O. This caused a power failure to the Warning Telephones as well as to all W/T equipment.

The hangar spraying pumps were started as a precautionary measure as fires were burning forward and aft of the hangars. Less important branch breakers, taken off automatically by the starting of the pumps, were put on again in local control by the electrical repair party, who also stopped the pumps when there was no danger of the hangars being involved in the fire.

A change-over from electric to steam steering was made directly the bomb damage occurred, but was not necessary as all four steering motor breakers remained on and supply was intact.

No. 2 150 ton pump was fed by emergency supply due to a small defect developing in the breaker.

Emergency lighting was rigged at the scenes of the damage.

Pumping and Flooding Table

Compartment	Deck	Stations	Flooding Board Data			
			Tons sea-water	Heel degrees	Draught increase inches Forward	Aft
Rapid flooding due to Damage, Uncontrolled, Port side aft.						
Oxygen Store	Lower	122½–125	10	0.1	−0.1	0.2
No. 2 Naval Store	Lower	121–127	118	0.9	−0.8	2.6
After Armament Store	Lower	127–135	89	0.9	−1.0	2.1
Decontamination Store	Lower	135–139	38	0.3	−0.5	1.0
No. 5 Naval Store	Platform	121–127	20	0.2	−0.1	0.4

No. 6 Naval Store	Platform	127–133	47	0.4	−0.5	1.1
No. 6 Naval Store	Platform	133–139	35	0.3	−0.5	0.9
W.T.C.	Hold	113–121	70	1.0	−0.2	1.3
O.F.T.	Hold	121–127	105	1.2	−0.8	2.2
Plummer Block Compartment	Hold	121–127	59	0.5	−0.4	1.2
Port Gland Space	Hold	127–139 113½– 121	96	0.8	−1.1	2.3
No. 2 Small Arms Magazine	Hold		75	0.5	−0.3	1.4
			762	7.1	−6.3	16.7

Pumping Port Side

Air Space	Hold	61–73	42	0.5	1.0	−0.1
		73–88	58	0.7	1.0	0.2
		88–97	36	0.4	0.3	0.3
		97–113	61	0.8	0.2	0.9
		113–121	29	0.3	−0.1	0.5
			226	2.7	2.4	1.8

Counterflooding Starboard

Torpedo Warhead Magazine	Platform	54–61	51	0.1	1.5	−0.2
No.1 Pom Pom Magazine	Hold	61–65	36	0.2	0.9	−0.1
No. 3 Pom Pom Magazine	Hold	65–70	55	0.4	1.3	−0.1
Air Space	Hold	61–73	60	0.7	1.4	−0.1
Air Space	Hold	73–88	82	1.0	1.4	0.3
Air Space	Hold	88–97	50	0.6	0.5	0.5

Air Space	Hold	97–113	87	1.0	0.3	1.1
Air Space	Hold	113–121	40	0.5	–0.2	8
			461	4.5	7.1	2.2

Counterflooding Middle Line

No. 2 Pom Pom Magazine	Hold	61–65	52	0	1.4	–0.2
No. 1 Fireworks Magazine	Hold	65–70	77	0	1.8	–0.1
			129	0	3.2	–0.3

Counterflooding Port

Small Arms Magazine	Platform Deck	54–61	51	0.1	1.5	–0.2
No. 4 Pom Pom Magazine	Hold	61–65	36	0.2	0.9	–0.1
No. 2 Fireworks Magazine	Hold	65–70	55	0.4	1.3	–0.1
			142	0.7	3.7	–0.4

Total entry of water into ship 1,268 tons
Resultant port heel 0.6°
Increase of draft forward 5.3 inches
Increase of draft aft. 16.3 inches

Damage Control

The damage control officer has reported as follows :–

A. <u>Immediate Action Taken by Damage Control Parties</u>

On 12 August, at approximately 1845 with ship closed up at "Action Stations", three explosions were heard, in damage control headquarters and within a few minutes ship listed 10° approximately to port.

The following is the approximate sequence of orders and reports received and action taken:-

From Captain –

(i) "A" turret on fire, flood "A" magazine.

No. 1 sectional headquarters were ordered to flood for'd group of magazines. Nos. 1, 2, 3 and 4 pom-pom and Nos. 1 & 2 fireworks magazines, torpedo warhead and war small arms were flooded, and pumped out early on the morning of August 13.

(ii) Correct list.

Previous to explosions, ship had been on an even keel, and five port air spaces between protective bulkhead and water jacket contained water to counterbalance natural list to starboard; ten port wing oil fuel tanks contained 75% oil fuel, and starboard tanks 75% B. & C. oil tanks were empty.

Nos. 2, 4 and 6 rapid flood positions were ordered to pump out their respective port air spaces, and Nos. 1, 3 and 5 to flood starboard air spaces, between protective bulkhead and water jacket. This was carried out under the direction of double bottom chief stoker and ship returned to even keel about 30 minutes after listing, when order was given to stop flooding starboard.

Report from No. 3. Sectional Headquarters

(1) Petrol system drained.

(2) Large fire aft, lower hangar decks.

(3) Main naval store 121 to 127 stations, main deck, flooded 3 to 4 ft.

Aircraft on fire in upper hangar put out by hose and armoured doors closed.

Fire in torpedo body room and cabins extinguished by hose.

Fire in fabric store in hand.

Manhole of hatch to naval store was found open and 4 ft. water in store; manhole in hatch under, to No. 2 naval store was also wide open. (F.A.A. had been down to oxygen store 10–15 minutes previously). Manhole No. 2 naval store was eventually shut and shored.

All adjacent compartments had been examined and found watertight; no doors or hatches were opened to check this.

Portable pump was rigged and main naval store pumped out.

Later it was found by test plugs that decontamination store and gunners arm store were flooded, and decks were shored.

One fresh water pipe was fractured, and fresh water pump was stopped temporarily to prevent loss of water.

More firemain pressure was asked for; at least 17 hoses were in use on the after fire excluding those run along flight deck. Firemain at 121 and 139 was therefore de-isolated and starboard engine room ordered via the machinery control room to boost pressure as much as possible; this gave four in number 75 ton pumps supplying water, and this was ample.

H.P. Air leaking aft.

Line isolated in wing workshops.

Report from No. 1 Sectional Headquarters

(1) Dense smoke in central communications office and switchboard flat. This was drawp in through ventilation supply from fire in boys' mess-deck; ventilation valve shut.

(2) "A" pump out of action; firemain de-isolated; more pressure required; fire in chief petty officers mess.

Firemain was further de-isolated at 61 starboard and second pump in centre engine room started, and running pumps in engine room and starboard boiler room boosted; this gave 100 lbs./in. pressure at pump. After 30 minutes fire reported under control.

(3) Small fire in boys' mess and fire in torpedo body room. Fire in boys' mess soon under control, but torpedo body room caused trouble due to calcium store adjacent catching fire; after much water had been poured on, fire was eventually taken under control by using chemical fire extinguishers and sand.

Additional fire fighters and equipment were sent for'd to torpedo body room, petty officers' mess and "A" turret by damage control headquarters, this depleted No. 2 damage control party, until some Fleet Air Arm ratings arrived.

(4) Kit locker flat flooding through ventilation trunk. Found that hangar spray flushing pipe had burst and water entering trunk. Flooding ceased when spray shut off.

(5) For'd fresh water pumps out of use, and fresh water line damaged in petty officers' mess. Fresh water line isolated.

(6) C.0.2 machine stopped; one condenser leaking and isolated; slight leak of gas; all valves shut; compartment evacuated.

(7) Small fire in wardroom caused by bombs soon extinguished.

(8) H.P. air line cut in torpedo body room – shut off in seamen's washplace.

Report of Action Taken in Hangars

(1) Lower hangar reported no damage.

(2) Fire occurred in upper hangar, for'd, due to large lubricating oil drip tray full up catching alight, and also a petrol hose aft. Both fires extinguished with foam generators.

Spray pumps were started as soon as fires were seen, and attempts made to drop curtains; No.1 fire curtain came down electrically; after fire curtain was jammed by blast.

A large fire was raging starboard, for'd of upper hangar, rendering access impossible; hangar became full of smoke and lit by red glare from end to end; it could not be ascertained whether hangar was on fire or not, so it was sprayed from port for'd starboard aft and starboard midships positions, maximum was 6 inches (depth) at 8° List to port; water cleared quickly.

A fire was seen to be raging in film store and hoses were sent to assist.

Assistance and 4 hoses were sent to fight fire in forward torpedo body room.

Hangar spray pumps were shut off.

B. Action Taken by Damage Control Parties

(1) Auxiliary hydraulic line tested and found fractured abreast "A" turret; water had been lost from hydraulic tanks and fresh water was not available. Adaptor was therefore fitted to "shore reserve feed tank filling connection" on lower gallery deck and hose run aft to tank filling funnel. Evaporator then discharged distillate to hydraulic tank and system was in working order except for

isolated damaged portion. It was considered urgently necessary to raise starboard wireless masts to enable destroyer to assist in fire fighting.

(2) Salt water was being continuously discharged through deckhead of Captain's quarters and flooding keyboard flat. Leak amongst the debris could not be found, so 158 firemain bulkhead valve was shut.

(3) Firemain pressure was lost for'd through cooling water to "A" turret pump fracturing, so lead from main deck shut off.

(4) All (4) portable pumps were rigged and used to pump out messdecks, kit locker space and flats.

(5) Compartments adjacent to those flooded were tested, plugged and shored as necessary. Certain compartments which appeared to be flooded owing to indicator test plug showing an air pressure were found later to contain only a few inches of water (e.g. flour store).

(6) It was considered possible that a lead of firemain was fractured in a flooded compartment (No. 2 naval store). Pressure to this lead was therefore shut off.

(7) 'Z' Petrol tanks were tested to check for leaks.

C. Ship's Conclusions and Recommendations Concerning Damage Control

(1) All damage control organisation worked calmly and efficiently; telephones remained in use and information was received and passed and orders carried out with very little delay.

(2) Firemain pressure, numbers of hoses and branch pipes were ample to cope with fires, but more spray nozzles are required to cope with smoke.

(3) Indicator test plugs were used successfully. The leather joints of these fittings did not stand up to salt water and it is submitted that in future washers be made of red fibre, and the securing nut of plug be made tight with a set screw.

(4) The portable "Snorer" pumps were a great asset and gave no trouble whatsoever. Discharge hoses had to be led up to weather decks as drains of bathrooms could not cope with discharge; this entailed a number of watertight doors and hatches remaining open; it is submitted, therefore, that discharge hose connections and watertight sluice valves be fitted in ship's side just above main deck level.

(5) Manhole doors of hatches are difficult to make watertight properly unless closed by an experienced officer or rating. Some simpler means of clipping is considered necessary, or double wedges, as it is not obvious which way the clip should be moved, when door is being shut from above.

(6) Magazine door keyhole fittings had been left in "open" position; it is submitted that these fittings be made larger and more definite in action and that they be made more accessible by fitting them further away from door frame.

(7) A number of magazine doors were found to be non-watertight under pressure – pressure tending to keep door shut. In one case compartment was pumped out, and all clips hammered up evenly, but as soon as compartment flooded up again clips became slack and water leaked through. It is considered that there is insufficient "bite" between clip and wedge, and it is submitted that clips be made an inclined plane to contact surface of wedge.

(8) Watertight hatch to Nos. 1 and 2 small arms magazines had been secured with one clip only; this together with items 6 and 7 is considered the cause of the lower magazines of the after group becoming partially flooded.

Comment by D.N.C. Department

(1) The firefighting organisation worked well.

(2) C.2. The allowance of spray nozzles has been increased to 30% of the total number of branch pipes. A.F.O. 3023/42.

(3) C.3. A better joint is being arranged. A.F.O.2425/42.

(4) A.F.O. 167/42 ordered the provision of side scuttle blanks fitted with hose connections for overboard discharge from portable pumps.

(5) C.5. This matter is frequently raised by ships' officers. Where single wedges are fitted, the positions and directions of movement of the clips should be painted on the manhole covers, and stops fitted in order to prevent the openings being closed with the clips on the wrong sides of the wedges.

(6) C.6. This will be borne in mind in future designs.

(7) C.7. A comprehensive series of experiments has been in hand for some months with the object of strengthening designs of watertight doors and hatches. A number of conclusions from these experiments has

already been put into practice, as described in A.F.O.3905/42, and A.F.O.5051/42.

Ship's General Recommendations

(i) Hangar spray pumps take their sea suction from salvage pump discharges. Small quantities of oil have been seen to come through the spray nozzles. Hangar spray pumps should have separate sea suctions.

(ii) Foam generators are fixed. They should be movable within limits, a short length of canvas hose being used between the generator and the salt water supply, in order to allow changes of position as required by variations in aircraft parking arrangements, bearing in mind occasional changes in types of aircraft embarked.

(iii) 75-ton pump starters should be above the datum deck.

(iv) Ventilation exhaust trunks from pump rooms should carry up to above the datum deck, with W.T.S.Vs. at that level.

(v) Portable diesel driven pumps are necessary.

(vi) More portable electric pumps are necessary. Only four are at present in the ship, two having been lent to another ship.

(vii) About a dozen portable Wilcox semi-rotary pumps are necessary. Only two are at present in the ship, and they are invaluable for rapid action when it is difficult to get the portable electric pump working.

(viii) Ventilation trunks require stiffening to withstand blast pressure.

(ix) Experience in this action emphasized the need for improvements in size of sick bay, facilities for transport of stretcher cases from flight deck to sick bay, and access to cots in the sick bay for nursing.

Comment by D.N.C. Department

(i) Separate sea suctions for hangar spray pumps are arranged for in later ships.

(ii) The disadvantages of having foam generators portable would outweigh any advantages. The proposal is not concurred in.

(iii) If the pump starters are arranged to operate from above the datum deck, there will also be a demand for the valves in connection with the pumps to be remote controlled. In action all the 75 ton pumps should be working and they can work quite well with the pump compartments closed down.

(iv) This is arranged in new construction.

(v) Concur. These are being provided.

(vi) C.A.F.O. 336/42 allows the ship 12 portable electric pumps.

(vii) Present supplies will not permit the adoption of this proposal.

(viii) Concur. This is being done in new construction.

(ix) Sick bay arrangements in new construction are on a more generous scale.

Effect on Fighting Efficiency

Armament

A1 and A2 4.5" BD mountings out of action; "A" T.S. slightly flooded, but never out of action. "B" director out of action.

Aircraft

Forward lift completely wrecked.

After lift temporarily out of action until faired up by ship's staff. Aircraft accelerator track warped.

Casualties

Casualties consisted of 6 officers and 40 ratings killed, and 70 ratings wounded.

Two very serious fires occurred in *Indomitable* involving aircraft in the upper hangar, torpedo body room, cabins, fabric store, boys' mess deck, "A" turret, wardroom, film store and parts of the upper hangar where a tray of lubricating oil and a petrol hose were ignited.

These fires in *Indomitable* were dealt with satisfactorily. Flag Officer Force F. in his remarks on this Fire Fighting Organisation stated: –

"The rapidity with which two large fires were extinguished in *Indomitable* had a stimulating effect on all who were in a position to observe. The success was largely due to the excellent equipment provided and also to the availability of large numbers of hands to back up the fire parties."

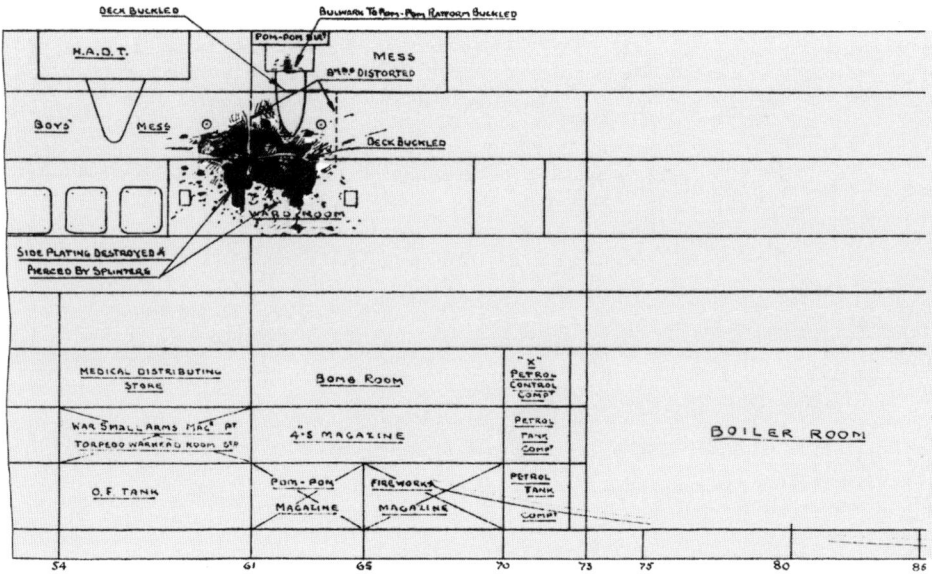

NEAR-MISS N°1

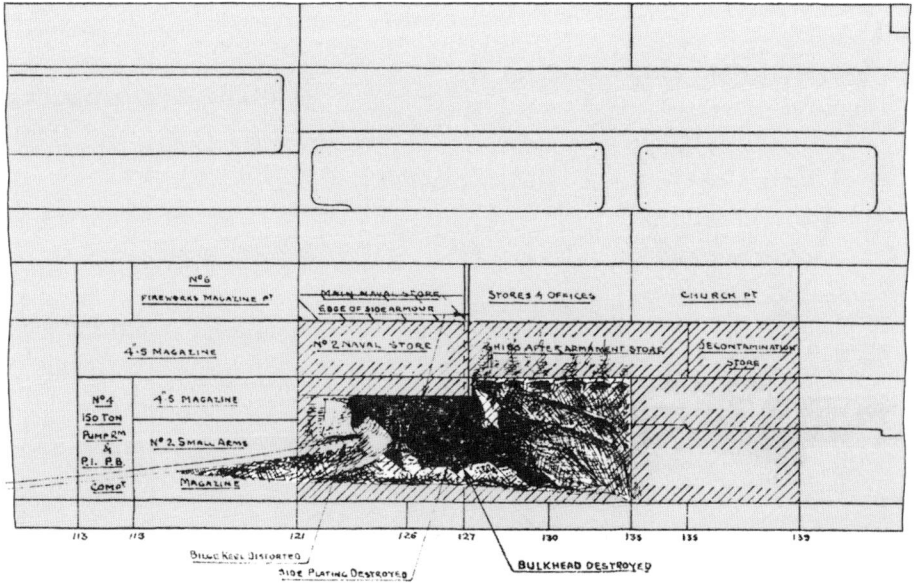

NEAR-MISS N°2

H.M.S. INDOMITABLE.

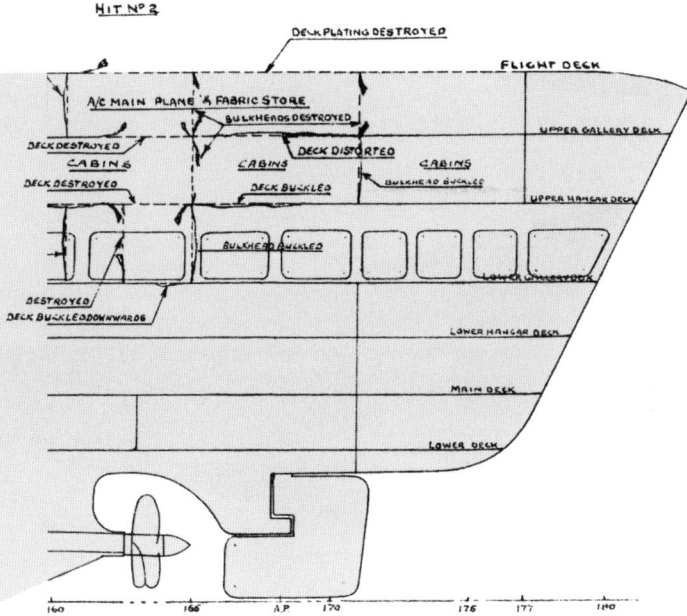

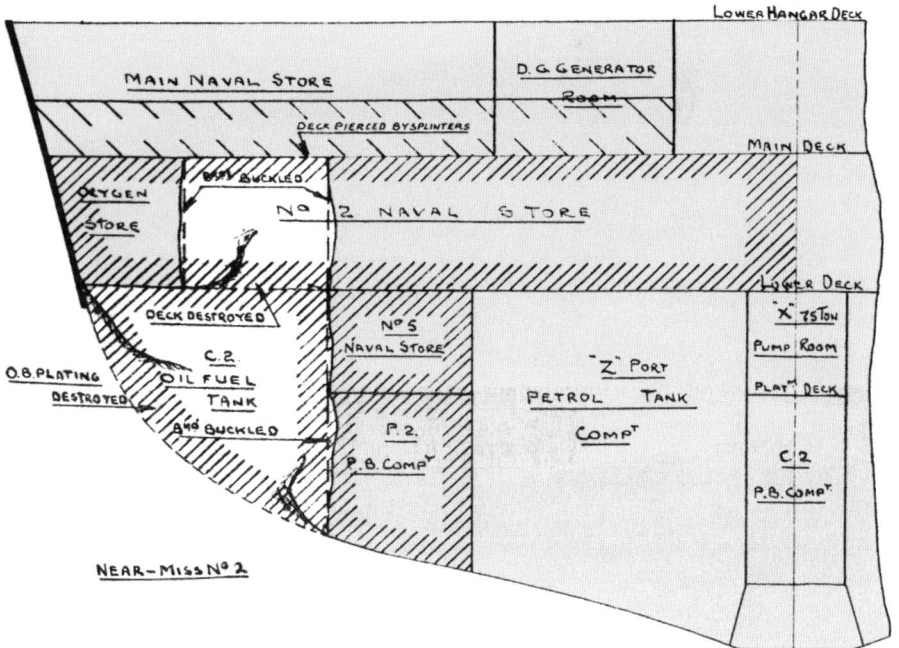

HIT Nº 2

DECK PLATING DESTROYED

FLIGHT DECK

A/C MAIN PLANE & FABRIC STORE

BULKHEADS DESTROYED

UPPER GALLERY DECK

DECK DESTROYED

CABINS

DECK DISTORTED

CABINS

CABINS

DECK DESTROYED

DECK BUCKLED

BULKHEAD BUCKLED

UPPER HANGAR DECK

BULKHEAD BUCKLED

LOWER GALLERY DECK

DESTROYED

DECK BUCKLED DOWNWARDS

LOWER HANGAR DECK

MAIN DECK

LOWER DECK

160   165   A.P.   170   175   177   180

LOWER HANGAR DECK

MAIN NAVAL STORE

D. G. GENERATOR Room

MAIN DECK

DECK PIERCED BY SPLINTERS

OXYGEN STORE

DECK BUCKLED

Nº 2 NAVAL STORE

LOWER DECK

DECK DESTROYED

Nº 5 NAVAL STORE

"X" 75 TON PUMP ROOM

O.B. PLATING DESTROYED

C.2. OIL FUEL TANK

"Z" PORT PETROL TANK COMPᵗ

PLATᵐ DECK

8ᴴᴰ BUCKLED

P.2. P.B. COMPᵗ

C.2 P.B. COMPᵗ

NEAR-MISS Nº 2

323

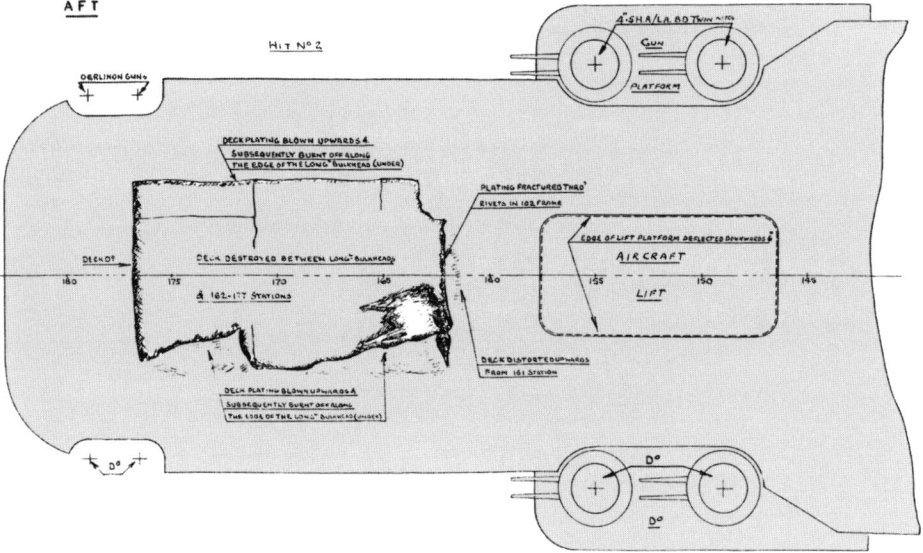

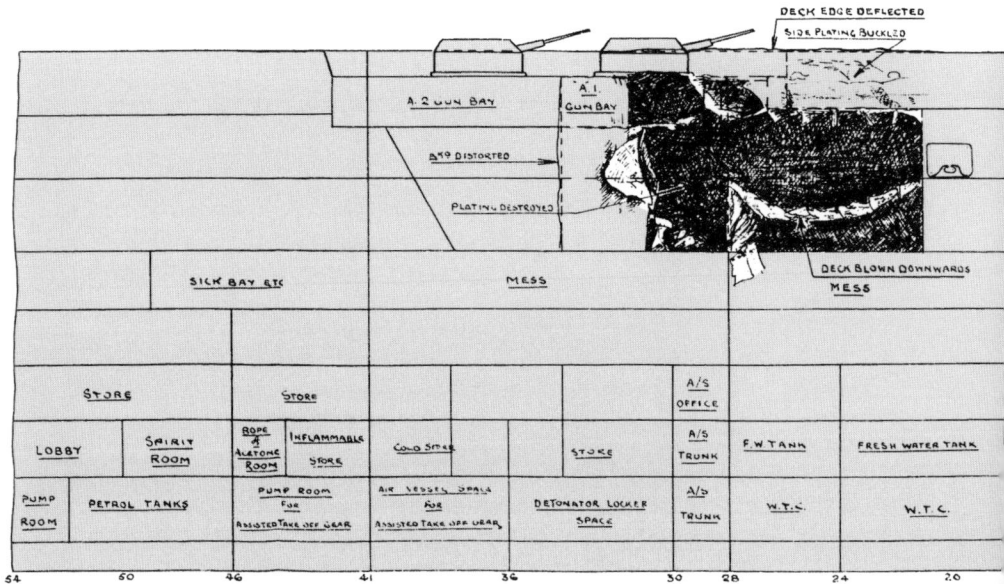

H.M.S.INDOMITABLE.

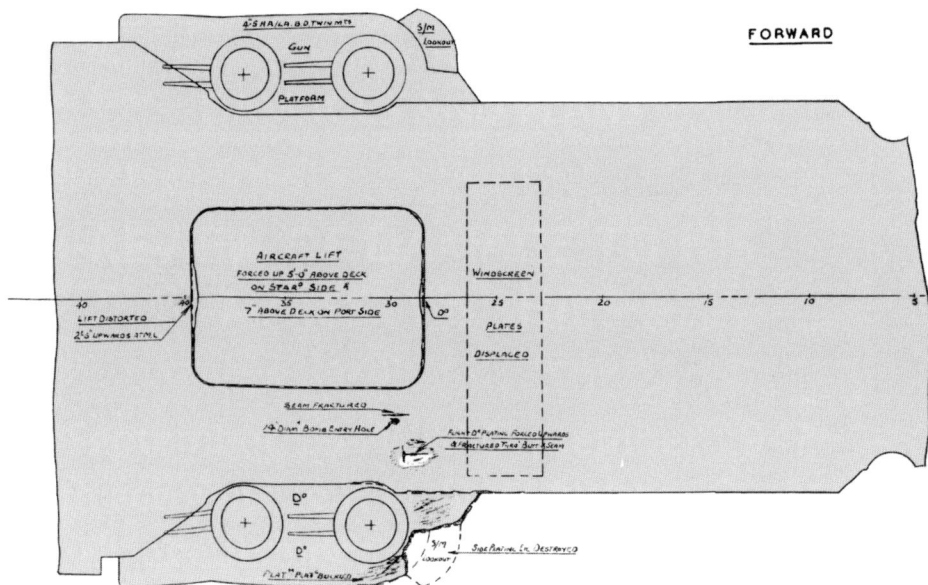

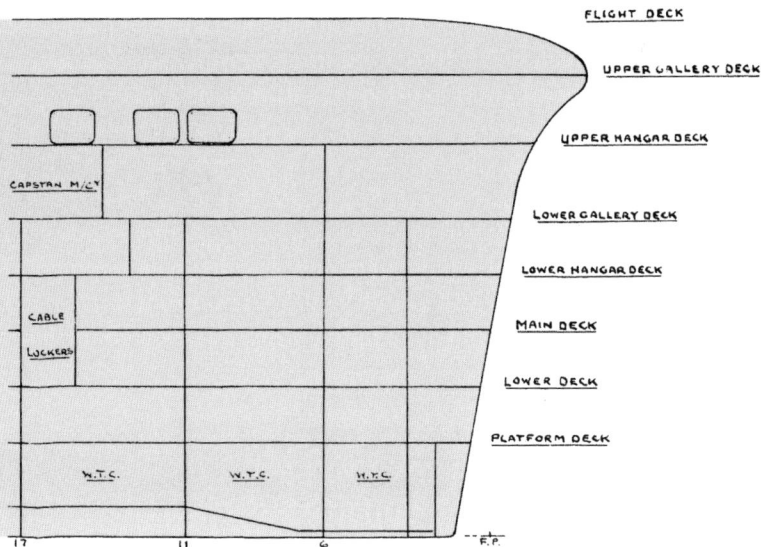

FORWARD

FLIGHT DECK

UPPER GALLERY DECK

UPPER HANGAR DECK

LOWER GALLERY DECK

LOWER HANGAR DECK

MAIN DECK

LOWER DECK

PLATFORM DECK

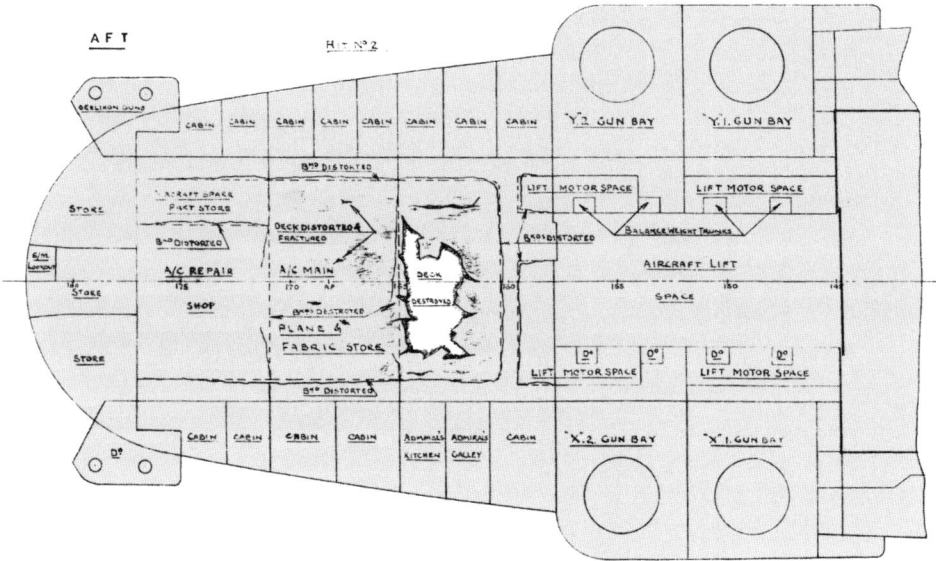

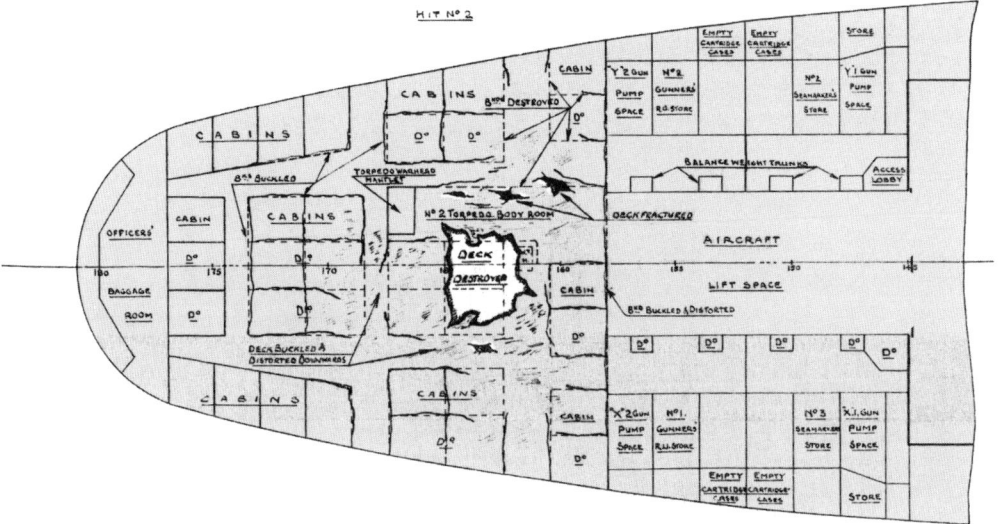

H.M.S. INDOMITABLE.

FORWARD

S/M LOOK OUT POSITION

EMERGENCY CONNING POSITION

B.2 GUN BAY

B.1 GUN BAY

B.M STORE

AERO ENGINE
STRIPPING SHOP & STORE

LIFT MOTOR SPACE

LIFT MOTOR SPACE

MESS

MESS

MESS

BALANCE WEIGHT TRUNKS

DECK BUCKLED & PIERCED BY SPLINTERS

SUMP DISTORTED

AIRCRAFT LIFT

SPACE

PANTRY

AIR ARTIFICERS'
MESS

BULK DISTORTED

DECK BUCKLED
FRACTURED

MESS

MESS

Dº

Dº

Dº

Dº

Dº

TRUNKS BUCKLED

DECK
DISTORTED

TORPEDO
B/W STORE

A.2 GUN BAY

A.1 GUN
BAY

MESS

PLATING BUCKLED

SIDE PLATING & S/M LOOKOUT DESTROYED

BULK BUCKLED &
PIERCED BY SPLINTERS

BOMB PERFORATION OF DECK
BEFORE DETONATION

HIT Nº1

WASHPLACE

EMPTY
CARTº
CASES

EMPTY
CARTº
CASES

B.2 GUN
PUMP
SPACE

TORPEDO
BLOWING
Hº COMP

DUPLEX
PISTOL
WORKSHOP

B.1 GUN
PUMP
SPACE

ACCESS
LOBBY

DECK
BUCKLED
Nº 1. TORPEDO

CABLEHOLDER

CHAIN PIPE

BALANCE WEIGHT TRUNKS

CAPSTAN

AIRCRAFT

LIFT SPACE

SORT ROOM

3º

2º

Dº

Dº

Dº

BULK BUCKLED & PIERCED BY SPLINTERS

TRUNKS DISTORTED

Bº FRACTURED

A.2 GUN
PUMP
SPACE

MESS

Bº BUCKLED &
PIERCED BY SPLINTERS

DECK BLOWN DOWNWARDS

SIDE PLATING DESTROYED

DECK & BULKHEADS DESTROYED

HIT Nº1

NEAR-MISS Nº 2

PLATFORM DECK (AFT)

O.B. PLATING DESTROYED

W.T. COMP.ᵗ

W.T. COMP.ᵗ

O.F. TANK

O.F. TANK

O.F. TANK

AIR SPACE (50% FULL) (60% FULL) AIR SPACE

Nº 6 NAVAL STORE

2ᴺᴰ DESTROYED

Nº 5 NAVAL STORE

Nº 8

4·5 MAGAZINE

Nº 4. 150 TON PUMP ROOM & P.B. COMP.ᵗ

ENGINE ROOM

O.F. TANK

O.F. TANK

PETROL TANK COMP.ᵗ "Z" PORT

Nº 9 4·5

C.I.P.S. COMP.ᵗ

ENGINE

WARD ROOM

WARD ROOM STORE

"Y" 75 TON PUMP ROOM

ENGINEER'S SPARE GEAR STORE

"X" 75 TON PUMP ROOM

MAGAZINE

ROOM

STORE

PROVISION ROOM

O.F. TANK

O.F. TANK

PETROL TANK COMP.ᵗ "Z" STᴰ

Nº 7

ENGINE

AFTER SPARE ARMATURE STORE

AFTER SPARE ARMATURE STORE

ENGINEERS SPARE GEAR STORE

4·5 MAGAZINE

Nº 5. 150 TON PUMP ROOM & P.B. COMP.ᵗ

ROOM

O.F. TANK

AIR SPACE

AIR SPACE

O.F. TANK

O.F. TANK

W.T. COMP.ᵗ

W.T. COMP.ᵗ

NEAR - MISS Nº 2

LOWER DECK (AFT)

O.S. PLATING DISTORTED

W.T. COMP.ᵗ

W.T. COMP.ᵗ

OXYGEN STORE

O.F. TANK

O.F. TANK

8ᴺᴰ DISTORTED

AIR SPACE (60% FULL) (50% FULL) AIR SPACE

SHIPS AFTER ARMAMENT STORE

8ᴺᴰ DISTORTED

Nº 4

4·5 MAGAZINE

AIR SPACE

ENGINE ROOM

DECONTAMINATION STORE

Nº 3

FLOUR STORE

Nº 4 BREAKER ROOM

DECK BLOWN UPWARDS & HOLED

Nº 3 NAVAL

MARINES' STORE

NAVAL

"Z" PETROL

Nº 6

4·5 MAGAZINE

ENGINE

FRESH WATER

STORE

CONTROL

ROOM

TANK

W.Os STORE

COMP.ᵗ

AIR SPACE

Nº 3 BREAKER ROOM

Nº 1

PROVISION ROOM

CHART & CHRONOMETER ROOM

IMPLEMENT STORE

Nº 5

4·5 MAGAZINE

ENGINE ROOM

STORE

AIR SPACE

AIR SPACE

O.F. TANK

O.F. TANK

W.T. COMP.ᵗ

W.T. COMP.ᵗ

H.M.S. INDOMITABLE.

MAIN DECK (AFT)

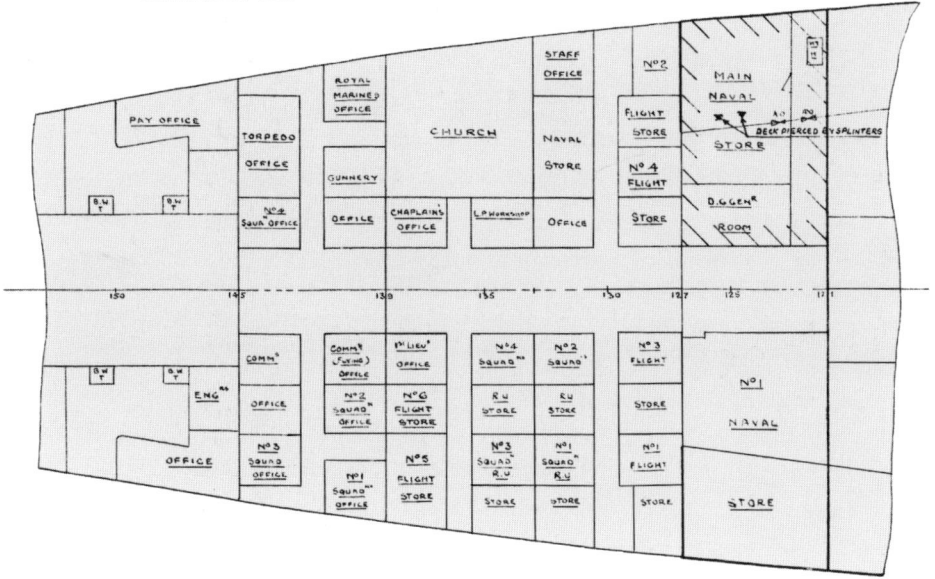

HOLD (AFT)

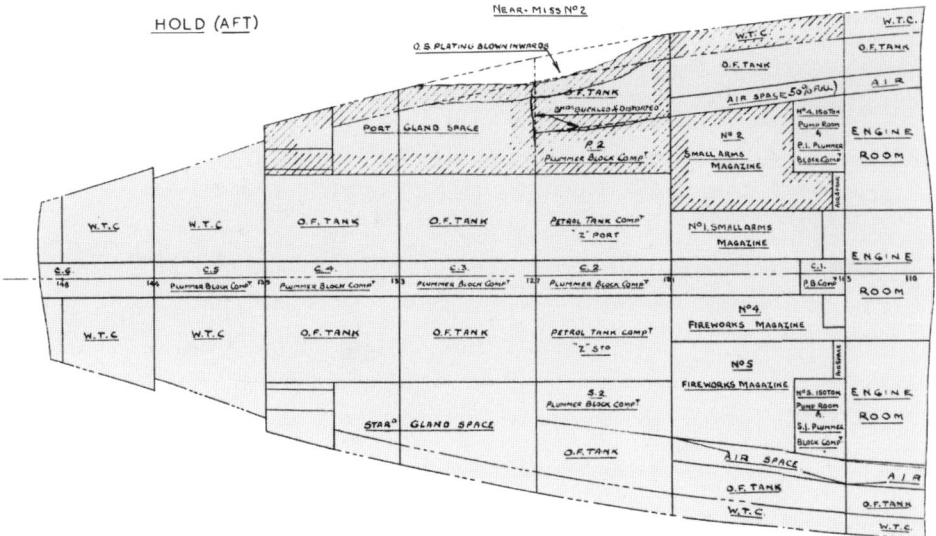

Damage Reports
H.M.S. *Liverpool*

Torpedo Damage

Type of Ship	Cruiser, completed 1938	
Principal Dimensions	Length overall	558 ft. 0 ins.
	Breadth on waterline	64 ft. 2 ins.
	Displacement	11, 930 tons. – deep condition
	Draught (mean)	20 ft. 11 ins. – deep condition
	Draught before damage (forward)	20 ft. 10 ins.
	Draught before damage (aft)	19 ft. 11 ins.

Circumstances

On 14 June, 1942 at 1125C hours H.M.S. *Liverpool* was leading the starboard column of a Malta convoy, then in position 037° 55' N, 007° 38' E.

Weather was fine and sunny, wind N.W. force 1, cloud nil, sea calm, visibility 30 miles. Depth of water was 1500 fathoms. These conditions changed little during the following day.

The Attack

Air attacks had been in progress for half an hour when 26 Italian S.79K torpedo bombers were sighted flying low on the port bow. These divided into two formations which Carried out synchronised attacks on the port side and starboard quarter. *Liverpool* turned to starboard and increased to 21 knots to counter the first attack. As the ship started to swing the second group dropped their torpedoes two of which passed ahead, one astern, and one running well at shallow depth hit at an angle of 40 to 50° to the starboard side at 165 station abreast the after engine room. The immediate effect was to put the ship practically out of control. The starboard telegraphs could not be moved but the port telegraphs were free and were put to STOP. The explosion made a hole 24' x 19' in the bottom and immediately put out of action the starboard outer and both inner shafts. The speed fell to 3 knots in 3 minutes. The ship heeled 7°.

The rudder which was 35° starboard could not be put amidships and the ship continued to swing to starboard until the port outer engine was put astern. After a short interval emergency leads were run to the steering motors, the helm put amidships and the ship was able to proceed at 3 knots on the remaining shaft.

Liverpool was taken in tow at 1300C by H.M.S. *Antelope* at 9 knots. At 1630 the tow parted and shortly afterwards a dive-bombing attack developed. Two bombs, probably 100 kgm., fell within 15 feet of the starboard side throwing up a column of water which fell on the air defence position and Type 273 office. The list increased to 9½° and the ship settled by the stern. The tow was restored and the ship arrived at Gibraltar at 1700B on 17 June.

The torpedo is thought to have been Italian, 17.7 inches diameter, speed 35 knots, range 3200 yards with a charge weight of 440 lbs. T.N.T. and fitted with an inertia pistol. After each attack a series of under water explosions was heard which was thought to have been the warheads exploding very deep at the end of the run. No surface disturbance was seen.

Damage Control

After the torpedo hit, the ship immediately heeled 7° to starboard. Preparations were made to counterflood but nothing further was done until it was found that the list was slowly increasing and had reached 7½°. The wing compartments abreast the forward engine and boiler rooms were then flooded by hose from the fire main, the contents of Y3 oil fuel tank were jettisoned, and feed water was transferred from 'A' starboard to 'A' port reserve feed tank. The boilers were set to steam from A3 oil fuel tank. The oil fuel was jettisoned by means of a 'Snorer' portable pump taking its suction from the residue suction pipe and discharging overboard via a deadlight fitted with hose connections.

A rough calculation made from the flooding board indicated that a list of 1° to starboard would probably remain after these counter-measures were complete but in fact a list of 6° remained. This discrepancy was attributed to water remaining in the compartments which were being pumped out and to the large free surface. It was later found that 80 tons of fuel which D.C.H.Q.

thought was transferred from A3 to A2 tank had not in fact been moved and that the cable passage abreast A engine room had flooded.

A rough estimate of the new GM was made and, although not considered an immediate necessity, all unnecessary top weight was jettisoned. This included:–

Walrus aircraft	stowed on Catapult
Loading bogies	stowed on Forecastle deck
Aircraft spare gear	stowed in Hangars
2 in No. paravanes	stowed on 'B' gun deck
25' fast motor boat	stowed on Forecastle deck
16' motor dinghy	stowed on Forecastle deck
Starboard torpedoes (3 in No.)	stowed on Upper deck
Ammunitioning, derricks	stowed on 'X' gun deck
Depth charges (9 in No.)	stowed on Quarter deck
Spare wire rope	stowed on Upper deck
Misc. derricks and davits	stowed on Starboard side

After the aircraft had been jettisoned, it was considered that the petrol carried on board represented an unnecessary risk and as the L.P. air compressor fitted in the after engine room was out of action a spare reducing valve which had previously been fitted to cross-connect the H.P. and L.P. air systems was used to provide L.P. air for jettisoning the petrol.

These countermeasures and the pumping of partially flooded compartments were nearly complete when at 1637 two bombs exploded to starboard abreast 105 and 150 stations. The list rapidly increased to 9½° but as no further flooding could be found apart from an increase in the depth of water on the lower deck, it was concluded that the increased list was due to a further loss of GM caused by the water in the washplaces (127–155 stations lower deck) becoming freely connected with that in the after boiler room so increasing the inertia of the free surfaces. In order to increase the metacentric height and at the same time to increase the freeboard aft, 'A' and 'B' magazines and shell rooms, the inflammable store and the bomb room were cleared and flooded. The following compartments were also partially flooded due principally to the failure of the flooding E.R.A.'s to close the seacocks when the flooding of magazines etc. was completed:–

No. 1 store, compressor room, cooling machinery compartment, paint store, canteen store. These measures together with the pumping of partially flooded compartments on the lower deck decreased the list to 6½° and increased the freeboard aft by 3 feet.

It was uncertain whether the remaining list was due to unsymmetrical loading or instability and it was therefore decided to work the oil fuel so as to maintain this list as it was feared that attempts to get the ship upright might result in a heavy list to port.

Shoring and Pumping

"B" Boiler Room

This compartment flooded rapidly immediately after the explosion, and it is estimated that the rate of entry must have been in the neighbourhood of 2,000 tons per hour. The water was seen to be entering through a large hole in the starboard after corner of the compartment, and an attempt was made by Shipwrights to place a patch over the hole. This attempt failed due to inaccessibility of the hole coupled with the fact that there was nothing suitable to take the heels of the shores. Subsequently it was found that nearly all the rivets in the lower boundary angle of the bulkhead (155) had fractured, leaving a large number of holes connecting directly to the flooded engine room.

The bilge ejectors were started; but before they had time to take charge of the water, the flooding reached the furnaces and steam supply failed.

Clothing Issue Room (179–198 stbd. Platform Deck)

This compartment was reported flooded at a very early stage in the proceedings, and it is estimated that about 50 tons of water entered the compartment during the first ten minutes after the explosion. It is not clear how the water entered the compartment, but it is thought that it must have come up through the starboard outer gland space, though there is no concrete evidence to support this theory. It was not possible to examine this compartment at any later stage since the lower deck was below sea level.

Starboard Lubricating Oil Store (143–155 stbd. Platform Deck)

This compartment flooded up rapidly through holes in the after bulkhead. Attempts to control the flooding and to repair the bulkhead met with no success since the rate of flooding was increased to surpass the pumping capacity of two portable pumps as soon as the lagging was removed from the bulkhead for access to the damage.

<u>Port Shaft Passage</u> (127–155) <u>and Port Outer Gland Space</u> (186–190)
The former flooded up between two consecutive examinations in the evening of 14 June, the water entering through damaged shaft gland at 155 bulkhead. The latter was found to be flooded when first examined. Neither compartment was pumped out because it was considered undesirable to change the status quo of the plummer blocks which were running very nicely in the flooded compartments.

<u>Cable Passage</u> (143–155 stbd. Platform Deck)
Electrical gear in this compartment functioned well until about 0300 on 16 June. It was therefore assumed that the compartment had been flooding slowly through its access door.

<u>Bathrooms</u> (127–155 stbd. Lower Deck)
These flooded through a split in the deck about three feet forward of 155 bulkhead. The rate of entry of water before the damage was increased by near misses was very small. Later, after the near misses, the water level rose rapidly up to sea level, and it was necessary to cover the split in the deck with planks and shores before the water could be pumped out. After repairs had been effected, the water was pumped out by means of two portable pumps. Once the water was removed the leakage was such that one pump could be removed and the other, working intermittently, was able to keep the spaces dry.

<u>Main W/T Office</u> (179–198 M.L. Platform Deck)
This compartment became flooded to a maximum depth of 2 ft. by water entering from the after engine room through a split in 179 bulkhead. A pad was shored over the split and the seepage was dealt with by a portable pump working intermittently.

<u>Lower Deck</u> (155–179 Starboard)
This deck was shored down. Considerable difficulty was experienced owing to the fact that hammock bars were attached to all the transverse beams while the firemain was slung beneath the only longitudinal girder. It was therefore necessary to place the upper ends of shores against upper deck plating.

<u>Engineers' Electrical Spare Gear Store</u> (179–183 port Platform Deck)
It was thought that the section of 179 bulkhead in this compartment was showing signs of strains. The bulkhead was accordingly shored.

<u>Provision Room</u> (198–209 stbd. Platform Deck)
When first tested it was thought that this compartment was flooding rapidly since the test cock showed that there was pressure in it. The hatch was therefore shored down. Shortly afterwards it was found that the clothing issue room was not yet completely flooded and the provision room was re-examined. Water was found to be entering through faulty electric lead glands. Attempts to deal with leaks met with no success and the compartment was cleared by portable pump working intermittently until the ship finally docked at Gibraltar.

<u>Port Inner Plummer Block Compartments</u> (186–190 stbd. Hold)
Water entered these compartments from the after engine room through leaky main shaft glands. They were pumped out from time to time by means of a portable pump connected to the main suction line.

<u>Forward Engine Room</u> (105–127 M.L. Hold)
Water entered rapidly through the damaged gland of the starboard outer shaft. The water was pumped out by means of the starboard main circulator which was run on bilge suction until the ship reached Gibraltar. The rate of flooding was too great for a 75 ton fire and bilge pump to deal with. The after bulkhead of the forward engine room was shored as a precautionary measure in view of the possibility of further damage.

Liquid Conditions

Compartment	Position	Capacity Tons	Condition before damage Tons	Condition after damage Tons	Entry of water Tons
Immediate Flooding					
O.F.T. B5	D.B. 127–155 S.	60	50	Full	10
W.T.C.	D.B. 147–155 S.	30	Empty	Full	30
W.T.C.	D.B. 155–179 S.	21	Empty	Full	21
W.T.C.	D.B. 147–155 S.	7	Empty	Full	7

O.F.T. X5	D.B. 155–179 S.	69	29	Full	40
O.F.T. X6	D.B. 155–179 P.	69	32	Full	37
O.F.T. X7	D.B. 155–179 S.	34	11	Full	23
W.T.C.	D.B. 155–157 S.	9	Empty	Full	9
W.T.C.	D.B. 155–157 P.	9	Empty	Full	9
O.F.T. Y1	Hold 179–198 S.	204	150	Full	54
'B' Boiler Room	Hold 127–155 M.L.	600	Empty	Full	600
R.F.T.	Hold 148–155 S.	34	31	Full	3
'B' Engine Room	Hold 155–179 M.L.	875	Empty	Full	875
Main Feed Tank	Hold 155–157 M.L.	20	16	Full	4
Plummer Block Compt.	Hold 186–190 S.	17	Empty	Full	17
Gland Compt.	Hold 186–190 S.	17	Empty	Full	17
Gland Compt.	Hold 186–190 P.	17	Empty	Full	17
Shaft Passage	127–155 P.	41	Empty	Full	41
Shaft Passage	127–155 S.	41	Empty	Full	41
Lubricating Oil Store	Plat D^k 143–155 S.	47	Empty	Full	47
Cable Passage	Plat D^k 143–155 S.	27	Empty	Full	27
Cable Passage	Plat D^k 155–179 S.	40	Empty	Full	40
Clothing Store etc.	Plat D^k 179–198	108	Empty	Full	108
Cabins, Offices, Lobby	Lower D^k- 155–179 S.		Empty	80	80

Controlled Flooding

"A" Engine Room	Hold 105–127 M.L.	900	Empty	about 100	100
Plummer Block Compt.	Hold 186–190 P.	17	Empty	about 8	8
Main W/T Office	Plat D^k 179–198 M.L.	160	Empty	35	35
Provision Room	Plat D^k 198–209 S.	70	Empty	20	20
Washplaces	Lower D^k 127–155 S.		Empty	50	50

Counterflooding (a) After Torpedo Hit

W.T.C.	D.B. 87–105 P.	31	Empty	Full	31
W.T.C.	D.B. 105–127 P.	20	Empty	Full	20

C.F.T. Y3	D.B. 198–213	130	128	Empty, oil jettisoned	-128
	(b) After near miss Bombs				
Inflammable Store	Hold 6–11 M.L.	16	Empty	Full	16
'A' Shell Room	Hold 25–30 M.L.	45	Empty	Full	45
'A' Handing Room	Hold 33–39 M.L.	21	Empty	Full	21
'A' Magazine	Hold 30–41 M.L.	43	Empty	Full	43
'B' Shell Room	Hold 41–47 M.L.	44	Empty	Full	44
'B' Handing Room	Hold 51–57 M.L.	22	Empty	Full	22
'B' Magazine	Hold 47–59	44	Empty	Full	44
Bomb Room	Hold 59–65 M.L.	35	Empty	Full	35
	(c) Accidental Flooding				
Paint Store	Plat D^k 6–11 M.L.	26	Empty	15	15
No. 1 Store	Plat D^k 25–30 M.L.	58	Empty	45	45
Compressor Room	Plat D^k 30–41 M.L.	64	Empty	6	6
Canteen Store	Plat D^k 30–41 M.L.	45	Empty	11	11
CO$_2$ Room	Plat D^k 41–53 M.L.	65	Empty	3	3

Net increase of liquid in ship <u>2,643</u> Tons

Water admitted for counterflooding = 321 Tons

Oil fuel jettisoned = 128 Tons

Structural Damage

Outer bottom (40, 30 and 25 lbs.) was holed over an area extending 19' from 3rd to above the 6th longitudinal starboard and 157 to 169 stations i.e. 24'. Distortion of outer bottom extended from 1st longitudinal to 4 feet above platform deck and 149 to 180 stations.

Inner bottom (15 lbs.) was holed from 3rd to just above the 7th longitudinal and 157 to 167 stations. Buckling of inner bottom extended from 151 to 181 stations.

The 4th, 5th and 6th longitudinals starboard were missing in way of the hole and badly twisted and distorted over the length of the engine room.

3rd longitudinal was fractured at 165 station but was not otherwise seriously damaged although the inner bottom had pulled away from it.

7th longitudinal was holed and broken at 165 station.

All plate frames from 3rd to 7th longitudinal and for the length of the engine room were missing or badly crippled and fractured.

The engine seatings supporting the cruising turbine and starboard end of the box girder in the after engine room, were badly distorted and torn from the inner bottom. The box girder was bent upwards from a point 4 feet to port of the middle line and buckled upwards again where it joined the starboard engine bearer.

127 bulkhead was undamaged but leakage occurred via the starboard shaft gland due to the racing of the starboard inner machinery following the damage.

In 155 bulkhead a hole 6½ ft. x 2½ ft. was made by the starboard outer shaft gland and coupling being dragged through the plating. The hole extended upwards and inboard from the shaft gland to a point 2 feet inboard of the longitudinal bulkhead of "B" boiler room. Two smaller holes (6 ins. x 2 ins.) were made in 155 bulkhead by the impact of pieces of machinery. The boundary bar at the foot of 155 bulkhead had carried away from the inner bottom and the bulkhead was buckled near the inner bottom on the starboard side.

179 bulkhead was only slightly distorted. There was a small split (12 ins. x ½ ins.) 1 foot below the lower deck and 2 ins. inboard of the starboard longitudinal bulkhead of the main W/T room. Some slight damage also occurred in way of the recess to the starboard outer shaft.

Lower deck (50 lbs. D) to starboard of the middle line and between 155 and 179 bulkheads was bulged upwards a maximum of 3 feet at 164 station. The second seam from the starboard side was open 4 ins., all rivets in the outboard side of the edge strip having sheared. The edge strip which was thus still attached to the inboard plate was resting on top of the outboard plate. At 154 station where the 50 lb. deck joined the 15 lb. deck the rivets had sheared and the butts were open 2 ins. over a length of 12 feet on the starboard side.

All minor bulkheads between 155 and 179 stations starboard side on the lower deck were crippled.

Machinery Damage

The starboard inner engine seatings supporting the cruising turbine and the starboard end of the box girder were badly distorted and thrown upwards and to port, wrecking the turbines and gearing. The cruising turbine was touching the lower deck.

The H.P. turbine rotor shaft was fractured at the after gland and the after cast iron bearing bracket broken.

The L.P. turbine bottom half casing was fractured at the after end and the rotor spindle was bent.

The gear casing was broken and the main gear wheel and pinions damaged.

The forward door of the condenser was fractured and the supporting pedestals broken.

Port inner L.P. turbine was thrown out of alignment by the movement of the box girder, the sliding foot keeps distorted and bolts broken.

Bolts in the starboard outer shaft couplings in the after engine room and shaft passage were broken and the 3rd intermediate shaft was badly bent. The 2nd and 4th intermediate shafts were bent at their after and forward couplings respectively. The machinery oversped causing the L.P. rotor to become distorted .054 ins. at centre. All reaction blading tipped and the rotor was slightly grooved by the casing blades.

The port outer machinery and shafts were undamaged.

The starboard turbo generator in the after engine room in way of the damage was entirely destroyed. The L.P. general service air compressor and the starboard F. and B. pump both in the after engine room were damaged beyond repair.

The only damage in the after boiler room was that due to flooding.

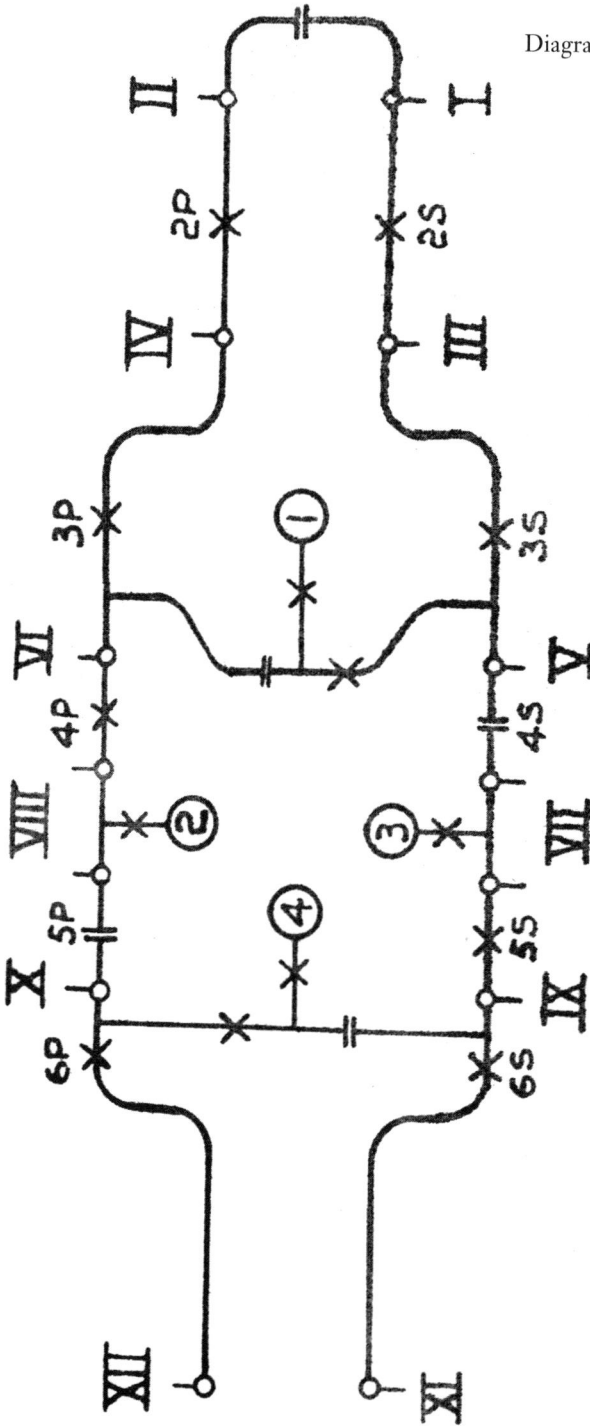

Diagram of ring main

Electrical Report

H.M.S. *Liverpool* had completed an extensive refit in U.S.A. at the end of 1941 followed by a short refit on Clyde in February 1942. All ring main switchgear had been equipped with the 1940 overload relays but H.R.C. fuses had not been delivered to the ship, and therefore branch breakers and group connection boxes were still equipped with links and Admiralty pattern fuses respectively.

Other important outstanding items were:–

(a) Fitting of complete emergency supply system (C.A.F.O.307/40).
(b) Improvement of shock resisting qualities of the lower power circuit breakers (C.A.F.O.2219/41) and replacement of lower power motor generator starters (A.F.O.1732/41).
(c) Modifications to supply and ring main breakers to increase their resistance to shock (A.F.O.1806/41) had been completed in No. 2 supply breaker only.
(d) Modifications to ring main and feeder breaker wiring to prevent blowing of retaining fuse (A.F.O.2637/42).

To increase the reliability of supplies to important machinery in the engine rooms, ship's staff had fitted change-over switches and semi-permanent alternative supplies direct from the dynamo side of supply breakers to:–

(a) One supply and one exhaust fan in each engine room,
(b) One fire and bilge pump in each engine room (the pump which could be connected to the main line suction was chosen).

When the dynamo in the engine room was running, these change-over switches were normally kept to dynamo supply.

Oil secondary lighting had been replaced by automatic emergency lanterns.

Organisation in Force Before the Action on 14 June, 1942

Electrical Organisation No. 1 was in force and all hands were at action stations. The chief E.A. was in charge at the main switchboard, assisted by two seamen and in direct touch by sound-powered telephone with the Torpedo Officer on the bridge (No Warrant Electrician was borne). The

Secondary Electrical Control Position was in the E.A.'s shop (adjacent to the secondary D.C.H.Q. and Midship Section H.Q.) where the H.P. E.A. was in charge.

There were four Electrical Repair Sections stationed as follows:–

> No. 1 Section, 40 Station, upper deck, 1 L.T.O., 2 ST.
> No. 2 Section, 70 Station, lower deck, 1 L.T.O., 2 ST.
> No. 3 Section, Workshop flat – E.R.A. (El.);
> 2 L.T.O.   3 Sto. (El.)
> Diesel dynamos 1 E.A., 2 ST.
> F.E.R. and A.E.R. 1 E.A., 1 L.T.O. each
> No. 4 Section, 281 Station lower deck, 1 L.T.O., 4 ST.

Communications from the M.C.B. were maintained by the sound-powered telephones of the D/G generator control group.

<u>Arrangement of H.P. Supply System Before the Action</u>
All four dynamos were running with the ring main split into four sections, No. 1 dynamo feeding starboard and No. 4 dynamo feeding port. Nos. 1, 4S and 5P R.M.B.'s were open.

Loads were:-

> No. 1 dynamo 300 amps.
> No. 2 dynamo 500 amps.
> No. 3 dynamo 400 amps.
> No. 4 dynamo 500 amps.
> Total 1700 amps.

The action load with all the turrets working was stated to be about 2800 amps.

All supply breakers and Nos. 6P and 6S ring main breakers were in local control and the overload trip gear of Nos. 2P and S ring main breakers had been rendered inoperative (C.A.F.O.714/42). All steering motor breakers were closed and in local control. All other breakers were in switchboard control. Shunt regulators were in switchboard control. No. 1 steering motor was being supplied from No. 5 breaker room and No. 2 from cable passage 155–179 port.

Emergency cables were coiled up except for the connections between the emergency switches in the dynamo M.S.S.'s and the permanent vertical connections to the lower deck. These were rigged while the emergency switches were kept in the central position by holes cut in the M.S.S. covers which held them firmly.

Arrangement of Low Power Supply Before the Action

Only Nos. 1 and 2 L.P. M/G's, supplied from Nos. 1 and 4 dynamos respectively, were running in parallel. The auto selector switch was on No. 4 dynamo.

Effect of Torpedo Damage on Electrical Installation

No. 4 Turbo Generator was destroyed by the explosion. The prime mover was shattered, while the dynamo itself apparently dropped out through the hole in the ship's hull. Power therefore failed to the port after quarter of the ship immediately.

No. 5 starboard ring main breaker opened with the explosion so cutting off power to the starboard after feeder.

The Chief E.A. at the M.C.B. immediately tried to restore power by closing Nos. 5P and. 5S R.M.B.'s, No. 5P re-opened on heavy short circuit, bringing off No. 2 supply breaker as well, while No. 5S opened on overload after a few seconds. No. 2 supply breaker was reclosed at once, and the system stabilised with Nos. 1 and 3 dynamos in parallel feeding I, II, III, V and VII sections, while No. 2 dynamo fed IV, VI and VIII sections. The two after sections each side were dead.

Note: After docking it was found that the starboard ring main was intact but that No. 4D. F.R.S. starboard and No. 6S ring-main breaker must have flooded quickly due to damage to their cases. The strain on the cables had pulled the glands out of the ring main breaker case while the lower part of the dynamo fuse release switch case had been damaged. The port ring main was undamaged but the port fuse release switch for No. 4 dynamo had failed to open; when a spanner was applied to the fuse cap to examine the switch it was heard to open. The fuse element had blown, but a careful examination failed to establish the cause of failure.

No. VIIA service fuse release switch opened with the shock of the explosion. It was recocked and did not open with subsequent shocks, which seems to indicate that it was not correctly cocked initially. Some branch breakers on section VIIB also opened on shock.

Action taken to restore H.P. Electrical Supplies

After a short telephone consultation between the Torpedo Officer, who had seen the position of the hit, and the Chief E.A., who reported the symptoms as seen from the M.C.B., it was quickly realised that serious damage, involving both sides of the ring main, had occurred in the after engine room. Orders were at once given to supply the steering motors from No. 2 dynamo by emergency cables.

As there were no bulkhead terminals on the port side of the lower deck in 155 and 179 bulkheads, the cables had to be jointed by clamps, pattern 5494, and taken through open doors to 198 bulkhead and thence aft. No. 1 steering motor was supplied, but omission to open the by-pass valve before attempting to start the motor, led to the starter burning out. The emergency cables were transferred to No. 2 motor which was running by 1200.

Meanwhile emergency lighting was being provided by portable floodlights and a portable fuse board was fed from 198 bulkhead terminals for supplies to portable pumps.

Power was then restored to group connection boxes Nos. XIA and XIIA, connections being made via the risers at Nos. 5 and 6 Breaker rooms to the temporary steering motor feeders at 209 bulkhead port. It was assumed that the ring main cables were short circuited, so the group connection box fuses were removed. Actually No. XII section of the ring main could have been energised by emergency cables and would have fed the watertight turret breakers so restoring power to the after turrets. However, this was done by taking emergency cables to "X" turret, C.O.S. Only one turret was considered as the capacity of the fuses fitted at No. 2 M.S.S. feeding the emergency leads was 500 amperes.

Effect of Torpedo Damage on L.P. Supplies

No. 2 L.P. M/G stopped with the failure of No. 4 dynamo, and No. 1 machine came off due to overload or shock. This resulted in a complete temporary L.P. supply failure. No. 1 L.P. M/G was immediately put back on the board, and No. 3 L.P. M/G started and put in parallel with it.

The auto-selector switch was sluggish in movement, probably due to the heavy load on the battery (see next paragraph) and had to be helped round by hand. During this process all starters of machines fed from the switch opened but restarted satisfactorily, except for the T.S. main drive motor, the overload of which operated and had to be reset by hand before the motor could restart.

The main telephone exchange became heavily overloaded due to flooding of telephones and one junction box, and the main fuses blew a few minutes after the explosion. This caused a breakdown of communication until the fuses controlling the flooded sections had been removed and the main fuses replaced.

Subsequent Events and Electrical Failures

Considerable anxiety was felt during the afternoon of 14 June on the score of possible dynamo failures. It was feared that No. 2 dynamo circulating water might fail and that No. 3 dynamo might be flooded should the list to starboard increase. Emergency cables were therefore led from No. 1 dynamo M.S.S. via the permanent risers, and thence via the weather deck to the quarter deck hatch forward of 'Y' turret, so that an emergency supply would be instantly available for the steering motors should No. 2 dynamo fail. All supply breakers were put into switchboard control to facilitate the handling of the electrical supply system.

No. 1 dynamo itself, however, was the only one to fail. It had to be stopped for ¼ hour at 1230 because of contaminated feed water. At 1435 No. 1 dynamo overspeeded, which caused the supply breaker of No. 3 dynamo which was in parallel with it to open on reverse current. A number of indicating lights on the main switchboard burnt out due to the increased voltage at this time.

This governor failure also caused a complete L.P. failure. No. 1 L.P. M/G speeded up, its starter opened on overload, while the circuit breaker of No. 3 L.P. M/G opened on reverse current. The temporarily increased L.P. voltage burnt out some indicating lights on the L.P. panels and blew some fuses on the Evershed System. No. 2 L.P. M/G was run up and put in parallel with No. 3 L.P. M/G whose breaker had been re-closed immediately. Fuses and indicating lamps were replaced.

No. 1 dynamo was taken off, while No. 3 dynamo was put back on the electrical supply system, which was then split fore and aft with each diesel dynamo supplying its own side.

At 1510 No. 1 dynamo was running properly again, only to fail at 1620 due to further engine trouble.

At 1630 an attack by fighter bombers developed. At 1650 a heavy delay-action bomb exploded starboard side abreast No. 3 dynamo causing a severe shock.

No. 3 dynamo fuse release switch opened on shock causing a supply failure on the starboard side of the ship. The circulating pump was damaged by shock and the diesel engine had to be stopped. For a time the whole electrical system had to be supplied by No. 2 dynamo.

Other shock damage caused was:–

(a) "Pointolite" lamp filaments in both H.A. tables,
(b) After gyro compass gymbal springs broken, allowing compass to drop into the bottom of the binnacle.

Nos. 1 and 3 dynamos were repaired by 1740 and 1750 respectively and put back on the system. 10 minutes later an attack by torpedo-bombers developed. There were no hits but several explosions were felt attributed to torpedoes exploding at the end of their run one of which was near enough to cause No. 3 port ring main breaker to open due to shock. On attempting to reclose this breaker it refused to "stay on" and the retaining fuse was found to have blown. The fuse was renewed and the breaker reclosed. The Torpedo Officer stated that the blowing of the retaining fuse is a common fault when breakers are opened on load whether accidentally or deliberately, and suggested that this may be due to an inductive surge, passing through the retaining circuit, if the main brushes open before the auxiliary contacts.

Events on 15 and 16 June

During the night difficulty was experienced with the fuel supply to the diesel dynamos. The only pump was in the flooded "B" boiler room and the ready use tanks had to be kept filled by portable hand pumps and buckets. No. 3 dynamo eventually failed and was not restarted till 0630/15 June.

By this time power had been restored to most circuits. The "sided" distribution of power was regained by supplying No. 5 breaker room from No. 1 dynamo M.S.S. via the weather deck emergency cables instead of by cross-connection from No. 6 breaker room emergency supply.

During 15 June, further trouble with contaminated feed water led to No. 1 dynamo being stopped, and it remained in a "standby" condition all that day and the next.

Events on 17 June

At 0515 a heavy load appeared on No. 3 dynamo. Manipulation of the ring showed the fault to be on No. VII section (into which No. 3 dynamo feeds). This was correctly attributed to a breakdown of some of the watertight switchgear in cable passage 143 to 155 starboard due probably to the damage sustained by the ship and the subsequent shocks caused by near miss etc.

Note: Examination after docking showed that this passage had been partially filled and that the following switchgear had leaked:–

(a) No. 5S ring main breaker, through one of the fuse caps which had been insufficiently tightened.

(b) VIIB service fuse release switch, through a defective sealing end in the group connection box. Serious burning had occurred inside the switch mechanism.

No. 3 dynamo could therefore not be connected to the main supply system. No. 1 dynamo was run up and put on to I and III sections. Emergency cables were taken from No. 3 dynamo M.S.S. to VIIA and VA group connection boxes so that it could feed No. VIIA section direct and the foremost part of the main supply system via No. VA service fuse release switch.

By 0835, No. 3 dynamo was again feeding Nos. 1, III, V and VIIA sections with No. 1 dynamo again standing by.

<u>Faults subsequently discovered</u>

It was later found that the retaining fuse of No. 5P ring main breaker had blown. This R.M.B. opened on overload when an attempt to close it was made immediately after the torpedoing.

The L.P. main run cables and H.P. control cables in the damaged cable passage 155 to 179 starboard were undamaged. One L.P. junction box, pattern 99, for telephone circuits was flooded.

The D.G. cables were damaged in this passage. One was A.P.6183A, while the other was U.S.N. type S.D.G.A1000. Both had flooded for a distance of 60 feet abaft the wounds.

<u>Damage Control. (Remarks by Ship's Officers)</u>

<u>Communications</u>. Although the Damage Control telephone system was functioning after replacement of main fuses at the Main Exchange, telephone communication was not found to be effective. The telephones provided are not good enough for a coherent conversation to be carried on in competition with the various extraneous noises which are inseparable from action conditions. Most of the business of D.C.H.Q. was carried out through the medium of written and verbal messages which led to considerable success in the directing of the operations of Damage Control Parties. The Officers of the Damage Control Parties frequently found it expedient to go to D.C.H.Q. to give and receive information in person. The successful working of D.C.H.Q. was

largely due to this.

Ship's staff consider that the difficulties would be greatly reduced by the introduction of a special telephone system running throughout the ship on the lower deck, fitted at frequent intervals with points at which portable handsets could be plugged in. It would then be possible for the Officers of the Damage Control parties to remain in constant touch with D.C.H.Q. without having to leave the scene of operations.

Further, the job of the Damage Control Officer would be considerably simplified if the D.C.H.Q. end of the telephone system could be suitably amplified and led to a loudspeaker. It would then be possible to supervise telephone conversations without being constantly attached to a telephone lead.

Portable Pumps

Ship's staff had fitted special adaptors to the portable pump leads which enabled rapid connection of pump starters to the fuse clips of any available section boxes or portable emergency fuse boards, with provision of a crocodile connection for the earth lead.

Portable Sill

The top of the portable sill fitted to the Starboard Diesel Room Access was about 6 inches above the flood level and so this compartment remained accessible.

Armament Damage

No serious damage occurred due to the torpedo hit but the entire main armament was put out of action by secondary effects as described in the following paragraph.

Effects on Fighting Efficiency

The immediate effects of the torpedo hit were as follows:–

(i) <u>Manoeuvrability.</u> Port outer engine only available and capable of slow speed. Steering gear out of action due to loss of power. List to starboard of 8° and ship 4 feet down by the stern.

(ii) <u>Gunnery</u>. High power electrical supply failed to the after 6" group, after H.A. director and 4" ammunition hoists. "X" and "Y" turrets were not damaged in any way but both found great difficulty in training due to the list: it was therefore impossible to use them against aircraft. All

4" hoists were strained, the starboard outboard unit so badly as to be almost unworkable in hand.

(iii) <u>Torpedo</u>. Nil

(iv) <u>Communications</u>. Main W/T Office out of action due to flooding, fumes and loss of power.

(v) <u>R.D.F.</u> All sets out of action due to shock and loss of power.

The immediate effects of two simultaneous near misses were as follows:–

(i) <u>Manoeuvrability</u>. List increased from six to nine and a half degrees.

(ii) <u>Gunnery</u>. The "point-o-lite" lamp carriages in H.A. Tables were shifted by the explosions giving incorect focus. Three guns in the starboard Pom Pom mounting stopped.

The immediate effects of the cannon shell fire from the attacking aircraft were as follows:–

(i) <u>Gunnery</u>. Two Oerlikon guns were put out of action.

The subsequent effects on fighting efficiency were as follows:–

(i) Starboard torpedoes and all depth charges were jettisoned as part of the measures taken to correct heel and trim.

(ii) It was found necessary to flood "A" and "B" Magazines, Shell Rooms and Lower Cordite Handing Rooms after the two near-misses. Thus all main armament was out of action.

(iii) The gradual leakage of oil fuel into the 4" Magazine combined with the list very seriously reduced the rate at which ammunition could be supplied.

<u>Casualties</u>

The after engine room staff of 12 were killed by the explosion. One of the medical party who was stationed in the Bathroom Flat (127–155) was asphyxiated by the thick fumes which filled the compartment after the explosion. Two men were killed by cannon fire from the attacking aircraft making a total of 15 killed.

Ship's Officers' Remarks

(a) Portable Pumps

(i) Adaptors to convert the discharges of the pumps from single No. 4 Nunan and Stove connections to double No. 3 connections had been made and fitted to all pumps since there is never a shortage of 3" hoses in the neighbourhood of any pumping operation.

(ii) Adaptors to accommodate the pump suctions of No. 4 Nunan and Stove connections had been made so that the pumps could be set to suck from the main suction line. It was only by means of these adaptors that it was possible to jettison the contents of Y3 O.F.T.

(b) Main Suction

(i) The main suction system consists of a single pipe line down the port side of the ship with direct connections to port side and centre line compartments. Starboard compartments are pumped using leather hoses. The disadvantages of this system are:–

    (a) Leather hoses are stiff and unwieldy and it is difficult to make an airtight joint at the standpipes.

    (b) The use of the main requires a fire and bilge pump. Of the remaining four pumps two were required to pump machinery spaces and two for fire main use.

    (c) Two separate parties cannot operate the main suction line simultaneously, hence damage control parties cannot rely on it.

D.N.C Department Comments

(i) Ships should draw from store for each pump delivery hoses as follows:–

    2, 40 ft. lengths with No. 4 bayonet joint connections.

    1, 20 ft. length with No. 4 bayonet joint connections.

(ii) Suitable adaptors are being supplied to ships of the class for pumping out oil fuel tanks filled with water. A drawing of the adaptor is given in C.A.F.O. diagram 145/42 accompanying C.A.F.O.1965/42.

(i) The difficulties experienced with the main suction system as fitted in *Liverpool* are appreciated. In new construction ships an entirely different suction system is being fitted. For existing ships in order to meet the difficulty with the leather hoses A.F.O.2083/41 authorised the supply of wire wound canvas hose up to half the quantity of leather hose carried.

(d) To use the main suction necessitates opening bulkhead valves below the lower deck and, frequently, several hatches on lower and platform decks.

In this action the main suction line was not used except when a portable pump was connected to it for pumping out the plummer block and gland spaces.

(ii) It is suggested that suitable risers should be fitted so that portable pumps can be used on this main. This would be valuable as sections of the main may be isolated due to damage or F. and B. pumps may be required for other purposes – e.g. firefighting.

ii) To connect the portable pumps to main suction by risers is not considered efficient from the pumping point of view. Also the air exhauster on the portable pump is of small capacity (suitable for evacuating air from the 20 ft. of hose and priming in 30 seconds). If connected to suction main, a considerable quantity of air would probably require evacuation and the pump must not run dry for any length of time.

(iii) Strainers fitted over hose connections on suction system need to be re-designed to enable the connection, to be tightened. At present it is necessary to remove the strainer to tighten the h.c. when the joint is made.

(iii) Action is being taken to correct this in ships affected.

(c) Hanger Spray Pump

(i) This is a pump of 150 tons capacity fitted in 'A' boiler room. Immediately after the explosion this pump was connected to the fire main and was run continuously through the remainder of the day. It was, however, necessary to "bleed" it to avoid the possibility of bursting hoses rigged to bridge the gap in the damaged fire main.

(i) A.F.O.2406/41 gave reasons why 150 ton hangar spray pumps should not be run in parallel with fire and bilge pumps designed for different heads, and restricted its use on the fire main.

(d) Sills in Watertight-Door Frames

(i) A portable sill was fitted to the starboard diesel room access trunk. This sill was of 5 lb. plate and was attached to the door frame by 7 in No. lugs and studs, the joint being made by rubber sheeting.

The water in the flat immediately outside the access to the diesel room rose to a level about six inches below the top of the sill. No water found its way into the diesel room and it is considered that without the sill great difficulty would have been experienced in keeping the starboard diesel running.

(i) *Liverpool*'s experience demonstrates the great value of the door sills now being fitted in all ships to limit the spread of free water. The sills being fitted are generally welded, but portable portions are being provided in some doors to permit the passage of bulky gear.

(e) Blanking of Watertight Doors on the Lower Deck

(i) It is considered that the difficulty of dealing with flooding and repairs to electrical services would have been very greatly increased if the door at 155 station (specified for blanking) had been blanked. In order to restrict the spread of flooding, it was necessary to shut and clip tightly the door at 155 station starboard. In this particular case, communication via the upper deck was possible, but it is easy to visualise circumstances in which this might not be the case.

(i) The door in 155 bulkhead port is an armoured door, scheduled to be bolted shut. If upper and forecastle decks became impassable it should be possible for the ship's staff to unbolt the door. It is preferred to retain the additional security afforded by the bolting of the door.

(f) Watertight Hatches

(i) When the forward 6 inch magazines were flooded, the hatches of these compartments proved to be leaky. These hatches are made watertight by means of a strip of rubber placed on edge in a groove in the hatch opening and secured by means of a metal strip screwed to the deck. Passage of personnel through the hatch causes the rubber to be torn from its fastenings and it is not possible for ship's staff to replace it in an efficient manner.

(i) The disadvantages of the arrangements for watertightness of this type of hatch were recognised some time ago, and to overcome them certain recommendations were promulgated in A.F.O.986/40. In new construction armoured hatches are being fitted with the rubber and the clips on the hatch cover.

(g) Bathroom Drains

(i) Where bathrooms are only a short distance above the waterline, steam ejectors should be fitted. In the case of *Liverpool* some flooding of bathrooms abreast 'B' boiler room was caused by the valves not being closed.

Owing to the large number of people using these bathrooms it is very difficult to ensure that the valves are kept closed.

(i) In new construction steam or hydraulic ejectors will be fitted to bathroom drains near the waterline. The effort involved in modifying arrangements in existing ships is considered to be unjustifiable.

(h) Counterflooding

(i) Arrangements should be made for rapid flooding of suitable compartments for the purposes of counterflooding. In *Liverpool* the watertight spaces abreast 'A' engine room and 'A' boiler room were counter-flooded by hose from the fire main – a very slow process. When it was necessary to flood compartments forward the only spaces to which water could be rapidly admitted were magazines and shell rooms. Thus counterflooding put the main armament out of action.

(i) Rapid flooding arrangements are being fitted in existing and new construction ships where the size and position of spaces afford the possibility of substantial correction of heel. Flooding the spaces abreast 'A' engine room and 'A' boiler room in *Liverpool* will correct only a small degree of heel.

(i) Air Escapes

(i) There are a number of air escapes which could be dispensed with as they might lead to extension of flooding in the event of damage.

(i) C.A.F.O. 1403/41 ordered the removal of such air escapes.

D.N.C. Department Comment

With reference to Clause dealing with damage control, it is observed that counter flooding of 'A' and 'B' magazines and shell rooms was carried out to gain stability and increase freeboard aft. 'X' and 'Y' turrets were already out of action due to loss of power and thus none of the main armament could be used. The ship was not unstable and it would have been much preferable to adjust trim by flooding store rooms and less important compartments low in the fore end of the ship.

H.M.S. LIVERPOOL.
TORPEDO DAMAGE. 14·6·42.

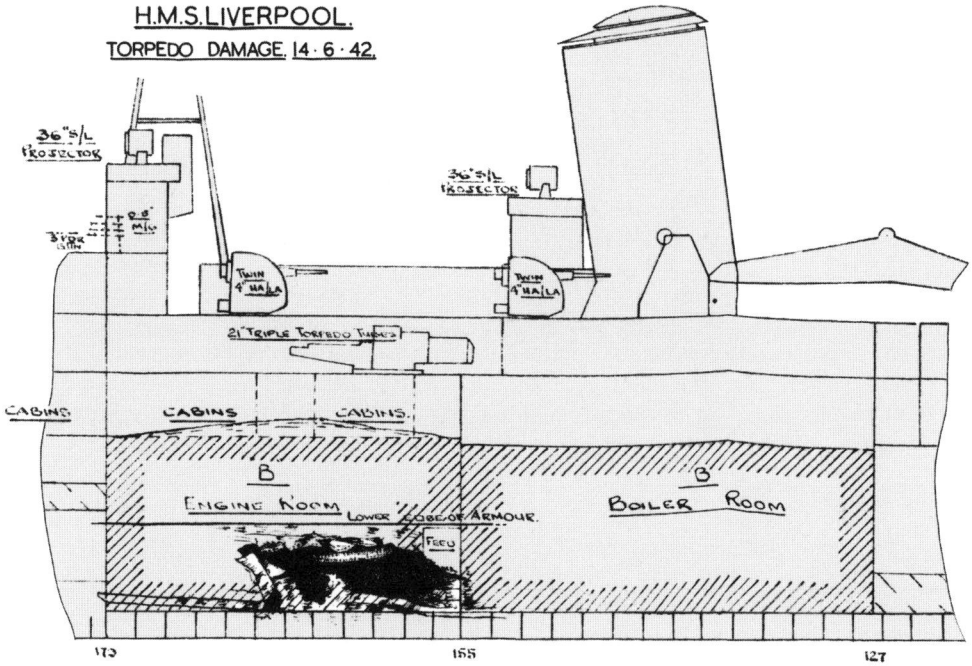

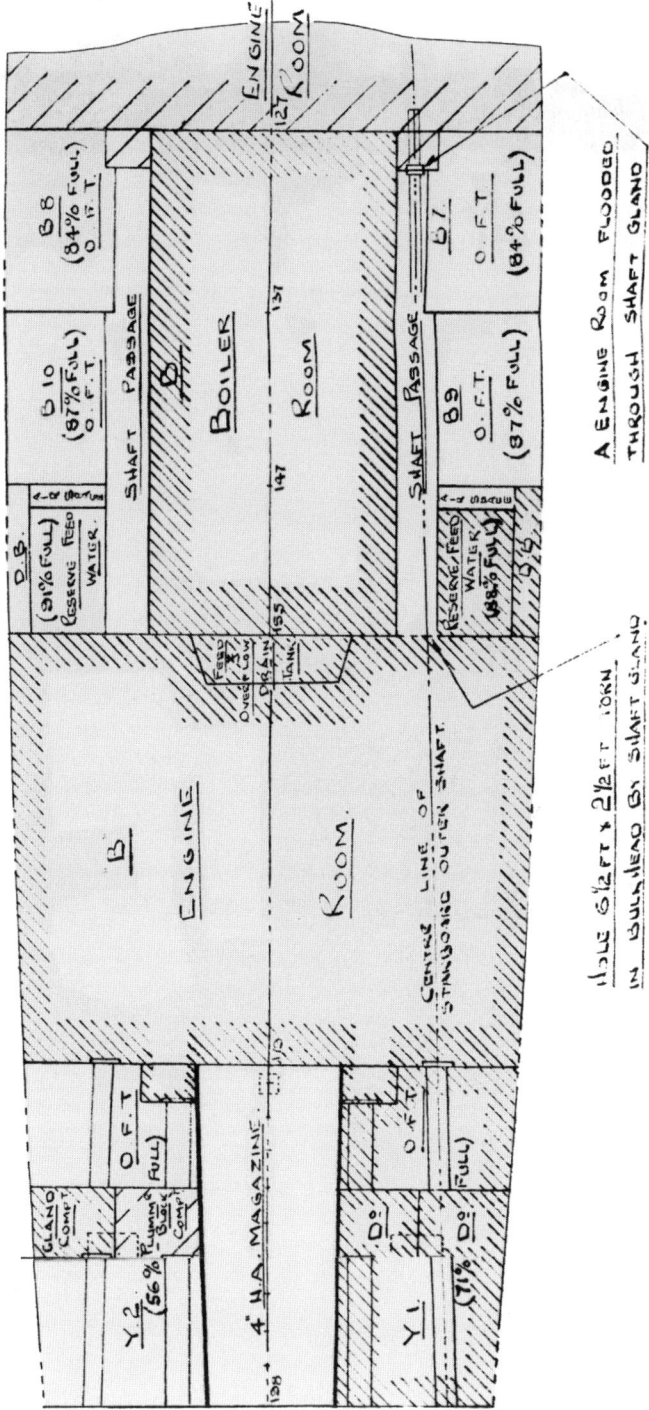

ENGINE ROOM

B8 (84% FULL) O.F.T.

B10 (87% FULL) O.F.T.

D.B. (31% FULL) RESERVE FEED WATER

SHAFT PASSAGE

BOILER B ROOM

B7 O.F.T. (84% FULL)

B9 O.F.T. (87% FULL)

SHAFT PASSAGE

RESERVE FEED WATER (88% FULL)

A ENGINE ROOM FLOODED THROUGH SHAFT GLAND

B ENGINE ROOM.

CENTRE LINE OF STARBOARD OUTER SHAFT.

HOLE 6½FT x 2½FT TORN IN BULKHEAD BY SHAFT GLAND

GLAND COMP'T

O.F.T. (FULL)

4" H.A. MAGAZINE

O.F.T.

Y2 (56%)

Y1 (71%) D°

D° D°

BULKHEAD STRAINED
AND SHORED.

CABLE PASSAGE

CABLE

PASSAGE

MIDSHIPMENS
CHESTS

SPARE
ARMATURE
STORE

ENGINEER'S
STORE

ENGINEER'S & LUBRICATING
OIL STORE

DIESEL DYNAMO
ROOM

MAIN W/T

ENGINE

BOILER

OFFICE

ROOM

ROOM

N° 4 TURBO-
GENERATOR)

ENGINEER'S & LUBRICATING
OIL STORE

DIESEL
DYNAMO ROOM

CLOTHING
ISSUE
ROOM

SOAP &
TOBACCO
STORE

GUNNER'S
ARM'T
STORE

CABLE PASSAGE

CABLE

PASSAGE

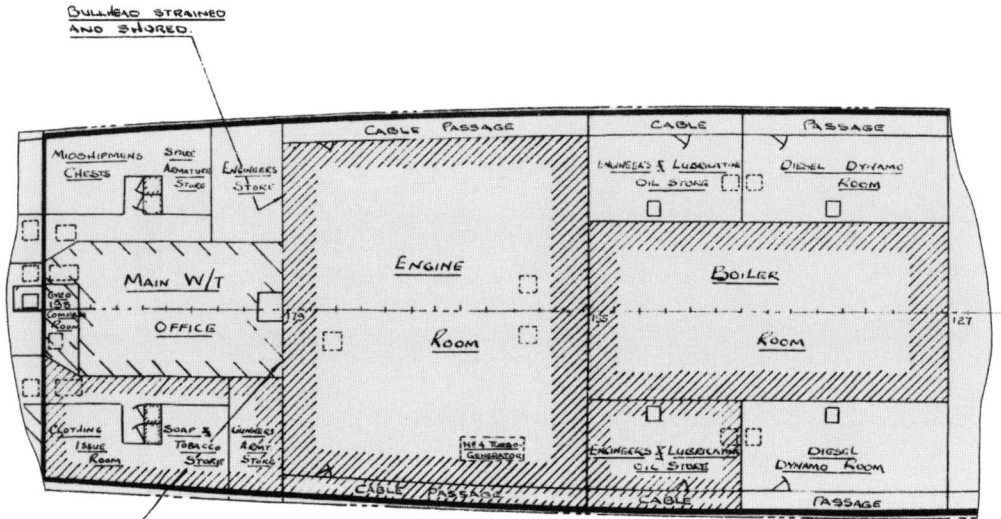

PAD SHORED OVER
SPLIT IN BULKHEAD

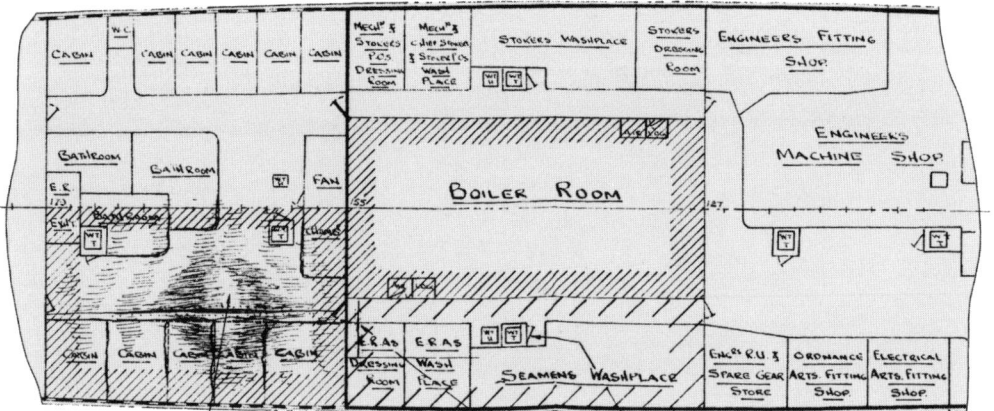

CABIN

CABIN

CABIN

CABIN

CABIN

CABIN

MECH'S &
STOKERS
P.O.S
DRESSING
ROOM

MECH'S &
CHIEF STOKER
& STOKERS
WASH
PLACE

STOKERS WASHPLACE

STOKERS
DRESSING
ROOM

ENGINEERS FITTING
SHOP.

BATHROOM

BATHROOM

FAN

BOILER ROOM

ENGINEER'S
MACHINE SHOP

CABIN

CABIN

CABIN

CABIN

CABIN

ERAS
DRESSING
ROOM

ERAS
WASH
PLACE

SEAMENS WASHPLACE

ENG'S R.U. &
SPARE GEAR
STORE

ORDNANCE
ARTS. FITTING
SHOP.

ELECTRICAL
ARTS. FITTING
SHOP.

DECK BULGED UP 3 FT
AND SHORED DOWN.

SPLIT COVERED WITH PLANKS
AND SHORED DOWN.

DOOR SILL PREVENTED FLOODING OF
DIESEL DYNAMO ROOM (UNDER), AND
ENABLED DYNAMO TO BE KEPT
IN ACTION.

H.M.S.LIVERPOOL.
TORPEDO DAMAGE. 14·6·42.

AFTER ENGINE ROOM. VIEW LOOKING AFT
AT 161 FRAME.

Richard Ibbotson

Vice Admiral Sir Richard Jeffrey Ibbotson KBE CB DSC excelled in a Royal Navy career serving as Deputy Commander-in-Chief Fleet. After Durham University, Ibbotson was promoted to Lieutenant within two years, then to Lieutenant-Commander in 1985, and Commander in 1990.

Ibbotson was awarded the DSC after being given command of HMS *Hurworth* before serving in the Gulf War. He went on to command the frigate HMS *Boxer* before joining the Ministry of Defence, specifically, the Directorate of Nuclear Policy. He was Staff Operations Officer to the Commander United Kingdom Task Group, Adriatic Sea. He was present during the British withdrawal from Hong Kong in 1997.

Ibbotson was given command of the First Frigate Squadron as Captain in 1997, then served as Assistant Director, then Acting Director, of the Directorate of Operational Capability at the Ministry of Defence. He became Commander of British Forces in the Falkland Islands in 2002 and was appointed Commander of the Standing Naval Force in the Atlantic Ocean (2003) and Commodore of the Royal Naval College, Dartmouth (2004). Naval Secretary in 2005, he was promoted to Rear Admiral in June that year. In 2007 he was appointed Flag Officer, Sea Training and then Deputy Commander-in-Chief Fleet in 2009.

In the 2011 New Year Honours, he was appointed Knight Commander of the Order of the British Empire (KBE).

Michael Pearce

Mike Pearce served with the Ministry of Defence (Navy) for nearly 40 years and was on the staff of the Britannia Royal Naval College, Dartmouth for 12 years. Closely connected with the Royal Navy throughout his career, he held planning and management roles within many different fields of MoD activity and on numerous projects for the Royal Navy in London, Hampshire and at the Naval Base at Devonport. As a naval historian, he has been a trustee of the Britannia Museum since its inception in 2007 and is a series editor for the BRITANNIA NAVAL HISTORIES OF WORLD WAR II (published by University of Plymouth Press). He co-authored, with Dr Richard Porter, the introduction to *Fight for the Fjords* in this series. His particular area of expertise is the period 1860–1960 and he continues to undertake research, both on behalf of the Trust and in his own specialist area.

Pearce traces his first spark of interest in naval matters back to the age of four, when his father lifted him shoulder-high on the Isle of Wight ferry so that he could see HMS *Vanguard*, the last British battleship. His interest in naval history took off in his teens when he started reading and buying naval history books – he has never stopped. At school, he was often found tucked away in a corner, avidly reading naval history and he counts himself fortunate that his career enabled him to put his knowledge to effective use.

Married to Anne, they have two grown-up children and live in South Devon where Mike is a qualified watchkeeper with the National Coastwatch Institution at Prawle Point.

Britannia Naval Histories of World War II

BRITANNIA NAVAL HISTORIES OF WORLD WAR II is a series containing reproduced historical material, newly commissioned commentary, maps, plans and first-hand accounts of specific battles. Each foreword is written by naval veterans of the highest order, including HRH Prince Philip, Duke of Edinburgh.

Turning the Tide The Battles of Coral Sea and Midway
Foreword Capt. John Rodgaard USN
Paperback ISBN 978–184102–333–5 **Hardback** ISBN 978–184102–334–2

Bismarck The Chase and Sinking of Hitler's Goliath
Foreword Commander 'Sharkey' Ward
Paperback ISBN 978–184102–326–7 **Hardback** ISBN 978–184102–327–4

Dark Seas The Battle of Cape Matapan
Foreword HRH Prince Philip
Paperback ISBN 978–184102–304–5 **Hardback** ISBN 978–184102–303–8

Fight for the Fjords The Battle for Norway 1940
Foreword Admiral Lord Alan West
Paperback ISBN 978–184102–306–9 **Hardback** ISBN 978–184102–305–2

Hitler's Ghost Ships Graf Spee, Scharnhorst and
Disguised German Raiders
Foreword Admiral Sir Jonathon Band
Paperback ISBN 978–184102–308–3 **Hardback** ISBN 978–184102–307–6

Hunting Tirpitz Naval Operations Against Bismarck's Sister Ship
Foreword Admiral Sir Mark Stanhope
Paperback ISBN 978–184102–310–6 **Hardback** ISBN 978–184102–309–0

www.uppress.co.uk/nav